STEPHEN HARPER

and the Future of Canada

STEPHEN

WILLIAM JOHNSON

HARPER

And the Future of Canada

A DOUGLAS GIBSON BOOK

M&S

Library and Archives Canada Cataloguing in Publication

Johnson, William, 1931-
    Stephen Harper and the future of Canada / William Johnson.

"Douglas Gibson Books".
ISBN 0-7710-4350-3

    1. Harper, Stephen, 1959-   2. Conservative Party of Canada.   3. Canada
– Politics and government – 1993-   4. Canada. Parliament. House of Commons
– Biography.   5. Legislators – Canada – Biography.   6. Politicians – Canada –
Biography.   I. Title.

FC636.H37J63 2005   971.07'2'092   C2005-902570-0

We acknowledge the financial support of the Government of Canada through the Book Publishing Industry Development Program and that of the Government of Ontario through the Ontario Media Development Corporation's Ontario Book Initiative. We further acknowledge the support of the Canada Council for the Arts and the Ontario Arts Council for our publishing program.

Typeset in Sabon by M&S, Toronto
Printed and bound in Canada

This book is printed on acid-free paper that is 100% recycled, ancient-forest friendly (100% post-consumer recycled).

McClelland & Stewart Ltd.
The Canadian Publishers
481 University Avenue
Toronto, Ontario
M5G 2E9
www.mcclelland.com

1 2 3 4 5   09 08 07 06 05

Writing a book is setting out on a pilgrimage. Along the road to Canterbury I encountered three memorable pilgrims, John Weissenberger, Tom Flanagan, and Doug Gibson.

CONTENTS

Foreword   ix
Prologue: The Ancestor   xi

Chapter 1   A Dreadfully Happy Childhood   1
Chapter 2   Books, Love, and Politics   13
Chapter 3   Power and Glory in Ottawa   25
Chapter 4   Crossing the Desert   38
Chapter 5   The West Wants In   58
Chapter 6   A Party Is Founded, a Star Is Born   71
Chapter 7   Spreading the Word   90
Chapter 8   Elections Are Not Won by Prayers   104
Chapter 9   Redefining the Reform Party   111
Chapter 10   Invading Ottawa   126
Chapter 11   The Question of Quebec   139
Chapter 12   Democracy in Ottawa   154
Chapter 13   Choosing One's Canada   162
Chapter 14   The 1993 Elections   188
Chapter 15   The Reformer in Parliament   201
Chapter 16   The 1995 Referendum   226
Chapter 17   New Horizons – Politics by Other Means   258
Chapter 18   Saving the Vision   279
Chapter 19   Leader of the Canadian Alliance   302
Chapter 20   Coming Together   326
Chapter 21   Coming Close   347
Chapter 22   Positioning the Party for Decisive Elections 374

Epilogue   399
Index   408

FOREWORD

Stephen Harper's life largely coincides with a period of Canadian history when the country, divided, struggled over four and a half decades to find a workable formula for national equity, identity, and unity. At times, amid the fractious confrontations, the very nature and existence of Canada was imperilled. Harper, as he matured, was to be drawn into politics by the conviction that something was gravely wrong with his country and its political culture. Increasingly, he became involved in the struggle for the very soul of Canada. He came to his own original vision of what Canada must become and of the actions required to bring about the transformation. He eventually moved into a position of national leadership so as to implement his vision. Now, he seems poised as never before to challenge the status quo, the facile assumptions which are commonly ascribed as "Canadian values."

Soon, Canadians will decide, after the indecisive elections of June 28, 2004, whether they are willing to follow Stephen Harper and the Conservative Party of Canada in the new direction where he offers to lead. But first, since it involves a leap of confidence into the future, the citizens are entitled to know far more accurately than they did last election day who Stephen Harper is, where he comes from, where he would lead, and what credentials he offers to justify his break with the long Liberal and Tory ascendancy.

To meet that challenge as accurately and responsibly as possible is the objective of this book. It requires not merely evoking the main episodes of Stephen Harper's life, but placing his life at every stage in the context of his times. Harper is unusual in that he did not choose politics as a career, as did Jean Chrétien, or as the fulfillment of monumental ambition, as did Brian Mulroney, or as the completion of a dynastic duty, as did Paul Martin Jr. In fact, despite their flagrant differences in most other respects,

Stephen Harper shares this with Pierre Trudeau – that each was drawn to politics by a sense of mission. If Quebec had not been frozen in reactionary clericalist institutions before 1960, if Quebec had not threatened Canada's existence after 1960, Pierre Trudeau would never have become prime minister. If Alberta had not been treated with flagrant injustice from 1973 to the present, if Canada had not been threatened with disaster by spendthrift politicians and Quebec nationalists, Stephen Harper would never have become leader of the Conservative Party of Canada.

Both Trudeau and Harper were, first and foremost, public intellectuals, seeing clearly what conventional leaders of their time could not see. Both were unusual in combining with vision a keen sense of strategy and a flair for leadership, once they felt leadership imperatively thrust upon them.

Trudeau, in his time, changed his country and made history, for better and for worse. Harper's most important years have yet to be written.

PROLOGUE: THE ANCESTOR

WAS IT PROPHETIC? The first Harper ancestor to set foot in what is now Canada changed his life and headed west out of concern for high taxes – and soon found himself caught up in a struggle over unity and secession.

On March 11, 1774, Christopher Harper left his Yorkshire farm and set sail from the port of Hull with his wife, their children, and a nephew who was a blacksmith, as well as the horses and cattle and equipment that would give him a chance to establish an even better farm in Nova Scotia.

After fifty-seven cold, miserable days at sea, punctuated by the terror of running aground on Sable Island, they reached Halifax. There another settler bound for the same destination noted "the account given us of Cumberland was enough to make the stoutest give way." They sailed on. Another ten days took them to the head of the Bay of Fundy, in the shelter of what had been Fort Beauséjour. Now Fort Cumberland, it gave its name to the district lying on the Fundy side of the narrow neck of land between what is now Nova Scotia and New Brunswick. This was frontier country, with no roads to the east, and it was still receiving new settlers. The Acadians had been expelled from there twenty years earlier and the vacated good farmland had been only partly filled by New Englanders. Ironically, this first Harper came as part of a government settlement scheme, one aimed at Yorkshire farmers. The chief inducement was low taxes in the new land.

Taxes were the main incentive to go into exile. The victories that were establishing the British Empire around the world, including Canada, came at a huge continuing cost to the people at home, and the taxes to build the ships, feed the sailors, and arm the soldiers guarding the empire were hard on even an abstemious farmer like him. In the New World, taxes were mostly wrung out of liquor so he took the great gamble, sailed west, and made a new home.

A contemporary account tells us that Christopher Harper settled on "a considerable quantity of fine cleared land, with a good house upon it, elegantly furnished, with barns and other conveniences, besides woodland at a distance, and twenty cows, with other cattle, etc., for which, we were told, he gave five hundred and fifty pounds."

He was fortunate that, unlike most settlers, he did not have to clear the fields, which had been created by the now expelled Acadians. But history was not yet finished with the new land, ruled by the Fundy tides. As a settler, Harper had chosen well in every respect but one. Within months of his arrival, Cumberland was to become a war zone.

Just five weeks after Christopher Harper's arrival at Cumberland, the Quebec Act received royal assent in London on June 22, 1774. The colonies in North America, already in furious revolt against the Crown, saw it as a last straw. In September that year, the first Continental Congress met in Philadelphia, a rebellious gathering that forecast the storm to come. The next April Paul Revere rode through the night alerting the now-prepared militia, and shots were exchanged at Lexington and Concord. The war was on.

Nova Scotia was full of New Englanders torn in their sympathies. The frontier country around Fort Cumberland contained the two most ardent leaders of the pro-rebel faction, John Allan, who had been elected Cumberland's member in the Nova Scotia House of Assembly, and Jonathan Eddy, a commander in the military police. Committees of Safety (a phrase borrowed from the Massachusetts rebels) were formed among the settlers and they sent petitions of support for the American Revolution.

Nova Scotia's governor Francis Legge countered the threat of secession by forbidding all assemblies and ordering the presence of any strangers to be reported. He instituted the draft, but when his recruiters showed up in Cumberland County, they were forced out of town. The governor then sent a garrison to occupy Fort Cumberland and prevent the settlers from joining the rebellion.

Jonathan Eddy travelled south and met with George Washington at his Harvard headquarters as he supervised the siege of Boston. Eddy urged the general to agree to an invasion of Nova Scotia with five hundred to six hundred men. Washington put off that decision, preferring a plan to invade Canada, which succeeded in capturing Montreal and attacking Quebec, where the rebels were repulsed. The Cumberland men, amid rumours of impending invasion, continued to agitate. A plan then propounded by John Allan as he dined with Washington, according to Ernest Clarke in his book *The Siege of Fort Cumberland, 1776: An Episode in the American Revolution*, "Contemplated a force of 3,000 men, eight armed schooners and sloops. Fort Cumberland was to be taken, Halifax taken or cut off from the western part of Nova Scotia, if it could not be destroyed, and sympathizers with America set free to its ultimate support."

Those sympathizers were so numerous in Cumberland that the authorities in Halifax decided to appoint as justices of the peace men of good reputation and strong character whose loyalty to the Crown was beyond suspicion. And so it happened that on July 1, 1776 – just three days before another significant date – Christopher Harper was appointed justice of the peace in the township of Cumberland. He took firm measures against the seditious, arresting several individuals, as one American sympathizer complained, "for being suspected to be friendly to the United States."

He was to pay the price. In October 1776, Jonathan Eddy received supplies and ammunition and staged his attack, culminating in a full-blown siege of Fort Cumberland. (This little-known piece of civil war on Canadian soil is fully described in the book of that name.) In a daring episode the rebel forces seized a supply sloop under the fort's guns and sailed off with it, taking away most of the provisions intended to carry the garrison through the winter, and capturing many pursuers.

The invaders had the run of the countryside and terrorized those known to be loyal to the Crown. At dead of night they paid a call on Christopher Harper, leaving him, as he later testified, "much frightened." Shortly thereafter he rounded up local Loyalists and they moved into the fort with their families to help the garrison fight off the invaders when they launched the expected assault on the fort. On November 9, the roving rebels returned to Harper's farm, stole what they could, and burned the house and barn to the ground. We know this – and about the earlier threatening visit – from legal proceedings for redress later taken by Harper, when the Loyalist side (ironically reinforced by refugees from the defeats in Boston and New York) eventually triumphed in Nova Scotia.

After the war, with Crown support he eventually gained redress, receiving property in Sackville by way of compensation. There he became a successful, prosperous citizen. W.C. Milner's *History of Sackville, New Brunswick* records the social note: "Mr. Harper is said to have owned the first two wheel chaise that appeared in Westmoreland County." In the Nova Scotia elections of 1785, the citizens of Cumberland County elected him to represent them in the provincial Legislative Assembly. But, as explained in *The Legislative Assembly of Nova Scotia 1758–1983: A Biographical Directory*, "the election was declared void, 7 December 1785, on the grounds that Harper was not a resident of Nova Scotia. He does not appear to have ever taken his seat." By moving to Sackville, Christopher Harper became automatically a citizen of New Brunswick rather than Nova Scotia when, in 1784, New Brunswick became a province.

He left to his family and his descendants an example as a man of integrity, a man of courage, a man who hated taxes, and a man who came to the aid of his country in its hour of crisis.

Chapter 1

A DREADFULLY HAPPY CHILDHOOD

THERE'S NO UNDERSTANDING where Stephen Harper came from, how he developed, and what he was to become as a man, without understanding his relationship to his family, and above all to his father, Joseph Harper, which was unusual for being so close, supportive, and loving. During the turbulent period of the 1960s and the 1970s when the generation gap was taken as a given, when youth rebelled theatrically at home, on campuses, and in the streets, when the times were a-changin' and you couldn't trust anyone over thirty, Stephen Harper trusted and never lost his trust. In 1991, when at thirty-two he submitted his master's thesis in economics to the University of Calgary, his dedication was only nine words long:

Dad and Mom, for all your love and support.

In 2003, when Joseph Harper died of the heart condition that had afflicted him for years, Stephen delivered the eulogy at Calgary's Westminster Presbyterian Church. By then the leader of the Official Opposition, with a reputation for being cold, even icy, Harper gave an emotional, deeply touching tribute to his father that had many of the assembled mourners in tears. One sentence stood out: "There is no adequate way of saying goodbye to the most important man in your life."

Even then, at the age of forty-four, in the middle of a career which had him sparring daily with the prime minister, Stephen declared that his father had been his greatest influence. The following year, when he had just won the leadership of the now united Conservative Party of Canada, Harper was asked on television by Peter Mansbridge to name the people who had most influenced him. He replied unhesitatingly: "My dad was certainly the greatest influence in my life."

So who was this Joseph Harper that he made such a mark on the son who now aspires to be the next prime minister of Canada? Stephen saw in him an admirable success as father, husband, man of the world – as a human being. The boy's views of other people evolved as he matured and went his own way. But, though from childhood Stephen developed an inner-directed personality in contrast to his father's extravagantly outgoing and talkative style, he never had reason to reject the attitudes and values that guided his father and infused their relationship. Unlike so many of his generation, Stephen never resented his father or rejected him.

Joseph Harper was born in Moncton, New Brunswick, on September 20, 1927. He turned eighteen just too late to serve in the armed forces during the war that ended in Europe in May 1945. But he was faithful to the family Loyalist tradition set by his ancestor Christopher Harper. Joseph's own father, Harris Harper, had been only twelve when the First World War broke out. But his older brother served in that war. And Harris, while attending normal school in Fredericton, served in the militia as a sergeant in the Seventh Battalion Canadian Machine Gun Corps. Eventually he moved to Moncton as principal of Prince Edward School, where he soon established a cadet corps. He himself was a crack shot and he led his cadets in the 1930s to first place in the national competition for the Dominion of Canada Rifle Championship for Cadets. Later still, during the Second World War, he was commissioned as a lieutenant in the Fifth Reserve Armoured Regiment of the Princess Louise's Hussars. He would spend his summers drilling and instructing recruits to the militia.

Joseph spent much of his youth in an atmosphere permeated by the military. He was not quite twelve when the Second World War broke out, but two of his father's brothers enlisted. During his high-school years, which coincided with the war, Joseph had marched as an army cadet. He developed early a fascination for Canadian military history and began collecting every form of military insignia. Later in life, while successive Canadian governments dismantled the Canadian military services, Joseph Harper published two monographs on military insignia, *Old Colours Never Die: A Record of Colours and Military Flags in Canada* (with Francis Dunbar), and *A Source of Pride: Regimental Badges and*

Titles in the Canadian Expeditionary Force, 1914–1919. He became a consultant to the Department of National Defence.

After graduating from Grade 11 in 1944, Joseph spent the following school year at Robinson Business College, then joined a Moncton firm of chartered accountants and articled until, in 1950, he became himself a chartered accountant. During those five years of apprenticeship, still living at home, he was sent out to perform accounting duties for firms in different parts of New Brunswick and Nova Scotia. At a young age he saw up close the problems and opportunities of businesses in the Maritimes. He would later note the impact of the programs brought in by the Trudeau government, notably the 1969 extension of unemployment insurance to seasonal workers. In the October 25, 1999, issue of *Report Newsmagazine*, Mike Byfield quoted Joseph Harper on the contrast between the New Brunswick of his youth and what he saw there later.

> "At that time, the inshore fishermen all had large gardens or small farms, and many of them worked in the woods during the winter," Mr. Harper recalls. On a recent return to his childhood haunts, however, the retired Imperial Oil accountant was surprised at how overgrown the same lands look now. "I'm told they don't need the income, thanks to unemployment insurance," the Calgarian says. Shell fishermen, for example, routinely earn $100,000 during a brief season of work, then collect UI for the remainder of the year.

Stephen Harper, after becoming leader of the Canadian Alliance in 2002, would shock the Maritimes by speaking of "a culture of defeat" fostered there by federal government policies. Like his father, he believed that such policies, far from alleviating collective poverty, exacerbated it by creating disincentives for the pursuit of more productive, better-paid, year-round jobs. The accountant father and the economist son were of one mind.

Joseph was still living at home on January 21, 1950, studying for the exams that would earn him the letters C.A. after his name, when a calamity befell the family. His father, Harris, well known in Moncton as the high-school principal, suddenly disappeared, totally, without a trace. No one would ever know what had carried off this pillar of the

community, whether a terrible accident or a scandal. The police investigated, the local newspaper published stories. There was speculation
and gossip. Joseph's mother was devastated. Five years later, Harris
Harper was declared legally dead. But the mystery of his disappearance
was never solved.

The impact on the family was incalculable. Stephen said of his father:
"It made him appreciate that all the good things in life, all of the best
things in life, in work and play, in friendships and family, are still just
passing things. And it made him deeply cherish these things all the more
and, especially, to be thankful for the eternal God that provides them."

Perhaps to put the turmoil behind him, Joseph left Moncton in
August 1951, a year after acquiring his C.A., and moved to Toronto.
Arriving there as a twenty-three-year-old bachelor, he joined Danforth
United Church, where while attending a youth-group event in late 1951,
he met eighteen-year-old Margaret Johnston. She had come from the
country to Toronto the year before to attend secretarial and business
school, making the transition from the farm to the big city. Joseph immediately fell in love for life. They had their first date on February 6, 1952,
the day that King George VI died, and were married in 1954.

Margaret, like Joseph, had long-established roots in Canada. Her
paternal ancestor, William Johnston, had migrated to Ontario in 1838
from Lincolnshire, on the east coast of England. He and his son Hinman
Johnston settled on adjoining homesteads in Grey County not far from
Hanover, in Southwestern Ontario. Margaret's father, Rupert Johnston,
still on the family farm, and her mother, Catharine Jane Herd, had six
children. Margaret, looking back, would recall that they were very poor
during the Depression years but they didn't really know it, as all their
neighbours were in the same state. They always had food from the
farm, a roof over their heads, and two parents who loved their children.
They had faith in God, they went to Sunday services at the Presbyterian
Church in Durham whenever weather and the state of the roads permitted. They grew up supported by strong family bonds in a still stable
rural community.

Stephen was to witness the loving, harmonious relationship between
his parents. Joseph, perhaps sensitized by his own family's tragedy, was
a totally committed husband, and an attentive father. He confided one
day to Stephen, "Before I met your mother, I had never really been a

really happy person. After I met her, I have never really been unhappy since." They remained a close-knit couple for the forty-eight years that remained of his life. For Stephen, family values would be more than a slogan. He'd experienced them at first-hand, at their best, and he saw no reason to rebel against them, in his youth or later.

Some time after their marriage, Joseph and Margaret decided to buy a house in a neighbourhood where children could be brought up safely. They chose Leaside, population 18,579, a dormitory community that was then a separate municipality located just northeast of the City of Toronto. A main artery, Bayview Avenue, had just been extended south to link Leaside with downtown Toronto. And so it was in Leaside that Stephen, born April 30, 1959, spent the first twelve years of his life, living in a house located at 332 Bessborough Drive. His younger brothers, Grant and Robert, were also born while the family lived there. Years later, in the midst of the 2004 federal election campaign, Stephen Harper was asked by the *National Post* to name his closest friends. "My brothers," was his reply. They were then both at his side fighting in the political wars.

Leaside boasted that it was Ontario's only municipality built entirely according to a pre-designed plan. Many of its streets were curved, some into crescents. Stop signs were frequent, discouraging through traffic. The ubiquitous trees and lawns gave a pleasant green look, and the narrow lots each contained a single-family dwelling flanked by a driveway leading up to a small garage. The Harper home, a red-brick two-storey house with a bay window and a small fireplace in the living room, sat on a lot that was 33 feet wide, and 138 feet deep. It had a tree growing on the front lawn and another tree in the fenced backyard.

Leaside was then the quintessential WASP middle-class Toronto suburb. The 1961 census indicated that 84.2 per cent of its residents had origins in the British Isles while 4.6 per cent were French. No other racial or national group lived there in notable numbers. Most houses sheltered the young families of ambitious people rising in the world. Few were old or poor or very rich. A notable community spirit encouraged participation in organized sports and other activities. The Leaside Lawn Bowling Club offered croquet as well as lawn bowling. Leaside fielded strongly competitive baseball and hockey teams. The Leaside Garden Society held flower shows and planted flowers on public property, including the grounds of the Leaside Public Library. A couple of years before Stephen was born a young woman named Margaret Atwood attended Leaside High School, a few blocks from his home.

Toronto the Good was not yet buried in Leaside at a time when the province required that adults wishing to buy alcohol obtain a permit, fill out a form listing name and address for every purchase, and drive directly home with the unopened package. The Leaside Council was recurrently preoccupied with forbidding bowling on Sunday, the day the Lord rested. On February 23, 1963, when Stephen was not yet four, the Leaside Council rebuked two local enterprises that had engaged in commercial activity on Sunday. According to the minutes, "The Theatre of Bayview has been opened on Sundays and now Bowlerama in Thorncliffe Park. A letter will be sent informing them of the violation of the Lord's Day Act." But, already, the community was going to the devil. The minutes of Leaside Council for March 1, 1965, reported: "Tennis was added to the list of games permitted on Sundays." On Sundays, though, *competitive* matches between members of the House Tennis League remained prohibited until 1969.

It was a safe, healthy, comfortable, and very conservative environment for a little boy growing up. The family regularly attended Sunday services at the Leaside United Church. Margaret was then a full-time homemaker. She devoted her energies to making a good life for her husband, raising her three sons, and cultivating her garden. Only later, when her youngest son was approaching the end of elementary school, did she return to part-time office work and serve as a volunteer at the Queensway Hospital Women's Auxiliary.

I once asked Margaret what Stephen was like as a child. She replied: "He was the way he is now – quiet and thoughtful." When he reached school age, Stephen attended Northlea Public School, housed in a long, low two-storey red-brick building just two blocks away from his home. The school, with an entrance at one end marked "Boys" and one at the other end marked "Girls," had an enormous grassy yard which also served as the public park for the northern section of Leaside. The boys especially met there to play games after school and on weekends. The school also housed the public library's collection for children. Stephen was, from the start, an apt pupil and as his teachers confirmed, he was attentive and well-behaved. His favourite subject was math, he recalled on a return visit to the school in November 2004. And he was deeply involved for years in the Scouting movement. As a Wolf Cub, he advanced to the position of Sixer – leader of a group of five to eight Wolf Cubs – and then to Senior Sixer – one who leads the Sixers. He then went on to become a Scout.

Meanwhile, Joseph's career progressed. When he first moved to Toronto, he had worked for the chartered accounting firm of George A. Touche and Co. After four years, he joined the accounting department of Imperial Oil and soon displayed a notable talent for the precise, logical analysis that was required by the new instrument known as the computer. He became a pioneer in applying the computer to the needs of very large business firms. He was a leader of the team assembled in 1958 that contrived for Imperial Oil what was to be one of the first large commercial mainframes to be put in service in Canada or the United States.

As his professional life prospered and his sons grew, Joseph began to feel that the family had outgrown its small house in Leaside. He and Margaret found what they were looking for sixteen kilometres to the west, in the borough of Etobicoke. There, a development called Princess Anne Manor offered spacious modern houses built ten or fifteen years previously on large lots. The new Harper home was at 57 Princess Anne Crescent, a large ranch-style bungalow, with big picture windows, a grey stone front, red brick at the side, three fireplaces, and a spacious two-car garage. A maple tree grew on the front lawn. To the side of the driveway a pole bore a netted hoop for basketball practice. No sidewalk ran between the lawn and the wide street. Presumably everybody drove. Here Stephen would live from 1971 until he left in 1978 for a new life in Alberta. Here he would attend Grades 7 and 8 at John G. Althouse Middle School, then five years of high school at Richview Collegiate Institute. Here the family would attend St. Luke's United Church. Here he would come to the verge of manhood and demonstrate that he was not an ordinary guy.

———◦———

When you speak to people who knew "Steve" in high school, they all agree: he was intelligent, serious, disciplined. And he was quiet. "Very, very smart. And quiet. Very conservative," says Bob Scott, who taught Harper in a course in American History in Grade 13. He described him as having "a very reserved and private manner." Scott, now retired after a career of teaching at Richview C.I., was not only Stephen's teacher. He also accompanied six graduating students, including Stephen, as they made a week-long canoeing and camping trip in Algonquin Park in August 1978. It was a farewell adventure in three canoes, a last coming together of high-school friends before they broke off in different directions to pursue their lives.

Also on that trip was Stephen's friend Paul Watson, who has since made a name for himself in journalism, first as a reporter-photographer for the *Toronto Star*, and now as a reporter-photographer based in India for the *Los Angeles Times*. Noted even among war correspondents for his derring-do, he has covered such world trouble spots as the NATO bombing in Kosovo – he was on the ground, among the bombs – war and warlords in Afghanistan, the clashes between India and Pakistan over Kashmir, and the American invasion of Iraq, where he was stabbed by an angry mob. In 1994, while he was still at the *Star*, his photograph of the bloodied corpse of a U.S. soldier being dragged through the streets and jeering mobs of Mogadishu appeared in newspapers and on television everywhere and won him the Pulitzer Prize.

But during that summer of 1978, his performance on the camping trip was rather less glorious, as he recently recalled. "I was sent forward to scout a river to see if we could pull a canoe through it to skip a portage, and wrongly advised the group that we could. When we got one of the canoes unstuck and onto the proper portage trail, a passing Boy Scout leader – whose kids were hauling huge knapsacks strapped to their foreheads – guffawed and said, 'Did you see those idiots back there trying to pull through that creek?'" Watson was no great success as a canoeist. He'd been born missing one hand and wore a prosthesis – a kind of claw. He generally rode in a canoe with two of his classmates, took a turn at paddling, and then sat in the bottom.

Even then, Watson was an aspiring journalist and submitted reports on high-school life to the *Star*. His fellow students recognized his gift for expression by voting him as their valedictorian. He was also passionately interested in politics during those anxious years after November 1976, when the separatist Parti Québécois came to power promising a referendum on Quebec's secession. Watson was a fan of Pierre Trudeau. He even founded a Liberal student club at Richview and recruited Stephen

Harper as one of its members. Harper was also then a fan of Pierre Trudeau, as he would later recall with some irony.

Though neither Joseph nor Margaret was active in politics, there was much talk about politics around the dining-room table. Margaret recalls that, when they were younger, "the boys talked hockey, hockey, hockey." Carl Brewer, star of the Toronto Maple Leafs, was married to the daughter of Joseph's first cousin and the three Harper boys, ardent Maple Leaf fans, discussed his every exploit. Every Saturday night, they watched *Hockey Night in Canada*. Stephen applied his methodical mind to the lore and statistics of professional hockey, and soon became a master of its mysteries. Occasionally, the boys were brought to a game at Maple Leaf Gardens. But, as they got older, Margaret said, the boys' conversations turned to "politics, politics, politics."

Did the adventurous seven talk politics on that canoe trip? Not according to Bob Scott. "We didn't have political discussions or anything like that." And he adds: "Steve was very quiet." That camping trip was mostly organized by another friend Scott Pezzack, the most active of the group in sports. He played on the high-school football team and played squash competitively. He helped put out the annual yearbook, titled *Rizmah*. One year, he'd served on the student council. He'd been a Boy Scout in his younger years and, unlike the others, he had done a lot of camping. As Pezzack describes the group, none of them smoked, either tobacco or marijuana. They were not much into alcohol or partying. "We were all nerdy. We were the clean-cut kind."

And Stephen? "Steve was really smart," Pezzack recalled. "He matured a lot earlier than most of us. He was very bright. And studious. He did spend a lot of time on his studies. I think most of the years he got close to 100 per cent. Paul, and I think Steve, were always the more mature of the group and had a big focus on what they wanted to do."

Peter Newton was another friend. He came originally from what he called "the Republic of Alberta" and never felt quite like a central Canadian – though he lives in Ontario to this day. He, like Pezzack, played on the football team and describes their group as straight, unlike "the in-crowd. The in-crowd smoked. They were always doing wild and woolly things. They were more rambunctious. We were more straitlaced."

Larry Moate, another friend, could be described as straitlaced. Larry was a member of a fundamentalist religious group, the Christadelphians, who accept the Bible as literally the word of God and recognize no other religious authority. They frown on alcohol, tobacco, and drugs. "There was a time period that, when I would go to parties, I would occasionally experiment [with alcohol] but decided pretty early on that drinking didn't do anything for me. You'd see people at some of the parties who probably had a bit too much to drink, but Stephen and I would never be counted amongst those."

Larry was into track and field, as was Stephen, and both served on the student council. Occasional asthma attacks kept Stephen out of competitive team sports. But he and Larry both ran in long-distance races. Stephen was tall and thin, several months older than Larry, and raced in a more senior category. Stephen was fast, Larry says, though never an intercollegiate champion. "He was probably the best distance runner on the Richview team, but none of us was really at the level to win and blow away the competition in the race. Stephen would be respectable."

What most impressed Larry about Stephen was his intellectual versatility. "I was smart in the humanities. Stephen was smart in the humanities, math, science. Anything he wanted, he excelled at it. He worked hard at it. He had, obviously, the brainpower and was versatile enough to excel in everything he wanted to."

His former teacher Bob Scott agrees. "Stephen was very intelligent. He was just a very quiet, very decent, very intelligent, very diligent, very hard-working person. And very disciplined." Scott was impressed that Harper did not take the easy courses in high school or aim merely for high marks. He studied French, including advanced French. In the summer after graduation he spent several weeks studying French intensively. At Richview he had studied Latin and had taken American History, courses which were non-compulsory, demanding options. Scott had only one reservation about his student: Stephen never asked questions in class. Scott would have expected a more challenging give-and-take from a student with a serious interest in history.

During that fifth year of high school, Stephen's classmates speculated that the gold medal, awarded to the student with the highest grade point average, would go to either Stephen Harper or John Clark, both recognized as outstanding scholars. In the event, it was Stephen who won the gold. His name was displayed in gold letters on the wall facing the school's main entrance. He was offered as a model for other students to emulate.

So it was that Stephen's childhood years came to a happy ending. Happy childhoods, to paraphrase Guy de Maupassant, make for sad biographers. A writer prefers to relate how his subject began in abject poverty, suffered through early neglect or abuse, survived persecution, overcame dreadful difficulties to emerge triumphant, crowned as a success. But not every important life begins with the pathos of Oliver Twist. Stephen had a home that was financially and emotionally secure, and he saw his father as a model of scrupulous rectitude. "My father was not merely honest, he had flawless integrity. In spite of his ambitions, he jealously guarded the interests of others as if they were his own." Joseph, like his ancestor Christopher Harper, was a lifetime teetotaller, but never dour or distant. He brought stimulating company into their home. He was a talker. Stephen remembers accompanying Margaret once when he was a young boy when she visited some friends. One turned to his mother and said, "Margaret, Stephen is sure a quiet boy. Doesn't he ever talk?" and Margaret replied, "Well, he really doesn't get a chance to talk," because Joseph talked constantly. "He loved to talk," Stephen recalled. "He talked to a fault. He talked all the time, I have to tell ya."

And there was music. Joseph Harper loved jazz. He went to many jazz concerts. He revered Duke Ellington as the greatest jazz musician ever. He joined the Duke Ellington Society, which published a monthly newsletter on the artist. Joseph collected every piece of music that the Duke ever recorded or wrote, including pirated recordings. Stephen's early years were lived against a constant background of music. He himself took piano lessons and passed Toronto's Royal Conservatory of Music exams at the Grade 3 level in musical theory, and Grade 9 for playing.

In his love of music as in everything else, Joseph was serious and hard-working. He was a lifelong self-improver, highly motivated, taking courses to increase his range of knowledge. He cultivated several hobbies, and each hobby brought him into contact with a different network of people sharing his interest. Young Stephen, always an attentive listener, picked up odds and ends of information on a wide range of topics. His versatility led to an adventure. In 1976, he was one of four Richview students picked to represent the school in an intercollegiate competition on CBC's popular television quiz show *Reach for the Top*.

Though they were beaten out by the team that eventually won the national championship, being chosen for the Richview team was already an accomplishment.

Graduation ended this idyllic phase of Stephen's life. In the school yearbook of 1978, Harper, like the other graduates, was asked to declare what he intended to do after high school. His answer, in the third person: "He's off to the U of T for Commerce or Law." And, in fact, he did enroll at the University of Toronto and begin taking courses in the fall. But something happened, something totally unexpected. After all his hard work and outstanding academic success, straight arrow Stephen Harper decided to drop out. After less than two months at the University of Toronto, he announced that he was quitting. He was going to look for a job.

His parents were shocked. His father had always regretted never having attended university. Now Stephen had the golden opportunity that he had lacked, and he was rejecting it. Margaret tried to reason with her son, as she explained to me. "I told him that, if he dropped out of university, he would never go back. He told me that he didn't know what he wanted to do. He would get a job, but he would return to university in two years."

What had happened? The outstanding student suddenly found that success at studies was not enough. Success for what? What was success? He sensed that something important was missing in himself, and he would not find it simply by continuing on the education track. He needed to see the real world in order to find himself.

And so, in the fall of 1978, he left university, left Toronto, left his friends, and headed west to find work in Edmonton, to fill a low-level office job for Imperial Oil. He was starting over again. He was going his own way.

Chapter 2

BOOKS, LOVE, AND POLITICS

FAST-FORWARD TO 1981. Stephen Harper was registered at the University of Calgary to pursue a bachelor's degree in economics. Politics was far from his mind. He was thinking about economics and world affairs. His favourite reading was the very serious and highly reputed British magazine *The Economist*. His ambition was to join the Department of External Affairs and represent Canada abroad as a diplomat. One year of study, then two went by.

He lived in a university residence, taking his meals in a cafeteria shared by students from other residences. There he noticed a blond young woman who seemed outgoing and full of laughter. Without ever having met her, he got hold of her phone number and rang her up. "He just phoned me and asked me out one day," she now recalls. "We didn't know each other. He just came and asked me if I would go to a movie with him." She accepted this invitation out of the blue and they went to see a Steve Martin film. She didn't tell Stephen until much later that she hated Steve Martin movies. But they clicked immediately.

Her name was Cynthia Williams and they became inseparable. She had completed two years of journalism at Calgary's Mount Royal College, which did not have a residence of its own, so Cynthia, whose parents lived in Fort Qu'Appelle, Saskatchewan, had a room in a University of Calgary residence.

She found "Steve" attractive with his wavy blond hair coming down almost to his shoulders. And, though he was rather shy, she soon found him funny, stimulating. "He was excited about life and he had a passion for things." She, like him, came from a family where current affairs were discussed. With her ambition to become a journalist, she followed the daily news. She discovered that he was a news junkie as well. "He was very interested in the world; it was an exciting place. That, to him, was a good drama, better than any show we could watch. One of the things we used to do was watch the news together. And he was quite the reader."

She remembers their first involvement with politics. Steve had been advised by a student counsellor on how he could prepare for a diplomatic career. "The counsellor had seen his grades and Steve could not get less than A-plus if his life depended on it. So his counsellor had basically said, to get into the foreign service he already had the grades, but he needed to show community activity, and that could be political involvement."

Together, they considered the possibilities, none of which appealed. Then they spotted an advertisement in the *Calgary Herald* announcing that their member of Parliament, Jim Hawkes, would hold a town-hall meeting the following Saturday. They checked it out. At the meeting, they were among the few young people in attendance. They questioned Hawkes about the goings-on in Ottawa – Steve in particular was disgusted with the Liberal government. Hawkes, as an opposition Tory MP, also criticized the Liberals. Steve and Cynthia found him intelligent and articulate. And, despite their youth, he didn't talk down to them. They came away impressed. From then on, they attended all of Hawkes's public forums.

Hawkes also recalls that first encounter. "He came to a public meeting with Cynthia, his girlfriend, and the two of them had obviously prepared. They sat in the front row. Stephen did most of the talking. But they both had questions and comments throughout the whole two hours, off and on. Very polite and very thoughtful. When the meeting was over, we talked a little more. My recall is that he did not know very much about the organized political party aspect of politics. How a riding was organized, and the business of membership and so on, were things he didn't know. He had concerns about the policy part of politics. They started coming regularly. They joined the association. Then the next thing I knew, they were working within my riding association as volunteers, and members of the executive."

Jim Hawkes was no ordinary politician. He'd been a university teacher and was used to dealing with young people. As a boy in Calgary, he'd been active in the Scouts and the YMCA, then worked at the YMCA in Calgary and in Westmount, Quebec, while he studied for his B.A. at Montreal's Sir George Williams College. He joined the University of Calgary as a professor, eventually taking two years off to obtain a Ph.D. in experimental psychology at Colorado State University. His specialty was research on job training and evaluating the efficiency and effectiveness of organizations. In the early 1970s, he had conducted for the federal government a two-year study of a pair of job-creation pump-primers, the Local Initiatives Program and Opportunities for Youth. That brought him to the attention of Joe Clark, then a special assistant in Ottawa to PC Leader Robert Stanfield. Clark invited Hawkes to chair a party advisory committee to study the advisability of a guaranteed annual income. Following the report of Hawkes's committee, the PC convention of 1972 adopted a guaranteed annual income as part of the party platform for the 1972 elections. Clark was elected to Parliament that year and, when Stanfield resigned as party leader, Clark succeeded him in February 1976. Hawkes had worked on his leadership campaign and then took a year's leave of absence from the university to help the new leader get his office in running order. He decided to run for Parliament himself, in the riding of Calgary West. He was elected in the PC victory of 1979, and there followed a few heady months when he was part of Joe Clark's short-lived government. That government fell on a budget vote in December, the party was reduced to opposition in the 1980 elections, and Clark's leadership was thereafter under constant attack. At the party convention in Winnipeg in January 1983, when Clark received only 66.9 per cent support from the delegates in a vote of confidence, he chose to call a leadership convention. PC party politics became frenzied. On June 11, 1983, Brian Mulroney defeated Clark for the leadership, and it was the start of a new era.

But the internal party struggles were not over. One day in early 1984, Hawkes's secretary, Joyce Smith, called Cynthia Williams. Steve was with her at the time. Joyce said that Hawkes was being challenged for the nomination as PC candidate in Calgary West. He needed all the help he could get. Would they come out and support him?

The challenger was a local businessman who had opposed Clark in the leadership campaign and wanted to replace Hawkes, the pro-Clark MP in Calgary West. "I was challenged for the nomination by people who had backed Mulroney," Hawkes recalls. "They had outsold us in terms of memberships. They had used a commercial outfit to sell memberships." Steve and Cynthia thought they already had the ideal member of Parliament in Jim Hawkes, so they took out memberships in the PC Party and recruited others to join as well. Hawkes's riding included the University of Calgary. "Steve and I – it was mainly Steve – turned out a lot of people from residence. We brought out a good portion of the residents of the University of Calgary to back Jim."

In the end, with the enthusiastic support of the university students, Hawkes won overwhelmingly at the nomination meeting. Stephen and Cynthia were hooked. Now they were part of Jim Hawkes's campaign team. His political friends were their political friends. One friend who was under heavy challenge for his renomination was the MP for Calgary Centre, Harvie Andre. He, like Hawkes, had supported Joe Clark. Stephen and Cynthia again swung into action. "The Youth Wing worked their butts off to help at both nominations, leadership selections and general elections," according to Hawkes. Harvie Andre also won his nomination battle. "Stephen was rapidly promoted within that Youth Wing to be the president, because of talent, because of interest and the way he was considered by the others." Cynthia became the vice-president.

Looking back, Hawkes recalls his impression of Steve. "Very studious. Always well prepared for whatever the discussion was. As a riding youth president he would do the homework necessary to run a good meeting, recruit members, participate in board meetings and election campaigns, and do the kinds of things that volunteers do. A hard worker."

He saw that Stephen was gifted, and he soon invited Stephen and Cynthia to his home to meet his wife, Joanne, and their two children. Cynthia says he made them feel like part of the family. Cynthia and Steve were now swept up in party politics. A young man named Brian Wik, whom they had met in the nomination campaigns, was running for the presidency of the PC Youth of Alberta. The convention was to be held in Edmonton, so Steve and Cynthia went off to Edmonton to attend the convention and support Wik. He had a vacancy on his slate of candidates for the position of vice-president for communications. He asked Cynthia, with her background in student journalism, to run. Steve promoted her campaign at the convention. By the time they returned to

Calgary, Wik was president of the PCYA and Cynthia was vice-president for communications.

Meanwhile, in Ottawa, Prime Minister Pierre Trudeau had decided to step down and John Turner won the Liberal leadership on June 16, 1984. Turner became prime minister on June 30 and, on July 9, when polls showed him in the lead over Brian Mulroney, Turner dissolved Parliament and called elections for September 4. In Calgary, Jim Hawkes mobilized his supporters and appointed Stephen as youth-campaign coordinator for Calgary West. All Alberta was determined to punish the party that had imposed the hated National Energy Program, but nowhere more than in Calgary West. Stephen Harper proved a strong organizer for the influx of young volunteers who turned up to help throw the rascals out. That was now more than a slogan, it was a passion, a cause that could mobilize a horde of volunteers. For Stephen, this campaign consecrated his passage from being a Torontonian to a true blue Albertan.

He had left Toronto almost six years earlier and headed to Edmonton to work for Imperial Oil in the regional office of the company that employed his father. At first, his duties were nondescript. He worked in the mailing room, sorting letters and parcels, and trundling a cart from office to office to deliver the mail to the appropriate departments. His bosses soon discovered that he had a natural flair for the language of computers. Soon he was busy in the computer department. After two years, he was asked to take charge of the computer system in the Calgary office. He accepted, even though it put off his return to university by one year more than he had planned. And so he arrived in the city with which his name and fortunes would be identified.

By 1984, Stephen had come to see the country from Alberta's vantage point rather than Ontario's. The geopolitics of oil had driven the two provinces far apart. While Stephen was a high-school student living at home in Etobicoke, Israel was attacked on October 6, 1973, by Egypt and Syria. Israel eventually won the Yom Kippur War, but the Arab-dominated Organization of Petroleum Exporting Countries (OPEC) retaliated against Israel's ally by restricting the output of petroleum and banning exports to the United States. The price of a barrel of oil rose from $1.80 to $32. In the United States, gas suddenly became expensive and scarce; motorists waited in long lineups at service stations where the supply of gas had not yet run out. Emergency conservation measures included reducing the legal speed limit on U.S. interstate highways to fifty-five miles per hour.

In Canada, after the elections of October 1972, Trudeau led a minority Liberal government with 109 seats in the Commons to the 107 held by Robert Stanfield's Tories. The Liberals relied on the thirty-one New Democrat MPs to govern. They held only seven seats in all of western Canada and none in Alberta where most of the country's oil was pumped. In Quebec, though, which had no oil, the Liberals held fifty-six seats, more than half their caucus. For historic reasons, the sharp rise in oil prices particularly affected Quebec and the Atlantic provinces. Since 1963, provinces west of the "Borden line" between Quebec and Ontario were compelled to take their oil from domestic western producers. They paid a higher price for this domestic oil than the five provinces east of the Borden line paid for the less expensive oil that they imported from offshore. Now, suddenly, when the price of imported oil rose dramatically at the end of 1973, the once-privileged provinces were at a disadvantage. So Trudeau imposed an export tax on the oil that left Canada to be sold in the United States. By April of 1974, that export tax was used to subsidize a single cross-Canada price for oil, one that was lower than the international price. The following month, the minority Liberal government fell and the country went to the polls on July 8. The grateful eastern provinces returned a majority Liberal government even as Albertans were outraged that they were being made to subsidize their fellow citizens in other provinces by a tax that fell singularly on a resource – petroleum – that actually belonged to the province.

Still, despite the tax and the controlled price, Alberta prospered from the windfall of higher oil prices during the remaining years of the 1970s. But then, on October 18, 1980, the Trudeau government intruded further when it announced the National Energy Program, along with various bills that gave Ottawa almost total control of petroleum, a provincial resource. It was a highly nationalist and socialist enterprise, premised on the assumption that the world price of oil would keep rising into the indefinite future. That turned out to be utterly wrong. The NEP maintained price controls on oil and natural gas, forced partial Canadian ownership of all new petroleum discoveries, and put in place measures to ensure that available petroleum met the needs of all Canadians, with only the surplus available for export. The federal government, in effect, shouldered aside the Alberta government to take control of its petroleum.

The NEP was popular in the East: it protected Ontario and the eastern provinces from the shock that was causing recession throughout the rest of the industrialized world. But it provoked a fierce backlash in Alberta, causing one of the most bitter conflicts between Ottawa and a province in Canadian history. Premier Peter Lougheed took to the radio to announce a defiant reduction in Alberta's production of oil. In the East, they spoke of Alberta's "blue-eyed sheiks." In Alberta, bumper stickers appeared with the message: "Let the Eastern bastards freeze in the dark."

In 1977, Stephen Harper had admired Pierre Trudeau as the champion fighting off the threat of secession in Quebec. But now, as an Albertan, he had a double reason for hating the NEP. It was an attack on the petroleum industry in general, and it also discriminated against petroleum companies that were foreign-owned – like Imperial Oil. And now Harper witnessed the flight from Alberta of a caravan of oil rigs. Exploration slowed almost to a stop. It wasn't only the view from Imperial Oil that appalled him. As an Albertan, he shared in the general distress of the recession that hit the entire province and, above all, Calgary, where he was now living. By 1983, when the world price of oil had dropped sharply because of fallen demand in the industrial countries which were in recession, Calgary's sumptuous construction boom of the 1970s froze. Idle cranes towered beside the skeletal frameworks of unfinished buildings as practically all activity died.

Harper, at the time an economics major at the University of Calgary, was marked for life by the experience of the NEP, as he was later to evoke in a column written a few days after Pierre Trudeau's death in 2000. "In 1977, I received an invitation to have lunch with Pierre Trudeau," he recalled. "Sudden and unexpected circumstances did not permit it to come about. It wasn't until last year that I would actually meet Mr. Trudeau, simply by chance, on the streets of Montreal. There I came face to face with a living legend, someone who had provoked both the loves and hatreds of my political passion, all in the form of a tired out, little old man."

It was the NEP that had made the difference between his earlier "loves" and his later "hatreds" for Trudeau, as he made clear. "By the time Mr. Trudeau embarked on the National Energy Program, I was living in the West. I witnessed first-hand the movement of an economy from historic boom to deep recession in a matter of months. A radical, interventionist blueprint of economic nationalism, the NEP caused the oil industry to flee, businesses to close, and the real-estate market to crash. The lives of honest, hard-working Albertans were upended, and I came to know many of those who lost their jobs and their homes." Eventually, that experience would cause Harper to commit himself deeply to politics. As he wrote in that same column: "In 1977, economics and finance didn't much matter to me. Beginning with the NEP, Mr. Trudeau would show me that they did matter – a lesson he never bothered to master himself."

So he and Cynthia threw themselves into the 1984 campaign in Calgary West. Together, it was their responsibility to recruit young volunteers for the Hawkes campaign. Together, they engaged in the flurry of activities that go with a campaign at the riding level. Cynthia worked on communications and spent much of her time accompanying Jim Hawkes as they went around the riding, knocking on doors and greeting the constituents. Stephen was mostly at campaign headquarters, working directly with the senior managers of the campaign, and helping organize the youth volunteers who were making phone calls to pinpoint supporters, putting together signs, placing them on lawns where the occupants consented, distributing pamphlets door to door, phoning to remind people to get out and vote. So many young volunteers turned out to help that the biggest problem was finding something to keep all of them busy. The experience acquired by Stephen and some of his friends in this professionally run campaign would prove invaluable in the future, but in ways that could not have been foreseen that summer.

It wasn't all work for the volunteers, as Cynthia Williams describes their tenure as youth president and vice-president. "Our attitude was that, if you want people to be involved in politics, you have to realize that it's coming out of their social time. So you need to make it social. We were just typical twenty-year-olds. Right? So we'd do fun things. We would talk about stuff, but we wouldn't go to a community hall and talk about it, we'd go for a beer at the pub of the University of Calgary. We went to dances together, we did sleigh rides and . . . a hayride in which every-body went out to the country to have a barn dance. We'd put on parties like that."

Cynthia was clearly the more sociable of the pair, and she did most of the social organizing. But she remembers Steve, clad in jeans and T-shirts, loving music, loving movies, and a good dancer. "When it came to fashion, he was just more like your average guy." When asked, she shies away from discussing Steve's religious views at the time. But she does say: "We were not churchgoers." They each kept separate resi-dences. "We were obviously together a lot. But I think Steve and I kind of both felt . . . if you're going to make the commitment to live together, you might as well make the commitment to marry."

As the election campaign heated up, Stephen liked what he saw and heard of Brian Mulroney. As a student of economics, Harper was most impressed by those economists who emphasized the importance of the free market for economic efficiency and democratic development. He thought he found that commitment in Mulroney, with his background in business, unlike Pierre Trudeau, with a career in the public service and universities, or Joe Clark, whose entire career was in politics. During his campaign for the party leadership in 1983, Mulroney had constantly sounded right-wing themes, calling for government restraint, for control of the federal deficit, for improved productivity, and more harmonious labour relations. He had denounced the Parti Québécois as socialist, and challenged Premier René Lévesque by name: "Before I give away a nickel of Canada's money, I want to know what Lévesque's going to do with it."

One of Mulroney's first acts after he became leader of the Opposition was to visit U.S. president Ronald Reagan and proclaim: "Canada is open for business." Most Albertans did not share the anti–U.S. nationalism common in Southern Ontario, and they liked what they heard from the new PC leader. During the 1984 election campaign, Mulroney denounced Canada's restrictive regulator of foreign investment, the Foreign Invest-ment Review Agency, which had been instituted amid the economic nationalism of the 1970s to ensure that all takeovers by foreign firms and all direct investment were of "net benefit" to Canada. The cumbersome procedure was a deterrent to foreign investment. Moreover, Mulroney promised to ensure "first-class" treatment for the armed forces. All this gave an economic conservative like Harper reason for hope.

Cynthia and Steve met the Mulroneys when the glamorous pair came to Calgary on a campaign visit. "When Brian Mulroney and Mila came into town, they had a big rally. We met Brian and Mila. I believe it was at Prince's Island Park. We liked them. Actually Brian, to this day, has an amazing memory. When we met him again later, he actually did remember both our names. Either that or he has a really good prompter who did."

One of the Calgary West youth volunteers attending the rally at Prince's Island Park on the Bow River, just north of downtown, was John Weissenberger, a University of Calgary student who was to play an important role in Stephen's life. He recalls: "The event on Prince's Island with Mulroney was unbelievable. They had bused people in and just packed the place. There was a double-sided receiving line about 500 yards long. I've never seen anything like it. I shook Mulroney's hand and spoke to him in French."

Finally, election day arrived. Cynthia spent the day serving as an outside scrutineer, supervising the voting in one poll on behalf of Jim Hawkes. Stephen was at campaign headquarters, assisting the leadership. The turnout of voters was particularly impressive. There was a sense of expectation in the air, as if the citizens of Calgary West wanted to send their message across the country. By day's end, all was jubilation at Hawkes's campaign headquarters. As soon as the polls closed in the east, despite the ban on broadcasting results before the polls closed in Alberta, Hawkes's people were on the phone to acquaintances in the east and kept relaying the results as they rolled in. The picture that emerged was stunning. In every region of the country, in every province, Mulroney's Progressive Conservatives had crushed every other party. Even Quebec, the graveyard of so many Tory hopes, returned fifty-eight Conservative MPs and only seventeen Liberals. By the end of the evening, Mulroney had won 211 of the country's 282 seats – 75.8 per cent. He had also won just over 50 per cent of the popular vote, a rare feat in Canadian political history.

Late that night, when the magnitude of the victory was confirmed, Brian Mulroney went on television in the hometown of his childhood, Baie Comeau: "The country has spoken – the real country nurtured by its past sacrifices, by the latent strength of its people, and by its awareness of its place in the world. Canada has responded to the call to unity."

That was no exaggeration. Region by region, the country had overcome its internal divisions and asserted a rare consensus.

In Calgary West, Jim Hawkes took 74.7 per cent of the vote. His closest rival eked out a mere 11.4 per cent. Stephen and his friends went to the victory celebration in a large, crowded hall. The riding, including the university, had responded with enthusiasm to Mulroney's call and Hawkes's reputation. There were many young people sharing in the joy, hugging each other, dancing, delighting in the glow of their historic success in Calgary West and across the country. Cynthia Williams remembers being "very excited. It was our first experience of being a part of something like that. Steve had a lot of respect for Brian Mulroney. He was very excited about what Brian Mulroney could bring to the country. And we were happy for Jim."

A blessed peace descended on Canada on that September 4, 1984, when Brian Mulroney's Progressive Conservatives rallied the entire country. It was a rare and historic coming together. The Atlantic provinces, Quebec, Ontario, the Prairie provinces, British Columbia, all spoke for once in harmony. After two decades of national turmoil, of divergent regional demands, of threats and resentments, of tensions that strained the very bonds of a common citizenship, a new government was elected that promised an era of national reconciliation. And the voice of the West, long stifled, would again be heard loud and clear in the land.

That sense of emerging from turmoil, from recession, from long conflict and dislocation, was projected by *Maclean's* in its 1984 year-end issue. *Maclean's* had commissioned from Decima Research a national poll on the mood of the country and the response was remarkably buoyant. *Maclean's* trumpeted on its front cover: "A Confident Nation Speaks Up." Robert Miller summarized the findings: "Perhaps not since 1967, Canada's centennial year, when the country impressed the entire world and amazed itself by successfully staging Expo 67 and a host of other celebratory events, have the Canadian people been as sure of themselves and their future as the poll suggests they are today."

Peter C. Newman provided the opening essay which hinted broadly that the passage of Pierre Trudeau from the political scene and the emergence of Brian Mulroney were critical factors in the change of the national mood. "After 16 punishing years of Trudeau telling us how ungrateful we were for not appreciating his presence, Brian Mulroney seemed as welcome as the rebirth of green at the end of winter. Mulroney's arrival was cause for optimism, even if he has yet to earn it." And Newman ended on this note: "On September 4, Canadians deposited their hopes, dreams, and expectations on Mulroney's unshrugging shoulders."

For Stephen Harper, too, this was a period of grace. He breezed through his last year of studies for his first degree in economics. And he had something exciting to look forward to. Jim Hawkes had invited him to come to Ottawa to act as his legislative assistant. Just before leaving for Ottawa, Steve gave an engagement ring to Cynthia Williams. All seemed right with the world.

Chapter 3

POWER AND GLORY IN OTTAWA

STEPHEN HARPER HAD arrived in Ottawa. The Peace Tower became the landmark of his new life. The grey gothic Parliament Buildings, with their network of interconnecting tunnels, were now his haunts. He walked the corridors lined with paintings and photographs of long-dead former prime ministers, forgotten Speakers of the Commons and obscure Speakers of the Senate. Tradition emanated from the walls. His footsteps echoed where once echoed the footsteps of John A. Macdonald, Mackenzie King, John Diefenbaker, and Pierre Trudeau.

In 1985, great changes for Canada were in the air and were already under way. They would be debated and decided in these very buildings. And he would be part of it. Prime Minister Brian Mulroney, now in power almost a year, had made it clear that the two priorities at the top of his political agenda were restructuring the economy and delivering national reconciliation. Both were close to Harper's heart and mind. Having just completed his first degree in economics, he felt passionately the need to change the political direction of the economy, to remove the shackles from the private sector and let it perform. And, after the trauma of the National Energy Program, national reconciliation meant something important to him, as long as it applied to Alberta and not only to Quebec. Now Stephen Harper was there at the centre of power and ready to make his mark.

Going from Calgary to Ottawa was a culture shock. He was now surrounded by ambitious young men in blue suits who bustled about self-importantly, letting everyone know what important secrets they could tell if they were free to talk. Stephen referred to them ironically as "the future prime ministers." He discovered intense rivalry between the political assistants staffing the offices of members of Parliament and cabinet ministers. Your status was defined by whom you worked for. Jim Hawkes, so respected in Calgary, was a backbencher here, one of about 170 on the government side. His expertise was recognized, and he was chairman of the Commons Standing Committee on Labour, Employment and Immigration. But he was also tainted by his close association with the loser, Joe Clark. Past rivalries and resentments still festered. This was so different from the congenial politics Stephen had known in Calgary, where it was as much about making friends as it was about winning. In Ottawa, ambition and competitiveness ruled even among people in the same party. Between parties, it was cutthroat. Stephen was not happy, recalls Cynthia Williams. "The whole Ottawa lifestyle, the glad-handing, the wine and cheeses, being with the right person, saying the right thing – that all seemed just too plastic to him."

He lived in Sandy Hill, a twenty-minute walk from the Confederation Building, where Hawkes had his office and where Harper spent most of his waking hours. He was lonely. He missed his fiancée. They spoke on the phone each night. Occasionally, he would see Cynthia when Hawkes returned to his riding and Harper accompanied him. But it wasn't the same. He spent most evenings doing research in a branch of the Library of Parliament in the basement, then he returned to the office upstairs where his closest confidant in Ottawa was his boss and now his friend, Jim. "The year he spent in Ottawa provided an unusual kind of closeness between us," Hawkes remembers. "He was lonesome, in part. He didn't really make friends easily, and I don't think he made a friend in that whole year in Ottawa. But quite often at night we'd be there until ten or eleven, making phone calls back to Calgary because of the time difference. And then we'd sit and talk for an hour about what was on his mind. Lots of times it was policy and politics. At other times it was very, very personal. More so than I had experienced with other staff people. So we talked a lot about Stephen Harper and where he was going and why he was going, and so on."

Stephen's problem was not just loneliness. There was something about Parliament Hill's atmosphere and political culture that he found repellent. During the day, he sometimes watched the forty-five-minute verbal scrimmage when John Turner, NDP Leader Ed Broadbent, and various opposition MPs assailed Prime Minister Mulroney and his ministers. It was called Question Period and was the focal point of the daily parliamentary ritual, the only time, except when votes were counted, that all MPs were normally expected to attend in the Commons. It was when the reporters of the Parliamentary Press Gallery turned their attention to the Chamber, waiting for an honourable member to reveal a scandal, utter a quotable put-down, make an embarrassing faux pas, or say something, anything, that could pass as newsworthy. The questions were almost never true questions: they were traps. The answers were almost never true answers: they were evasions, counter-charges, taunts, sallies of scorn and derision. Total hostility separated like a knife one side of the Commons from the other. Commonly, honourable members displayed their wit by catcalls, shouted interruptions, or by crude hand gestures that weren't immortalized in the written record of Hansard. The august Chamber often had the allure of a boarding school for undisciplined adolescents.

Harper was depressed by the triviality of it all. He came to realize how powerless government backbenchers were. Their most visible role was to applaud the responses of the ministers when these prima donnas rose to answer a question from the Opposition. And they invariably voted the party line. He had arrived full of enthusiasm for the significant work that he was eager to undertake. "He was excited," Hawkes recalls. The Mulroney government had performed rather spectacularly in its first year. When Brian Mulroney had spoken in Calgary before the '84 elections, he had denounced in vivid terms the National Energy Program, describing it as "exactly like a hold-up at the corner gas station at 3 a.m." Once in power, he chose a cabinet that had forty ministers, with the real power to make decisions vested in a fifteen-member inner cabinet called the Priorities and Planning Committee. Apart from the prime minister himself, precisely half of its fourteen members were from western Canada. Only three were from Ontario. It suggested where Mulroney's priorities lay, and they were not in Ontario.

Mulroney appointed a westerner as Minister of Energy, Mines and Resources where, by contrast, Pierre Trudeau had relied on Marc Lalonde, a lawyer from Quebec. Mulroney's choice, Pat Carney, had made a name for herself as a business journalist for the *Vancouver Sun* and the *Province*. What she thought of the NEP was entirely consonant with Mulroney's view that it was robbery. "As a newly elected MP from the West, full of dreams about the West's place in Confederation, the brutal unfairness of the NEP was like a slug in my gut," she wrote later in her memoirs, *Trade Secrets* (2000). "I reflected the burning resentment of many westerners, fuelled by the fact that an energy minister and prime minister from Quebec were stealing the resource revenues – owned by the western provinces under our Constitution, and which we needed to finance our own development – in the interest of national 'fairness' but essentially for the benefit of Ontario and Quebec consumers." As she relates in her memoirs, she moved quickly to meet demands by Newfoundland and Nova Scotia over offshore petroleum resources. On October 29, 1984, in the month after she was sworn in as minister, she signed with the western energy ministers an interim agreement setting a new price for petroleum that was more favourable to the provinces. It was an impressive display of speed and determination to reverse the energy policies of the Liberals, so hated in the western and two Atlantic provinces. And it was all done while circumventing the usual bureaucratic requirements. As Carney explained, "With the prime minister's backing, I bypassed the normal cabinet process of committees and discussion and consensus. He told my cabinet colleagues that while the process was unorthodox, our energy decision-making was going ahead full steam, thus discouraging their interference or comments. He justified the procedural shortcuts by saying our caucus had already approved our energy policy while we were in Opposition." Carney was ecstatic at the time. She would be less happy two years later when Mulroney would use the same unorthodox tactics to give Quebec rather than Winnipeg the contract to service the CF-18 fighter aircraft.

Her greatest triumph came on March 28, 1985, when she and the western energy ministers signed what was called the Western Accord. It completed and finalized the interim agreement of October 29 and ended the federal government's assumption of control over the energy sector. It restored market pricing, and promised to phase out the tax on natural gas. The government of Alberta was happy, Stephen Harper was proud to be a supporter of Mulroney's government, and for a brief time, western alienation was out of fashion. But all this happened before Harper arrived in Ottawa.

———◈———

Brian Mulroney had come to power with boundless ambition and a towering self-confidence. Some might call it hubris. Within three months of taking office, he went to the United States to deliver a speech to the Economic Club of New York. Rereading it even today, after the ashes of the years have accumulated, one is struck by the boldness of his commitments and the grandiloquence of his tone. He was about to remake Canada. He would turn its gaze outward. He would restore tarnished relations with the United States. Within Canada, he would restore peace and co-operation where there had been regional conflict and distrust. Such was Brian Mulroney's euphoric vision at the beginning of his mandate. Would he realize it in the end?

During that first year, just before Harper came to Ottawa, it seemed that his deeds would be as good as his words. In Opposition, he had blamed Pierre Trudeau for the bitterness of federal-provincial relations. By the time Trudeau stepped down, in fact, there was not a single Liberal government left in any of the ten provinces. Mulroney was confident that, with his extraordinary personality, his charm, his truly remarkable magic as a negotiator, he could bring peace to the federal-provincial scene. A month before the 1984 election, he had insisted: "Our first task is to breathe a new spirit into federalism. I am convinced that the serious deterioration of federal-provincial relations is not exclusively the result of the constitutional deficiencies. Centralistic and negative attitudes are much more to blame." "Centralistic" and "negative attitudes" were clearly code words for Pierre Trudeau. Mulroney would espouse, rather, the "sunny ways" of Wilfrid Laurier.

And it worked, then. Mulroney had proposed that the prime minister should meet with the premiers at least once a year. Shortly after he took office, he invited the premiers for a November meeting in the relaxed, rustic atmosphere of Meech Lake, in the Gatineau Hills, north of Ottawa. The event turned into a love-in, with the premiers emerging to praise the new, co-operative attitude that they had experienced. Mulroney followed up that meeting by proposing a more formal, more

structured meeting with the premiers three months later, to share views
with them on the national economy. Moreover, he proposed that they
should meet in Regina rather than Ottawa. His proposal conveyed the
symbolic message that he was going more than halfway to meet the premiers on their ground. Again he carried off a triumph of personal diplomacy. At that meeting it was resolved to hold conferences of First
Ministers at least once a year.

He followed through, too, on his promise to promote a consensus in
the whole of society. In March 1985, he took a leaf from the agenda
book of René Lévesque who, a few months after he came to power in
Quebec in 1976, convened an "economic summit" at a resort – the
Manoir Richelieu – in an Arcadian setting by the Malbaie River with a
view over the Gulf of St. Lawrence. Lévesque had invited not only politicians from all parties, but also business leaders, union leaders, bankers,
credit-union executives. It had been deemed a great success. Mulroney's
National Economic Conference was held in Ottawa, bringing together
about 150 prominent people drawn from all sectors of society. There,
again, Mulroney preached his consensus gospel: "Consensus is the only
way to let Canada adapt, compete, and prosper."

He repeated his mantra on consensus when, on April 2 and 3, 1985,
he again gathered the premiers, this time to meet him, along with aboriginal leaders, in what was called the First Ministers' Conference on the
Rights of Aboriginal Peoples. "You know of my commitment to national
reconciliation. You know of my determination to breathe new life into
and restore harmony to federal-provincial relations. We have seen the
advantages of moving to consensus and the new hope it offers us."

But, somehow, the magic was losing some of its effect. The problem
was that charm and rhetoric and the evocation of the bad old days of
Pierre Trudeau could carry Mulroney only so far. When it came time to
cut the cash, the premiers, the union leaders, the citizens' groups, the
aboriginals, the bankers, the interest groups receiving subsidies, all
came to a somewhat different consensus from the mellifluous, harmonious speeches delivered at the conferences. Now the common theme
was "show me the money."

Finance Minister Michael Wilson had delivered an economic statement on November 8, 1984, expressing the new government's determination to cut spending and reduce the deficit. His statement, *A New*

Direction for Canada: An Agenda for Economic Renewal, was followed up the next May with more concrete actions when he brought down his first budget. Wilson then announced that the deficit projected for 1985–86 would be greater than it had been in 1984–85. Strong measures were needed to curb the deficit. He announced that pension benefits for seniors would no longer be fully indexed to rise with the cost of living. This was not exactly what Mulroney had promised when, still in Opposition, he had pronounced the entitlement programs to be "a sacred trust." He got his comeuppance on June 19, 1985, when a phalanx of fierce, grey-haired seniors held a demonstration on Parliament Hill against the erosion of their pensions. One little old lady, Solange Denis, caught the public imagination with her vivid denunciation of Brian Mulroney: "You made promises that you wouldn't touch anything . . . you lied to us. I was made to vote for you and then it's goodbye, Charlie Brown." Mulroney didn't have the fortitude to stand up to an outraged, extremely vocal pensioner of sixty-three. He backed down. The announcement in the budget remained a dead letter. And Mulroney was in full retreat in his battle against the deficit.

This happened just as Harper was finding his way around Ottawa. With his own strong commitment to fiscal restraint and balanced budgets, he took it as a very bad portent. In future years, he would often ironically evoke "sacred trusts" to stigmatize the unwillingness to make hard but necessary decisions. Still, he had reason to be enthusiastic about his new job. In August 1985, the Royal Commission headed by former Liberal heavyweight Donald Macdonald presented its final report. The commission had been appointed out of desperation by the Trudeau government in 1982 when Canada was in recession, its productivity was falling behind that of other industrialized countries, and its economy was under the constant threat of growing protectionist sentiment in the U.S. Congress against the all-important export industries. So Trudeau had named his trusted former finance minister to head the Royal Commission on the Economic Union and Development Prospects for Canada.

In its long-awaited report, the Royal Commission had made one particularly dramatic recommendation to restructure Canada's economy: that Canada make "a leap of faith," in the words of Donald Macdonald, and enter into a free-trade agreement with the United States. Would it happen? Mulroney had given the thumbs-down on free trade when it had been put forward by his rival, John Crosbie, during the 1983 Tory leadership campaign. Free trade with the U.S. had been, for a century, too hot to handle. But Macdonald, with his impeccable Liberal credentials, had just given Mulroney credible cover to reverse his position and become a proponent of free trade. At his "Shamrock summit" meeting in Quebec with U.S. president Ronald Reagan on March 17, 1985, Mulroney had signalled his interest in new arrangements to expand trade between the two countries. On that, both leaders could sing "When Irish Eyes Are Smiling."

Harper was, of course, entirely in favour of free trade with the United States, but of more immediate interest to him as Hawkes's assistant were the Macdonald commission's recommendations regarding Canada's uniquely generous regime of unemployment insurance. While praising the good intentions that had inspired it, the commission had been highly critical of its unintended results. A program originally intended to protect workers against the calamity of unforeseen unemployment had been extended into a program to subsidize seasonal workers. It encouraged workers to remain in seasonal jobs rather than look for year-round employment, just as Harper's father had observed on a trip back to New Brunswick. It raised the level of unemployment in some provinces. It encouraged regions with high unemployment to retain their low-paying and unstable jobs, which would then be subsidized by industries and employees in the rest of Canada. Because there was little incentive to replace marginal jobs with more productive employment, this program acted as a drag on the economies of both the richer and the poorer regions of Canada. And so the commission recommended that the unemployment insurance program be reformed to function strictly as insurance rather than disguised welfare. The money saved could then be applied to targeted welfare measures, such as a guaranteed annual income.

This was good news for Harper. As an economist, he agreed that the UI program had unfortunate effects and needed reforming. And, by happy coincidence, even before the Macdonald commission had submitted its report, the Mulroney government, shortly after it took office, announced that it was setting up its own commission specifically to review the unemployment insurance program. Its chairman was the economist Claude Forget, who had served as minister of health and welfare in the Liberal government of Robert Bourassa. It was called the

Commission of Inquiry on Unemployment Insurance. Before the Forget commission had even begun its work, Mulroney named Harper's patron, Jim Hawkes, as chairman of the Commons Standing Committee on Labour, Employment and Immigration. "In that following year, we did a lot of major work on immigration," Hawkes remembers. "We did five major studies that had a lot of influence on what the government did about that." Harper soon found himself studying the intricate relations between immigration and the economy, demography, and politics. But, of greater consequence for Harper's own understanding of how the Mulroney government operated, the Hawkes committee decided to conduct its own review of the unemployment insurance program.

"My portfolio at that time was related to unemployment insurance and immigration and there are always issues, and they're always very, very difficult," Hawkes recalls. "One of the shocks I got as a younger man was attending a caucus and having people from Newfoundland talk about unemployment insurance, and I'd been raised in Alberta. The attitudes were so different. It was hard to believe that you had two MPs from the same party in the same room at the same time talking about it. And I think Stephen experienced that as well."

As Hawkes's legislative assistant, Harper was soon plunged into reading, analyzing, and absorbing everything he could find on the structure, the functioning, and effects of Canada's unemployment insurance program. This was exhilarating for the young economist. He now had the opportunity to put his previous studies to practical use on a subject that carried immense economic and political consequences, and the Mulroney government was, he thought, determined to deal with it decisively after the years of muddled Liberal thinking and perverse policies. As he saw it, reform of the unemployment insurance program would help the Atlantic provinces to raise their economic performance, while at the same time it would lessen the burden on industry and workers in the three wealthier provinces, including Alberta. As an added benefit, the improved economy would help the government to bring down the dangerously high deficit, as Mulroney had promised to do.

In fact, while Harper investigated the mysteries of UI, still another commission was launched. In 1985, about the time that Harper arrived in Ottawa, Newfoundland premier Brian Peckford appointed a sociologist from Memorial University, Douglas House, to chair a Royal Commission on Employment and Unemployment. Its mandate was broadly defined: to "investigate all aspects of employment and unemployment in the Province of Newfoundland." It conducted its inquiry at the same time as the Forget commission and the Hawkes committee were doing their investigations, and the staff members working on all three inquiries kept in communication with each other. Everything seemed to converge toward a fundamental reform of UI. The timing in the economic cycle seemed ideal: the sharp recession of the early 1980s had turned into a period of strong, sustained growth. Jobs were being created; unemployment was receding. It was now or never.

In fact, two of the three investigating bodies produced proposals for reform that underlined the negative effects of the existing UI system. A summary of Newfoundland's House commission report, titled *Building on Our Strengths*, stated: "The commission argued that the status quo undermined the intrinsic value of work, good work habits and discipline, the importance of education, personal and community initiatives, and the incentive to work. It also discouraged self-employment and small-scale enterprise. In addition, the make-work aspects of the UI system encouraged political patronage and distorted the efforts of local development groups. Finally, the UI system had become 'a bureaucratic nightmare' which was vulnerable to manipulation and in which the role of officials had become distorted."

The Forget commission had held hearings on UI in forty-six communities across the country. Its research was thorough. Like the Macdonald commission, its majority report concluded that "fundamental transformation" of the UI program was "essential." It, too, spotlighted the perverse effects of the UI program, its disincentives to personal and economic growth. Both commissions proposed to separate the dual objectives of UI, an insurance program for job security on the one hand, and a welfare program for supplementing income on the other. The House commission stated that the UI program should be focused on its original role of providing income maintenance to people "in transition between permanent jobs or on short-term layoff, sick leave, or maternity leave."

But Hawkes's committee was made up of members of Parliament, politicians concerned with getting re-elected. In the event, the Hawkes committee proposed that the government broaden the coverage of UI to

extend it to new vulnerable social groups, expanding the welfare function of unemployment insurance. Instead of costing considerably less, as
proposed by the Macdonald, House, and Forget commissions, the
Hawkes report would have added $1 billion in additional payments, for
a total annual cost of $12 billion.

Harper was no longer in Ottawa by the time the Hawkes committee
reported, but he could see before he left which way the hearings and the
negotiations within the committee were heading, and he found it deeply
disenchanting. Hawkes recognized just how scarring the experience of
real-world politics was to the idealistic young man with his strongly held
beliefs, driven by economic theory, of the way the world should work.

"The policy part that Stephen was closest to was related to that whole
unemployment insurance thing. Starting with that, and then, how do you
work it through a caucus? We had a caucus of 206 members of
Parliament. That was probably the single biggest experience of his life –
certainly at that stage – of the need to compromise. Of what you gain and
what you lose. At that stage of his life he found some of that upsetting.
He felt there should be clear-cut answers to problems. You should implement the best economic decision, and then it would work over time. He
wasn't difficult in the sense of being stubborn, or in the way; but, in his
mind, from an economic point of view, there was a right way to do it. And
when we were reaching consensus, that wasn't the overriding concern.
The overriding concern was to have it working in the different parts of
the country in ways it needed to work to help the people in the different
regions, and that was not in accord with the pure economic model.

"I think with Stephen, at that age, you had to look at an economic
textbook, and in particular the school of thought favourable to free
enterprise. The rules or the findings related to the development of a free
enterprise economy were the ideas he held dearest. And so you wouldn't
have special adaptations, for instance, with unemployment insurance in
different geographic regions, because then that would keep people in
regions of high unemployment. They would continue to live there. And
if you didn't have geographic adaptations, then they would have to move
to where people needed to hire people. That's very much what a university can teach you to do, and I think that's what his economics background had taught him to do. That's the way he looked at the world at
that age."

Hawkes recalls an incident illustrating Harper's progressive disenchantment with the real world of politics, this time outside of Parliament. "I remember, near the end of his time in my office, I was going to go to an organized labour event in Calgary, to make a bit of a speech. It was a union meeting that would have related to the unemployment insurance [program]. I couldn't do it, at the last minute, and I sent Stephen to do it for me. It was the only time where he replaced me on a platform. He went without a text to read but with some pretty good notes from the day in and day out work he had been doing for months. I can remember his coming back, and I asked, 'How did it go?' And he said, 'It went OK, but I'd never been at a labour-union meeting in my life, and I can't believe the amount of misinformation that was being circulated by their leaders.'

"That's kind of the naïveté of Stephen at twenty-three or twenty-four years of age. It was not just his academic learning. I think it comes from his habit of paying attention to information, trying to be accurate about information, and thinking through the implications of that information. This bending of the facts disillusioned him. That whole experience, I think, disillusioned him. Just being there in Ottawa for a year and watching the compromises and the misinformation – that didn't just come from labour unions! Even political parties expressed their information completely differently about the same event, and the press was certainly capable of having a point of view. So, he left my office, I think, totally committed to pursuing a Ph.D. and teaching in a university as his primary career."

In the end, when it came to reforming UI, the Mulroney government chose to go with the elected politicians rather than the expert economists. On May 15, 1987, the minister of employment and immigration, Benoît Bouchard, delivered in the Commons the Mulroney government's considered reply to the vast expenditure of money, time, thought, and the research, consultation, analysis, discussion, and conclusions of four hard-working bodies over five years. The decision was that "the competing and conflicting opinions of all the interested parties are best reconciled within the current structure of Unemployment Insurance." In other words, the brave new future was to be more of the past.

As before with Solange Denis, the Mulroney government had backed down on a fundamental reform because it feared the political cost. And this time it was on an issue that was of immensely more consequence

to the long-term performance of the Canadian economy, to the eradi-
cation of poverty in the Atlantic provinces, and in most of Quebec, to
curing a subculture of dependency and consequent indolence, and to re-
establishing equity between the regions of Canada.

It was a hard lesson in the reality of politics in Canada at that time.
But by then Stephen Harper, who had believed in the politics of economic
rationality and had worked hard for Jim Hawkes, had left Ottawa, disillusioned, and was back at the University of Calgary to work on a
master's degree in economics, with the intention of pursuing it to a Ph.D.

Chapter 4

CROSSING THE DESERT

POLITICS WAS NOT FOR him. He did not want to be part of the politics he'd seen practised in Ottawa. But was there any other kind? He would find out.

Stephen Harper's year in Ottawa had not been wasted. Before his involvement in the 1984 elections, he had no interest in a career centred on Canada and Canadian issues. He was attracted to the world. He'd wanted to be a diplomat, representing Canada abroad. But now that he had seen Parliament in action, he had observed how the politicians failed to deal with the country's most pressing problems. He wanted to understand those problems and find their solution. The career path to fit his obsessions was the academic life. So, in June 1986, he was back in Calgary to work on a master's degree and then a Ph.D. in economics. Eventually, from a position in a university, he would develop and disseminate his own proposals on public policy.

The last thing on his mind was to become a member of Parliament. So says Jim Hawkes: "At that age I think he would have said very clearly he wouldn't ever want to be an elected member. I think he saw up close the kind of lifestyle that it was, the kinds of things that you had to do – sit for hours, sometimes months at a time, for people to reach consensus. It was a much clearer path, something he knew more about, being a university academic. It was something that he could do and do well, and you could still have influence from that kind of a platform. That's really what he came back to Calgary to do."

Cynthia Williams is equally certain. "I don't think he ever wanted to be on camera. I'm sure of it. He liked being behind the scenes. I think he always believed that he could find the candidate that he could get behind, and work for that person. I think he saw himself as an economist. There's a problem, now here's an answer, nothing to whine about, and let's just get it done. And you can't do that in Ottawa. All kinds of people have to be talked to, and feelings worked out – he would have just wanted to get it done."

Harper was at heart a political economist, as Cynthia Williams confirms. "His interests were economics. He's always believed that if you have strong financial management, then you can do all those other things that you want to do. With a good economy, you have more money for the arts, more money for social programs. I think he has always believed in the individual, too. He's always believed, get out of the way of the individual, don't take so much off their cheques with taxes, and let society make the right choices."

So, at the age of twenty-seven, Stephen began the life of a graduate student. But he would not wait until the end of his studies to develop his own views. He'd worked in the real world for three years after high school before returning to university for his first degree. He had then seen real politics from the inside. He was a mature student in every sense, and a quick study. He could not be content to absorb what his professors told him, read what they recommended, write papers, and get good marks, then get a good job in a good university. He was beyond that. Compulsively analytical, his character made him unable simply to play the game by the rules set by others. He had to know why and why not.

And so he now set off on a personal pursuit that was parallel to his studies. He began a vision quest that would soon lead him far from where he began. He deliberately entered into the labyrinth of human thought, down through the ages, on the human and political condition. He enrolled in a course on the history of philosophy and began systematically reading his way through the works of the great philosophers. Then, in one economics course, he asked his professor to recommend the great classical works in the field, the ones he should read to form a solid foundation. He was shocked when he was told, with a wink: "Steve, no one really reads the classic texts any more. We may talk about them, but we don't actually read them." In fact, Stephen set about reading Adam Smith, the exponent of the "invisible hand" that guides the marketplace. He read David Ricardo's *Principles of Economics and Taxation*, in which the economist argued that international free trade was the best policy because all would be best served when each specialized in the products where each enjoyed a comparative advantage. He read the classical economists, but also the social and political philosophers David Hume, Edmund Burke, and Jeremy Bentham.

He was on his own journey. Shortly after he returned from Ottawa, he and Cynthia broke off their engagement. Jim Hawkes puts the breakup in the context of all the changes that Harper had been through: "I think the year in Ottawa made Stephen less certain of a lot of things. It was quite an eye-opener kind of year for him. That analytic mind went to work on his relationship to people as much as it did on the policy proposals. They were in different parts of the country and he was a young man who had come immediately after graduation. He had to figure out what he was going to do with the rest of his life, and he had lots of time to think about those things."

Cynthia explains, "I think that Steve and I just grew apart." She says that neither originated the breakup. "We both just needed to go down different paths, and we'd both end up where we wanted to be. Politics isn't a two-person career. And I wouldn't have been here working for a television station if I was with Steve." In 2005, after a varied career which included writing on country music for the *Calgary Herald*, Cynthia Williams now produces advertising copy for A-Channel television, in Calgary.

Whatever the inside story, Stephen was deeply shaken, as Hawkes testifies. "It's a traumatic event and I think when you're younger it's maybe even more traumatic than when you get a little older. But that was a traumatic event at that time." Cynthia and Stephen were quite different in their attitudes toward politics. For Cynthia, politics was above all about meeting people and forming friendships. People mattered more than policies. "I got to know some really good people. And that's really what it's all about with me, the people. It never really was about winning with me, it's more about who I got to know and meet."

For Stephen, politics was above all about policies, good policies and bad policies. Politics, ideally, was about implementing good policies and defeating bad policies. And winning was important because the stakes were high in the struggle for better government. The wealth of nations, the well-being of people, mattered above all. He cared about the big picture, and the people he worked with were secondary. He showed this later when he actually ran against his political mentor and friend Jim Hawkes.

After Stephen returned from Ottawa, he and Cynthia both sat on the executive of Hawkes's constituency association. "He went right on the board immediately, he was attending meetings," Hawkes says. But, with the breakup, Stephen told Hawkes that it was too painful for him to attend the meetings where he would be encountering Cynthia. "The rift with the constituency association occurred when the engagement ended. We talked things over. With Cynthia at the meetings, he couldn't go. When he couldn't stand the emotional heat in the kitchen, he withdrew." Strategic withdrawal at turning points in his life was to prove a pattern.

Whether or not Stephen gave his full reasons for quitting the Calgary West PC association, he was clearly distancing himself from the PC Party. At the same time, he drew closer to a friend he had met in politics two years earlier, John Weissenberger, who had arrived at the University of Calgary in 1984 to study for a doctorate in geology. At a time when Stephen was recoiling from his political involvement and recovering from the breakup of his engagement, when he was full of doubts and perplexities and feeling compelled, once again, to find his own way, he and Weissenberger began meeting almost daily, often over a lunch or dinner of Chinese food at a mall across from the university campus. They were both disciplined thinkers, trained in the academic exercises of writing papers, participating in seminars, and critically dissecting ideas. Together, they began systematically to carry through a critique of what they saw happening in their country, to question conventional wisdom, discard easy assumptions, develop together their own political philosophy. They embarked on a program of reading, exchanging books, and then meeting to discuss what they had found. For Stephen, at a turning point in his life, John became the companion who accompanied him on a journey of discovery. They were to be friends for life. Weissenberger would be closely involved in Harper's future political ventures. And when both had married and become fathers and pursued their separate careers, their families would meet and go off together for a respite from the battles of life.

Born in Montreal, brought up just across the river on the South Shore, John Weissenberger lived through the October Crisis of 1970 when the Front de Libération du Québec kidnapped British diplomat James Cross and Quebec's deputy premier Pierre Laporte, who was soon found assassinated. He remembers the tanks moving into Montreal and the proclamation of the War Measures Act. "I always had that interest in history and politics," Weissenberger reminisced. "Growing up in Quebec at that time, I think you'd have to be absolutely insensitive not to be caught up somehow in politics. I was ten years old at the time of the October Crisis, so I remember all that very vividly. Laporte's body was found at the air base up there in St. Hubert, which was a mile from my house. In fact, the FLQ kidnappers were living close by. So we were definitely in the middle of it."

For Weissenberger, as for Harper, politics mattered deeply, though their backgrounds and their experiences differed. John was the son of an immigrant father from central Europe who had seen the Second World War. John had not only grown up in Quebec, he had taken a master's degree in geology at the Université de Montréal's École Polytechnique, where all his courses were in French. He had a knowledge of Quebec's political culture that Harper lacked. Both had been precocious high-school students with a serious cast of mind. John, in high school, had subscribed to the conservative U.S. publication *National Review*, and revelled once a week in watching the political television talk show *Firing Line*, hosted by the *National Review*'s editor, William F. Buckley. He shared with Stephen the adventure of having been chosen to represent his high school on the CBC-TV competition *Reach for the Top*, and his team went all the way to the national finals. His interest in public affairs was sharpened by the dramatic political events he witnessed in Quebec. After the FLQ crisis of 1970, there followed the 1976 victory of the separatist Parti Québécois, the restrictive language laws adopted against English in 1977, and the referendum on secession in 1980. He saw the mass exodus of English-speaking Quebeckers, including many of his friends, that reached a peak between 1976 and 1981, when homes in English neighbourhoods emptied, prices fell, and moving vans streamed up the 401 to Toronto. He observed the determination of the Quebec government to control intrusively so many aspects of communal life, including the economy, education, municipalities, labour relations, and communications.

His experience as an adolescent and young adult gave vivid meaning to the pleas in the *National Review* and on *Firing Line* for the freedom of the individual, the freedom of the marketplace, the urgency of restraining the power and the intrusiveness of the state, of resisting communism, creeping socialism, and state *dirigisme*. Weissenberger grew up as a committed conservative, what was then called a "neo-conservative" and what had been called in the nineteenth century a liberal.

He found an intellectually and politically congenial companion in Stephen Harper, the one-time Trudeau Liberal who was now drawing conclusions from his studies in economics and philosophy, and from his political experiences. Harper was pursuing his own evolution as a principled, explicit conservative. "I think we hit it off pretty well right from the start," Weissenberger recalls. "We were both philosophical conservatives, and we were both interested in public policy."

While he was studying for his first degree at the University of Western Ontario, he joined a political party for the first time – the PC Party – and he worked as a volunteer in both the 1979 and the 1980 federal elections. He discovered little enthusiasm for Joe Clark in the university milieu. Then, while he was studying at Montreal's École Polytechnique, the Tories held the leadership contest provoked by Clark. Weissenberger was impressed by the conservative economic rhetoric of Brian Mulroney and gave him his support. So, when he arrived in Calgary in the spring of 1984, he immediately signed on with the PC's youth campaign in Calgary West, where he worked with its president, Stephen Harper, to re-elect Jim Hawkes. They both also attended the PC university club on campus, but soon gave up. It was run, recalls Weissenberger, "by Red Tory egotists and buffoons," with little interest in policy. One whole meeting was spent debating the complexities of Robert's Rules of Order. After that, Stephen and John never returned.

After the '84 campaign, John remained active in the constituency association's youth club as they held fireside chats with prominent invited guests, attended PC Party events where ministers from the government were in attendance, or merely went out as a group to a horse race or a concert of western music. During the following year, while Harper was away in Ottawa, Weissenberger replaced him as the youth president. At the request of Jim Hawkes, Weissenberger also sent his MP periodic reports on the issues that concerned his constituents in Calgary

West. When Hawkes held his public forums in the riding, it was often Weissenberger who presided, maintaining order and recognizing those who rose to put a question to Hawkes or to voice a complaint. Hawkes was pleased with the member of his association who could field questions in French as well as English.

John is a surprise for a scientist, a geologist. One would expect a taciturn man most at home in the silent spaces of the northern tundra. Instead, he breaks into explosive peals of laughter, loves to talk, and speaks in vivid language. As personalities, he and Stephen were opposites. But they clicked, sharing an intellectual approach to politics. Their reading concentrated particularly on the neo-conservative thinkers reacting against the long liberal hegemony. They read Buckley's shocker of 1951, *God and Man at Yale*, in which the young Yale graduate flayed his university for rejecting conservative values while promoting agnosticism and socialism. That book launched the conservative counterattack in the United States against the liberalism dominant in the leading universities. They discussed Buckley's 1959 book, *Up from Liberalism*, the manifesto in which Buckley attacked the statism that was current in the political thinking of the U.S. elites after the Second World War. Buckley presented statism as an ultimate threat to human freedom. They pondered Buckley's definition of liberals: "They are men and women who tend to believe that the human being is perfectible, and social progress predictable, and that the instrument for effecting the two is reason; that truths are transitory and empirically determined; that equality is desirable and attainable through the action of state power; that social and individual differences, if they are not rational, are objectionable, and should be scientifically eliminated; that all people and societies strive to organize themselves upon a rationalist and scientific paradigm." Every week, they watched *Firing Line*, during which the jaunty, witty, irreverent, and erudite Buckley took on all the major liberal figures of the day and usually bested them in debate.

Weissenberger recalls that Harper wanted to think through issues of social ethics like reconciling the pursuit of self-interest in a capitalist society with the greater common good. Harper gave Weissenberger a copy of an essay on the subject by theologian Reinhold Niebuhr, who had advocated socialism and pacifism early in his career as a minister, but then later shifted to the right. "We had quite a discussion about human nature and human interests, or self-interest. Stephen wrote an essay about that in one of his graduate courses. And one book that Stephen introduced me to was Ian Hunter's biography of Malcolm Muggeridge."

Muggeridge had been a reporter in the Soviet Union for the *Manchester Guardian* in 1932, at the height of the famine deliberately imposed by Josef Stalin, when millions starved to death while their grain was exported to finance the forced march to industrialization. Muggeridge, without permission from the authorities, set off on a journey through the Ukraine and described what he saw in reports smuggled out through diplomatic pouch. He had seen the dying and the dead, had seen peasants kneeling in the snow, crying and begging for a crust of bread. Muggeridge was fired by the *Guardian* for his efforts and denounced as a liar. The press corps in Moscow, led by Walter Duranty of the *New York Times*, systematically covered up the state-enforced catastrophe. It was a classic example of the treason of the intellectuals, who were blinded by their sympathy for a Marxist-Leninist regime. It began with adulatory reports on the 1917 Bolshevik Revolution by journalist John Reed, who was a witness to the events he described in *Ten Days That Shook the World*. He was followed by Lincoln Steffens who, in 1919, uttered the memorable endorsement: "I have seen the future, and it works." That phrase was repeated by the prominent British Fabian socialists Sydney and Beatrice Webb, who visited the Soviet Union about the time that Muggeridge was there, at the height of the famine. They produced a book, *Soviet Communism: A New Civilisation*, that saw nothing but sweetness and light in the Stalinist state. Weissenberger remembers: "I read Muggeridge's autobiography as well. They weren't all totally dry philosophical texts that we were reading."

The wonder is that the two graduate students, one in economics, the other in geology, found so much time to read and grapple with fundamental human and social issues so remote, apparently, from their professional disciplines. "I was still doing my Ph.D.," Weissenberger recalls. "So those were the days when the kernel of our political ideas was formed, as a reaction to the failure of the Mulroney government, and particularly the unwillingness to tackle the deficit. And then we both started reading – in graduate school we had a fair bit of time [he laughs], so we read. We used to have a lot of political discussions and we would trade books that we were reading. And Steve got me interested in the Austrian school of economics."

Harper and Weissenberger pored over the 1944 classic work of Austrian economist Friedrich Hayek, *The Road to Serfdom*. Hayek had begun his intellectual career as a socialist, but soon became disenchanted with the logic of a planned economy. He had obtained doctorates in both law and economics at the University of Vienna in the early 1920s, when the old European order had been destroyed by the First World War, especially in Austria, Hungary, and Germany. The Bolshevik Revolution had triumphed in Russia and competing ideologies struggled to impose themselves on the European continent. Intellectuals were attracted to theories that promised to make the world over and bring about a new order of justice and prosperity. Hayek also witnessed the Depression of the 1930s and the state actions taken in country after country to impose protectionism and exclude foreign imports, which aggravated worldwide impoverishment. He saw the clash of ideologies between communism, fascism, and liberal democracy, which led to world war and military occupations. He saw emerging in the final years of the 1930s and the early 1940s the movement in liberal democracies toward planned economies as the cure for depressions, for poverty, and insecurity. He argued that it was the wrong way to go. He rejected the theories of John Maynard Keynes, who began his critique of capitalism as far back as 1919 and, in 1936, in the depths of the Depression, published his *General Theory of Employment, Interest and Money*, which had enormous impact on politicians and academics. It explained how states could control the economic cycle of boom and bust by intervening in the economy with countervailing measures. Then, in 1942, in wartime Britain, the economist Sir William Beveridge headed a committee which produced a massive proposal for post-war reconstruction, titled *Social Insurance and Allied Services*. The Beveridge Report laid down the outlines of what would be adopted after the war as the welfare state. It took as its first principle a statement that Hayek, from his experience after the First World War, could only abhor: "Now, when the war is abolishing landmarks of every kind, is the opportunity for using experience in a clear field. A revolutionary moment in the world's history is a time for revolutions, not for patching."

The second principle of the Beveridge Report was to vastly increase the role of the state. The proposal was that the state would have the responsibility to overcome "Want, Disease, Ignorance, Squalor and Idleness." The state should attend to all the stages and conditions of life from childhood to old age. The report proposed a free national health service, children's allowances, unemployment insurance, compensation for accidents in the workplace, maternity benefits, widow's pensions, retirement pensions, and retraining for the unemployed.

Hayek, by contrast, rejected a planned economy on two grounds. First, it was a threat to freedom. It logically led to a cycle of planning, followed by economic failures, because no planner could anticipate all the complexities of reality over time. The failure would be followed by more planning to remedy the failure, and then again more failures. The logic of a planned economy was to engage society on a course toward totalitarianism. But, secondly, Hayek opposed the planned economy also on strictly economic grounds. He argued that an economy involved an incalculable number of decisions and choices spread over time in a process that went from planning, to production, to delivery, to consumption. No single mind, no committee of minds, was knowledgeable enough and wise enough to make those decisions for all the members engaged in the economy. On the other hand, a "spontaneous order" emerged if millions of people were left free to make their own choices and decisions in the marketplace, taking the consequences of those decisions. This spontaneous order appeared messy to technocrats wanting to control the flow of events, but the millions of individuals, each and all pursuing their own judgments, ultimately produced a more flexible, adaptable, self-correcting, and productive economy, than one constructed by planning.

For Harper and Weissenberger, reflecting on the Canadian economy in the 1980s, what Hayek had written made sense. In the early 1970s in particular, the Trudeau government had embarked on a much more planned economy, creating the Foreign Investment Review Agency, buying Petro-Canada, fixing the price of oil. And the result was exactly what Hayek had predicted: in the short run, inflation; in the long run, inflation accompanied by stagnation, or what came to be called "stagflation." Trudeau then tried to cope with the stagflation by calling on industry and labour to co-operate with the state in agreeing to restrain salary and price increases. When that failed, Trudeau went further with state planning, imposing wage and price controls, to be monitored by an Anti-Inflation Board. Then, in 1980, Trudeau brought in the National Energy Program, a massive undertaking to plan and control a major sector of the economy. The results, again, were about what Hayek would have predicted. A mess.

In their examination of the critiques formulated by both Buckley and Hayek, Harper and Weissenberger were impressed by the emphasis on the limitations of human reason, no matter how intelligent the proponents of a new order. They accepted, as did Hayek, that the role of the state was to establish general rules that were to apply to all. This was the rule of law, impartially enforced, without fear or favour. But it was not up to the state to determine the outcome for particular individuals or groups in the society. There was more wisdom in the efficacy of the free market, with its millions of decisions made daily, independently, by individuals, than in central planning, or in state intrusion into economic decisions, especially when intrusions involved the state deciding which individuals or firms would benefit from state largesse. That was the road that led to economic inefficiency and to political corruption – the road to serfdom.

For a time, Hayek's teachings had lost favour as Keynes and Beveridge became the cornerstones of public policy in Britain and, to greater or lesser extent, in other industrialized countries. But, by the 1970s, a reaction had set in. The industrialized countries were now experiencing structural inflation. Inflation had become a spiral in which the value of money was depreciating at an accelerating rate and as the various groups and classes in society strove to protect their standard of living against future devaluations, there was a multitude of industrial strikes. At the same time, people on fixed incomes saw their worth deteriorating. To stem the inflation, and to compensate for the anticipated diminished future value of money, central banks raised interest rates, at times as high as 20 per cent. But the high cost of money then slowed the economy. Stagflation, once thought to be an oxymoron, was now the reality.

Hayek suddenly was studied again. In 1974, he was awarded the Nobel Prize in economics and his principles were taken up by a new generation of intellectuals and politicians. Harper and Weissenberger read them avidly. Weissenberger recalls that they were very impressed with a book by the Boston University sociologist Peter Berger. In *Democracy and Capitalism*, Berger argued against the Marxian view, fashionable in some universities, that capitalism resulted in the masses being kept in chains. On the contrary, Berger maintained (in the Hayek tradition, though with qualifications) that capitalism was a condition of democracy and secured the freedom of the individual. Berger wrote, "Capitalism creates 'escape hatches' from political power; socialism makes such escape very precarious if not impossible. This understanding of the political effects of capitalism and socialism has been propounded in the work of F.A. Hayek; and at least to date, has been amply confirmed by the empirical evidence."

Stephen and John followed with fascination the turn toward free markets that had taken place in Margaret Thatcher's Britain, Ronald Reagan's United States, and in New Zealand, where the Labour government's minister of finance, Roger Douglas, initiated in 1984 a package of radical reforms that were called "Rogernomics." He had published in 1981 a manifesto, *There's Got to Be a Better Way*, which called for the reforms which he then implemented as finance minister, with dramatic results. After he cut income taxes, introduced a goods and services tax, deregulated financial markets, and privatized the state monopolies, New Zealand was lifted out of its stagnation. Harper and Weissenberger asked themselves: Why could Brian Mulroney not have done what Roger Douglas did? Why did he not follow the example of Thatcher and Reagan?

Harper asked Weissenberger to dig up the Conservative Party manifestos under which Margaret Thatcher had fought her first elections, as leader of the opposition in 1979, and then as prime minister in 1983. They admired the clarity with which she nailed her theses to the wall. "No one who has lived in this country during the last five years can fail to be aware of how the balance of our society has been increasingly tilted in favour of the State at the expense of individual freedom," she began in her 1979 campaign manifesto. "This election may be the last chance we have to reverse that process, to restore the balance of power in favour of the people. It is therefore the most crucial election since the war. Together with the threat to freedom, there has been a feeling of helplessness, that we are a once-great nation that has somehow fallen behind and that it is too late now to turn things round."

In both Great Britain in 1979, and in the United States in 1980, there was a sense of something being profoundly wrong. In the United States, the 1980 election campaign pitted the challenger, Ronald Reagan, against the president, Jimmy Carter. There, too, the country suffered from a sense of economic and social dislocation. Interest rates were at record levels and unemployment was at its highest in years. And the United States stood by helplessly while its diplomats were held hostage month after month in a revolutionary Iran under the Ayatollah Khomeini. Jimmy Carter acknowledged that there was a "malaise" in the land. But Reagan, ever the sunny optimist, claimed that it needn't be so, if only the proper policies were implemented. "It's morning in America!"

Why, then, in Canada, was there not a recognition of the profound problems that undermined the country? Why were "Thatcher" and "Reagan" terms of contempt here, considered synonymous with heartless and reactionary leadership? In Britain, the Iron Lady stood fast on conservative principles. She implemented counter-inflationary policies. Then, fifteen months after she came to power, when the unions were threatening to use every means to bring her down, she stood defiant: "To those waiting with bated breath for that favourite media catchphrase, the U-turn, I have only one thing to say: You turn if you want to. The lady's not for turning!" And, unlike Brian Mulroney, she was as good as her word. For the first four years, her policies actually resulted in increased unemployment, which later receded. But she won election three times, and Tony Blair, years later, even as the leader of the Labour Party, kept most of her reforms.

In the United States, Reagan cut taxes and greatly increased the defence budget. He was till the end a popular president, and sixteen years after he left office, his reputation has grown. His successors, notably Bill Clinton, maintained many of the changes he had initiated.

But the conservative renaissance seemed to have bypassed Canada. As prime minister, Mulroney had undertaken some modest measures to bring public spending under control and restrain the growth of the state. But they had been largely half measures. The annual federal deficit remained above $30 billion even during the several years of unusual prosperity. The national debt doubled.

Harper and Weissenberger wondered why Canada was different. They received a powerful lesson when, in October 1986, the Mulroney government – their government – made public a decision that shook all of western Canada. It announced that the maintenance of the newly acquired fleet of 138 CF-18 fighter jets would be done by Montreal's Canadair rather than Winnipeg's Bristol Aerospace. The $1.2-billion contract went to the Montreal firm despite the fact that the jury appointed by the government to evaluate the two bids had found the Winnipeg bid represented "the most favourable price and technical proposal," according to the briefing paper prepared by the PC caucus' own research staff. Though Bristol Aerospace offered to service the aircraft at lower cost and with a superior performance, Canadair won the contract.

The CF-18 maintenance contract became a *cause célèbre*. Former energy minister Pat Carney gave the inside story in her memoirs, *Trade Secrets*. She noted, for example, that "all the major decisions I have been involved in have rarely been made at cabinet. . . . Decisions are typically reached in private with the PM, or in private meetings with cabinet colleagues, or in committee. An example is the decision over the CF-18s. . . ." Mulroney, in fact, announced this decision to the cabinet. The ministers never had an opportunity to debate it.

It would be hard to quarrel with Carney's conclusion that it was "a decision that, in my view, changed Canadian history by hardening western alienation, breathing life into the Reform movement, and bringing on the slow death of the Progressive Conservative Party." Certainly for Harper and Weissenberger the impact of that decision was dramatic. "That was the big eye-opener for me," Weissenberger recalls. "It was just so blatant. We had all those cabinet ministers from Alberta, the West had resolutely supported the PC Party for years, and then Mulroney did this, obviously very much focused on appeasing Quebec."

———◦———

Once again, as so often in our history, western Canada was treated as a colony destined to serve the interests of central Canada, and specifically Quebec. This decision, like others of the Mulroney government when Quebec's interests were involved, led the pair to reflect on the place of Quebec in recent Canadian politics. By coincidence, a book on the subject had been published shortly before, *The Patriot Game: National Dreams & Political Realities*, by Peter Brimelow. It was a shocker, a bombshell, a call to arms. For bright young men trying to make sense of their country at a time of disillusionment, it offered powerful medicine.

"Brimelow's book, that was a big influence at the time," Weissenberger says. "Whether you believe his analysis completely or not, it was strong. We both read it with great interest and discussed a lot of the points in it. Brimelow identified a number of areas of conflict within Canada that the current system was papering over, the Quebec question being the largest one. We were so impressed we actually went to one bookstore and we said, 'OK, we want to buy ten copies of this book, what deal will you give us?' So we bought ten copies and gave them to all our friends."

Brimelow was a Brit who had received an M.B.A. from Stanford University and had then worked in Canada as a staff writer for the *Financial Post* and as business editor for *Maclean's* magazine. He wrote *The Patriot Game* as a kind of Parthian shot aimed at Canada after he left for the United States, where he would become a senior editor of *Forbes* magazine, and a senior editor of the conservative *National Review*. He wrote with wit and irony. His perception of Canada was depressing. He turned topsy-turvy all the political platitudes and pious assumptions of Canada's right-thinking (left-thinking) elites. Brimelow invited Harper and Weissenberger on a new voyage of discovery, and they willingly embarked. He described many fault lines in Canada. They included the inherent conflicts between central Canada and the other geographical regions, and the struggle for wealth and power between the mainstream society and the natives. But the one fundamental conflict that he saw as undermining Canada, past, present, and future, was that which opposed French and English speakers, Quebec and the rest of Canada. "The history and politics of Quebec are dominated by a single great reality: the emergence of the French-speaking nation. The process has been slow, complex, and agonizing. There have been false starts, reversals, and long periods of quiescence. But for over 200 years its ultimate direction has remained the same: toward ever-greater self-expression, as the growing plant seeks the light."

For Brimelow, the Liberal Party is the villain of Canadian history. It imposed a way of thinking about the country, a vision, that was detrimental. In effect, the Liberal Party became the surrogate of French Quebec, ruling the country because our parliamentary and electoral system allowed a minority to rule the majority: French Canada voted as a bloc, while English Canada was split. "Some time this century, English Canada lost its nerve," Brimelow wrote. "As the Anglophones retreated,

the Francophones advanced. But their movement was not simply opportunistic. They were also impelled by the seismic upheaval in Quebec
society that led to the so-called Quiet Revolution in the 1960s." Brimelow
saw the history of the previous century as essentially a competition
between French and English to assert their nationality through the state,
with the Liberals representing the French speakers, the Conservatives
representing the English. But the competition proved unequal, in part
because the Liberal ascendancy managed to impose a false consciousness
on English speakers whereby the latter were seduced into accepting a
political vision that was contrary to their reality and to their interests.
"The Canadian Liberal Party has been able to persuade English Canada
that preserving the Canadian Confederation and common morality itself
requires continual concessions to Quebec. . . . The Liberal Ideology to a
considerable extent is the projection of internal Quebec concerns onto the
national stage, so that Canadian politics in the Liberal era have been
essentially those of a sort of Greater Quebec."

The Liberals had a left-wing philosophy. They tailored their policies
to attract needy minorities wanting protection and favours from the
(Liberal) state. This included buying the loyalty of client constituencies
with the money of the taxpayers with, for instance, "the bewildering
variety of subsidies and incentives orchestrated by Ottawa in the 1960s
and 70s to stimulate development in the peripheral regions. If you have
convinced yourself that economic growth is not best left to market forces
but always requires government direction, it is easier to justify what might
otherwise appear a crude attempt to bribe the regions to shut up about
federal trade policies that benefit only Central Canada." So it happened,
according to Brimelow, that Canada acquired a hypertrophic welfare
state, with a "New Class" of politicians, civil servants, employees of the
multiple Crown corporations such as the CBC, welfare workers, teachers,
journalists. And these opinion leaders were tributary to the Liberal ideology which they then propagated as the true national vision and the New
Nationalism. Any other view was politically incorrect.

The Liberals were defeated in 1984, and Brian Mulroney brought the
Progressive Conservatives to power. But, for Brimelow, this was again
playing the same old Liberal game. Mulroney was from Quebec, he was
perfectly bilingual, and Quebec's concerns were his priorities. He maintained and promoted the same old "Liberal Ideology."

The focus of Canadian politics on the concerns of central Canada, and especially of Quebec, was causing powerful strains east of Quebec and, above all, west of Ontario. The attempt to remodel Canada into a Greater Quebec would provoke a reaction, Brimelow prophesied: "*The sectional divisions within English Canada will be a continuing problem.* This is particularly true of the western provinces. They may lead some sort of rebellion against the Liberal hegemony, perhaps by supporting a right-wing, fourth party." The Reform Party would be founded the following year.

Weissenberger commented: "This was the time when Mulroney was bringing nationalists into his caucus – separatists, let's be honest. He was trying to play both sides against the middle. And then there was what we perceived as the crisis of the welfare state in Canada, with the debt problem. And there seemed to be essentially an ideological consensus between the three major parties. Everybody had essentially bought into the system; they weren't willing to consider an alternative – certainly not from the right. If anyone had a question about what to do in public policy, well, 'we're not spending enough money in this area,' right? [peals of laughter]. So we were looking at it from the other side and thinking, there have to be some other possible solutions to this. So, in retrospect I may not agree with all of Brimelow's points, but certainly it was a very important book for us at that time."

As Harper and Weissenberger saw it, Weissenberger in particular, Mulroney's attitude toward Quebec revealed a fundamental problem which made the much-needed conservative shift in the country nearly impossible. Quebec had gone through its Quiet Revolution after 1960, demolishing an order there that had been built for more than a century on an ultra-conservative Catholic ideology which rejected liberalism and modernism. When this order was swept away, Quebec reacted much like the central European powers after the First World War. Quebec wanted to build everything anew, and everything seemed possible. One ideology after another contended for acceptance in Quebec, from existentialism, to decolonization theory, to Marxism, socialism, Maoism, federalism. The recurrent question for the past generation, "What does Quebec want?" was in fact unanswerable. Quebec wanted many incompatible outcomes, and so the kaleidoscopic demands were continually in flux. The one constant, dominant thrust was nationalistic statism. All the provincial political parties – and there were many that came and went – wanted a bigger and better Quebec government. Quebec could have enunciated as its own the first and second principles of the Beveridge Report, notably: "A revolutionary moment in the world's history is a time for revolutions, not for patching." This was called "the Quebec model."

Harper and Weissenberger, from their study of Edmund Burke's *Reflections on the Revolution in France*, were entirely unsympathetic to revolutions, even one called "Quiet." With Quebec embarked on a left-wing ideological adventure, and the rest of the country – especially Ottawa – trying to cope with Quebec's post-revolutionary surges, the country lacked the political resources to deal with the growing crisis in public finances and the imminent threat of a run on the Canadian dollar. All the efforts of the best and the brightest were concentrated on containing or appeasing Quebec.

It seemed to the two young men, as they discussed and searched for solutions, that throughout their lives, from the time that they became politically aware around 1970, national politics had been chiefly taken up with responding to the demands of Quebec. It had meant trying to revise the Constitution, trying to entrench the French language federally and provincially, trying to complete Canadian sovereignty by patriating the Constitution as originally demanded by Jean Lesage. The quest had meant decades of regional tensions over issues that seemed peripheral to most westerners. Ross Thatcher had put it straight when he was premier of Saskatchewan: If the people of his province had one hundred priorities, revising the Constitution was the one hundred and first.

That long bruising struggle had seemed completed and closed with the Constitution Act of 1982. But now Mulroney was proposing to reopen the whole process. The West, notably Alberta, was once again being sacrificed to Quebec. And Mulroney, despite his rhetoric, was doing very little, they thought, to deal with the monstrous and crushing dimension of the state in Canada. As Brimelow had pointed out: "Canada suffers from a particularly acute form of the generalized late-twentieth-century crisis of the welfare state. Its politicians apparently feel unable to respond to this problem, partly because of what they believe is the danger of exacerbating sectional and linguistic divisions by withdrawing any subsidy or privilege."

The two young conservatives concluded that something was fundamentally wrong with politics in Canada, and that more of the same would not do. Weissenberger recalls a conversation he had at that time at a cocktail party with Harvie Andre, the MP for Calgary Centre, who had recently been appointed minister of consumer and corporate affairs. John asked him what the government was going to do about the postal unions that were periodically disrupting the mail service. In the United States, the law stipulates that any federal employee who goes on strike against the government must be fired; there has never been a generalized strike in the U.S. Postal Service.

"So I was standing with Jim [Hawkes] and with Harvie, and we were talking about the problems they were facing and the challenges, and I said, 'Now look, what's going on with these postal workers?' Having come from Quebec where there were always problems with the unions, I said, 'Can't anything be done to restructure this and make something work?' And Harvie said, 'Well, you know, John, it's really tough dealing with these unions, they're so intransigent. You know, to tell you the truth, John, our hands are tied.' This is a senior minister in the government, with a huge majority, and here I am, a young, idealistic guy, thinking, well, things can change. He's basically telling me, 'I'm a senior minister in the government, and, really, *our hands are tied*. We can't do anything.' It was clear that, in Canada, there was no political will to change anything. So that was a pretty stark realization for us in the mid-eighties."

Harper and Weissenberger became increasingly disenchanted with the policies and the actions of the Mulroney Tories. But the Liberals under John Turner were no better, and would be unacceptable to the West. As for Ed Broadbent's New Democrats, they were a good example of the problem. So what was left? They settled on a reform movement within the Progressive Conservative Party. There were others, many others, who thought as they did. Harper had got to know some of them in Ottawa. But the Red Tories or the Pink Tories controlled the party, controlled its key institutions. Fundamental reform was blocked while they remained in charge. A strong right-wing movement within the party was needed to impose a clear change of direction like that in Britain, the United States, even New Zealand.

"We sat down and we said, look, this party, this government, is not implementing the policies we thought they were going to, that we thought

they should. What are we going to do? Looking back on it, it sounds kind
of improbable or implausible that two young guys would sit down and
say: 'Well, you know, you've got this huge majority government and it's
going the wrong way. What are we going to do about it?'

"But that's exactly what we did, oddly enough. Not that we expected
to accomplish anything at that time, really. But we knew we wanted to
stay politically involved. At that time the only vehicle was the Progressive
Conservative Party. So we said, OK, well, how are we going to do this?
We know there are guys across the country who hold the same views as
we do. We would have tried to work within the system, and build up our
own network and proceed that way."

So now Harper and Weissenberger began focusing their meetings
on working within the system to create what they called a "Blue Tory
network," systematically encouraging people with the same views as
themselves to become members, to take positions on riding executives, to
become candidates, to begin exercising influence at all levels of the party.

Steve and Cynthia were no longer engaged but they still met and
talked. Cynthia was aware of the direction in which Steve was moving.
"I know that he had some ideas of having a group within the Conservative
Party – that there could be a strong enough voting bloc, that they would
influence the party, influence the nominations, and the leadership of who
became leader. So that was where he was originally going. Because he
thought the party needed to be reformed."

But something happened on the way to a Blue Tory network. Two
things, actually. One of them: as Cynthia says, "He met Preston Manning
and everything changed." And the other turn of events: Brian Mulroney
announced triumphantly that he had met with all the premiers on
April 30, 1987, and they had all come to an agreement with Quebec.
The Meech Lake Accord was born. And everything changed.

Chapter 5

THE WEST WANTS IN

STEPHEN HARPER, WHO had always felt like an outsider when he was in Ottawa, now felt right at home. He was staying at Vancouver's Hyatt Regency Hotel along with about 180 other people who had come together for what was billed as the "Western Assembly." The table on the podium at the front of the hall had a banner strung in front of it that announced: THE WEST WANTS IN! In the hall and later, in the corridors, he found himself rubbing shoulders with people who thought much as he did. At the formal meetings, he heard others speak out loud what he had been thinking. And he was at one with the tone of indignation, the sense of betrayal, that he heard delegate after delegate express when each rose to speak.

An advertisement that was run in advance in the major western metropolitan newspapers set the tone for that meeting on the last weekend of May 1987: "Something is grievously wrong in western Canada. Farmers can't afford to seed their crops, mines are closed, oil rigs lie derelict, shipyards are idle, food banks are besieged, the savings of many lifetimes have vanished, homes have lost their value, and a host of unemployed bursts the welfare rolls of every town and city. In vain we look to Ottawa, but more and more we find that Ottawa's first concern must be with the Big Vote, and the Big Vote is not here. And though we demand action, often we ourselves have little to propose."

Harper had something to propose. He and John Weissenberger had spent months meeting, discussing, reading, dissecting, criticizing, and thrashing through their views on Canada's economic and political future. And now this "Western Assembly" came along just when they were eager to share their ideas with others. So, when it was decided that Stephen would attend the assembly as an observer, they put together on a single piece of paper a précis of their thoughts on what the country needed, and they both signed their names. It was just a bare-bones outline, really, because they judged that hardly anyone would read a handout from two unknowns if it ran to more than one page. And they printed it out on bright yellow paper to catch the attention of the participants. It was titled "A Taxpayers Reform Agenda." They were placing themselves from the start outside of partisan politics, giving the point of view merely of ordinary citizens, of concerned taxpayers. They then listed, in order, eleven one-sentence proposals, highlighting the first few words of each. The very first proposal asserted their conservative philosophy, which they put forward in contrast to the left-wing approach of the three parties in the Commons: "*The articulation of strong conservative principles* as an alternative to the unanimity of the NDP–Liberal–Red Tory philosophy, i.e., a democracy of real debate, not 'sacred trusts.'"

It was something of an accident that a graduate student like Harper found himself attending this conference reassessing the West's future in Canada. Almost all the participants were older and established in life. But, through a chain of circumstances, Harper had become acquainted with one of the moving spirits behind the meeting Preston Manning. It had happened this way. As a student, Harper was not content with absorbing economic theory, but was preoccupied with trying to establish the link between economics and politics in accounting for Canada's economic problems. This would eventually be the subject of his master's thesis. He found in the Department of Economics at the University of Calgary a professor who had similar interests. Robert Mansell had made a specialty in the 1980s of studying the effects of federal fiscal policies on the various regions of the country. In particular, he had demonstrated the role of the federal government in extracting many billions of dollars from Alberta to be distributed in the seven poorer provinces, with about half of it going to Quebec. The sheer figures were staggering in their immensity, and Harper was fascinated. His own work in Ottawa on unemployment insurance had made him all too aware of one of the mechanisms for this redistribution of wealth. Harper made a point of meeting and getting to know Mansell outside of the lecture hall and they had many conversations together on their shared interests.

> Mansell was also concerned about the spiralling debt of the federal government and the risk that Canada was running of a severe monetary crisis in the not-too-distant future. If the investors of the world were to come to the conclusion that Canada's debt was out of control, they would stage a run on the Canadian dollar that would sharply depreciate its value compared to other currencies. The entire economy of Canada would be devastated. Mansell was sounding the alarm, but in the 1980s, there was little awareness in the country of the dangers of deficits and public debt, even as the Mulroney government kept increasing both.

Mansell had a concern that was close to Harper's heart, from his aborted experience of working with Jim Hawkes on the reform of unem-
> ployment insurance. Mansell was convinced that the programs that transferred wealth to the poorer provinces were so constructed that they had the perverse effect of maintaining poverty and dependency rather than creating prosperity. He was in full agreement with the conclusions of the Macdonald Royal Commission, the Forget commission, and the House commission: "What turned Stephen off was the corruption in Ottawa. This guy has a very definite sense of what's right and wrong. I remember our having lots of conversations about how business is done in Ottawa, and we'd always come to the conclusion: it doesn't have to be done that way. That's the way it's done in Ottawa, special deals and, you know, it's all about manipulating the system; but it shouldn't be done that way. It should be much more transparent, open. So that was a big concern with Stephen."

Another person who was interested in Mansell's research and in his conclusions was Preston Manning. At that time Manning lived in a suburb of Edmonton and ran a consulting firm. An important part of his consultancy involved working with the petroleum industry and the local people in northern Alberta to stimulate community development. Preston Manning had practical problems needing practical solutions, and Mansell's research seemed pertinent. And so Manning had invited Mansell on several occasions to speak to groups of people Manning had brought together. Manning often found himself in Calgary and he enjoyed stopping by Mansell's office to engage in discussion with academics from the

University of Calgary whom Mansell had invited for the occasion. "There was a group at the university, a bunch of frustrated policy wonks," Mansell explained. "We'd sit around with coffee once in a while, Preston would be around, and we'd have a chat about what's wrong and how can you fix it." Harper was invited more than once. Weissenberger also participated.

A common theme in these discussions was the perversity of federal fiscal policies, as they affected all of Canada, but Alberta in particular. "We discussed bringing integrity back to Confederation. We'd say that, instead of having decisions made on the basis of whining and threats, there should be better mechanisms that incorporate equity. So, for example, you don't just make transfer payments based on some narrow measure of historic need, or some obscure measure of tax capacity. Make the transfers based on how well the province is doing in terms of investing, and helping to create wealth, helping themselves out. Remove some of the policies that provide incentives *not* to adjust, incentives *not* to invest. It's about time that we started paying some attention to the fundamentals."

Manning was paying attention to the fundamentals and so was Harper. It was at one of these informal get-togethers organized by Mansell that Harper had met Manning in the early months of 1987. "I remember introducing Stephen to Preston Manning and him being very heavily involved in a very short time," recalls Professor Mansell. "Preston, to his credit, also saw him as a real talent, right from the beginning. I mean, they really hit it off. Harper is very thoughtful, very logical, very analytical."

These discussions with the economists, historians, and political scientists brought together by Mansell were stimulating for Harper and Weissenberger. They confirmed them in the direction they had already been moving, and gave them access to a new fund of facts and figures to back up their views. But what could they do to change the way politics was done? They were still turning that question over and planning a Blue Tory network when, one day, at one of those informal meetings organized by Mansell, Preston Manning told their group that several people in western Canada shared the same concerns and were determined to take action. He had received a call from Vancouver economist Stan Roberts, well known throughout Canada as a past president of both the Canadian Chamber of Commerce and the Canada West Foundation. Roberts told

Manning that a rich man by the name of Francis Winspear was willing to put up the money to hold a conference on the problems experienced particularly by western Canada. Would Manning be interested in co-sponsoring it?

Manning was indeed interested. Since the previous summer he had been telling people that a new reform movement was needed in western Canada. He had proposed holding what he called a Parliament of the West, to deliberate on the region's future. Manning, Roberts, and a like-minded Calgary lawyer, Robert Muir, past president of the Canadian Petroleum Law Foundation and former general counsel for Dome Petroleum, proceeded to form what they called the Reform Association of Canada. They set a date for the conference, May 29 to 31, 1987. And they sent out invitations broadly, even, optimistically, to the leaders of the three major parties, Brian Mulroney, John Turner, and Ed Broadbent.

Mansell was among those invited to participate in the Western Assembly on Canada's Economic and Political Future, but he had other commitments and suggested that Stephen Harper go in his stead. So it was that Harper packed a stack of yellow sheets of paper containing in outline the political vision that he and Weissenberger had worked out together and set off for Vancouver and the Western Assembly. He would deposit them on a table at the back of the meeting hall in the hope that they would be picked up and discussed.

This meeting had received considerable advance publicity in the four western provinces, but practically none east of Manitoba. Ted Byfield, notably, the publisher of the sister publications *Alberta Report* and *Western Report*, had given the event extensive advance coverage. In fact, Byfield, a passionate *engagé* journalist, conservative on both economic and moral issues, a defender of the Christian faith and western Canada, in constant indignation at politicians and journalists in central Canada, had for some time been calling for the creation of a regional party to defend western Canada's interests and had been involved in some of the discussions which had led to convening the Western Assembly. He was almost a co-founder.

Despite the numerous invitations, there were few currently elected politicians at the gathering in Vancouver. Not surprisingly, Prime Minister Mulroney chose not to attend, and he ordered all the members of the PC caucus to keep away. In a letter to the organizers, he surmised that the real purpose of the assembly was to form a new party to compete with the PC Party for western votes. "It seems to me that another regional party risks fracturing and reducing the influence of western Canadians on national policy. That would be contrary to Canadian interests and contrary to western Canada's interest, so you will understand that I would not want to designate representatives to such a conference."

Among those invited to speak on the Saturday evening was Peter Brimelow, whose book *The Patriot Game* Harper and Weissenberger had found so inspiring. But his past scathing criticisms of Mulroney and the Tories, of the Liberals and the NDP, were hardly likely to draw prominent members of the established federal parties to the assembly. The provincial parties also boycotted the meeting, with only a handful of former provincially elected members showing up. One independent member of the Alberta legislature did participate: Ray Speaker, a former minister in a Social Credit government. He would be heard from again later. There as observers: the Tory maverick from Calgary, Alexander Kindy, and the NDP's MP Simon de Jong from Regina. No Liberal MP attended.

At the opening session on Friday evening, the delegates held back, apparently uncertain about the significance of their coming together. But as the weekend advanced, they moved forward, more seats were filled, the atmosphere got warmer, and enthusiasm took over.

The unquestioned high point of the weekend came on the Saturday afternoon when Preston Manning gave a speech that blew his audience away. Manning was a paradox. A self-described populist, he was nonetheless shy, and when dealing with people up close, he rarely looked directly at them. His fingernails were bitten to the quick. His oversized glasses, his prominent Adam's apple, his long thin frame, all gave him the stereotypical look of a nerd, while his voice quavered oddly up and down the register. He was anything but a firebrand, a barnburner, a charismatic arouser of the throngs. But when he addressed the delegates that Saturday, he spoke directly to the minds and the hearts of those disenchanted citizens. He articulated their views, only better. He placed their discontents in a vast historic context that gave them grandeur. They, that weekend, were suddenly marching with William Lyon Mackenzie, with Louis-Joseph Papineau, with Louis Riel. They were taking up the torch of Frederick Haultain, who had fought for the provincehood that created

Saskatchewan and Alberta. They were acting against intolerable conditions, as William Aberhart had done during the Depression. They, in that room, were no longer simply angry people who weren't going to take it any more; they were part of a surging movement of the grassroots people that pulsed recurrently down the generations like an erupting volcano and made history.

"Let me make clear from the outset that when we refer to the possibility of creating a new political party to represent the West we are not talking about another splinter party or single-issue party, or yet another party of the strange and extreme. The West has produced too many of these in the past years, and there is no need for another. Rather, if we think at all about the creation of a new federal political party to carry our concerns and contribution into the national political arena, we should be thinking about the creation of a new vehicle to represent the great political 'reform tradition,' which runs like a broad and undulating stream throughout the length and breadth of Canadian politics, but which currently finds no suitable means of expression in any of the traditional federal parties. . . . If we talk about creating a new federal political party in this context, we are talking about reviving a tradition which is older than Confederation itself and as western as Riel and the Farmers' Movement."

Manning spoke of the hopes that Brian Mulroney had aroused in the West, and of the deep sense of disenchantment which followed. "Some people mention their high expectations that the Mulroney government would introduce major changes in the scale and structure of the federal government during its first 18 months in office, and their profound disappointment when these changes didn't occur. Others mention the government's slowness to remove the iniquitous Petroleum Gas Revenue Tax, its mishandling of the CF-18 contract, its slowness to enunciate a western diversification policy, the continuation of patronage politics and appointments, and the failure to implement proposed reforms in the unemployment insurance program after spending years and millions of dollars on developing reform proposals."

Manning, after considering various alternative courses, recommended to the assembly that they create a new political party in the great reform tradition. He obviously was inspired above all by the great Social Credit victory at the polls in 1935, when a movement led by William

Aberhart transformed itself into a political party and, a few months later, swept into power in what was a protest by the whole province, not just by a particular class. Preston Manning wanted to repeat that phenomenon. He wanted a party that attracted people for reasons beyond their class interests. He envisaged a populist movement that would suddenly cause a shift in the paradigm of politics as it was then practised. "Obviously, if the West were to choose a new political vehicle to advance its agenda, we would be careful to position that vehicle ideologically and policy-wise so that it would have equal potential for drawing the support of western Canadians from both the Liberals and the NDP, as well as the Conservatives. In fact, one could go so far as to say that if a new federal political party cannot be positioned in this way, it should not be initiated."

Manning was expressing his vision, his faith in a populist surge that moved a whole people at the same time in a new direction, one which shattered the status quo and displaced the established parties. This faith would later lead to conflicts between Manning and prominent members of his party, including Harper. He was, from the start, rejecting the purely economic conservatism that animated most of the people at the Vancouver Assembly, who would be most active in the Reform Party later. For Manning, a reform movement was as irresistible, when it occurred, as the tides, or the alternation of the seasons.

The paper which Harper and Weissenberger had prepared was much more modest, much less exalted in its ambition. They did not look to the past for a constant in Canadian history. They sought, rather, to bring about in Canada a realignment of politics along a left-right axis, as had occurred in the U.K. and the U.S. Their commitment, expressed in the first principle of their paper, was to "strong conservative principles." That was quite different from Manning's insistence that a new party must be equally attractive to westerners who voted Liberal, NDP, and Conservative. When they titled their paper "A Taxpayers Reform Agenda," they knew that they were implicitly opposing the taxpayers to the New Class of clients of the state – the public servants, those who worked in Crown corporations, as well as the provinces, businesses, interest groups, and individuals depending essentially on the largesse and subsidies of the state. This was a right-wing perspective. It was one that was suspicious of the state and that wanted to restrain the state's power

and economic control. Their sixth principle was in the same vein. It recommended "*The development of a randomly chosen Taxpayers Council*
to help legislators assess real public opinion, counteract funded political
lobby groups, and suggest ways of obtaining direct taxpayer input on
government spending." The real people – the taxpayers – would not
condone so many perverse actions of governments run by professional
politicians. Such a council of citizens chosen at random could at least act
as a conscience for the real people to bring them stern messages of
common sense and publicly rebuke them for their excesses.

This expressed a populism quite different from Manning's. His populism was somewhat mystical. The common people, when suitably
informed, were in the long run always right, Manning believed. When the
institutions of government departed too much from the right path, a
reform surge arose from the people to sweep away the old unsuitable institutions and create the new institutions, necessarily better than the old.
Manning's populism was essentially radical. It celebrated revolution, the
taking up of arms. The populism of Harper and Manning was conservative. It was law-abiding, suspicious of extreme, rapid change, and
opposed to revolution. Where Manning saw the people as having a
welcome revolutionary impact on government, Harper and Weissenberger
looked to the people – the taxpayers – as a constraint on the excesses of
government, as a conservative influence. And this countervailing concept
of populism was expressed in their second principle: "*The establishment
of a Party controlled by private citizens*, independent of its politicians
and government insiders, and their tactics of phony involvement, stack-
ing of meetings, and instant memberships." The same suspicion of the
professional class of politicians was expressed in their third principle:
"*The replacement of the carnival atmosphere of political conventions* –
orchestrated campaigns, balloons, songs, and free booze – with the active
recruitment of solid candidates and the examination of philosophy and
policy, not image and personality." And the same skepticism reappeared
in the fourth principle: "*The unveiling of the mysteries of party solidarity* – free and public caucus votes before a unanimous position is taken
in the Commons." This principle reflected the old complaint against
party discipline which forced MPs to defend the party line rather than the
true interests of their constituents. Proposals to abolish this kind of party
discipline had been recurrent among reformers, going back at least to the

Progressives right after the First World War. Harper and Weissenberger did not reject party discipline absolutely, but they demanded that it be tempered by being made transparent – that the discussions in caucus before a party line was enforced should be made public, so that the public would be better able to judge whether their representatives were really representing their interests to the party, or merely representing the inter- ⌐ ests of the party to them.

The suspicion of the politicians was again in evidence in the tenth and the fifth principles: "*The implementation of the new economics* – ⑤ of smaller government, regional diversification, non-discriminatory or discretionary spending, privatization, fair trade, and less expensive and less bureaucratic income transfers," and "*The termination of patronage* ⑥ appointments and positions, as well as of the public funding of special interest groups." Harper, in particular, knew from his experience on Parliament Hill, how the power of the prime minister and of the party lay in large part in their ability to reward their friends and sycophants with the money of the taxpayers, with the publicly remunerated positions that were often created precisely to purchase favour. In fact, whole regions of the country could be seduced in this way, for example, by the current program of unemployment insurance and the regional development grants. Instead of favouring regional development by lowering taxes for any and all businesses in a poorer region, the federal government chose to dole out public money to chosen businesses – a less efficient form of regional development and one that lent itself to nepotism, cronyism, and corruption.

The seventh principle made a specific application of the general suspicion of the state and of politicians and reflected the distaste Harper had felt for the antics of the politicians in Question Period: "*The ending of* ⑦ *special status of the political class* – the ending of heckling and juvenile behaviour in Parliament, of the exemption of Parliament from its own laws, of the right to slander private citizens with impunity."

The remaining three principles were more specific in their intent. The eighth principle was aimed at protecting western interests by proposing ⌐ reform of the Senate and ensuring the right of the province to control its resources against any repetition of a National Energy Program: "*The furthering of constitutional changes* for regional representation, as well as property and resource rights." The ninth principle was aimed at attacking the Meech Lake Accord, which Prime Minister Mulroney had announced just four weeks earlier, on May 1, and which almost the entire country had greeted with a Hallelujah chorus. Harper and Weissenberger had opposed the accord from the first day, seeing in it the conferring of special status on Quebec and a repudiation of the equality of the provinces: "*The organization of opposition* to the attempt to permanently entrench constitutional arrangements (Meech Lake)."

Finally, the eleventh principle was a practical one, intended to create a vehicle by which to further all ten previous principles: "*The identification of Western PC MPs* ready to accept this convention's agenda." It was in the spirit of creating a Blue Tory network, on which Harper and Weissenberger had been working. But given the western focus of the Western Assembly, their proposal concentrated on luring western Progressive Conservative MPs to their conservative taxpayers' agenda. It proposed to confront members of Parliament from the western provinces, who would be summoned to form a right-wing caucus within the PC Party, or to leave the party altogether. This, of course, was very different from Manning's intent to lure grassroots supporters equally from all three parties.

Did the paper have any effect on the course and direction of the Western Assembly? Probably not. But, just as the assembly itself turned out to be an unexpectedly important event in the political history of Canada, this paper, schematic and skeletal as it was, constituted the first public expression of Harper's political philosophy, his vision of what public life should be, just as he was about to appear on the public stage for the first time. Unlike most manifestos, it used a minimum of words that could almost have been chapter headings. The ideas, while idealistic and perhaps verging on the utopian, clearly constituted a condemnation of existing and past practices entrenched in Canadian political institutions and Canadian political culture. They projected an alternative, a populist and economically conservative vision of government. With hindsight, what is also notable is that they offered not the slightest hint of social or moral conservatism.

To a large extent, these ideas were to govern Harper's thinking over the following two decades. As Mansell said of him, "Stephen's got a very well-developed framework. He doesn't get jerked off the track based on all kinds of winds. He's thought about these things a lot, and he never usually says anything unless he's kind of come to a conclusion."

In the event, the assembly voted to launch a new party in the fall. The vote was 76 per cent in favour of the course proposed by Manning. As *Western Report* wrote at the time, "A modest, affable, and quietly brilliant man, Mr. Manning was the guiding light throughout the convention and the chief reason a party emerged." But he did not get everything his own way. When it came to voting on social policy issues, notably the treatment of aboriginals, the assembly was divided and chose not to take a position. Manning was disturbed. In his speech, he had made it clear that, for him, economic conservatism was not enough. A party that did not have a platform for the poor could not attract the people as a whole. "A new federal party which embodies the principal political values of the West will transcend some of the old categories of left and right. It will provide a home for the socially responsible businessman and the economy-conscious social activist. It should be a party whose members and leaders are characterized as people with 'hard heads and soft hearts,' i.e., people who attach high importance to wealth creation and freedom of economic activity on the one hand, but who are also genuinely concerned and motivated to action on behalf of the victims of the many injustices and imperfections in our economic and social systems."

For Stephen Harper, the assembly had provided some disappointments, but also much cause for enthusiasm. Above all, he was disappointed that the assembly had been divided on the Meech Lake Accord, which he so strongly opposed. Though it seemed to him to be a serious threat to western interests, Manning had not so much as mentioned it in his major speech. A motion had been put forward demanding that the four provincial legislatures not give legislative assent to the Meech Lake Accord unless it also included a Triple-E Senate – elected, equal, and effective. That motion was defeated by a vote of 78 to 67. The assembly also failed to adopt a motion to entrench property rights in the Constitution, as he and Weissenberger had advocated. But, on the Triple-E Senate itself, the vote was almost unanimous: 151 to 1.

The assembly also showed itself favourable to a populist approach to politics. It voted 130 to 1 for the principle of holding referendum votes on specific policy questions simultaneously with the vote to elect federal and provincial members in general elections.

Harper left Vancouver with the sense that he had participated in history. He had gone to Vancouver still a member of the Progressive Conservative Party. When he got back to Calgary, he gave Weissenberger a detailed account of what had taken place at the assembly. And the two newly inspired young men turned their back on the past and looked forward to taking part in founding a new party.

Chapter 6

A PARTY IS FOUNDED, A STAR IS BORN

ON THURSDAY, OCTOBER 29, 1987, Stephen Harper and John Weissenberger climbed into Weissenberger's Volkswagen Jetta and set off across the prairies on the fourteen-hour drive from Calgary to Winnipeg. The fall sun shone brilliantly in a big prairie sky and they were in high spirits: they were off to found a new political party. And Stephen Harper had a special reason for anticipation: he was slated to give a speech.

John was at the wheel, Harper sat beside him, and in the back seat was Donna Hallett, a graduate student in economics and a philosophical libertarian, also on her way to the Winnipeg founding convention. They had much to talk about. The convention would be asked to give the new party a name, to adopt a constitution, a statement of principles, and, most important, to elect the leader. Picking the right leader was critical for a new party with a bold agenda but without a history or an established membership. The best constitution would little avail unless the leader could embody it and present it winningly to the electorate. Over the past two decades, Alberta had seen its landscape littered with the roadkill of protest movements that failed to find the right leader.

They talked of the Vancouver assembly, where Manning had so impressed Stephen. He and John told Donna that they'd resigned during the summer from the Progressive Conservative Party. John had even written a letter to Brian Mulroney explaining why he, the president of the Calgary West PC Youth Association, was quitting. He had first written to Mulroney in June of 1983, after the leadership convention, to congratulate him for defeating Joe Clark. Then, John had high hopes for the party. Now his disenchantment was final.

They discussed the big speech that Stephen had prepared. This convention would be very different for him than the Vancouver assembly. In August, Stephen had written a long memo to Manning in which he elaborated on the proposals he had brought to Vancouver. His memo was titled "Political Reform and the Taxpayer." He expressed the ideas, the conclusions, the philosophy, the vision, the alternative approach to government, which he and John had come to as a result of their months of reading and meditation. He denounced the statist, left-leaning vision shared by the three major parties, characterized by "sacred trusts." To redress the political imbalance, Harper proposed that the new party should be "a genuine conservative option, a Taxpayers Party." Manning must have been impressed because he asked Harper to prepare a full-scale speech on the mistreatment of western Canada, with proposals for remedy. Harper would be speaking to a plenary session for the convention's major speech on political economics.

His first sentence would go right to the heart of the matter: "This paper is about justice and injustice, fairness and unfairness, and compassion and selfishness, in the economic treatment of western Canada under Confederation." The speech was long. He had so much to say. Would they listen to the end? He did not have Manning's lofty philosophy of history or his folksy technique, learned from innumerable religious broadcasts, of embodying high principles in vivid, down-to-earth expressions. But Harper felt passionately about what he would say, and he hoped that passion would be contagious even if conveyed by facts and figures.

After his return from Vancouver, he and John helped set up the interim Calgary West Reform Constituency Association. There had been a first meeting, held at the Village Park Inn on October 7, 1987, for all those, Calgary-wide, who were interested in the party-to-be. A corporate lawyer, Marv MacDill, gave a pep talk to about fifty people on the need for political reform and he explained how they were to proceed. The people living in the same riding were to meet, elect officers, and choose delegates to the Winnipeg convention. And so Harper, Weissenberger, and five other people met in the kitchen of a young tax lawyer named Siân Stephenson, in northwest Calgary. The others, with Stephenson, included an engineer, an accountant, a retired military man who now worked as a contractor, and a retired oil and gas executive. Harper was named president. After some discussion they agreed that anyone interested could go to Winnipeg as a delegate. So did the magnificent seven modestly establish a constituency association that would become famous and so it happened that Harper and Weissenberger were speeding to Winnipeg.

On arrival after dark they met a howling wind that cut them to the bone. They'd not dressed for what felt like the depths of winter. The next morning, they walked the two blocks to the Winnipeg Convention Centre. The atmosphere was much warmer inside.

The first order of business was to choose a name for the new party. The delegates soon rallied to one name. Of some thirty proposals – ranging alphabetically from Acumen Party to Western Reform Party – they chose Reform Party of Canada. They rejected "Western Reform Alliance" or "Western Reform Party" because they wanted to give the new party "room to grow." Its first priority would be to address western discontents, but its vision would always be national, with the objective of reforming in time the federal government of Canada.

Robert Muir, the Calgary lawyer who had co-convened the Vancouver Western Assembly along with Stanley Roberts and Manning, had prepared over the summer a draft constitution. The delegates in plenary session debated, amended, and adopted the draft. The constitution included a sunset clause: the party would cease to exist in the year 2000 unless two-thirds of its members then voted to keep it alive. This met Manning's view that, as a populist movement, the new party must soon sweep all the way to power or it would lose the dynamism that justified its birth. Also populist was the requirement that the leader be bound by the policies adopted by the members; major changes of policy would require that the members be consulted first. The delegates voted down a proposal that authorized the executive to name fifty delegates to party conventions. They wanted this party to be controlled by the grassroots members, not from the top-down. Harper fully agreed.

The constitution aimed at pre-empting two common sources of abuse. To qualify for membership, one had to be of voting age, not the fourteen years of age permitted by the established parties. Also, to vote for candidates at nomination meetings, one had to have been a member for at least forty-five days. This was meant to prevent the influx of "instant members" choosing the candidate. The delegates also determined that the leader must be subject to approval by secret ballot after every general election in which the party did not form the government.

Both Harper and Weissenberger went to the microphone to speak against creating a youth wing for the new party. They cited their experience in the PCs, where the constitution required that 30 per cent of all delegates to conventions be under twenty-five years of age. This huge voting bloc was a tempting target, and was inevitably manipulated by seniors in the party. Joe Clark, in the 1976 leadership convention, had owed much of his support to youth clubs and youth delegates from the constituency associations: Joe had once been national president of the Young PCs. John Crosbie, in the 1983 leadership campaign, took advantage of a provision in the constitution that stated that a PC club affiliated to a post-secondary institution could send three youth delegates to a convention. Crosbie's organizers produced three delegates from a range of dubious institutions such as driving schools, flying schools, schools to train beauticians, as well as academic institutions. Newfoundland, as a result, sent more youth delegates to the 1983 Tory leadership convention than delegates from constituency associations. Harper and Weissenberger won their point. Creating a youth wing was rejected.

While Bob Muir had prepared the draft of the body of the constitution, Manning had drafted a preamble and a twenty-one-point "Statement of Principles." The preamble expounded Manning's vision of current reformers as the heirs of a constellation of dissidents, from Egerton Ryerson's crusade for public education in Upper Canada, Louis-Hippolyte Lafontaine and Robert Baldwin's struggle for responsible government in the United Province of Canada, Louis Riel's two rebellions, Frederick Haultain's struggle to attain provincial status for the Northwest Territories, all the way to Quebec's Quiet Revolution and the Committee for a Triple-E Senate. These various phenomena, so utterly different, had in common only the attack on the status quo. But Manning's vision expressed in the preamble carried. As he later wrote: "The preamble recapped the reform tradition of Canadian politics, identifying contemporary reformers with the 'reform tradition in Canadian politics whereby far-sighted and courageous men and women have sought to correct injustices and inequities and to achieve more responsible and representative government in Canada.'"

Manning's "Statement of Principles," also to be part of Reform's constitution, bound together quite a package of propositions, some as general as approval of motherhood and apple pie, others specific and current. Each appealed to some constituency of the Reform movement. The first principle was the most concrete: "We affirm the need to establish a Triple-E Senate in the Parliament of Canada – that is to say, a Senate which is Elected by the people, with Equal representation from each Province, and which is fully Effective in safeguarding regional interests." A much less specific principle was the sixth: "We affirm the value and dignity of the individual person and the importance of strengthening and protecting the family unit as essential to the well-being of individuals and society." Almost everyone could support it, from those who read it as inoffensive, to others who could read into it a condemnation of the welfare state, of abortion and divorce, even of homosexuality.

Other principles supported free enterprise, private property, free markets, balanced budgets, regional equity, appreciation of the land and its resources, education and skills training, the accountability of elected members to their constituents rather than to their party, and good relations with the United States. All these principles, because they were put positively, in general terms, and without a single "Thou Shalt Not . . . ," could rally support without condemning any discernable constituency. Even Brian Mulroney could have piously assented.

Though the general tenor was allusively right wing, this was softened by a non-specific commitment to compassion in the tenth principle: "We believe that Canadians have a personal and collective responsibility to care and provide for the basic needs of people who are unable to care and provide for themselves." The principle affirmed "a soft heart," in the phrase that Manning often favoured, without dividing the sheep from the goats. Was succour to be provided by the welfare state, or by private benevolence and voluntary associations encouraged by the tax system? In the real world of politics, the devil would be identified only when such details were known.

The populist thrust of the Statement of Principles was expressed somewhat clearly – but, again, leaving room for interpretation – in the twelfth and fourteenth principles: "We believe that public policy in democratic societies should reflect the will of the majority of the citizens as determined by free and fair elections, referendums, and the decisions of legally constituted and representative Parliaments and Assemblies elected by the people." This certainly would suggest a disagreement with representative democracy as Edmund Burke defined it, where the people elected their member of Parliament to exercise his best judgment, not to reflect theirs. But not necessarily. The fourteenth principle was clearer in its populist inspiration: "We believe in the common sense of the common people, their right to be consulted on public policy matters before major decisions are made, their right to choose their own leaders and to govern themselves through truly representative and responsible institutions, and their right to directly initiate legislation for which substantial public support is demonstrated."

The delegates debated all these questions with unflagging interest and high seriousness. Harper and Weissenberger, who had both attended the most recent Progressive Conservative convention, held in Montreal, could appreciate the contrast. In Winnipeg, there were 262 delegates, all from western Canada. They assiduously attended the policy discussions. Few chairs were empty during the plenary sessions, or when the delegates split into twelve workshops of twenty people each to sit around in a circle, study the information provided by the organizers, discuss, and vote on the proposals. In Montreal, there'd been hordes of Tories from all over the country. The policy resolutions were moved, debated, and duly voted on, but with the hall half empty; people came and went, the party's stars – the ministers – were rarely present unless they appeared to pronounce a high-profile statement. Only the naive and the ambitious took the policy debates seriously: the others knew that the Mulroney government would do what it wanted, whatever.

At lunch on the Saturday, Harper and Weissenberger sat at a table with David Somerville, president of the National Citizens Coalition, which had been founded in 1967 by a millionaire from London, Ontario, named Colin Brown. Its motto was "More freedom through less government." Ideologically, it stood clearly to the right. At one point, according to Weissenberger, Somerville, who attended as an observer, asked if any of the eight people at the table were members of the NCC. All of the other seven, including Harper, raised their hand.

An important order of business was to elect the new party's leader. The choice was between Preston Manning and Stanley Roberts. The campaigns of the two contenders were as different as their careers.

Roberts had a hospitality suite where alcohol was freely available. His supporters wore specially made colourful scarves. Posters bearing his picture plastered the walls and the columns in the room where the meetings were held. The caption above his photo, in big letters: STAN. Below, in smaller letters: The voice of the west. Manning had no picture on the wall, just a banner with his name. His only campaign gimmick, worn by him and his supporters, was a round white button which said, in black letters: MANNING: A VOICE FOR THE WEST. Even their slogans contrasted in style. Roberts claimed to be *the* voice of the West, Manning merely *a* voice *for* the West.

By the usual criteria of politics, Stan Roberts was the more obvious choice. A handsome man with a ready smile and a good speaking style, he had at the age of sixty an impressive resume and, unlike Manning, a national profile. Raised in Manitoba on a farm near the village of Saint-Adolphe, he was bilingual, held a bachelor's degree in agricultural economics from the University of Manitoba, and an M.B.A. from Western. While running a farm, he had twice been elected as a Liberal to the Manitoba legislature and later served for two years as president and acting leader of the Liberal Party of Manitoba. He had also made a name for himself outside politics. In 1971, he was appointed vice-president of Simon Fraser University. In 1976, he assumed the presidency of the Canada West Foundation, just when the separatist Parti Québécois had come to power and was preparing to hold a referendum on secession. Amid the prevailing mood of a national emergency, Roberts gave the Canada West Foundation a high profile as it formulated a western response to the crisis by sponsoring academic studies and holding public meetings. Roberts became known as a leading voice of western Canada.

In 1980, Roberts became president of the Canadian Chamber of Commerce and now, in 1987, he planned a second career in politics, and had the financial backing of an Edmonton millionaire now retired to Victoria, Francis Winspear.

How could Preston Manning compete? True, he carried the name of one of the most revered figures in Alberta's history as the son of Ernest Manning, but Preston had never established a public persona of his own. While still a college student, he had got a summer job working in San Francisco for the giant U.S. defence contractor Bechtel, through the head of its Canadian subsidiary, who did business with his father. Preston obtained in 1964 an honours degree in economics from the University of Alberta, but never went on to graduate school. At the age of twenty-three, in the federal elections of 1965, he ran as a Social Credit candidate but came in second even though his father, who had been re-elected as premier two years before with 55 per cent of the vote, had sent a personal letter recommending his son to every household in the riding.

Preston's first regular job was as a researcher with the National Public Affairs Research Foundation, a conservative Alberta think-tank close to the Alberta Social Credit Party provincially and to the Tories federally. His biographer Frank Dabbs, wrote: "Preston's initial assignments at the foundation sprang from his father's interest in reconnecting Social Credit to the reforming passion upon which it had been founded and rewriting that ardour in an idiom suited to the last quarter of the century. . . . Father and son were working as a team, with Preston's patrons footing the bill."

Dabbs informs us of Preston's "second initiative at the foundation: an exploration of the basis for merging the federal Social Credit and Progressive Conservative parties." The provincial PC Party was now led by a dynamic Peter Lougheed, and Ernest Manning's support had slipped badly in the 1967 elections. He and Preston were in favour of merging the two parties, and Lougheed was at least curious. Exploratory talks were held, with Preston and one other representing Social Credit, while Joe Clark, then executive assistant to Lougheed, represented the PC Party, along with Tory MLA Merv Leitch. The talks hardly got beyond finding a name for the merged parties: the Social Conservative Party.

Preston's next venture was to publish a book with his father in September 1967, proposing a party merger at the federal level. The book, *Political Realignment: A Challenge to Thoughtful Canadians*, was mostly written by Preston though it bore Ernest's name on the jacket. It proposed that a single party be formed on the right of the political spectrum by the merger of Social Credit with the PC Party. Its publication came just before the Progressive Conservative leadership convention that was to dump Diefenbaker and elect Robert Stanfield. Some saw it as Ernest Manning preaching for a call to lead the federal party. In any event, it evoked little interest outside of Alberta. Both federally and provincially, Social Credit was in sharp decline. Ernest Manning stepped down from the premiership in December 1968.

Within weeks of Ernest's resignation, he and Preston formed a company, M&M Systems Research Ltd. Almost twenty years later, in 1987, Preston was still president of the family firm, now called Manning Consultants Limited, and Ernest was chairman. In the intervening years, Preston had become his own person as a problem-solver to businesses and communities. He helped firms operating in the energy industry to resolve conflicts with local communities – notably Indian bands – by working co-operatively on community development. But, to the general public, he still remained known chiefly as the son of Ernest Manning, the long-time premier and then, for fifteen years, a federal senator.

And yet, when he arrived in Winnipeg on this Halloween weekend of 1987 to help found a new party, Preston was obviously the delegates' overwhelming favourite for the leadership. He was not a classic politician, but they were not the classic crowd attending a political convention. Most had had no previous experience working in the campaigns of established parties. They hadn't come to make new contacts or renew old ones, to rub shoulders with the powerful, or to spend a convivial couple of days as part of a mighty organization with great ambitions. They were mostly serious people, of the middle of the middle class, with a conviction that something was wrong with their country and they must do something about it. They, like Manning, had a sense of mission, and they were willing to pay the two-hundred-dollar registration fee and travel to Winnipeg to help found a protest party.

With this audience, Stan Roberts's past and his style worked against him. He was a Liberal or former Liberal spending big money on his leadership campaign compared with Manning, who spent almost nothing. And he was part of the national elite. These delegates had assembled because they were not part of the elite, did not share the attitudes and values of the elite, felt the elite did not understand them and looked down on them, and felt the elite had badly mistreated the West.

Roberts, in his speech for the leadership, made the mistake of saying that he expected about one hundred of his supporters to arrive the next day in time to register for the leadership vote. The agenda called for registration to end at 5 p.m. on Saturday. Roberts, to judge from later events, was bluffing and wanted to look like a winner even if he didn't have a winner's support in the hall. Only fifty-one delegates had registered from Manitoba, even though the convention was being held on his former home turf. Now he lived in Vancouver and there were seventy-six delegates from British Columbia. But Alberta had sent 129 delegates. The figures suggested the relative effectiveness of the two men as leaders and organizers.

Roberts's evocation of an influx of local people who hadn't troubled to attend the policy discussions but would arrive on the Saturday by the busload, staying just long enough to elect their former neighbour, panicked the delegates, who saw it as an example of the "instant members" who distorted electoral outcomes in the established parties. On Saturday morning, a motion was passed to close nominations immediately. Roberts and Winspear protested but the motion carried.

Roberts walked out, with a score of his supporters. The others carried on, and Stephen Harper went to the podium to give his speech, titled "Achieving Economic Justice in Confederation." He was introduced as "a part-time lecturer with the University of Calgary economics department and former executive assistant to Calgary MP Jim Hawkes." No doubt the audience expected the traditional Albertan denunciations of central Canadian perfidy. In fact, Harper delivered a tightly reasoned, fact-filled indictment against the treatment meted out to western Canada throughout its history and especially since 1973, that had the audience repeatedly interrupting with applause and giving him, at the end, a standing ovation.

Harper started slowly, enumerating a series of numbers that were little known outside the economics department of the University of Calgary, numbers that were abstract and lifeless in themselves, but, taken together, spoke powerfully of dispossession, and the people in that room grasped their impact for their own lives.

"Figures compiled by Robert Mansell at the University of Calgary show that from 1961 to 1985, a roughly $70-billion net surplus – or positive difference between what the federal government collected in revenues from the region and the expenditures and transfers it returned to the region – was extracted from western Canada. . . . On a per capita basis, nearly $2,000 per person per year was taken from Alberta, fifteen times the contribution of Ontario. British Columbia's per capita annual contribution also exceeded Ontario's, though it clearly has lower income levels. It is also interesting to note that in the 1980s, Ontario has joined Quebec as a major net beneficiary of regional transfers, while Alberta has remained a net loser. However, the two central economies have generally had a strong performance, while Alberta has consistently been on the ropes."

The parade of statistics went on, always showing the West in the red, bleeding for the benefit of other parts of Canada. "Remembering that the West contains roughly 29 per cent of the country's population and roughly 34 per cent of its economic activity, it received 15 per cent of regional development grants in 1985–86, 19.5 per cent of job creation funds in 1984–85, 14 per cent of federal procurement by the Department of Supply and Services in 1980 to 1983, and only 11.5 per cent of all federal procurement last year. [It received] less than 10 per cent of programming on CBC's national English-language television, 19.5 per cent of employment in the federal Department of Public Works, 14.5 per cent in Veterans Affairs, 9 per cent in Energy, 6 per cent in the Secretary of State, and only 2 per cent in the Federal-Provincial Relations Office."

Harper recalled one of the West's constant grievances from even before Saskatchewan or Alberta became provinces: the protective tariff that forced westerners to buy Canadian goods manufactured in central Canada, at prices higher than they could have bought them close by across the border in the United States. "Tariff structures continue to remove up to 6 per cent of western GDP, of which about half is a transfer to central Canada."

Another current source of unfairness to the West was the policy of bilingualism in the public service, which the Mulroney government was in the process of reinforcing by Bill C-72, an amendment to the Official Languages Act. It would push bilingualism in all areas of the country and into the private sector as well as the public service, taking it far beyond what the Trudeau Liberals had legislated. "The concentration of the Canadian bureaucracy in Ottawa is three times per capita that of the American bureaucracy in Washington. As well, it is probably much more difficult for a westerner to fit into that bureaucracy. Federal bilingualism policies work unevenly in a region where the majority language is English and the [most spoken] minority language is only rarely French. Fully 94 per cent of westerners are not 'officially' bilingual, and this must disadvantage hiring and promotion in a federal public service which is already centrally oriented."

After the cannonade of figures from the recent past, he returned to the West's history under the shadow of John A. Macdonald's National Policy of 1879. But Harper presented the National Policy, not merely as the tariff structure imposed in the past, but as the prototype of federal policy ever since. "In historical terms, the principal economic factor in the bias against the West has been the National Policy. . . . Over one hundred years later, the National Policy continues to function, federal government policies not only continue to diversify and strengthen the central core of the country at the expense of the periphery, but even actively resist peripheral developments. Despite its unprecedented elements, the National Energy Program was in many ways simply a direct descendant of the old National Policy. Today central Canada remains a strong, diverse, and stable industrial economy, which is highly protected. Western Canada – a weaker, narrower, far more cyclical economy – survives on its international competitiveness and pays the protectionist bills."

Harper then extended the logic of the National Policy to cover another phenomenon of contemporary Canada: the growth of the welfare state, which he argued, "has placed unprecedented power in the centralizing hands of the federal bureaucracy, both in terms of its new reaches into Canadian life and its insistence on standardizing all policies and practices on a national scale. . . . The key point, however, is that the unlimited appetite of the welfare state for funding has led to unprecedented tax grabs. One principal target of these tax grabs – indeed a very logical target – has been the windfall profits of western resource industries during boom times. It is critical to understand how such centralized handout economics works. On the one hand, its inevitable drain during boom times continually hampers any attempts to put resources into the kind of productive investment which could diversify the western economy. On the other hand, the trickle-down of bureaucratic enterprise aids a peripheral region only when, like Atlantic Canada, Confederation has reduced it to a state of permanent dependency."

This was a powerful charge. It supported Preston Manning's view that the welfare state was more effective at delivering dependency than in helping people to achieve self-sufficiency. But whereas Manning was by temperament and by professional practice a reconciler, one whose criticisms were generally more implicit and allusive than smashing, Harper defined clearly, concisely, and devastatingly the various strands that caught the West in a paralyzing net.

He evoked another obstacle in the way of the West wanting fair and equal treatment: The constant appeasement of Quebec. The Meech Lake Accord, agreed to by all the First Ministers five months earlier, was only the latest example of an entrenched partiality that worked to the West's disadvantage.

"One more modern source of unfairness to the West is in the special treatment accorded the Province of Quebec. The issue of Quebec's financial position in Confederation was a major part of the independence debate. An analysis of fiscal transfers between regions indicates unmistakably that the balance tipped greatly in favour of Quebec during this period. Moreover, the costs of these transfers were paid exclusively by western Canada. In many ways, the Quebec question has actually become a barrier to genuine decentralization and regional fairness. This is because, regardless of Quebec's gains, it has never been asked to make any significant concession – like surrendering a clear option to secede. Thus, the Quebec question has been made a perpetual puzzle, occupying permanent centre stage in the national unity debate. It is therefore paramount that the West's demands remain a 'hot second' in priority. Truly regional questions have become permanently subordinated in the two-nations dilemma."

The Quebec question was clearly a concern of the westerners who had come to Winnipeg, but Manning had never yet made it a major issue. He was reluctant to target one province and preferred to advance positive solutions rather than negative analysis. Harper was not only targeting Quebec, he was identifying it as a major obstacle to a West searching for justice, on a par with the National Policy and its contemporary extension, the welfare state. He denounced the ideology of the central Canadian opinion-forming elites for justifying a systematic injustice.

"Around the National Policy, the welfare state, and the Quebec question has grown a highly centralized political culture which is inherently and righteously biased against western Canada in its basic values and rhetoric. Whenever challenged, it wraps itself in a flag called 'Canadian identity,' 'Canadian nationalism,' 'national unity,' or the 'national interest'. . . . The whole concept of 'Canadian culture' no longer means the values and lifestyles of Canadians in a diverse country. Instead it means the protection of narrow arts and media interest groups based in Toronto.

Unilingualism in Quebec is a legitimate desire – *Maîtres chez nous*. In Manitoba, it is 'redneck' and 'racist.'"

In Harper's view, the official nationalism was (as with the "National" Policy) a cloak for regional interests, the interests of central Canada. His demonstration led to the conclusion that a new political party was needed to represent the interests of the West, because all the parties had demonstrated their unwillingness or their inability to do so. "The leadership of Canada's national parties has shown a fear of real debate and a desire to relegate politics to a game of images and image-makers. Thus quibbling over a few cans of tuna can continue for weeks on end, but there was no party willing to carry the ball for the West on the CF-18 contract. There is no party that will challenge the Meech Lake Accord. There is no party that will put the economic, political, and constitutional priorities of the West first. By failing to offer a clear vision of the future, they have us exist in the shadow of our past. And the shadow cast by Confederation has been western alienation."

So what should be the program of the new party? In the first place, it must demand fairness, that is, equality of treatment for people in similar circumstances, regardless of the region in which they live. There should be no more privileged individuals, privileged groups, or a privileged province. "A fair shake requires the immediate dismantling and restructuring of all policies and discretionary decisions that discriminate against the West. Economic justice begins with an equality of concern that must be matched by equality of action resulting in equality of treatment."

Without a commitment to fairness, he warned, " 'National Reconciliation' becomes simply another stage in the appeasement of Quebec nationalism." And he had an implicit warning for Quebec, though he did not name which "partner" he had in mind: "If the partners are not willing to live up to the requirements of a partnership, fairness requires that they pursue an equitable dissolution of the partnership." Those words, that view, when Manning did finally come to espouse them two years later, were to make the fortune of the Reform Party in western Canada in the years leading to 1993.

The current preferential treatment given to Quebec, even at the sacrifice of western interests, demonstrated the need for a structural change in the governance of the federation. The Constitution left the

West too little power to protect its interests. More than a change of attitude was needed. "It is time to balance the adjustments made in Confederation for Quebec with a set of policies that will establish equal treatment for all regions. We obviously require stronger forms of regional representation, like a Triple-E Senate, to balance the population dispro-portions caused by historical policies. In order to achieve this, it will be critical that we view any further demands of Quebec for more conces-sions, including passage of the Meech Lake Accord, as opportunities for the West to push its constitutional agenda." In other words, if Quebec wanted the terms of the Meech Lake Accord, they should receive the assent of the western provinces only if and when Quebec had also assented to their demands for constitutional change.

There was much, much else in that long speech. It offered red meat for people who hungered for straight talk in the form of a western man-ifesto. It had a prophetic tone; it offered a vision of what the West could be and what Canada must be – or else.

"All this requires is a different vision of Canada. This vision must not simply be western; it must be reforming. . . . The Joe Clarks may succeed in making themselves more at home in Ottawa, but to their constituents, they sound more like the same old song. In the stale air of politics, what Canada really requires is the sweeping winds of change. This will chal-lenge the vested interests of the National Policy, the welfare state, and the Quebec question, and they will resist. In the end, these groups will have to cast aside their narrow definitions of Canada – the country they claim to love – because that country can no longer be built on the eco-nomic exploitation and political disfranchisement of western Canada."

When he finished speaking, the applause was long and enthusiastic. Harper's hard-hitting talk complemented Manning's more ethereal, more diplomatic proposals. This speech at the founding convention had the same effect as Manning's had had at the Vancouver assembly. It lifted the anger, the frustrations, the hopes and aspirations, to a higher plane. *Alberta Report* reprinted large passages of the speech with a big picture of Harper, with this annotation: "The speech was acknowledged by del-egates, party officials, and media as a highlight of the convention." Manning himself, when he published his memoirs in 1992, under the title *A New Canada*, was generous and accurate in his assessment: "The best speech and most influential presentation at the Founding Assembly of the

Reform Party of Canada – and there were numerous strong presentations – was that given by Stephen Harper on the subject of 'Achieving Economic Justice.'" After describing Harper's background, Manning continued: "Harper's address to the Winnipeg Assembly was more germane to western concerns and more detailed in its analysis and its policy prescriptions than any speech by any cabinet minister to a western audience since the Conservatives came to power. At the same time, Harper's delivery was eloquent and understandable to those not well versed in economics, marking him as a potential spokesman, candidate, and member of Parliament. People who have been told that the Reform Party consists of well-meaning simpletons mouthing naive solutions to complex problems should study Harper's speeches on behalf of Reform."

Clearly, Harper's speech, and the reaction to it by the delegates, were a revelation to Manning. This was someone who must have a special role in the construction of this new party that Manning saw as redeeming the West and changing Canada. He enthused: "Harper's address shattered all the stereotypes (reactionary, backward-looking, narrow, simplistic, extreme) that are often applied to a new political party struggling for legitimacy from a western base. It combined youthful enthusiasm and idealism with wisdom, breadth of vision, and practical solutions to real problems. It was greeted with a prolonged standing ovation from all who heard it, and I knew that the party had found a potential policy chief."

There remained the business of electing the leader. Roberts's fate was already sealed. He did not fit in the party that had received its style and its vision from the non-politicians, Manning and Harper. Returned from his ostentatious walkout, Roberts tried to have the vote put off by six months, but those who had come to found a party and choose a leader refused a postponement. Roberts would not accept that he, with his brilliant career and national reputation, could be defeated by a nonentity like Preston Manning. He claimed that the idea of the Vancouver assembly and the founding of a new party was his, and that Francis Winspear had supported him by putting up the money. He had at various times dismissed Manning and his delegates as "fanatics" and "small-minded evangelical cranks." When, on the Sunday morning, before the vote was taken, he announced that he was withdrawing from the race, his voice quavered and he was tearful.

Meanwhile, as Kenneth Whyte and Mike Byfield related in *Alberta Report*, "Instead of campaigning for the leadership, Mr. Manning simply assumed the role. He has had his way on all major points so far, from the decision to form a party last spring to the decision to wait another year before tackling potentially explosive social issues." So Manning became leader by acclamation, and his leadership would remain strong over the next twelve years. But Roberts's departure broke the link with the Liberal Party. Manning had envisaged the party as transcending left-right ideology and appealing equally to disenchanted Tories, Liberals, New Democrats, and people never before aligned. But, from the start, Manning was out of sync with the party he had founded, since the traditional parties were almost entirely absent from the founding convention, except for former Tories. Harper's own speech – and the mood of the delegates – were clearly positioned on the right.

Shortly after the convention, Manning appointed Harper as chief policy officer, the only person besides Manning authorized to speak in the name of the party. To Harper's relief, the new party had taken a stand against the Meech Lake Accord and for a Triple-E Senate, for free trade with the United States, and for entrenching property rights in the Constitution of Canada. He later collated all the various policy positions and put them in a coherent order to represent a statement of what the party stood for. Later still the statement was rewritten in the form of a booklet that was called *The Blue Book*.

But, despite the high intellectual calibre of the presentations by Manning and Harper and other speakers, the reports in the news media – with the exception of Ted Byfield's publications – were generally patronizing at best. On Sunday morning, November 1, the day after Harper's speech, the Reformers woke up to this first sentence in a *Toronto Star* story by Val Sears reporting on their convention: "WINNIPEG – A broomstick load of revolutionary ghosts rode Winnipeg's Halloween sky last night, summoned by the West's newest political bloc, the Reform Party of Canada." But Sears did take Harper seriously: "Harper's speech, likely to be the foundation document at a later policy conference, spells out western grievances." The following Sunday, Val Sears was even more sarcastic: "There are a good many sodden cigars in western Canada these days, as more and more flatlanders and mountain men wind themselves up about the threat to their way of life from the East – that wicked, grasping, foreign land somewhere beyond the Manitoba border. This is not, of course, novel. Louis Riel found himself at the end of rope for translating his complaints into action. But there is a certain new focus in the formation of the Reform Party of Canada in Winnipeg last week, a group passionately devoted to winning the West by whining about the East."

John Weissenberger recalls ruefully: "As long as you were still a Tory, you were a fine upstanding person, but as soon as you left, and you were part of this new thing, all of a sudden they considered you to be kind of a radical yahoo, or reactionary or whatever. Overall, the sessions were very positive from a policy standpoint. So I was shocked at the reaction from outsiders. This was just a group of average Canadians, most of whom had had no political involvement at all, just getting together and saying, 'This is what we think the country should be and how things should be changed.' And the reaction from the outside was just so vitriolic. There was a really vicious cartoon in the *Free Press* of Manning with bad pointy teeth and he carried one of those big marching drums, and the quote underneath was: 'Join Preston's thump for Jesus.' I was shocked, because religion wasn't even discussed at this meeting, it had nothing to do with what was discussed. I remember saying to Stephen, Were these guys even at the same meeting? I mean, this is just unbelievable, but these guys obviously came to the meeting with fixed ideas of what this was all about. I was just flabbergasted that they basically had the story written before they even showed up. So that was another eye-opener for me, or for us, I guess." That contemptuous treatment was to be recurrent in the news media at least until the elections of 1993. It would leave its mark. Harper developed a rooted distrust of the press.

The last day of the convention was November 1. That was the day when René Lévesque died suddenly. The news coverage of the life of the former separatist premier of Quebec the next day and until after his funeral was vast, and very different in tone from the treatment of Manning and the new party. It was reverential. Prime Minister Mulroney ordered the flags at half-staff on all federal buildings in Quebec and in Ottawa. Mulroney declared Lévesque "the ultimate democrat. He was the greatest democrat that this country has ever known." He even depicted Lévesque as a great Canadian: "We have just lost a very great patriot. It's a loss not only for Quebec, not only for all those who believe in democracy, but for all of Canada, because, all told, he built, to my mind, a better Canada. It's a simply splendid heritage."

Premier Robert Bourassa lamented "the loss of a brother-in-arms." He declared that Lévesque "will pass into history as one of our most generous and determined patriots." He decreed a three-day lying-in-state leading up to a state funeral. The funeral in Quebec City was attended by the prime minister, even though he was sick with the flu, and by federal ministers Joe Clark, Robert de Cotret, Benoît Bouchard, Michel Coté, Marcel Masse, Barbara McDougall, Monique Vézina, Gerry Weiner, and Pierre Blais. Nova Scotia premier John Buchanan and New Brunswick premier Frank McKenna also attended, as did France's former prime minister Pierre Mauroy and the Speaker of the French National Assembly, Jacques Chaban-Delmas. The members of France's National Assembly stood for a minute in silence to show their respect.

Pierre Trudeau visited the exposed coffin during the lying-in-state, paused there in reflection, then left without a word. He did not attend the state funeral.

So it was that one historical figure passed from the scene while a new party that would make history was born. And Stephen Harper emerged into public view, never to quite disappear again in the following years.

Chapter 7

SPREADING THE WORD

STEPHEN HARPER, AS chief policy officer for Reform, was often called upon to speak for the party. He appeared at press conferences and addressed meetings in Calgary. But the new Reform Party was also exciting interest in the small towns and villages of rural Alberta, and the requests came frequently to send a speaker to remote Legion halls or church basements. Harper was setting out on one of those missions with John Weissenberger in February 1988, during the time when Calgary was hosting the Winter Olympics. John was at the wheel of his Volkswagen Jetta.

"It was ridiculously warm and bright sunshine," Weissenberger remembers, "and we were trying to get out of town during the rush hour to this small place in southern Alberta called Granum, where we were going to meet about a dozen people. I was late, as usual, and . . . in traffic, I wasn't paying enough attention, the sun was in my eyes, and I slammed into the back of this woman's car, and wrecked the whole front end of my car. So Stephen had to walk all the way up the hill to the university to get his car while I was filling out the police reports. We were supposed to meet a fellow who was organizing for us down in southern Alberta for dinner, and then go to this meeting. And one bizarre aspect of this experience: the party had made tapes of some of its better-known speakers. They had made a tape of Stephen's famous speech at the founding convention and they'd distributed it to some of the organizers. So here we are, we ended up in Granum half an hour late after missing dinner, and we walk into this little town hall and we hear Stephen's voice on a tape recorder. It was his Winnipeg speech that they were playing. When we arrived, they turned off the tape recorder and Stephen gave a presentation to ten or twelve of the locals."

That was how the Reform Party was growing during the year between the founding at the end of October 1987, and the federal elections of 1988. At the time, Harper was in his second year toward a master's degree in economics and was also teaching undergraduates part-time. He was a busy man. After the founding convention in Winnipeg, Harper wasted little time setting up a Reform Party constituency association in his home riding of Calgary West. He and John Weissenberger lured a few Tories from the PC Calgary West association, but most of the attendees were new to politics, drawn to the policies of the new party. On January 16, 1988, they held their founding meeting and Harper, acclaimed president of the riding association, gave an inspirational speech. It was not like his speech in Winnipeg. He did not dwell on the grievances of the West. Instead, Harper insisted on the need for a principled party of the right in Ottawa, one with a comprehensive program of reform. Only the Reform Party could make that claim. Both the PCs and the Liberals were parties of expediency, of opportunism, and they would sell the West out whenever it was to their advantage. "Time may show you to be on the leading edge of political change in Canada today," he told the new recruits.

Policy was Harper's forte and his passion. So he found himself in the centre of the action during the year of preparing for the first confrontation at the polls. The two assemblies of the previous year, in Vancouver and Winnipeg, had endorsed the fundamental policy commitments that would define the Reform Party as it attacked the status quo. But those policy positions needed to be developed, refined, and embodied in language that could reach the minds and hearts of westerners. To distill the right words and paragraphs was now the shared responsibility of Manning as leader and Harper as chief policy officer. Strategically, their line of attack on the status quo would concentrate on promoting the need for a Triple-E Senate, while condemning the Meech Lake Accord, the hypocritical bilingualism policy of the Mulroney government, and its out-of-control spending.

The key was to identify the Reform Party above all others with the Triple-E Senate, a relatively recent proposal that had rallied the support of Albertans. Reform must so position itself that it was perceived as the only effective defender of the Triple-E Senate, and so the only reliable defender of the West. Only the Triple-E Senate – by giving new power to the outlying regions as a counter to the demographic dominance of central Canada – could bring an end to the long history of western exploitation; and only the Reform Party offered the supporting policies that would make the Triple-E Senate attainable. So, to demonstrate the seriousness of Reform's commitment, Manning and Harper set up a constitutional committee on which both sat, with a mandate to produce the text of an amendment to the Constitution that, if adopted by the federal government and the provincial legislatures, would entrench the Triple-E Senate as part of the fundamental law of Canada. In effect, Reform would produce a western-centred amendment as a deliberate counterpoise to the Quebec-centred Meech Lake Accord. No one, despite all the rhetoric, had ever done this. The constitutional committee, with legal specialists from different parties as well as Manning and Harper, worked out the points to be made and the final drafting was entrusted to Mel Smith, who had been British Columbia's deputy minister for constitutional affairs.

True to Reform's populist commitment, the draft constitutional amendment was then studied at a specially convened meeting in each of the four western provincial capitals, as well as in Vancouver and Calgary. The model that emerged from these deliberations called for a Senate with ten senators elected from each province, while the Northwest Territories and the Yukon would elect four senators each. The elections would be held on the same date across Canada every three years, each time electing half the senators, for a fixed term of six years. They would be elected in a province- or territory-wide election, by a single transferable vote. The Triple-E Senate would have approximately the same powers as the current Senate, but senators could not be part of the cabinet, nor could they cause the fall of a government.

The Triple-E Senate had its conceptual birth in 1981, in a paper published by the Canada West Foundation, titled *Regional Representation: The Canadian Partnership*. Its authors were Peter McCormick, a political scientist teaching at the University of Lethbridge, Senator Ernest Manning, and Gordon Gibson, who had been executive assistant to Prime Minister Pierre Trudeau and later the leader of the Liberal Party of

British Columbia. Their proposal did not use the name Triple-E Senate. That came later, and was coined, according to the *Edmonton Journal*, by Ted Byfield, writing in *Alberta Report*. But the idea was launched, and launched by westerners, to meet specifically western grievances. The idea was taken up in 1985 in a report by the Alberta Select Special Committee on Upper House Reform, titled *Strengthening Canada: Reform of Canada's Senate*. It proposed that each province should elect six senators, they would be elected province-wide, with the six candidates receiving the most votes being declared elected. The PC government of Premier Don Getty, under fire in 1988 from the nascent Reform Party and from the Alberta Liberals and New Democrats, tried to get on the right side of the issue of Senate reform. On March 10, 1988, the Alberta legislature passed unanimously a resolution endorsing the Triple-E Senate, as recommended three years earlier by the select committee.

The vision of the federation defended by Premier Getty was very different from that enshrined in the Constitution in 1867, but also from the paper by McCormick–Manning–Gibson. It would have ended the commanding predominance of the federal government over the provincial governments, as set down in the British North America Act. Both *orders* of government (no longer called *levels* of government) would now become the equal "partners of Confederation." The "constitutional equality of the provinces" had become the Alberta government's cardinal principle, its mantra. It meant both the equality between provinces, but also the equality of each provincial government with the federal government.

Getty liked to suppose that Meech Lake would first redefine the role of the First Ministers as a directorate of eleven equals, meeting annually on the Constitution and on the economy. After Meech Lake was adopted, a constitutional conference would then follow which must consider Senate reform as a curb on the federal power to mistreat the provinces. Then, he trusted, the Triple-E Senate would triumph. Premier Getty's optimism was highly vulnerable to attack. So were the pro-Meech positions of the federal Tories, Liberals, and New Democrats. They all neglected to consider that, once Meech Lake passed, Quebec would have a veto over further constitutional change, and Quebec opposed the Triple-E Senate.

On May 18, 1988, having just put the finishing touches to their constitutional amendment for a Triple-E Senate, the Reformers carried off a publicity coup. The western premiers were meeting at Parksville, on Vancouver Island. Seizing the occasion, several hundred Reformers chartered a train and rode it to Parksville, where they delivered to the conference the text of their constitutional amendment and also the petitions they had been gathering across the West in favour of its implementation. They did not get to meet any of the four premiers, but their "Constitutional Express" escapade did make the news and draw attention to their campaign. They were able to contrast Prime Minister Mulroney's and the premiers' speed in responding to the Quebec Liberal government's five demands for constitutional amendments with the lack of any serious action on the Triple-E Senate.

On June 28, 1988, Harper was acclaimed as the Reform Party candidate in Calgary West. No one would have thought of running against him. "This campaign is not about political images or personal relationships," he said, in an obvious reference to his opponent, Jim Hawkes, with whom everyone in the room knew that he'd had a very close relationship. "A vote for Jim Hawkes is a vote for the kind of Red Toryism that appears so similar to the Liberals and NDP on dozens of public policy issues like the CF-18, Bill C-72 [the proposed new Official Languages Act], or reform of UIC. A vote for my candidacy is a clear vote for western representation and an agenda which would change the system to give a real voice in Parliament to the regions and to taxpayers. A vote for Jim Hawkes is fundamentally a vote for Brian Mulroney – a blank cheque for Mulroney to do whatever he wants, whenever he wants, and however he wants, to satisfy the voters of central Canada and to stay in power."

Harper appealed to his supporters to become involved as concerned citizens with a sense of civic duty. But he recognized that the coming election would be difficult because it would be fought on the Free Trade Agreement with the United States, and the West was for free trade. The Tories would rely, Harper warned, on the "Red Scare" in the West: " 'The Red Scare' is the old argument that the Reform Party will 'split the vote' against the PCs on the critical issue of free trade, and therefore help 'the socialists.' " The Reformers, like the Tories, were in favour of free trade because it was in the West's interests and had long been a western demand. But he noted with irony that the West had never obtained free trade, nor was the West really obtaining it now. "Like the Meech Lake

Accord, it is a Quebec policy initiative. The West has wanted free trade for over a hundred years, because protection is part of the historic bias against the West in Confederation. Suddenly, when the Province of Quebec is prepared to back free trade, we find the federal Tories changing their position on the policy."

He also took a swipe at the "Canadian" nationalists like Bob White, then president of the Canadian Auto Workers, and David Peterson, premier of Ontario, both strongly opposed to the Free Trade Agreement. "Free trade is exposing a real and long-standing division in this country, pitting the aspirations of the various regions of Canada against the rigid views of Canadian nationalists. The rhetoric of Canadian nationalists like Bob White or Premier Peterson is failing to capture the imagination of the country as a whole. This shows exactly what I've said before. That is to say, so-called Canadian nationalism does not represent the values or identity of most Canadians, but is simply the regional culture of Ontario, and the vested interests of central Canada's political elites."

Harper got in a dig at Lucien Bouchard, the separatist friend of Mulroney whom the prime minister had sent as his ambassador to Paris and, to strengthen his appeal to the Quebec nationalists, had recalled to join him in Ottawa. On March 31, Mulroney named Bouchard directly to the cabinet, before he had been elected as an MP. He was sworn in as Secretary of State, responsible for the official languages. A riding was opened up for him: Lac St. Jean, which included the village where Lucien had been born. A by-election was called. Mulroney pulled out all the stops in making promises to ensure that his prize minister won his seat. This is what Harper seized on in his nomination speech.

"You know, those who think things have changed should take a careful look at the Tory by-election in Lac-St.-Jean, Quebec. Brian Mulroney told the people there that if they elected Lucien Bouchard, he would be 'a bulldozer for Lac-St.-Jean.' Now that in itself isn't a bad idea. Having worked on Parliament Hill a while myself, I think it could use a bulldozer. There's a lot of 'bull' that needs to be 'dozed.' Let's, however, look at what it cost to get this bulldozer elected: $440,000 – old wharf – sold to Sainte-Rose-du-Nord for $1 by feds. Road to James Bay – $40 million to $50 million. The $1 billion Quebec Regional Development Fund – $120 million for Lac-St.-Jean. $1.4 million for local job creation centre – renovate a building, buy furniture, pave parking lot. No plans for job creation funds. Unspecified money to refurbish a local airport. Two million dollars to run the actual election where there already was a sitting member. With a price tag like that, this must be one of those nuclear-powered bulldozers!"

Then, in a sally that would have been considered most politically incorrect in Ottawa at the time, Harper taunted Bouchard the separatist. "The fact is that we spent all this money to elect a separatist to be the Secretary of State. Maybe I'm being unfair, calling Monsieur Bouchard a separatist. But he has never denied that he is still an *indépendantiste*. And recently, when accused by the PQ leader of having sold out the separatist cause by going federal, Bouchard replied, 'There's more than one road to Rome.' From that I conclude that either he's a separatist or he wants Quebec to join Italy." Nor was Harper finished with the theme of Bouchard as separatist. "Monsieur Bouchard was miffed that the PQ would not officially support his candidacy. He didn't ask the Reform Party to support his candidacy – because he knows that the Reform Party doesn't support separatists, unlike the Tories."

Harper then proceeded to attack the Mulroney government for its two standards on the official languages. It was much in the news precisely at that time. In June 1987, Mulroney had introduced in the Commons Bill C-72, officially titled "An Act Respecting the Status and Use of the Official Languages of Canada." It was also supported, like the Meech Lake Accord, by both John Turner's Liberals and Ed Broadbent's New Democrats. It went much further in promoting the two official languages than anything Trudeau had done. Section 38 of the bill proposed: "The Government of Canada is committed to ensuring that English-speaking Canadians and French-speaking Canadians, without regard to their ethnic origin or first language learned, have equal access to appointment and advancement in federal institutions; and [to ensuring that] the composition of the work force of federal institutions tends to reflect the presence of both the official language communities of Canada." This suggested that Canada was to be divided into two official language communities. And the person who would be called on to apply this much more statist and intrusive new policy was none other than Lucien Bouchard, the Quebec separatist who was known to favour Quebec's Charter of the French Language – the chief thrust of which was precisely to restrict English, its use or its appearance in public. Was this not the fox entrusted to promote the welfare of the chickens? Harper went after Mulroney's language policy embodied in the new secretary of state.

"Monsieur Bouchard may well be an honest man," Harper continued. "I say this because of his statements on Bill C-72. That's the new Mulroney language legislation that extends official bilingualism. Monsieur Bouchard assured Quebec politicians that Bill C-72 does not challenge Bill 101 and enforced unilingualism in the Province of Quebec. 'The French face of Quebec, its French character, we will respect it,' he said. Furthermore, Bouchard added that Bill C-72 is mainly intended to help francophones outside Quebec, not to assist Quebec's anglophone minority. At least Monsieur Bouchard will admit to us what our western Tories haven't got the guts to admit: that Mulroney's language policy is to push bilingualism in English Canada while giving Quebec a green light to remain unilingual French and placing at the highest level of government Québécois who support Bill 101. Canadians, particularly western Canadians, understand what's going on. Many are like me – individuals who once supported official bilingualism but now realize that federal language policy is collapsing under the weight of its own hypocrisy."

Harper went on to summarize Reform's language policy. "It is time for a new approach to federal language policy, one that recognizes that there is a predominantly French-speaking region of the country and predominantly English-speaking regions of the country, that recognizes this in a way that involves no double standards, in a way that respects minorities, and in a way that is fair to all Canadians, including the vast majority of Canadians who are unilingual. I say, let Quebec be Quebec; let the West be the West."

Harper's speech on that June 28 dealt largely with language policy because the controversy over Bill C-72, then still not adopted, was current, and Bouchard's election had taken place only eight days before. But language policy was not the first priority of the Reform Party and of its chief policy officer. That was the Triple-E Senate, and the Meech Lake Accord was its chief nemesis.

Harper worked all that spring and summer on the Reform Party's electoral platform. He prepared a draft, taking inspiration from the election manifestos of Margaret Thatcher, which he and John Weissenberger had studied and admired. The Reform manifesto was not to be a mere grab bag of promises to disparate constituencies, with a little something for everybody, in the tradition of the Progressive Conservatives and the Liberals, who usually brought out their election goodies one at a time, with the announcements spread out over the entire election campaign so as to get a maximum of publicity, and always to have something new to offer the media. The platform of the Reform Party was to project a vision. It was to offer a detailed critique of the major policies of the Tory government in Ottawa. It would demonstrate in detail why these policies betrayed the West. It would present and explain the Reform Party's own policies, and demonstrate why they were appropriate.

The draft was submitted to a special Reform assembly in Calgary on August 12 to 14. Harper, as chief policy officer, opened the meeting on August 12 with a speech to the delegates from the four western provinces, some 250 in number. "The platform talks about constitutional equality," he said. "It is not enough to just get handouts. The West requires fundamental changes to the system that will protect regional interests against the arbitrary will of central Canada and the federal government. The West can get these changes. Despite history and policy, the West is strong. It has one-third of Canada's population and is growing. It has over one-third of its economic activity. It has critical resources and the country's key industries. The West is not weak. The West is strong. It is our representatives that are weak – representatives who bargain away the issues in exchange for personal political gain. . . . The West needs fundamental change, and it needs it now. When the prime minister and his buddies gather in the kitchen to change the Constitution, the Triple-E Senate must be on the table, not on the back burner."

He briefly outlined the major sections of the policy document that he had prepared. His explanation of Reform's social policy is worth noting, because of widespread misunderstanding of the position: "We seek cost-effective and humane alternatives to the fading vision of Mother Government as the best and only way to care for the sick, the poor, the old, and the young. We seek to develop a society of real 'social conscience,' where all individuals and agencies re-assume their social responsibilities, and do not simply shove those responsibilities onto the poverty professionals in the bureaucracy. Furthermore, we seek to move away from universality and to target social spending and social caring on those unable to care for themselves."

Then, before sitting down, he spoke his last words: "With those thoughts, my contributions to the policy development are complete, and I leave the decisions to you."

The delegates then debated, amended, and finally approved the "Platform Statement of Principles." The overall title, "The West wants in," was the slogan that had defined the Vancouver assembly and that Manning had adopted as his battle cry. As with the manifestos of the Conservative Party in the U.K., the Reform platform was preceded by a signed statement by the leader, entitled "The Next Canada," in which Manning denounced in turn the policies of the three other federal parties. "Today, as the world rushes toward the Twenty-first Century, the leadership of Canada's old line parties marches backwards into the future. . . . Mulroney, Turner, and Broadbent parrot flawed and obsolete visions of Canada. These visions western Reformers reject. We reject once and for all the old Conservative model of the Canadian economy – the heartland/hinterland model that concentrates industry and economic opportunity in Southern Ontario and Southern Quebec, hides behind walls of protection and insecurity, and treats the rest of the country as a captive market and resource reservoir to be forever exploited. We reject as divisive and unworkable the Liberal definition of Canada as a 'meeting of two founding races, cultures and languages.' . . . We reject the fading social vision of the NDP – the concept that Mother Government and universal social programs run by bureaucrats are the best and only way to care for the sick, the poor, the old, and the young."

The pamphlet was printed on thirty-six pages, including a table of contents. It was a sober, serious document. The first of the pamphlet's four general topics, constitutional reform, was given a headline straight out of Harper's speech to the Winnipeg convention: "A Fair Shake for the West!" It began by putting forward the charge that the West was subjected to "unfair treatment" and the claim that "only the most fundamental of changes can rectify this situation." There followed an argument for the Triple-E Senate to safeguard western interests, and an explanation of the constitutional amendment developed by the Reform Party, with the comment, "It has been made abundantly clear to westerners that the current barrier to a Triple-E Senate is the lack of political will of our federal representatives."

The single longest section by far in the platform was titled "Opposition to the Meech Lake Accord." It contained no fewer than fifteen separate arguments against the passage of the proposed constitutional amendments. The most important arguments were those that emphasized that Meech Lake, once entrenched, would make a Triple-E Senate virtually impossible.

Underlying the utter rejection of the Meech Lake Accord was Reform's repudiation of the vision of Canada it projected. The West placed a high priority on equality in all its dimensions, especially the equality of the provinces, whereas Quebec's political class rejected specifically the equality of the provinces. That rejection was implicit in Quebec's insistence on being recognized as a "distinct society." The western vision, a legacy of John Diefenbaker, was one of equal citizens and equal provinces, and was profoundly antagonistic to the tradition of "two nations," "two founding peoples," which had inspired all Quebec provincial party leaders since Maurice Duplessis. Reform wanted to make the 1988 elections turn on the very vision of Canada, on Canada's future identity. It defined sharply its vision, in contrast to those that had been espoused by Robert Stanfield, Brian Mulroney, the Liberals under John Turner, and the New Democrats from their founding convention.

Reform's dissection of Meech Lake also resulted in two interesting criticisms that faulted the Accord for not requiring Quebec to play fair with the rest of the country. In this, it reflected Harper's positions rather than Manning's. It denounced, in point form, "The failure to secure from the Government of Quebec assurance that it will not seek independence in future constitutional negotiations. That is to say, the failure to show that the Accord in any substantive way promotes national unity. The failure of the Government of Quebec to explicitly acknowledge that its acceptance of the Constitution Act of 1982 must mean its surrendering of its claim to Labrador."

Then, as though all this accumulation of attacks was not enough, the section ends with a final assault: "We cannot overemphasize our opposition to this deal. We urge the Provinces of Manitoba and New Brunswick not to ratify the Accord [they had not yet done so] and all other provinces to rescind their ratifications."

The Reform Party's policy on the two official languages was in many ways similar in inspiration to its opposition to Meech Lake. In the name of equality, it found offensive the imposition of bilingualism on western Canada and on the private sector. It proposed, in effect, territorial bilingualism, with a compromise in key federal institutions. It repeated Harper's call in an earlier speech, "Let Quebec be Quebec. Let the West be the West." It viewed the national bilingual vision as an archaic residue of the struggles between Canada East and Canada West in the united Province of Canada.

Against the breathtaking hypocrisy of Mulroney's language policy, the Reformers offered a language policy that, at least, was honest and in keeping with the party's populist bent: "We believe that 'asking the people,' through a referendum, would create a language policy that reflects both the aspirations of Canadians and the demographic reality of the country. Such a policy, we believe, would include the following characteristics: a) A recognition of French in Quebec and English elsewhere as the predominant language of work and society; b) A removal of enforced bilingualism from the provincial level and of any forced language policy from private-sector institutions and personal lives; c) Official bilingualism in key federal institutions, such as Parliament and the Supreme Court, and critical federal services, where numbers warrant; d) Protection of minority education rights, possibly by interprovincial agreement. In no way do we discourage personal bilingualism, but language policy must be consistent to be fair. It must be fair to all Canadians, including the vast majority of unilingual Canadians."

The platform criticized the Tory government for its spendthrift ways. "Mulroney's 'deficit reduction' has resulted in a sustaining of $30-billion annual deficits despite exceptional economic performance in the central Canadian industrial heartland. The Mulroney government has thus, in its four years in office, nearly doubled Canada's national debt." To counter the easy acceptance of deficit spending in all three parties, Reform proposed a permanent solution: "To return government spending to a responsible course, we propose that the government be required to balance the budget in each three-year period or be obliged to call an election on the issue. The first period would commence April 1, 1991." This policy would largely explain Reform's success later, in the 1993 election.

Populism, of course, was the bedrock foundation of Manning's political philosophy, more than it was Harper's. In the future, their divergent views on populism would lead to a rift between them. But, in 1988,

Manning was the leader and the towering presence in the party. The section on political reform proposed free votes in the Commons so that the MPs could represent their constituents instead of the party leaders. It proposed that governments should be defeated on a vote specifically designated as a vote of confidence, so that the threat of being precipitated into elections could not so easily be used to enforce party discipline. Party leaders should no longer have the right to refuse to sign the nomination papers of candidates who had been duly chosen by their constituents. "In addition, we urge that the MPs' oath of office be amended such that they swear or affirm fundamental allegiance to their constituents as well as the Queen."

One proposal that would have a fruitful and controversial life in the subsequent years, dealt with pensions: "The Reform Party opposes the current pension schemes for members of Parliament. We would end full indexation of these pensions and postpone eligibility for benefits until a normal retirement age. The Reform Party would also reexamine MPs' and Senators' expense allowances, free services, staff privileges, and limousines in light of private-sector standards."

An issue that would bedevil the future of the Reform Party – and of its successor, the Canadian Alliance and the Conservative Party of Canada, was how to deal with contentious issues of conscience such as abortion or capital punishment. The platform proposed that they be resolved by government-sponsored referendums or citizens' initiatives. The government would be bound to implement the results of such a referendum. "We would also recommend consulting the people on matters that alter the basic social fabric such as immigration, language, and measurement." Harper's own view, as he would express it later, was different: he opposed parties taking party positions on issues of conscience.

Nowhere in the platform was the hand of Harper more evident than in the section on social policy. As an economist, he rejected as inefficient universal programs such as family allowance, the child tax credit, the spousal exemption, the child exemption, and "federal contributions to social assistance payments, retirement plans, federal social housing programs, daycare deductions, and minimum wage laws. We will explore options from among existing proposals such as the guaranteed annual income, security investment fund, and negative income tax." Rather than universal programs, which bred a big bureaucracy to administer them,

Reform proposed programs targeted to the needy. It was Reform's – and Harper's – view that the welfare state, with its array of entitlements for all the citizens, would in time be unsustainable.

Harper's experience in Ottawa was reflected in the plank on UI: "Unemployment insurance should be returned to its original function – an employer-employee funded and administered program to provide temporary income in the event of unexpected job loss. . . . We will urge the immediate elimination of discriminatory UI elements, such as regional entrance requirements and regionally extended benefit phases."

In principle, Reform disapproved of the federal government using its spending power to subsidize welfare programs that were within provincial jurisdiction. "We would prefer an agreement to provide unconditional transfers of the tax base from the federal government to the provinces, adjusted for differential provincial economic development." That way, the citizens could hold the appropriate government responsible for how it spent the taxpayers' dollars. There was one program, in particular, for which Reform opposed federal government financing: daycare. "We believe that children are our most precious resource and parents the most appropriate judges of their needs in upbringing. We believe that daycare programs should subsidize financial need, not the method of child-care chosen, and should subsidize children and parents, not institutions and professionals. We are opposed to state-run daycare. There is no room for bureaucrats in the raising of our children."

Chapter 8

ELECTIONS ARE NOT WON BY PRAYERS

IN THE LATE SUMMER of 1988, the phone rang at Jim Hawkes's Calgary home. It was Stephen Harper on the line. Stephen asked Jim how he would feel if he, his former assistant, were to run as a Reform Party candidate in Calgary West. "He phoned and asked me if I would be bothered if he ran against me," Hawkes recalls. "They were putting pressure on him to run. The logical seat for him to contest, because of where he lived, was the one in Calgary West. And he asked me if that would bother me, and would I be upset? My response was: 'No!'" Hawkes now believes that, had he objected, Stephen would have refused to contest Calgary West. "That would have been the implication."

The situation was unusual. Stephen was proposing to fight an election against the man he had worked so hard to get elected in the last elections, in 1984. Jim Hawkes had been Stephen's mentor and friend as well as his boss. He had given Stephen his start in politics. And there was more: Stephen told Hawkes there wasn't the slightest chance of the Reform Party winning in Calgary West, and that was part of the reason why he was willing to enter the contest. Hawkes: "A major reason for his wanting to run in Calgary West was that he could be sure he wouldn't win. He had no desire to be a member of Parliament. He wanted to avoid that, and the best way to keep his credentials was to run against me. He wouldn't win because the safest riding that he felt we had was Calgary West."

Elections are not clashes of policy. They are fought, won or lost, on the ground and in the air. Modern election campaigns are essentially a civilized and ritualized transformation of something much more ancient and basic: civil war. The parties mobilize their aroused supporters and seize every opportunity of terrain and circumstance to assail the adversary. This first election campaign of Reform in 1988 did not actually turn on conservative values so much as on regional discontent. Reform ran above all as the party of western anger, on a western sense of being exploited, a western sense of being betrayed by the Mulroney government, betrayed by its own western MPs. Reform was essentially mobilizing the West – Alberta in particular – against central Canada and the federal government. The membership had grown encouragingly in the months since the Winnipeg founding convention. But money was scarce. The party was too poor to invest in paid advertising on television and radio. To all intents and purposes Reform had to fight the elections on the ground, riding by riding, making itself known at all-candidates debates and, just occasionally, snaring a burst of regional and even national attention.

Manning, of course, was the single emblematic carrier of the Reform phenomenon in the eyes of the general public and the news media. He was the founding father, he was the son of Ernest Manning. Preston described in detail in his 1992 memoirs, *The New Canada*, his own 1988 campaign. He did some travelling, but mostly he campaigned in the riding he chose to run in, Yellowhead. He chose it because it was the riding held by Joe Clark, a former prime minister and still the best-known member of the Mulroney cabinet other than the prime minister. His voting record, in Manning's words, was "at considerable variance with the views of his constituents. Early in the year, five of Clark's constituency executives had resigned and joined the Reform Party. They told the local media that Clark had lost touch with the riding and was better suited to represent central Canadian bureaucrats in Ottawa than he was to represent the farmers, oil-patch people, forestry workers, miners, and small business–people of Yellowhead."

The fact that he was running against Clark won him far more interest in the national media when they confronted each other at all-candidates meetings than if he had run in his own riding of St. Albert, where he lived on the outskirts of Edmonton. Joe was in fact the perfect foil at which to throw all the complaints against the Mulroney government, from the CF-18 maintenance contract to the discriminatory new policy on bilingualism. Why had he and the other western MPs not prevented these outrages against the West? At the first all-candidates meeting, an unsuspecting Clark was ambushed by loaded questions and accusations from the floor, fired by Reform supporters. One question in particular became Manning's refrain, and it was taken up by almost all Reform candidates: "Why should we vote for you, when you won't vote for us?"

The contest in Calgary West, once the elections were called on October 1, 1988, must have been one of the most civilized and decorous in all of Canada. Stephen Harper and Jim Hawkes appeared on the same platform to debate at several all-candidates forums. But, Hawkes recalls, "Neither one of us ever said anything about the other that wasn't complimentary. I can't ever remember a row with Stephen at any time, public or not public. It just didn't happen. In '88, he was fully supportive of the free-trade agreement. We were both saying the same kinds of things about that. His main argument was, 'The West wants in.'"

There were a number of ironies in that contest. One was that Cynthia Williams, Harper's former fiancée, worked on that campaign as she had on previous campaigns – for Jim Hawkes, and this time, against Stephen Harper. "I stayed with Jim," she says. "Not out of a hostile thing. It's not about one against the other. It's more that I've always been a Jim Hawkes person. So it's not like I was against Steve. And I knew that the reason Steve was running against Jim was more about getting his ideas out. Steve wasn't running against Jim personally. Steve just had ideas, and he needed to give those ideas a forum."

There was another irony, though no one could appreciate it at the time. It involved a young woman by the name of Laureen Teskey, who now happens to be the chatelaine of Stornoway, the official residence of the leader of the Opposition. "In '88, the woman that Stephen is married to now, worked for me and not for Stephen," Hawkes says with a chuckle. "She wanted the free-trade thing desperately. She told me that one day. I have only spoken to her, I think, twice in my life. We were at a fundraiser after this last election and she told me, 'You may not know it, but I worked for you instead of Stephen.'"

Stephen Harper's campaign did not have its own exclusive headquarters. To save money, Reform candidates from several Calgary ridings – Calgary East, Calgary Centre, and Harper's Calgary West – joined together to share office space on 10th Avenue SW, just outside downtown

Calgary. Stephen had two co-campaign managers, Siân Stephenson and Ken Warenko. Neither had ever been in a political campaign before. Stephenson was the young tax lawyer who had been one of the seven founders of the Calgary West Reform Association. Warenko was also a graduate student with Harper, working on his master's degree in economics. They began with more enthusiasm than political savvy, but their learning curve rose sharply as Harper and John Weissenberger passed on to them the lessons they had picked up as part of Jim Hawkes's model campaign organization. A few volunteers showed up, then a few more, so that within a few weeks the number had grown to about 250. "I was the poll chairman," John Weissenberger recalls. "We made three literature drops. We hit every household in the riding. That was the beginning of our strength in terms of our on-the-ground support throughout western Canada. We have been strong ever since. What the party was saying struck a chord with the average person, people who had never been active before."

There were people of all ages working to get Harper elected, and for most of them, from the middle to lower middle-class, it was their first time taking an active part in a campaign. One exception was Margaret Whiteside. She was in her eighties, a shut-in. She actually had campaigned as a volunteer fifty-three years earlier, as a fervent supporter of William Aberhart, in the 1935 campaign that swept the Social Credit Party into government. This time around, from her home, she made constant phone calls to a list of electors, urging support for Reform and Stephen Harper; for her, it was the Manning name that drew her back into participating in politics. Others volunteered for a range of reasons. Many came because they felt the treatment of Alberta by the federal government was unfair. Some were angry at the Mulroney government for all the scandals that had come to light. For others, it was the failure to curb deficit spending. One couple volunteered to work for Harper because they were angry at Alberta's PC government. They had gone to apply for a government small business loan on the very first day the program became available, only to find that all the loan money had already been allocated, presumably to cronies of the Tory Party.

Harper and Weissenberger were among the only ones in their organization who had experience with the nuts and bolts of running a campaign on the ground: greeting the walk-ins, answering the phone, setting up the workspace, making up signs, printing up pamphlets, setting up a phone committee, sending out squads of people to blanket the riding with pamphlets, canvassing door to door. But they managed to get it all done. By election day, they had run a classic campaign, with their slender means, comparable to what Jim Hawkes was running with far greater means. And they had managed to raise fifty thousand dollars, in small donations.

"The general feeling in the riding was that the people were sympathetic to our position, but they didn't feel they could risk voting for us because of the free-trade issue," Weissenberger explains. "We lost at least 5 or 10 per cent because of that. 'We are sympathetic with what you're doing,' they would say, 'but we feel very strongly about free trade.'" So they would hold their nose and vote PC.

Stephen himself spent hours every day going from door to door, introducing himself, and making a pitch for votes. In the course of his campaigning, and especially when he took part in the all-candidates meetings, he would encounter some of the people he had worked with when he was president of the youth campaign for Jim Hawkes. Some of them resented Harper's defection to the enemy, as Hawkes recalls. "*Traitor*, I guess, is the kind of word that came to mind for a lot of people. He had an opportunity, he's learned a lot of things, and now all of a sudden he's using it against our candidate, against us." But Hawkes himself was not concerned in 1988. "When you're getting 70 to 75 per cent of the vote, it doesn't have the same impact as if you're facing something that's razor thin. In that particular time and place, when you were the Progressive Conservative candidate, in the end you were going to be the next member of Parliament."

The Tories were still secure in Alberta. The new Reform Party may have been striking a chord with more and more people, but history intervened to postpone by one election a Reform breakthrough. History took the form of free trade and John Turner. Had the election turned on the issues closest to the heart of Reform, such as Meech Lake and the Triple-E Senate, the results would have been very different. But John Turner decided to make opposition to free trade the fight of his life.

On January 2, 1988, the Free Trade Agreement was signed between Canada and the United States. It still had to be passed by both Houses of Parliament in order to go into effect the following first of January. And

Turner, with a reputation as an indecisive, impulsive man who had lost Quebec in 1984, who had even lost the respect and loyalty of his caucus, who came third in the opinion polls measuring esteem for the three party leaders, decided to wrap himself in the Canadian flag, sprinkle himself with maple syrup, evoke his inner *coureur de bois*, don his toque and snowshoes, and stand on guard at the Canada–U.S. border.

He made his big pitch in a speech on August 30, when the free-trade agreement was before the Commons. "We love this country. It is precious to us. And because we love this country . . . we will not allow it to be thrown away by this or any other government," he vowed. "They are telling us to give up that which is most precious to us – our sovereignty, our way of life." Turner evoked the vast expanses of wilderness, reflected in the paintings of Lawren Harris, A.Y. Jackson, and Emily Carr. But he did not limit his appeal to effete intellectuals. There was the lunch-box crowd also to be warned of their collective peril: "Sold out! Like what happened to Wayne Gretzky! What Peter Pocklington is to Edmonton, our prime minister is to Canada." In his nationalist fervour, Turner left no tune untoned. He came to the defence of the land, the water, the national potato. "To give up our right to develop our own resources – our oil, our gas, our coal, our hydro, even our own water . . . is it worth it to sell out our whole agriculture industry, our supply management system, our grain transportation subsidies, our potato industry? One of the first things the U.S. intends to do in this so-called free-trade deal is limit all trade in potatoes."

In the Turner canon, the free-trade deal was not just about meat and potatoes. Canada would be selling out to the Americans our minimum wage, our unemployment insurance, our maternity leave, our medicare, our hospital insurance. "We reject this deal because it turns us into little more than a colony of the United States."

The Liberals still held a leftover majority in the Senate and by getting the Senate to block approval of the Free Trade Agreement until after an election, Turner succeeded in precipitating that election and ensuring that free trade would be the defining issue. That was bad news for the Reform Party. As long as the polls showed the PCs comfortably ahead, and the Liberals threatened with coming in behind the New Democrats, western voters who favoured free trade could indulge their anger with the Mulroney government by considering a vote for the Reform Party. But that changed on October 25 when Turner triumphed in the English-language debate of the three major party leaders – a debate from which Manning was excluded. With several million Canadians watching the debate, Turner at last managed to score with his hand-on-the-heart appeal to Canadian nationalism and latent anti-Americanism. A Gallup poll taken after the debate showed, for the first time, the Liberals actually leading the other parties in vote intentions. That changed the whole course of the electoral campaign. Now the vote became polarized on the issue of free trade between the Liberals and the Tories. The other parties – the NDP and Reform – suffered as western voters in particular rallied to the Tories to save free trade.

For a while, Turner and the Liberals had momentum. But it soon slowed, then reversed itself. And, in the West, the Tories gained from Turner's determination to make this a second election on free trade, as in 1911. In Calgary West, on November 21, Jim Hawkes was re-elected with 32,025 votes, far ahead of "Steve Harper" who received 9,074. But Harper came second, beating out the Liberal and NDP candidates, plus two representatives of fringe parties. Hawkes, who had received 74.7 per cent of the vote in 1984, now saw his vote drop to 58.5 per cent. Harper's share was 16.6 per cent. He had his wish: he did not become a member of Parliament, and now he could concentrate again on his studies. And on policy.

In Yellowhead, Preston Manning received 11,207 votes, 27.9 per cent of the total. Clark won easily with 57.9 per cent, but that was a fall from the 74 per cent he had harvested in 1984. In Alberta as a whole, Reform had received 15.4 per cent of the vote, beating out the Liberals at 13.7 per cent. But the Tories triumphed again with 51.8 per cent. In British Columbia, Reform took just under 5 per cent. In Manitoba, just over 3 per cent. In Saskatchewan, less than 1 per cent. It was hardly a spectacular first performance. That night, when the results were known, Preston Manning ended his concession speech with these words: "The Reform Party is here to stay. We are building for the future, and tonight we have made a significant step forward."

Here to stay. Stephen Harper would repeat those words on a dark day fourteen years later.

Chapter 9

REDEFINING THE REFORM PARTY

AFTER THE DISAPPOINTING results in the 1988 elections, where would the Reform Party go? During the post-mortems that followed November 21, it quickly became clear that Preston Manning and Stephen Harper had conflicting visions for the future. Their premises would lead the party to quite different destinations. The ideological tension between them had become obvious even before the elections. Harper, as chief policy officer, and Manning, as leader, had had to agree on the text of the party platform submitted to the party delegates. It hadn't always been easy. Their disagreements were partly resolved by allowing Manning to express in the "Leader's Foreword" the views with which Harper disagreed. Manning wrote two sentences that went to the heart of what separated them: "We reject political debate defined in the narrow terminology of the Left, Right, and Centre. This vestige of the French and Industrial revolutions may continue to delineate our old-line parties, but it is increasingly out of place in the complex and multi-dimensional world that we live in today."

Fine. The leader could say what he wanted in the personal statement that prefaced the platform. But with the elections out of the way, Harper was not about to let that stand. In his view, the political cleavage expressed in terms of left, right, and centre was not an archaic term from a distant era. On the contrary. Harper's main reason for breaking with the Tories was precisely that they did not distinguish themselves from the Liberals and the NDP on the basis of right and left. All three parties, he believed, were more or less on the left. All three shared an ideological consensus on the role of the state, that is, a commitment to big government. Their differences were only a matter of degree and of consistency. If the Reform Party was to have a future, it would be precisely to the extent that it succeeded in defining itself unambiguously as the only true party of the right.

Harper knew that to challenge Manning's vision would not be easy. From the start, at the Vancouver assembly, Manning had demonstrated just how attached he was to the project of founding a party that transcended the division of right and left. "Obviously, if the West were to choose a new political vehicle to advance its agenda, we would be careful to position that vehicle ideologically and policy-wise so that it would have equal potential for drawing the support of western Canadians from both the Liberals and the NDP, as well as the Conservatives," he had said. And he had added these ominous words: "In fact, one could go so far as to say that if a new federal political party cannot be positioned in this way, it should not be initiated." One of Manning's favourite sayings was that the party must be like a hockey team, with a right wing, a left wing, and a centre.

Harper disagreed. He disagreed profoundly. But how was he to change the mind of the party's founder and leader, who bore the revered name of Manning? Going into general elections and trying to move into a space where three parties already covered the field, it was perhaps a good tactic to present Reform as equally attractive to disappointed Tories, Liberals, and New Democrats. But, in reality, the content of the platform was overwhelmingly right-wing, with an emphasis on free enterprise in the economy and thrift in government. Those who came to the party as volunteers and who voted for it were mostly people disappointed with the Tories for not keeping their promise to control government spending and eliminate the federal deficit. They would define themselves as definitely right-wing. So there was a discordance between Manning's proclamation of what Reform should be, and what it had become.

Manning took as the archetype of history, particularly in western Canada, the dramatic sweep into power of the infant Social Credit Party in 1935. A few months after its creation as a party, this movement beyond class took fifty-six of Alberta's sixty-three seats. A sweep of such magnitude was unprecedented in Alberta's previous electoral history. Manning constructed a grand historic synthesis in which the 1935 experience was seen as a variant, a specific case, of a chain of preceding and subsequent movements that recurred inevitably in the history of Canada, and especially of western Canada, and he raised these various movements into a philosophy of history, a metronome of movements that surged irresistibly from the grassroots and resulted in a new order that was better than the preceding one.

Harper's political philosophy was different. He, too, was interested in history, but primarily in the history of political economy – the relationship between economics and politics. He saw the last two centuries in the Western world as a constant tension between freedom and constraint, with freedom as the creative, liberating, and dynamic factor; political constraint was inhibiting, stultifying. Moreover, freedom, when accompanied by the rule of law so as to establish the same set of pragmatically determined rules for everybody, meant greater justice as well as greater prosperity. Constraints created privileges for the more powerful and also produced corruption in government. In the contemporary world, the tension was on the one hand between statism and big government, and the enhancement of the private sector on the other. In practical terms, Harper again took the examples of Margaret Thatcher in the United Kingdom and Ronald Reagan in the United States as the prime models for Canada to follow.

Harper's opportunity to bring to a head the differences between them arose on February 13, 1989, when Manning sent a memo to the constitutional task force, of which Harper was a member. It was this task force which, a year earlier, had developed a draft amendment to the Constitution to express the party's position on the Triple-E Senate. Now, Manning asked the task force to return to the subject "to help us arrive at a more definitive position on the Meech Lake Accord and the appropriate way to link the passage of a modified Meech Lake Accord with a Senate Amendment." It was an opening, and Harper would take it, to range far beyond the assigned topic. He would draft a memo which would go to the heart of his disagreement with Manning's vision.

The terms of reference he gave the constitutional task force suggested that Manning was looking for an accommodation with Meech Lake, an amendment that would allow Reform to get behind it so long as it did not threaten the Triple-E Senate. That was not Harper's view at all. He was opposed to the whole vision that underlay Meech Lake. In his eyes, tinkering with it could never save it. And he wanted Meech Lake to be treated, not just in the context of its effect on the Triple-E Senate, but in the broader context of the whole question of Quebec and of the policies toward Quebec of all three established parties. The issue of Quebec was also the issue of Canada. But the issue of Quebec needed to be placed in the still broader context of the political philosophy that Reform brought to its actions and that justified its appearance as a new political party competing for the votes of the citizens. And it was in this wider perspective that Harper wrote his memo.

That memo is worth examining in considerable detail. More than any other source, it reveals how Harper's mind works, what his fundamental political commitments are, and how he translates them into strategic positioning on wedge issues. The memo was not written for publication. It made no concessions to political correctness, to diplomatic niceties, to opportunistic euphemisms, or convenient silences. It was straight talk all the way. If there was one occasion when Harper bared his political soul, it was in this memo to Manning, with its twenty-one pages of tight argument.

He headed it with the words PRIVATE AND CONFIDENTIAL. He was not yet ready to have their deep divergences break out into the open. He wanted first to unfold in writing his full argument, explaining the differences between them and why he thought Manning should change his approach and come over to his own position.

He began by explaining his "Reason for Writing." He was concerned that, though Reform had received about 275,000 votes in the 1988 elections, it had not elected a single member of Parliament. Looking forward to the next convention to be held in Edmonton in October, Harper felt it was important to go back to first principles. "Specifically, Preston, it is my opinion that, at the October Convention, the Party will require from you a clear, written statement of the direction you wish to take the Party and the changes necessary to implement it." Already Harper was assuming that Manning must change his approach.

He was unapologetic about the fact that his approach would differ from Manning's. But, before launching into his argument, he presented his own credentials as a Reformer. He was not simply someone who had climbed aboard the Reform bandwagon. He had been through his own political pilgrimage before encountering Manning.

"As you know, I have been deeply involved in the effort to create a new political option for Canadians since I left the employment of the PC government in Ottawa in August 1986. I have sought change within the PC Party and have had contact with a number of parties and political organizations. Since May 1987, however, my principal preoccupation has been the Reform Party of Canada. This involvement has been rewarding and I am very thankful for the opportunities you have given me. . . . As you know, I have had concerns about the Reform Party's ulti-mate direction since the beginning. In the absence of long-run, system-atic thinking, there is a definite tendency for new parties to get locked into their initial base. . . . My biggest fear has always been that the Reform Party wants to avoid being 'labelled' at all costs. I hope this is not true. Labels can be erroneous and disadvantageous, but they are absolutely necessary to establish an electoral identity and create some viable base of support for a new party. Ironically, it appears to me that the ideological labels this Party may wish to avoid will ultimately cut off far less of the electorate than the labels the Party is drifting towards."

Harper then laid out what he called the "Current Direction of the Reform Party." These, of course, were the views of Manning. The first that Harper identified was the fear that the party was perceived as too right-wing. "Thus it must moderate its image, principally by shifting emphasis to issues of a non-ideological nature, such as the environ-ment." In fact, that was precisely what Manning was saying at that time; he was urging that Reform should give priority to developing a policy on the environment.

The second assumption was that, while the Reform Party must expand beyond the West, "it must seek to expand into areas similar to its Western and Northern base, i.e., 'hinterland' areas such as Northern Ontario, Outer Quebec, and Atlantic Canada." Again, this was precisely the language used by Manning.

The third assumption that Harper ascribed to the current direction of the party was the need to push further its "grassroots" approach to poli-tics. "The Reform Party will extend its participatory, 'grassroots' approach to the development of policy, spokespersons, and membership."

Against all three assumptions, Harper launched a barrage of argu-ments. But first came this summary and overall judgment: "The basic thrust of this [approach] is that the Party should emphasize its geographic nature while downplaying its ideological content. It should become a 'Hinterland-Grassroots' Party, a populist coalition of the 'thinly popu-lated resource-producing regions,' overwhelmingly concerned with rectifying imbalances between central Canada and the vast Canadian Hinterland. As an outgrowth, the Party would reflect a 'conservatism' consistent with the values and economic interests of hinterland regions. In my view, the analysis underlying this is erroneous and seriously out of date as a fundamental basis for understanding contemporary Canadian politics and creating a new political coalition. Let me begin by outlining what I believe are key 'myths' on which this analysis is based."

He certainly was unsparing in savaging Manning's most cherished pronouncements, which he now dismissed as outmoded myths. Small wonder that Manning, in 2002, would reflect harshly on Harper in his memoirs, *Think Big*. While recognizing his former favourite's "brilliant strategic mind, sound grasp of public policy, and good communication skills in both French and English," Mr. Manning called him, in effect, a big ego. "Stephen had difficulty accepting that there might be a few other people (not many, perhaps, but a few) who were as smart as he was with respect to policy and strategy."

The first myth Harper attacked was that the resource-producing regions, which Manning thought of as the prime prospects for his party, had essentially common interests. Harper countered: "On many con-temporary major issues (e.g., unemployment insurance compensation, oil and gas) the view of various hinterland regions (e.g., Alberta, New Brunswick) have often been diametrically opposed." Moreover, some of these hinterland regions, such as Atlantic Canada and Outer Quebec "have consistently and profitably supported the coalition in power" rather than make common cause with western Canada.

He presented the strategy of targeting the hinterland regions as a loser, because most people live in cities and "the urban electorate is largely left cold by the rhetoric and issues associated with primary pro-duction." He listed several other problems with the current approach and concluded that, if it were to be pursued, the "Party will end up being labelled 'right-wing' anyway, because it strongly reflects the conservative values of its rural base, not because it has any coherent economic agenda or any links with the intellectual right."

Moreover, he found that the "grassroots" approach to policy making could work well in a relatively homogeneous society, but not on a national scale, where the range of common interests would be narrow. This, he said, was why the Social Credit Party, so successful in Alberta, had never succeeded nationally. And Preston's father, Ernest Manning, had come to understand that. According to Harper: "In 1967, Social Credit premier E.C. Manning published *Political Realignment*, in which he argued that, to address the modern electorate and modern issues, Canadian partisan politics needed to be realigned into two more ideologically coherent parties, a Social Conservative Party and a Social Democratic Party. He did not call these 'Right' and 'Left' in the traditional sense. Nevertheless, since the key differences concerned the size and nature of the social role of government, that is what they would've been called had realignment happened. Manning made it clear that Social Credit could survive only in the context of the Right of such a realignment."

There was a clear irony in that reference to *Political Realignment*. Both the writer of the memo and its only intended recipient knew perfectly well that Preston had been the ghost writer for the book attributed to Ernest Manning. Harper, recalling the book, could have challenged Preston: *well, why did you change your mind?* Instead, by referring only to Ernest Manning, he left the question – and the reproach – implicit.

Harper was laying out for Preston Manning in this memo of March 1989 the conclusions of the political-economic analysis that he and John Weissenberger had carried through together during their vision quest of 1985–86. Harper had first put it down on paper in an essay he submitted for a graduate course under the title, "Thoughts on Self-Interest." Harper and Weissenberger then developed more fully their analysis of the crisis of the welfare state in Canada in an unpublished manuscript, cited by Tom Flanagan in his book, *Waiting for the Wave*. The second chapter was titled "The Political Class," and it was to the political class rather than urban central Canada that Harper wanted to direct Manning's attention as the real political adversary.

Realignment into right and left did not succeed in the 1960s, Harper argued, because the appropriate combination of factors did not then exist in Canada. But that was no longer true. "I maintain that the material basis now exists. In fact, there has been a distinct trend toward ideological realignment in most Western countries since the mid-1970s." The crucial factor for the change, in Harper's analysis, was the crisis of the welfare state. "The Welfare State, i.e., Big Government, became the most important institution in the Western world. The consequences of this were twofold. First, Western society laid the groundwork, through excessive economic intervention, that would eventually undermine the efficiency and growth of the market economy. Second, it created a new class of people whose vested interests and values would resist reform and lead to political conflict once economic growth slowed. This new class of people is urban and professional, just like the private-sector middle class from which it was drawn. It consists of social scientists, social researchers, political professionals, educators, bureaucrats, activists, and, to a lesser degree, journalists and communicators."

For Harper, the significant cleavage in contemporary industrial societies, notably Canada, was not between hinterland and centre, as Manning maintained, but between the private and the public sectors. The acceptance of the principle of the welfare state during the Second World War created a big government that constantly tried to do more and more, and so constantly taxed more and more. It created a new class – Harper called it the "political class" – which served the welfare state and its clients. This new class developed its own ideology, which pushed for the constant further expansion of the welfare state. It developed a constantly expanding clientele of people who looked to the welfare state to provide them with economic security, health care, business and regional subsidies, and subsidies to various interest groups. This clientele also had a vested interest in expanding the welfare state. But, at some point, the post-war economic expansion that made the welfare state possible slowed under the burden of constantly expanding taxes, and that is when the crisis began, pitting the private sector against all the interests served by the welfare state.

The polarization went beyond merely economic interests. The political class also developed its own values. "The value system of this new class must be mentioned. The urban middle classes have always been linked more closely to liberal values and lifestyles than other parts of society. However, the political class, since it is concerned largely with social problems and human underdevelopment, has tended to be openly hostile to those aspects of society which condition human relations (i.e., the market system, the traditional family) and the values attached to them. Hence we find the mindset of this group dominated by liberal intellectualism."

The crisis of the welfare state had already begun in Canada, Harper believed. "The Welfare State is dominated by a politically powerful class removed from the processes of wealth generation and normal standards of cost constraint. The consequence of all this is that the Welfare State ultimately begins to demand resources (i.e., taxes or, temporarily, deficits) beyond what the private sector believes it can afford. This began in earnest after the oil price shocks of the 1970s. In a democratic system, the phenomenon begins to provoke a reaction from the private sector. This becomes a battle, not only for tax dollars, but about social values and social organization, especially over the size and role of government. Thus the terms 'Right' and 'Left' come back into the political vernacular, although the original connotations are largely irrelevant."

And so Harper formulated his alternative theory of polarization in opposition to Manning's theory of the hinterland versus the centre. "My hypothesis is this. Political realignment in most Western countries today represents a battle over tax dollars between two groups of the urban, professional, middle-class voters – the taxpayers of the private sector (the "Right") and the tax recipients of the Welfare State (the "Left"). Viable political coalitions become based on these and seek allies among other groups of voters. The Left seeks allies in a way consistent with the survival and growth of the Welfare State. It targets very specific groups of voters with very specific programs, such as loans for students, funding for daycare needs, pensions for seniors, subsidies for dairy farmers, etc. . . . The Right seeks allies by appealing to ordinary people in a way that does not demand a radical expansion of the Welfare State. It targets growing hostility of large segments of society to the economic malaise and moral uncertainties that accompany Welfare State policies and values. These large segments are the urban working class and the rural sector."

Though the private sector's urban middle class was to be the "core" constituency of the right-wing party that Harper proposed the Reform Party should be, he did not write off the urban working class nor the people living in rural areas. For the working-class people in the private sector of the economy, he proposed to appeal to their interest in paying lower taxes than the burgeoning welfare state currently required of them. Despite the left-wing attitudes of most union leaders, the workers

themselves could appreciate the appeal of lower premiums for unemployment insurance and smaller deductions from their paycheques. He
recognized that members of the working class were often suspicious of
the free market. But they were also resistant to the appeals of the political class. "The most important appeals to both the working class and
rural class are usually based on a broader social agenda. These groups
hold social values that are dominantly conservative, far more so than the
private-sector middle class. In fact, these classes are outrightly hostile to
the liberal intellectualism of the Welfare State class, i.e., its indulgence of
unconventional lifestyles, its dislike of traditional family values, and its
crusades for minority causes and international priorities. These classes are
also increasingly hostile to the 'help' they tend to get offered by the
Welfare State. The inhumanity of bureaucratic social services, the pater-
nalism and arrogance of their social engineering schemes, the dangers of
its experiments in criminal justice policy, are better known by these people
than any other. They have been its victims." They tend to have a strong
sense of justice and a corresponding resentment of official laxity in
dealing with criminals who put at risk the personal security and property
of those people, above all, who live in working-class neighbourhoods.

Reform, he argued, had to stand for conservative values. It must
attract socially conservative voters who could not recognize their own
values in the policies of the three established parties, all three being predominantly liberal. But Reform was not alone in the field on the social
right. "We must look at fourth-party competitors," Harper proposed.
He then examined in turn the strategic significance for Reform of the
Confederation of Regions Party (COR), the Libertarian Party, and the
Christian Heritage Party. Of COR, he was utterly dismissive. COR was
the best example of what the Reform Party must not be, "the quintessential Party of the Extreme Social Right."

Harper had much more respect for the Libertarian Party. "The Libertarian Party is a free enterprise party advocating minimal government in
all aspects of public policy. Very radical in agenda, this party is actually
very moderate in tone, fairly well run, and contains many thoughtful
and articulate people." But he thought that the party's commitment to
minimal government contained the seeds of its own political impotence.

While dismissing the other two parties, Harper took very seriously
the third party that based its appeal largely on conservative social values.

"The Christian Heritage Party is the most interesting from our perspective. This party purports to be a party for evangelical Christians. However, its agenda, strongly pro-life, borders on theocratic and its current support is restricted mainly to ultra-conservative voters. Nevertheless, that community is strongly committed to the party, and the CHP, very well run for a small organization, promises to survive. The Christian Heritage Party at the moment is capable of getting no more than 1 to 2 per cent of the vote. I believe, however, that such a religious party, while it can never gain seats, is capable of hindering our development, given the ongoing attention that is likely to be paid to the abortion issue. The CHP's Ontario provincial wing, the Family Coalition Party, unites a pro-life mission with policies that are very acceptable to economic conservatives. Its base includes both evangelical Catholics and Protestants. Many of its members are urban professionals. The Party appears capable of pulling 5 to 6 per cent of the vote on an ongoing basis.

"In the United States, this element of the electorate has been critical in the development of the Republican coalition. It provides workers and funds disproportionate to its size as a voting bloc. It represents a definite social trend in North America – a small but stable part of urban society for whom religion is of primary importance in life, but who interact well with the rest of society. Typical urban, private-sector voters are poor political activists. I believe that the Reform Party cannot afford to lose moderate pro-life voters en masse to a religious option if it hopes to be a viable fourth party." This analysis will help to explain, several years later, his stance on same-sex marriage.

He spoke in passing of one other party that was not of the right, the Canadian Green Party. His treatment of that party is of interest because Manning was at that time thinking of making the environment the subject of Reform's next big policy push. Tom Flanagan quoted a Manning memo: "In one sense, the environmental issue is one of the few with the potential to cut completely across the traditional left-right-centre spectrum. The Reform Party should be well positioned to deal with an issue of this nature."

Harper, though, was rather dismissive of the strategic importance of the environmental issue in his treatment of the Green Party. "This party is, of course, environmentalist. Yet, despite the supposedly high priority given the environment in public opinion polls, the Green Party's electoral support is virtually non-existent, as it is throughout North America. In fact, my contention is that the environment, while extremely important, is still simply 'motherhood,' i.e., non-contentious and non-partisan."

While recognizing that the Reform Party should stand for conservative social values, Harper also warned against any departure from moderation, any partiality for "ultra-conservative values" such as nativism and excessive religious fervour. "A modern party of the Right cannot pander either to these minorities or to resentments of them." He warned against any immigration policy that discriminated on the basis of country of origin rather than on economic criteria for selecting immigrants. He also warned against the danger of anti-French prejudice. "I believe our current language policy is acceptable, provided we forever dismiss the heresy of 'one national language' (i.e., with Quebec still in Canada)."

He insisted that the Reform Party should accept the label of being right-wing, but also shape the public perception of what right-wing meant currently, in contrast with the past. It did not mean a return to a do-nothing state, but rather an appreciation of what should be done by the state and what would be better left to non-state community groups and to private enterprise. The state, for example, should invest seriously in education and training: "The agenda of the modern Right must recognize that provision for human resources and human capital development is an essential part of the infrastructure requirements of a modern economy. Without it the growth of a modern, socially stable, service-based market economy will not be possible. Indeed, without it, the growth of Welfare State interventionism, economic malaise, and social decline are assured." While advocating a clear right-wing posture, both for economic policies and social values, Harper insisted that both must be moderate. And he concluded: "In summary, it is the Social Right, not the Economic Right, issues, which are more likely to seriously harm the Party's image at some time." Those words would prove prophetic.

But, of course, the Reform Party did not see itself as principally competing with splinter parties. Its ambition was to displace a mainstream party and eventually form the government. So Harper turned a strategic lens on each of them. "Our principal competitor remains the PC Party. (Notice it rarely calls itself the "Conservatives.") The PC leadership under Mulroney has emerged as an alliance of Quebec Nationalist and English Red Tories (with a couple of exceptions in the East). It combines a high priority on Quebec's constitutional agenda (of course), with a hesitant market economic agenda and a weak liberal social agenda. This latter is peculiar considering that the Party's electorate is dominantly conservative, both economically and socially. We must gamble that the PCs have a vision too weak, a program too unclear, and a Quebec base too strong, for it to respond competently to the kinds of challenges it will face in the next four years. Otherwise I assume we would not exist."

Harper's positioning of Reform strategically in relation to the Tories – us versus them – went to the heart of his fundamental difference with Manning. The son of a founder of the Social Credit dynasty clung to the idea of appealing *equally* to people who had been voting Tory, Liberal, and NDP. His was to be a movement of the grassroots, a common impulse energizing *the people*, that would lead the Reform Party to power. Manning's strength was in building vast historical syntheses which linked together in one system many different phenomena from different times. Harper's strength was in creating a synthesis in which a multitude of contemporaneous phenomena were brought together into an interactive system. Manning, in dealing with the contemporary scene, was above all intuitive. Harper was insistently analytical. Harper insisted that Reform must identify a hierarchical priority of its adversaries. Manning preferred not to see actual human adversaries but merely obsolete and dying assumptions. Harper wanted Reform to label itself sharply, deliberately, strategically, the better to impose itself by grappling hand-to-hand with real adversaries and so displace them. Manning wanted to avoid labels in order to attract the ideologically undefined *people*.

Harper's implicit political vision was one of conflict. Manning's was one of finding the appropriate consensus. Harper worked with a quasi-Marxist model of contemporary society as inherently polarized between two broad classes of people with opposed material interests: the private sector and the public sector. Other factors also came into play, notably social and religious values which exerted strong political influences quite apart from material interests. But citizens tended to be drawn toward one or the other of the fundamental poles: social and religious conservatives were apt to be attracted to conservative economic policies. He saw the dynamic between the two class sectors, not as a stable equilibrium, but as an intensifying conflict leading in some not-too-distant future to a crisis. In his adult years, he had seen the public sector – what he called the Welfare State – grow continuously in relation to the private sector. In the previous decade and a half he had seen constant and huge federal government deficits, with the debt mounting rapidly, and an ever larger proportion of revenues being required to pay interest on that public debt. It was a spiral that could not go on indefinitely, and Harper anticipated the coming revolt, not of the masses as such, but of the private sector.

Within this conceptual framework, Harper was urging that Reform must target the Tories as the adversaries to be taken on and replaced, because the Tories had betrayed their natural conservative clientele in the private sector and the rural areas by their preoccupation with the Constitution, with Quebec, and with Welfare State commitments to "sacred trusts." The Tories were now hostages to their own muddled vision and to their Quebec praetorian guard. They were vulnerable to a concentrated attack from a clearly right-wing Reform Party.

The other two parties were given only cursory notice. "The Liberal Party is always capable of a sudden shift, including one to the Economic Right, but this is not likely considering its preoccupation with constitutional questions and its former Quebec base. The NDP, drinks thrown in its face, may seriously consider backing away from its flirtations with Quebec and even emphasize its macho Anglophone reality. Even if it does this, however, its clear "Left" agenda means it can do only limited damage to our potential."

The reference to the NDP must be understood in the context of the time. In 1987 and early 1988, the NDP under Ed Broadbent had soared to first place in the polls. The party also made a strong pitch for the support of the Quebec nationalists, which included endorsing "collective rights" as having priority over the Charter of Rights, which dealt only with individual rights. At best, the NDP under Broadbent had two policies on language and the Constitution, one in Quebec and another in the rest of Canada. And the policies of the NDP's Quebec wing were precisely aligned with those of the Parti Québécois. It did the NDP no good at all at the polls in November 1988, however; despite all the concessions and contortions, no NDP candidate came close to winning a seat in Quebec. That rebuff explained the "drinks thrown in its face" of Harper's memo.

Harper, having set up his alternative vision of the future of Reform Party politics, then came to the point of Manning's request for a more definitive position on Meech Lake. This will be the subject of a later chapter. But before leaving Harper's critical overview of the Reform Party strategy, there is one missing element in his analysis that deserves to be noticed: he never discussed the factor of leadership.

An established political party travels with much baggage, for better and for worse. It has a history, it has a core clientele. In Canada, for instance, the most notable factor traditionally separating the Tories from the Grits was religion. Though neither party as such professed a religious faith, Protestants flocked to the Tories, Catholics to the Grits. But, always, and in recent times particularly, the leader of the party has been an important factor in realigning parties. Wilfrid Laurier caused Quebec to move from being the Tories' bastion to being that of the *Rouges*. John Diefenbaker swung the Prairie provinces into the fold of the Progressive Conservatives.

Not merely the policies, so discussed by Harper, but also the style, the personality, the presentation of the leader, are important factors in a party's success or failure. Pierre Trudeau attracted yuppies by his swinging demeanour, his fast convertible, his cape and gaucho hat, his Barbra Streisands – and by the same tokens he repelled more conservative voters. Clearly, for a new party with national ambitions trying to establish itself on the political landscape, the style, the image, the presentation, the *modus operandi* of the leader are critical factors in gaining the party's acceptance. The discussion of Preston Manning's leadership, his strengths and weaknesses, could have occupied pages of the memo and ranged far beyond evaluating his eyeglasses and his coiffure. But there was not a word. Was the subject too sensitive for the man who was now viewed as Manning's likely successor? Or was Harper, so preoccupied with strategies of policy, left insensitive to the human and personal factor? That question will be worth taking up when Harper himself has become a leader.

Chapter 10

INVADING OTTAWA

STEPHEN HARPER WAS back working in Ottawa after an absence of three years. It was quite different now, in 1989. The first time, he had been an assistant doing research for Jim Hawkes, on the side of power. Now, he was the legislative assistant to one single, solitary, totally inexperienced Reform member of Parliament whose seat in the Commons was in the far corner of the last row on the Opposition side. It was quite a demotion, and he felt great.

It hadn't been an easy decision. Coming to Ottawa meant interrupting his studies again. Four years after his bachelor's degree, he still hadn't completed his master's. When the invitation first came to return to Ottawa, he had said no. But Preston Manning had been persuasive. Harper finally found that he couldn't refuse.

This was a challenge that suited him. He would be following up on the stunning victory pulled off by the schoolteacher from Dewberry, Deborah Grey. She had sent excitement and hope jolting through the Reform Party when, on March 13, 1989, she had swept a by-election in Beaver River, Alberta, where she had placed a distant fourth in the general elections of November 21, 1988. In less than four months, she had vaulted over the candidates of the Progressive Conservatives, the Liberals, and the New Democrats. If the miracle could happen in Beaver River, a rural riding northeast of Edmonton, it could surely repeat anywhere in Alberta.

Because Grey would be the first Reformer to set foot in Parliament, she would be watched closely. She would not have a friend in the House.

And the journalists would also be scrutinizing her for signs of ignorance, extremism, prejudice against the French language, or against Quebec. She carried the future of the Reform Party with her to Ottawa. If she made a major blunder in her first months or fell into a trap, she would confirm the negative stereotypes. It was important that she have an experienced and sophisticated counsellor at her side during that critical first year. So Manning turned to Stephen Harper.

Deborah Grey is a big, hearty, buxom woman who, when appearing in her public role, favours brightly coloured clothes. She also has an alternative wardrobe of dark leather when she grabs her visored maroon helmet and bestrides her red Gold Wing motorcycle. She would not qualify as a stereotypical politician. When I interviewed her in late 2002, shortly after she announced that she would not be a candidate in the next elections, I found her to be gutsy, down to earth, jovial, and genuine, an engaging extrovert who loves to talk for the sheer joy of talking and who loves to laugh and to use gleeful sounds like "*wooo*" and "*wooo-hooo!*" She never used profanity, but found substitute expletives like "*my lamb!*"

Though a city girl from Vancouver, she loved the bush and began her teaching career in northeastern Alberta, on the Frog Lake Indian Reserve. When she moved, it was to the Alberta farming community of Dewberry, three hours' drive from Edmonton, where she taught high-school English and social studies. When she went home after classes, it was to a house by a lake in the village of Laurier (pronounced *Laurior*). A devout evangelical Christian, she sang in a gospel group called HIS, the possessive referring to Jesus. Though single, she served over the years as a foster parent to six children, five of them Indians, in her house that did not have a television. But back in September 1988 – just over two months before the elections that would be held on November 21 – she was having dinner with a couple of friends at their farmhouse when the subject of politics came up. Here is her account, as she talked in her office on Parliament Hill in 2002.

> I had read something about the Reform Party. And I thought to myself, Here comes another western separatist group. Because we'd gone through the Western Canada Concept, which I hadn't paid a whole lot of attention to. I'm a proud and passionate Canadian. So I'd heard about the Reform Party and thought,

Hmm, I wonder if that's another one of these groups rearing its head again. So, while I was at their place for a birthday party, I said to my good friends Liz and Jack, 'What do you know about this Reform Party?' And I remember my words: 'Are they a bunch of western separatist wackos?' *Wooufff!* And my friend Liz said, 'No, I'm a member of the party, and I think it's the way to go.' So I thought, Well, for heaven's sake. You know, she's normal. She was a nurse, a farmer, they'd been my friends for years. And I thought, She hardly seems like a political activist. So I said, 'Wow!' So we got talking about it. And I said, 'Is this [Don] Mazankowski's riding still?' And she said, 'No, we have a new riding called Beaver River.' They'd gone through redistribution, and so the Beev, as we affectionately call it, was formed, and she said: 'I think this is the way to go.' So I said, 'Well, who's running for a candidate here?' I remember saying: 'I'm going to get really involved politically. I will go to an all-candidates forum, and listen to the candidates.' [She laughs] Little knowing . . . But my pal Liz said to me, 'We don't have a candidate yet.' And then she said those infamous words, 'We don't have a candidate yet, Deb. Why don't you run?'

Deb wasn't convinced, but she said she would look at the Reform Party program. She received it in the mail on a Friday, just before she was leaving for Vancouver to attend her brother's wedding. She took it with her, and while waiting to board her plane at the Edmonton airport, she started reading it. She found it a revelation.

At everything I read, I just thought: Yeah! That's me. You know that song that says 'I was country when country wasn't cool?' I was a Reformer. I thought, That's me: that all the provinces want to be treated equally; and I thought, Yeah. So I read it, and just agreed with it, and thought, Well! That's me!

While I was reading it, this older good-looking gent comes up to me, stands there. So I kind of looked up politely and smiled and he said, 'Oh, hello. Can't help but notice what you're reading.' And I thought, Ohhhh, he's going to ask me a question about it. And he said: 'My name's Gordon Shaw. I'm the vice-chairman of

the party. I've been up for meetings with Preston Manning. . . .'
And I thought, Holy man! So I said: 'Oh, it looks very interesting
[laughs], I don't know much about it.' Blah, blah. Anyway, we sat
together on the plane. He lived in Vancouver. So he was going
home. And we chatted. And he asked me where I lived, and I said
'Oh, just in the middle of nowhere.' He said, 'Whereabouts?' So
I told him: 'In Heinsburg, Alberta.' 'Oh, is that right?' he says.
'Well, that's in the new Beaver River riding.' And I thought, Holy
smokes, he knows. I said, 'Yes, I understand that. Somebody just
told me that.' And he said, 'We're looking for a candidate there.'
Then I said, 'Well, for goodness' sakes.' I said, 'I'm a schoolteacher, and I'm a Gospel singer. So we do travel around a bit. So
I'll keep my eye open. I'll let you know.' [Laughs hard] How
would I know what the right person is? But anyway, I said, 'I'll
let you know.' So he said: 'Well, what about you?'

So it was that accidental encounter and the Reform Party program
written up by Stephen Harper that eventually led to thirty-six-year-old
Grey's receiving the Reform Party nomination for Beaver River. After
finding a substitute teacher and preparing her lesson plans, she took six
weeks' leave of absence. And she began campaigning with a will. But
hers was an amateur organization. "We got a voters list. I had no idea
what to do with it, so it stayed at the back end of my truck for the entire
time. We had no organization, basically. Not a clue. A few volunteers.
A couple of dozen. We kind of had a person in most of the major towns.
No scrutineers. We didn't know what a scrutineer was if it came up and
bit us! So that was the general election. But we had a lot of fun." They
managed to raise eleven thousand dollars in small amounts. "We had
an ongoing garage sale, we just had junk. At the campaign office people
would come in and we had a KFC bucket, and we put red and blue
streamers around it – they were our colours. And, at meetings, we
passed around a cowboy boot, I remember taking money in cowboy
boots – that holds a lot of money."

  The Tory candidate, John Dahmer, was expected to win as usual in
Alberta. He didn't show up, though, for the all-candidates forums; they
said he was sick. So, mockingly, the Reformers would have an empty chair
on the platform for him on which they'd put a live chicken or a bale of

hay. They only learned after the election that he was seriously sick. Deb Grey had lost by a country mile. John Dahmer had taken 13,768 votes; the Liberal candidate 6,528; the NDP 6,492. With her 3,158 votes, she had bested only the Confederation of the Regions Party. She experienced the pain of loss. "It's a grieving. You work just as hard when you lose, as you do when you win. So, I was sad. Plus I was really sad because you have to get 15 per cent of the vote to get your deposit back. I got 13.5."

Then the totally unexpected happened. The following Saturday morning she received a phone call. John Dahmer had just died. He'd not lived long enough to be sworn in as MP. So Grey phoned Preston Manning, a man she'd never met, and spoke to him for the first time. She invited him to be the candidate in the coming by-election, and she promised him her full support. But after he had spent a few days talking to people in the riding, he decided that he would look like an opportunist if he ran there. She, on the other hand, had made a good impression. Now that Mulroney was re-elected and free trade would go ahead for sure, people would give her a second look. She might have a chance. So she was nominated at a meeting that drew about a hundred people.

Then the Tories had their nomination meeting in the Glendon Hockey Arena, attended by about 4,500 people, including Deputy Prime Minister Don Mazankowski and other notables from far and wide. Grey decided to crash the Tory event. "It was huge. There were people there from all over God's half acre. So my campaign team and I made up a brochure that had my sweet cheery face on it, and it was entitled, 'If your candidate didn't win today, perhaps you'd like to consider me.' There were nine of them running, I think. I got a whole bunch of young kids, and we went out – it was bitterly cold – and we plastered a pile of trucks and cars there. We put one of these brochures under everybody's windshield. Then I went inside. I was there from one o'clock until – it didn't end until ten o'clock that night. I was there the whole time. It was very funny."

As she went mixing with the massed Tories, introducing herself, shaking hands, and distributing her pamphlet, she was recognized by someone at the microphone – she thinks it was Mazankowski – who stood up and announced: "And we have a candidate from one of the other political parties here, to see how a real party conducts its nomination meeting." There were some boos and some cheers, and she was delighted. "It was hilarious, because then everybody knew I was there. And the TV cameras found me and came over and just did a great big long interview. And so I was on TV." [She laughs].

This campaign was different from the last. She could not get a leave of absence, so she was teaching full-time, and campaigning full out. "We had no idea I was going to win. Not a clue. We didn't have any money to do any polling. We had more scrutineers this time. But we didn't have a get-out-the-vote. We still didn't understand anything about that [laughs]. We didn't have enough volunteers to do that. And the first clue I had that anything was happening was when *Maclean's* magazine, CBC television, CTV, Canadian Press, all showed up in my campaign office when the polls were getting ready to close, in St. Paul, Alberta – that's two hours outside of Edmonton. And some of these people had come out from Ottawa. So I said to them, 'Well, welcome, but, what in the flip are you doing here?' And they said, 'We think you're going to win.' I said, 'Good grief!' And that was the first clue I had. So I took 50 per cent of the vote. There was a hockey game on TV. I remember there was a little thing that went across the bottom of the screen; you know, they didn't want to interrupt the hockey game. So it just went across the bottom: 'Reformer wins by-election in Beaver Lake.'"

It was a moment of newborn hope for all Reformers. This was a victory in the heart of Tory land. If they could win here, where could they not win? And their candidate was, in herself, a rebuttal to the stereotypes that circulated about Reformers, that they were bitter old men. She was a woman. She was young, only thirty-six. She was a fresh newcomer to politics, not some jaded old pol. She had made her campaign headquarters in St. Paul, perhaps the oldest established French-speaking community in Alberta, and she had carried the polls there, and in other traditionally French communities such as Lac La Biche and Bonneville. Who could credibly say that Reformers were anti-French? And her personality – her exuberant, articulate, totally idiosyncratic way of expressing herself – was a walking refutation of the calumnies. She would now be the itinerant face of Reform, along with the leader, Preston Manning, and Stephen Harper, the chief policy officer. And she had been consecrated by an election. She must not be allowed to fail.

And that's how Stephen Harper found himself back in Ottawa. He was even working in the same Confederation Building as before. He'd just changed floors: now he was on the seventh. Grey recalls: "As the guidance counsellor, I was always telling these high-school kids, 'You have to know the job description, you have to do a search, you have to know what it is you're getting into.' I didn't even know I had to come to Ottawa on a regular basis. In Alberta, they sit precious few weeks out of the year. I had not a clue I'd be down here this much, and I hated flying, I was terrified of flying." And so Miss Grey went to Ottawa. "I flew down here. Diane Ablonczy came, helped me find a place, spent two or three days. Preston phoned Stephen Harper; he told him, 'This girl needs serious help.' Stephen said he couldn't do it because he was working on his master's degree. But Preston pressed him to come. So Stephen took a year off from his master's. He was my legislative assistant."

The situation was anomalous. The Honourable Deborah Grey was the MP and Stephen's boss. But, at the same time, he was there to be her tutor, to write the speeches that she would be giving in the House, to educate her in the ways of Ottawa, and to provide her with the historical and political background she would need to comment on events and to take a stand on issues. He was the party's chief policy officer. She, the professional teacher and MP, was now the pupil and he was her Svengali. It was made for tensions and misunderstandings.

"Stephen is bright as a whip," she told me. "He's a good strategic thinker. But intense: 'You have to do this, you have to learn that.' He was industrious. A big-picture guy. It was very important for him and for everybody that Reform's sole MP not embarrass the party, not commit gaffes, which the press would have jumped on to tar the whole movement. So he was intense in terms of just trying to put more and more information in me. My style was fine, but for content. . . . So I had to learn about, not just procedural stuff in the House, but big-picture strategic thinking."

One senses the tension between them when one reads Grey's memoirs, *Never Retreat, Never Explain, Never Apologize*, published in late 2004. She devotes only one paragraph to summarizing her entire experience with Harper as her legislative assistant. It lacks the diplomacy of her words during our interview. She writes: "I talked with Preston at length about who would fit the role of legislative assistant and political advisor. As always, Preston was thinking far ahead of anyone else. Although he knew of my abilities and adventurous spirit, he was also aware of my complete lack of knowledge of parliamentary procedure and political experience. Preston had spoken with, and lobbied, our best political advisor in the party, someone who already had parliamentary experience as a former legislative assistant. He protested because he was working on his master's degree in economics at the University of Calgary and did not want to break off his studies and go to Ottawa. Preston persisted and managed to persuade him to spend just one year with me to give me a solid footing. He agreed, and so it was that Stephen Harper came to be my first legislative assistant."

That's it. Not one word of appreciation, of gratitude, though she recognizes that Harper made a sacrifice to come to her assistance and to that of the party. Not a word about what he was like, or what were their relations, or what he did for her. Her silence suggests that she holds a grudge against him. She is a flamboyant, capable, and self-confident woman in her own right, and she did not take easily to being under tutelage.

During our interview in 2002, she was more generous. "Stephen and I both were concerned that I give a good impression of the party. I mean, Preston was out and about across the country, but obviously his fortunes were riding on not having a bean-head down here who would say something or do something stupid. And if you're going to build a beachhead and have a flagship down here, you want to make sure that you basically know what you're talking about. So I was very grateful to have Stephen's mind and abilities because I always knew that whatever he was doing would be sound. Stephen wrote most of my stuff for in the House."

It had been understood with Manning that Grey was, above all, to concentrate her time and effort on serving her constituents of Beaver River. She was not expected to express a view on every issue that came up for comment. That, he felt, would be a sure way of getting her embroiled in controversy and giving her constituents the impression that their interests were far from hers. She must, from the start, be present, be visible, be inquiring, be responsive to them. That could ensure her re-election. Harper, on the other hand, had again a ringside seat to observe, moment by moment, day by day, the political evolution of the country, and it was not a happy sight.

When Parliament opened with the Throne Speech on April 3, 1989, the prime minister, its true author, once again sold the Meech Lake constitutional amendments hard, on the grounds that they would make further constitutional amendments possible and so open the door to the reform of the Senate. Mulroney was obviously sensing that the initial support for Meech Lake was ebbing across the country. At the same time, polls showed separatist sentiment in Quebec rising sharply.

It was imperative that Deborah Grey, in her new status as an MP, stand up in the House and let, at last, the voice of the ordinary people be heard. She would give the reply to the prime minister, she the schoolteacher from Dewberry. And now was the time when she would rely on Stephen Harper to guide her. His single most important duty was to prepare her for command performances, where all eyes and ears would be trained on her. Such was her maiden speech, which she delivered on April 12, 1989, just a month after her election victory. For the first time, a Reformer would rise in the very political heart of the country, and speak with the authority of a member of Parliament on behalf of her electors, but also on behalf of a different vision of the country, one which the elites had banished from the Chamber. As she told me later: "I was the only one in the House of Commons that spoke against Meech Lake. So you could just guess how popular I was."

"Mr. Speaker," she began, "as a new Member speaking for the first time in the House of Commons, I wish to congratulate and thank those who make this institution what it is." Her first words proclaimed that the Reform MP intended to do things differently, would not stoop to the partisan rough-and-tumble that held sway in that Chamber and that Harper had so deplored from his earlier stay in Ottawa. He and Weissenberger, in their statement for the Vancouver assembly, had proposed that the antics in the House were in need of reform. Now, as Grey's speechwriter, he could have her display conspicuous dignity and graciousness. And so the member for Beaver River congratulated the Speaker on his re-election, thanking him and the staff of the Commons "for all the help and assistance they provide to new members."

Then she extended her courtesy to her opponents, even to Brian Mulroney. "I wish to congratulate the prime minister and each member of the government on their re-election and, as a western Canadian, thank them for the willingness to pursue the free-trade initiative. I also wish to congratulate the leaders and members of the [Liberal] Official Opposition and the New Democratic Party on their re-election."

She thanked the two MPs who had introduced her when she appeared in the House for the first time on April 3. She extended her condolences to the family and friends of John Dahmer. Then, having demarcated herself by her non-partisan goodwill, she got down to the business of explaining and selling Reform.

"I am especially pleased to note that the word *reform* is creeping into the government's vocabulary, and appears at least four times in the Speech from the Throne in reference to tax reform, reform of Canada's legal system, parliamentary reform, and reform of the electoral process. The word *reform* means constructive change and represents a long and honourable tradition in Canadian politics from coast to coast."

The spoken words were Deborah Grey's. The written words were almost all Harper's. Grey launched into an historical exegesis in the manner of Preston Manning. She gave the Reform Party cover and legitimacy by presenting it, not as a passing protest party without a history, but as part of the vital pulse of Canadian history. Then, as is the tradition in a maiden speech, she paid tribute to her electors and described the geography, economy, and diversity of Beaver River. "Beaver River is the home of seven major Indian reserves and four Métis colonies. It includes the towns of Lac La Biche, soon to be the site of a new pulp mill, and St. Paul, one of the oldest Francophone communities in Alberta." That was implicitly a riposte to all those who portrayed the Reform Party as racist, anti-aboriginal, and anti-French.

She then began a critique of the government's economic and constitutional policies that had all the ring of Stephen Harper. "Rightly or wrongly, many of our people believe that the legislative programs of the federal government are too centralized in their orientation, focused on managing Toronto's economic boom and meeting Quebec's constitutional demands, to the neglect of the needs and interests of the more thinly populated resource-producing areas of the country." She criticized the executive federalism that made policy and took decisions "beyond the reach or involvement of the common people." She criticized the high interest rate policy of the Bank of Canada and the government, the new Goods and Services Tax, and, above all, the Meech Lake Accord.

This was when she delivered her rebuttal to Mulroney's utterly mis-leading statements about Meech Lake in the Throne Speech. Mulroney said: "As my government renews its commitment to national unity, it believes the ratification of the Meech Lake Accord is indispensable to the further evolution of the Canadian Constitution. With Quebec at the table as a willing participant, future constitutional development – including the important issues of Senate reform, of aboriginal and linguistic rights, of roles and responsibilities in relation to fisheries, and of ways to strengthen the Charter of Rights and Freedoms – will become possible and will be a priority of the government." Grey – and Harper – knew that Meech would end forever the hope of a Triple-E Senate. And what chance would there be afterward to "strengthen the Charter of Rights and Freedoms" when Bourassa had repeatedly made clear his insistence that the "distinct society" must never be overridden by the guarantees of the Charter? Meech would give Bourassa the power to veto any attempt to reinforce the Charter. And Grey was the only MP in the House who could deliver home truths to Mulroney, because all the other members were committed by their party leadership to defending Meech Lake.

"Our people are not unsympathetic to constitutional amendments to make Quebec more at home in Confederation," Grey began, "but they want concurrent constitutional amendments, namely, meaningful Senate reform, to make the West feel more at home in Confederation. In the past generation, it is the West which has experienced the National Energy Program and the CF-18 decision, not Quebec. It is the West's grievances which the government should be addressing with at least as much fervour as it brings to Quebec's demands. In its present form, the Meech Lake Accord thus fails completely to win the support of the people of the West, and the executive-dominated process under which the Meech Lake Accord was developed is even more unattractive to our people than its contents. To us, Meech Lake is not an example of democratic Constitution-building, but executive federalism run amok."

There! She was not just speaking for herself or for her party, but, as a true Reformer, for her constituents. And so she spoke these memorable sentences: "The Beaver River, I must report, is not a tributary of Meech Lake. Its waters come from different sources and flow in a different direc-tion." She announced that she would distribute throughout her riding summaries of the Throne Speech and the Budget Speech, and would hold a meeting in each of the major communities to discuss both documents, expressing her faith in the common sense of the common people of Beaver River, who were not swayed by the partisan passions of the members in the Commons. "They will be more objective. They will ask and expect answers to simple, blunt, common-sense questions concerning each of the government's legislative and budgetary proposals. They will ask: Is it necessary? Is it fair? Who gets help and who gets hurt? Is it practical? What does it cost? Can we afford it?"

She anticipated that there would be a favourable response from her constituents to some of the government's proposals, notably to environmental conservation. Her constituents would appreciate the commitment to a strong economy and to deficit reduction. By saying this, she demonstrated that Reform would rise above partisanship and praise the government when praise was due, as well as condemn when condemnation was needed. And so, after the praise, she did give some warnings. Her constituents in Beaver River, she said "will be looking for signs of real cost-cutting at the top, and in the thick layer of middle management that characterizes so many government programs, before they will be willing to make sacrifices at their level." She added a warning about constitutional amendments. "They will also ask why the government does not feel, in response to the demands of western Canadians, the same sense of urgency to pursue meaningful Senate reform as it feels in pursuing Meech Lake in response to the demands of Quebec. They will ask why the government insists on subordinating Senate reform to the Meech Lake Accord. . . . The people of Beaver River are uneasy patriots, and look forward to the day when they become truly fair and equitable partners in Confederation."

She could not expect a standing ovation at the end of her speech, in that House where Reform was new and a rebuke to all three parties established there. But Deborah Grey had, so to speak, nailed her theses to the door of the House, making clear how she would be different and what would be her most important priorities. She did receive a compliment from John Turner: "I want to congratulate the Member for Beaver River on her excellent debut in the House of Commons, and excellent speech. We can all understand why she got elected."

So Deborah Grey was off to an excellent start in Ottawa. When I asked her in an interview how she was accepted by other MPs, she replied:

"Oh, as a bit of an anomaly, I suppose. You know, some freakish redneck from the West. And the media as well. But I think when they got to know me just even a little bit, they realized that I had some things to say, and that I kind of knew what I was talking about." With her coach backing her, preparing her and warning her of what to expect and what to avoid, and her own spontaneous good sense, she soon disarmed those who feared the barbarians had crashed the gates of Parliament. But she soon had reason to be outraged by the antics of the barbarians already settled on the government benches.

Chapter 11

---◦◉◦---

THE QUESTION OF QUEBEC

A JUBILANT GATHERING of Reformers filled the Edmonton Inn on October 27, 1989, for the party's first biennial assembly following the founding convention of 1987. Just eleven days earlier, the Reform Party's candidate, Stanley Waters, had handily won the unprecedented province-wide Alberta election held to nominate the province's official candidate for the Senate of Canada. So the first order of business of the Edmonton assembly was a resolution summoning Prime Minister Brian Mulroney to appoint Stan Waters to the Senate forthwith.

Theirs was now a party vindicated. After the Senate appointment vote of October 16, in which the nominee of the governing Conservatives had actually come in a weak third, the Reform Party could see itself as the true voice of Alberta. And now Reformers had two stars to put on display at their convention, both consecrated by winning elections, Deborah Grey and Stan Waters.

That such an election for the Senate was even held testified to the pressures on Premier Donald Getty. In the Alberta elections in March, Getty had suffered an embarrassing defeat in his own riding. He was constantly harassed by the Reform Party to prove that he could deliver a Triple-E Senate, he who had had the Alberta legislature adopt the Meech Lake Accord. He had tried to convince the other First Ministers that they should hold a constitutional conference in 1988 on reforming the Senate, in accordance with the very terms of the Meech Lake Accord. But the governments in Quebec, Queen's Park, and Ottawa had turned down his request: they said that Senate reform could only be taken up after all the legislatures had adopted Meech Lake.

To force the prime minister's hand, Getty decided to follow the example of the State of Oregon. In 1904, for the first time, Oregon held a direct election for one of its two representatives in the U.S. Senate. The idea quickly caught on in other states, and by 1913 an amendment to the U.S. Constitution required that all senators be elected by the people of their state rather than delegated by the state legislatures. So Getty had his legislature adopt the Alberta Senatorial Selection Act, whereby Albertans would vote on their choice of nominee for the Senate of Canada. The vote would coincide with province-wide municipal elections on October 16, 1989.

The Reform Party nominated as its candidate Stan Waters, a Calgary businessman who had been a career military officer. As a paratrooper he had risen to the rank of Lieutenant-General and commander of Canadian Forces Mobile Command. He'd been a founding member of the Reform Party and displayed a forceful personality. He would tease Stephen Harper: "The trouble with you is that you have never killed a man." They got along famously. They were both economic conservatives rather than populists in the style of Preston Manning. Waters opposed universal social programs, federal policies on bilingualism, and the multitude of subsidies and grants distributed by the federal government and its agencies.

His candidacy was an important test of whether the Reform Party program could catch on with Albertans. The Beaver River by-election had been a great boost to the party's morale, but it could have been "just a blip" as Deputy Prime Minister Don Mazankowski maintained. After all, there was a sense in that riding that the Tories had deceived the voters by not revealing that their candidate was dying. But this election to nominate a candidate for the Senate was a fresh start. It had never been done before. And it would be province-wide, which was unprecedented. Of the three main candidates vying for the vote on October 16 – there were also three independents – Stan Waters was initially the least known outside Calgary. The Reformers spent $250,000 on the campaign, including $90,000 for television ads. A special edition of the party publication, *The Reformer*, carried the message: "YES to Senate Reform, NO to the Meech Lake Constitutional Accord, YES to reduced federal spending,

NO to the proposed Goods and Services Tax." All of the candidates were in favour of the Triple-E Senate, but the electors would decide which candidate would most effectively deliver their message to the prime minister and the country. Stan Waters won hands down. He received 41.5 per cent of the vote, almost the combined scores of his two closest adversaries. Equally significant, some 620,000 Albertans had taken part in the vote, and Waters had been endorsed by 257,523 Albertans, slightly less than the 275,767 votes Reform had received cumulatively in four provinces during the 1988 elections. His support was also broadly based, in the cities but particularly in rural Alberta, where he took 53 per cent of the vote.

Mulroney had announced long before that he would not be bound by the vote. The news media gave the contest little attention until almost the end. But, on election day, the turnout had been 42 per cent – extraordinary for what had originally been scheduled as merely municipal elections. Later that month, when Mr. Mulroney was back in the House after a trip abroad, Deborah Grey rose from her seat: "My question is for the prime minister on his stopover," she began. "Albertans have been anxious for the prime minister to return and celebrate the political reform that has begun in his own country. I ask the prime minister, in the light of an overwhelming victory on October 16, indeed, over a quarter of a million votes for one man, when – not if, but when – can Canadians expect to hear of Mr. Waters's appointment to the Senate of Canada?" Mulroney turned the question aside with a quip: "I have, as the Honourable Member elegantly pointed out, just returned. And, Mr. Speaker, I have a strong urge to leave again." He did not take Deborah Grey seriously, nor, apparently, the election of Stan Waters.

In Edmonton, as the 1989 assembly came to order, there was a strong sense among the members that their party was in the ascendant, that its opponents were on the defensive, and that Quebec was drifting away from the consensus in the rest of the country on the fundamental values expressed in the Charter of Rights. There was particularly a sharp cleavage between Alberta and Quebec on the role of the Senate. A poll conducted that same October for the *Financial Post* by Telepoll Research found that 63 per cent of those polled on the Prairies strongly favoured election of the members of the Senate. In Quebec, only 34 per cent wanted elected senators.

Quebec and the rest of the country, and most especially Quebec and
Alberta, were straining apart. Increasingly, the deadlock over Meech,
over reforming the Senate, and over language were leading to mutual
anger and rejection. In midsummer of 1989, the *Toronto Star* published
a massive, three-part, mood-of-the-country series by national columnist
Carol Goar under the title "Is Canada Starting to Fall Apart?" Her
answer to the national existential question was a qualified yes. The big
problem, she found, was a general indifference to the severe strains on
national unity. "The last time Confederation started to come unstuck, we
rallied to keep the country together. We met and talked and agonized.
This time, many Canadians don't seem to care."

The *Globe and Mail*'s Ottawa bureau chief, Graham Fraser, also
brought out a view-with-disquiet state-of-the-nation pair of articles.
"There is a new tone to relations between French and English and Quebec
and the rest of the country." He found discontent with Confederation in
Quebec spreading out beyond the traditional nationalist circles – the
labour elite, universities, intellectuals, and the left – to encompass for
the first time many businesspeople. He evoked a scenario of circular
anger between Quebec and the rest of the country if the Meech Lake
agreement should fail and should some cabinet ministers and members
of Parliament from Quebec quit Ottawa in disgust. Also, "English
Canadians may respond with impatience, if not anger, leading either to
a constitutional crisis or a further souring of the relationship between
Quebec and the rest of Canada. Suffused with a mood of sullen resentment, that could lay the groundwork for a revival of a new, more virulent form of Quebec nationalism."

The changing situation was reflected in the public opinion polls. Both
Mulroney and Robert Bourassa kept repeating a dangerous message, that
Quebec was outside the Constitution and outside the federation. The
message was registering with Quebeckers. As Quebec was headed for
provincial elections on September 25, 1989, a Sorecom public opinion
poll published a few days before showed 46 per cent of francophone
Quebeckers now in favour of sovereignty-association, with only 38 per
cent opposed. Even total independence for Quebec rallied 34 per cent of
francophones, about double the percentage recorded when Bourassa
came to power in December 1985.

Manning knew that the Edmonton assembly must take a firm and

clear stand with respect to Quebec's place in Canada. It must adopt resolutions that would deal specifically with the Meech Lake Accord, but
those resolutions must be justified in terms of Reform's founding principles. Manning's own attitudes toward Quebec's ambitions had been
ambivalent. He was torn between praising Quebec's Quiet Revolution as
an authentic reform movement, and denouncing a central principle of the
Quiet Revolution, that is, the demand for special constitutional status for
Quebec. And so, in preparing for the Edmonton assembly, Manning
took inspiration from Harper's important memo of March 10, in which
Harper had urged Manning to lead the party in a different direction with
respect to Quebec as with almost everything else.

For Harper the Quiet Revolution was not a grassroots reform movement at all. It was a top-down revolution, led by the "new class" that
Harper saw as buttressing statism: politicians like Jean Lesage, journalists like René Lévesque, in the employ of state-owned Radio-Canada;
technocrats like Education Minister Paul Gérin-Lajoie, with his Ph.D. in
constitutional law, and Jacques Parizeau, with a Ph.D. from the London
School of Economics; university professors like Jacques-Yvan Morin
and roving intellectuals like Pierre Trudeau; union leaders like Jean
Marchand, who was a university graduate on a mission to save the
working class rather than a blue-collar worker. The Quiet Revolution
was an urban phenomenon and the rural areas of Quebec were the last
to join. And the defining principle of the Quiet Revolution was statism –
the construction of an ever more powerful Quebec state to advance the
interests of the French-speaking majority.

Harper recognized that the Meech Lake Accord would further
strengthen Quebec's already exorbitant statism. Quebec was already,
before Meech, the province with by far the most omnipresent public
sector, with its Crown corporations in forestry and mining and steel, its
state intrusions into the corporate world with its investment arm, the
Société générale de financement, and its huge pension fund, the largest
single pool of capital in Canada, which allowed it to appoint directors
for leading corporations and select some businesses over others for state
support. Already, the Charter of the French Language committed the
state to extensive intrusions into the internal and external communications of businesses, hospitals, municipalities, even voluntary associations. Now Meech Lake proposed to extend the reach of the Quebec

government by giving it a constitutionally entrenched obligation to "promote the distinct identity" of Quebec. It was a blank cheque for state control, and as such, Harper was viscerally opposed to it. Manning also opposed the Accord, but mostly for the reason, also shared by Harper, that it made the attainment of a Triple-E Senate unlikely. But Manning did not have a philosophically rooted objection to Meech, as the future would show.

Harper, in his memo to Manning, had explored why a realignment between right and left had not occurred in Canada, despite the crisis of the welfare state which normally would have precipitated such a realignment. "I have become convinced that there is a more fundamental and obvious cause, which most English Canadians would prefer to ignore. As the Economic Crisis worsens, Canada and its political parties are preoccupied with a deeper crisis – the Crisis of National Unity. Specifically, Canada's political options have become paralyzed by the question of Quebec."

The threat of Quebec's separation over the previous twenty-five years had prevented a political realignment that would otherwise have occurred. "The situation has not simply made the Economic Crisis hard to notice. It has also made it harder to address. This is because the net benefits of federal government activity have been allocated in massive disproportion to Quebec. This has been both to get the Quebec bloc-vote and, in the period 1976–1980, to win the referendum. Therefore, the Quebec question not only stands in the way of any coherent ideological agenda. It is particularly a problem for an Economic Right agenda, especially if it is really only a windfall economic benefit that is holding Quebec in Confederation."

Harper estimated that the situation could not continue indefinitely because, as the economic crisis went from bad to worse, eventually the English-speaking majority would disengage from policies focused on pleasing Quebec to concentrate increasingly on policies corresponding to their economic interests. "The strategy of the Reform Party as regards Quebec must therefore be very careful. To pursue its agenda, it must insist that the Crisis of National Unity can be resolved only by Quebeckers making an emotional commitment to Canada, not by economic or constitutional appeasement. It must be prepared to negotiate a looser arrangement if this commitment is not forthcoming. Yet the

Reform Party must prefer unity, and therefore not toy with the nationalist or separatist vote. . . . It must be committed to Quebec's right to a
French society (along with concurrent rights elsewhere)."

Harper was, in effect, counselling that the Reform Party adopt a
policy of benign neglect toward Quebec, neither trying as the other
parties did to entice Quebec votes and stimulate federalist sentiments by
offering more bribes or constitutional preferential treatment, nor cultivating anti-Quebec sentiments in the rest of the country. He accepted
territorial bilingualism, which could also be called symmetrical unilingualism. This was already in the 1988 program, which proposed "a
recognition of French in Quebec and English elsewhere as the predominant language of work and society." Official bilingualism would be
restricted to "key national institutions." He judged that turning away
from the Quebec question was necessary to promote a political realignment on a left-right axis and so avert an inevitable economic crisis in the
long run. And, if this approach should entail some risk to national unity,
the Reform Party must be ready to face that risk.

In summary, Harper had written: "My hypothesis is this. Political
realignment has not occurred in Canada because of the major parties'
preoccupation with Quebec. The arrangements designed to include
Quebec in a national party, and ultimately the country, have been
incompatible with any coherent ideological agenda, especially an
Economic Right agenda. Therefore, a modern Party of the Economic
Right must be prepared to effectively ignore the National Unity issue,
neglect organizational effort in Quebec, and ultimately risk calling the
separatist bluff."

Harper raised one important issue on which the main parties were
resolutely silent. That was the issue of how Quebec could separate in a
constitutional democracy based on the rule of law. On the one hand, he
saw the 1980 referendum as a precedent that Quebec could invoke as
giving it a moral claim to a possible secession. On the other hand, he was
insistent on recognizing the constraints embedded in the Constitution.

"First, the Constitutional Crisis, epitomized by the referendum of
1980, has effectively acknowledged Quebec's independence as an option.
Thus the Quebecois have grown in self-confidence, sure, as few other
minority societies ever have been, that an attempt to separate will not risk
serious retaliation. Second, national leaders who have the Quebec bloc

vote (Trudeau, Mulroney) have themselves successfully used the separatist threat to bend the opposition parties to their personal agendas."

Harper was writing, obviously, before the Supreme Court's advisory opinion on Quebec's secession of 1998, which would reject the proposition that Quebec had a right to secede and state that secession could only be carried out legally by obtaining an amendment to the Constitution. But he was prophetic in raising the issue of constitutionality. His memo had formulated four principles that should guide the party in approaching the Quebec question. "The Reform Party must take the following position on the participation of Quebec in Confederation:

a. The Reform Party believes all Provinces, including Quebec, should remain in Confederation.
b. The Reform Party categorically rejects any suggestions that Quebec or any other Province is currently outside the country's Constitution.
c. The Reform Party believes that the participation of Quebec or any other Province in Confederation must ultimately be decided as an issue of emotional attachment to Canada and not in consequence of the economic benefits of participation.
d. The Reform Party believes that any Province wishing to pursue a separatist option should first put forward a separation procedure to be included in the Constitution."

Harper's insistent denial that Quebec was outside the Constitution, as Brian Mulroney and Robert Bourassa maintained, was timely and badly needed. But his insistence on "a separation procedure to be included in the Constitution" was prophetic. Its time would come.

Given his overall analysis throughout his memo, his final recommendation respecting Quebec is not surprising: "The Reform Party would not expect significant expansion in the Province of Quebec until such time as the National Unity issue there has lost importance." Manning would borrow from Harper's memo in preparing for his address on Saturday evening, which would be the highlight of the convention. He also instructed Harper to prepare the motion on Quebec to be submitted to the assembly. That motion is here reproduced in full, because it was to lead to much future controversy, and some misunderstanding.

QUEBEC MOTION

WHEREAS Quebec understandably wishes to preserve the language and culture of the majority of its residents, and

WHEREAS this feeling has, in the past quarter century, given rise to a movement in Quebec seeking independence from the rest of Canada, and

WHEREAS federal attempts to accommodate this movement, such as official bilingualism and the Constitution Act of 1982, have not been accepted by the Government of Quebec, and

WHEREAS Quebec politicians, both federal and provincial, appear increasingly unable to hold office without appealing to the separatist vote, and

WHEREAS concessions made on account of this separatist threat are, for many, proving to be costly, ineffective, a source of deepening friction between Quebec and the rest of Canada, and a barrier to the development of national purpose for the country as a whole,

BE IT RESOLVED that the Reform Party state clearly its belief that Confederation should be maintained, but that it can only be maintained by a clear commitment to Canada as one nation, in which the demands and aspirations of all regions are entitled to equal status in constitutional negotiations and political debate, and in which freedom of expression is fully accepted as the basis for language policy across the country.

IT IS FURTHER RESOLVED that, should these principles of Confederation be rejected, Quebec and the rest of Canada should consider whether there exists a better political arrangement which will enrich our friendship, respect our common defence requirements, and ensure a free interchange of commerce and people, by mutual consent and for our mutual benefit.

_____ AGREE   _____ DISAGREE

(NOTE: The chief policy officer wishes specifically to acknowledge contributions made to the development of this resolution by
T.W. Deachman, Vancouver Centre.)

The resolution followed closely Harper's argument in his memo that
Reform should no longer play the game of the nationalists, no longer
submit to blackmail, no longer try to buy Quebec's adherence by bribes
or concessions on language. It would call the separatists' bluff and show
that Reform was not afraid to face the truth or consequences. The
motion deviated in only two important areas from the argument of
Harper's memo. With respect to official languages, Harper had supported Reform's previous position in favour of dual unilingualisms,
French in Quebec, English in the rest of the country, and official bilingualism only in key national institutions. Now, the resolution proposed
as a condition of maintaining Confederation that "freedom of expression
is fully accepted as the basis for language policy across the country." The
positions are not necessarily contradictory, because the 1988 policy
assumed that the private sector would be free of language constraints; it
did not condone the compulsions against freedom of expression of a
Charter of the French language. Still, the resolution indicated a change
of emphasis. Manning and Harper both were aware of the surge of
repugnance in the West for Quebec's violation of freedom of expression
by its laws restricting the use of English. The defence of freedom of
expression was a response to that outrage. The second notable difference
was that the resolution spoke nowhere explicitly of the need to respect
the constitutional order if Quebec and Canada were to seek a new and
different relationship. This, again, almost certainly came from Manning,
in whose historical analysis, grassroots insurgency trumped constitutionality, even when arms were taken up against the state. But the resolution did speak of a new arrangement by "mutual consent." It did not
raise the alternative of a unilateral action by Quebec. The resolution was
hard-edged. It cut through the soft, wheedling, appeasing rhetoric regularly gushing from the country's political leaders, academics, and pundits
of journalism.

On October 28, Preston Manning gave perhaps the most memorable speech of his career. It is recalled as "the House Divided speech," and it was to ring throughout the country. Its central focus was the Quebec question, in the spirit of the Quebec motion.

Manning set up his discussion with a telling joke: "Last year, in a magnanimous effort to redress regional disparities, Edmonton allowed Calgary to win the Stanley Cup. While it is Edmonton's nightmare that this might be repeated this season, Les MacPherson of the Saskatoon *Star Phoenix* had an even worse nightmare. He dreamt that Mulroney and the federal government intervened after last year's Stanley Cup final, to give the cup to Montreal even after Calgary had won the series." That, of course, was a sly replay of the 1986 decision on the maintenance contract for the CF-18 fighter planes. Then Manning sent a barb to Ottawa over Meech Lake: "The genesis, content, and impending collapse of the Meech Lake Accord illustrates a lack of constitutional leadership. How ironic that Ottawa, the centre of our national government, will be the last centre in the country, rather than the first, to discover that there is no public support for Meech Lake." And then he came to the core of his speech, and sounded the themes that would resonate in the hearts and minds of citizens in the four western provinces and beyond.

"Of all the troublesome issues which will face Canada in the next decade, I can think of none which are more in need of a blast of fresh air from the West than the issue of relations between Quebec and the rest of Canada. It is now more than a quarter of a century since the Pearson administration committed Canada to governing itself as an equal partnership between the English and the French. It is now more than twenty years since the Trudeau administration declared the federal government rather than the Quebec government to be the primary guardian and promoter of the French fact in Canada. Based on those commitments and declarations, the Liberals gave us the Official Languages Act and the Constitution Act of 1982, and the Conservatives (following in the same rut rather than breaking new ground) have given us Bill C-72 and the Meech Lake Constitutional Accord.

"All of these measures have been advocated, promoted, and in some cases imposed upon the Canadian people for the avowed purpose and intention of making Quebec 'more at home in Confederation,' reducing the separatist threat, and strengthening Canada's sense of national unity, identity, and purpose. As the sun rises on the last decade of the twentieth century, it is imperative that Canadians fully assess the results of this course of action in the cold, clear light of a new and coming day."

For Manning, the current distemper so evident in Canada was the proof that the past assumptions had failed and that a new approach was needed. "Has this approach produced a more united, less divided, Canada? No, it has not. Has this approach produced a more contented Quebec? No, it has not. Has this approach reduced the use of Quebec separatism as a threat to wring more concessions out of the rest of Canada? No, it has not. Has this approach engendered in Quebec politicians an emotional as well as an economic commitment to Canada? No, it has not. Has this approach produced in Canadians a new sense of national identity, pride, and purpose sufficient to guide us into the twenty-first century? No, it has not. Instead, what the Pearson–Trudeau–Mulroney approach to constitutional development has produced is a house divided against itself. And as a great Reformer once said long ago, 'a house divided against itself cannot stand.'"

The audience listened, rapt. This was not the usual inflated droning of convention speeches. This was not the pussyfooting around the question of Quebec that had become the distinctive Canadian way. This was the boy standing up to say the emperor has no clothes. And the Reformers listened to their leader revealing openly, without apology or circumlocution, what had been hidden in the bottom of their hearts.

"Now if this is the unvarnished truth as we see it, then leadership demands that we rise to our feet in the federal political arena, and say at least three things on behalf of western Canadians: First, we do not want to live, nor do we want our children to live, in a house divided against itself, particularly one divided along racial and linguistic lines. Second, we do not want nor do we intend to leave this house ourselves (even though we have spent most of our constitutional lives on the back porch). We will, however, insist that it cease to be divided. Third, either all Canadians, including the people of Quebec, make a clear commitment to Canada as one nation, or Quebec and the rest of Canada should explore whether there exists a better but more separate relationship between the two. In short, we say that living in one Canada united on certain principles, or living with a greater constitutional separation between Quebec and the rest of Canada, is preferable to living in a 'house divided.'"

Manning anticipated that his words would be misunderstood, that the Reformers would be stigmatized as anti-Quebec. On the contrary, he protested, the Reformers were for a united Canada, one in which Quebec could be both prosperous and culturally secure. He recognized that Canada would be diminished without Quebec within the federation. But Manning went on to make Harper's argument that the current course itself was bringing the country to a crisis.

"If we continue to make unacceptable constitutional, economic, and linguistic concessions to Quebec at the expense of the rest of Canada, it is those concessions themselves which will tear the country apart and poison French-English relations beyond remedy. If Canada is to be maintained as one undivided house, the government of Canada must ask the people of Quebec to commit to three foundational principles of Confederation:

- That the demands and aspirations of all regions of the country are entitled to equal status in constitutional and political negotiations.
- That freedom of expression is fully accepted as the basis of any language policy.
- That every citizen is entitled to equality of treatment by governments, without regard to race, language, or culture.

"If these principles are accepted, our goal of one united Canada is achievable. But if these principles of Confederation are rejected by Quebec, if the house cannot be united on such a basis, then Quebec and the rest of Canada should openly examine the feasibility of establishing a better but more separate relationship between them, on equitable and *mutually acceptable terms.*"

Manning was introducing implicitly the concept which had been put forward explicitly in Harper's memo: the test of constitutionality. Quebec alone could not unilaterally determine the terms of a possible secession. "From the West's perspective, such terms will be judged satisfactory if they are fair and advantageous to Canada, if the new relationship with Quebec can be established and maintained without violence, and if the terms are *approved by a majority in both Quebec and the rest of Canada.*"

It was, surely, one of the great political speeches ever given in Canada. The next day, the assembly voted for the Quebec motion, and much of the country was aghast. Manning, when he met reporters, said more clearly than in his speech that it was about time "to call Quebec's bluff." And he added: "We think it's about time somebody stood up and said 'no, we're going to put some demands on you. If you can't respond to those, then maybe you better think about a separate relationship.'"

The *Calgary Herald* published an editorial on October 31 that expressed some grudging admiration, but mostly patronizing reproof. "The biggest benefit for western Canadians, and perhaps for Canada as a whole, is that the Reform Party has, once and for all, clearly articulated exactly how the majority of westerners feel about Canada. Feel, not think. Their policies are deeply felt but they are not those of the deepest thinkers. Reformers speak from the heart more than the head. They represent an honest reaction to the changes which have marked Canada including the West, in the past decade. . . . Reformers have a vision of Canada. Unfortunately, it is a blinkered vision, which withdraws from, and throws up barricades against, change."

The deepest thinkers at the Montreal *Gazette* had a predictable reaction to the speech: "Friends like that, English Quebec can do without; they stand for everything most English Quebeckers oppose." The *Gazette*, which supported the Meech Lake Accord, compared the Reformers to Quebec nationalists: "Small minds resemble each other the world over."

Manning and the Reform Party had now moved close to Harper's position on Quebec. Both now recognized that the country was at a crossroads and must choose between incompatible paths leading to quite different values, to a very different national identity.

Manning expressed this in his speech when he stated: "We say that living in one Canada united on certain principles, or living with a greater constitutional separation between Quebec and the rest of Canada, is preferable to living in a house divided." And that was what Harper expressed in the resolution when it affirmed that certain principles, certain values, and the visions of the country must be common and compatible: "A clear commitment to Canada as one nation, in which the

demands and aspirations of all regions are entitled to equal status in constitutional negotiations and political debate, and in which freedom of
expression is fully accepted as the basis for language policy across the
country." The alternative, as the resolution stated, was that the country
begin seriously to consider whether de-confederation might not be a less
costly option than constantly heightening tensions.

This clearly expressed ultimatum caused shock among the national
elites that it could even be raised aloud and in public. But it also provoked a great release of tension at the grassroots level among people who
felt that, at long last, the truth had burst out. Whatever one might think
in retrospect, Harper and Manning offered intelligent analysis and an
epic articulation. They raised to a much higher level the accumulating
gripes and prejudices and resentments voiced by ordinary people in different parts of the country. Grumbling was transmuted into the considered statement of a people refusing to be herded by its elites and insisting
on making a deliberate, principled choice of its future.

Chapter 12

---◆◆◆---

DEMOCRACY IN OTTAWA

STEPHEN HARPER WAS in Ottawa supporting Deborah Grey during the first half of 1990, when the country was breaking apart in slow motion. The tectonic plates of this continent-sized country were straining toward opposite compass points. East was east and West was west and the concern was spreading that just possibly, inconceivably, the centre could not hold.

The Meech Lake Constitutional Accord had to be passed by June 23, 1990, by every provincial legislature, or it would then become null and void. As the life or death deadline approached, the accord was in trouble. Liberal Frank McKenna had swept every riding in New Brunswick in 1987 after running a campaign in which he promised not to adopt Meech Lake unless it was amended to meet his objections. But Premier Bourassa would not countenance the slightest amendment. Then, Manitoba's all-party Task Force on Meech Lake had presented its report in October 1989, demanding important changes as a condition for Manitoba to adopt the accord. Finally, on March 8, 1990, the Newfoundland legislature opened with a Throne Speech in which Premier Clyde Wells promised to rescind the adoption of Meech Lake by the previous PC government of Brian Peckford. The agreement seemed doomed. But Prime Minister Mulroney, instead of backing off, kept raising the ante and heightening the rhetorical heat.

Typical was the 1989 year-end television interview he gave to Radio-Canada's Madeleine Poulin, in the very Meech Lake lodge where, in 1987, he and the premiers had negotiated the constitutional deal. In a suave baritone, he gave his revisionist history according to which Quebeckers had been betrayed, humiliated, and isolated by Pierre Trudeau. "He said, 'We put our seats on the block.' That's what Mr. Trudeau said. 'I tell you, Québécois, we put our seats on the block to favour this new climate and this new relation. There will be change,' he said. Well, there was change, all right. Twelve months later, Quebec was excluded from the Constitution." Mulroney told Quebeckers who had voted no in the referendum that they had been misled and betrayed by their prime minister, with the support of all the premiers of the nine provinces outside Quebec. Quebeckers were thrust out by treachery. And then a party was held on Parliament Hill, with the Queen invited to Ottawa for the party, to celebrate the signing of a Constitution from which Quebec was excluded. And then, according to Mulroney, the Quebec premier and the National Assembly made their reasonable proposals to permit Quebec to return to the constitutional fold. But the Meech Lake agreement was now threatened, and Mulroney said, "If this moderate and reasonable position is rejected, then we will have to reconsider many things."

The rhetoric was working. In Quebec, polls regularly showed that the people did not understand nor embrace the transformation of the Constitution called the Meech Lake Accord, which had been concocted by the First Ministers in 1987. And yet, paradoxically, the conviction was growing among Quebeckers in the early 1990s that the rest of Canada was rejecting Quebec's very identity, rejecting Quebec's distinctiveness, even rejecting Quebec itself, by showing reluctance to adopt the Meech Lake Constitutional Accord. It had become a flag issue, a matter of national honour. Premier Robert Bourassa gave a speech to his party's national council in which he warned: "I don't have a mandate to negotiate on my knees." "Quebec will not get on its knees," headlined Ottawa daily *Le Droit*. Montreal's *Le Devoir* played the story big under the headline: "Bourassa says no to any 'federalism on our knees.'" His Minister of Intergovernmental Affairs, Gil Rémillard, confirmed the message that English Canada wanted to make Quebec grovel. "We have had enough. . . . We will not turn the other cheek."

In December 1989, *Maclean's* magazine published its year-end opinion poll on the state of the nation. It showed 60 per cent of Quebeckers thinking that Quebec would separate from Canada if the

Meech Lake Accord failed to be adopted. At the same time, a majority of Quebeckers – 52 per cent – thought that Quebec would separate from Canada in the 1990s whether Meech Lake was adopted or not. Damned if you do, damned if you don't. So much for Brian Mulroney's policy of "national reconciliation." In the West, meanwhile, particularly in Alberta, rejection of the constitutional deal was hardening, on the grounds that it would consecrate the inequality of the provinces and prevent the smaller provinces from achieving true reform of the Senate.

While regional conflict intensified and a crisis lay ahead, the people's confidence in their federal government weakened, and Mulroney's Tories were setting records of unpopularity. As Val Sears reported in the *Toronto Star* on May 19, 1990, "Never in history has a mainstream party sunk so low in public esteem as the Conservatives. And the country – three years before another federal election – is sullen and bitter about language, taxation, and its very future as a unified nation."

The country was being riven apart by both of Mulroney's two major policies for securing "national unity." Meech Lake was one. The other was Bill C-72, passed in 1988, which expanded the scope of the Official Languages Act. It caused resentment especially after Robert Bourassa suspended Charter-protected freedom of expression in Quebec to restrict the right to put English words on commercial signs. On January 29, 1990, the municipal council of Sault Ste. Marie passed a resolution which stated that "the Council of the Corporation of the City of Sault Ste. Marie declares English to be the official language of the said Corporation." That vote was preceded by a petition, gathered door to door, which was signed by 25,000 people out of a population of 85,000. The campaign was led by an anti-French lobby, the Association for the Protection of English in Canada (APEC). It succeeded in eventually convincing a total of forty-seven generally small municipalities – of Ontario's total of 839 – to pass similar resolutions asserting English as their official language and implicitly negating French. The Sault resolution in particular triggered an immediate and widespread chorus of outrage. Prime Minister Mulroney denounced the action as "deplorable" and expressed concern about the "surge of intolerance" the country was experiencing. The premier of Ontario, David Peterson, disapproved, even while recognizing that Quebec's Bill 178 prohibiting English on commercial signs had poisoned the atmosphere. But among French-speaking

Quebec's opinion leaders, the Sault resolution was seen as the quintessential rejection of French by all of English-speaking Canada. Federal environment minister Lucien Bouchard, then still in Mulroney's cabinet, saw in the Sault's action possibly the beginning of the end of Canada. "It wouldn't take many Sault Ste. Maries for the rope to break," Bouchard declared ominously. He called the council's vote "the summit of a reaction of intolerance which will destroy this country."

Another action with vast consequences occurred in 1989 in Brockville, a municipality beside the St. Lawrence in Eastern Ontario. About a dozen former Quebeckers, with the support of APEC, invited the television cameras to a staged event during which they deliberately trampled on the Quebec flag. They later explained that they had wanted to protest Bill 178 and they had noticed that the nationalists succeeded in getting the attention of the cameras when they burnt a Canadian flag. The event drew little attention at the time. But, in the wake of the Sault outcry, the Quebec media rediscovered the Brockville footage and broadcast it on television incessantly. In newspapers, on television, in books, the Brockville incident became a stunning insult, an unspeakable outrage, the very prototype of English Canada's scorn for Quebec.

The actions in the Sault and Brockville did not escape the attention of John Turner. On February 5, 1990, Turner rose in the Commons and proposed that there be all-party support for the following motion:

> Resolved, that this House reaffirm its commitment to support, protect, and promote linguistic duality in Canada.

His motion received the support of Audrey McLaughlin, recently chosen as leader of the NDP. But Brian Mulroney noted that the motion contained the dangerous words *promote linguistic duality*. In Quebec, neither the provincial Liberals nor the PQ could countenance that English be promoted. So Mulroney hedged, hemmed and hawed. The next day, he finally declared, in response to Audrey McLaughlin's urging, that he could support the motion – if it were amended to include support for the Meech Lake Accord. "Surely, surely, when my honourable friend says she's concerned about the future of the country, I am very concerned about the future of a country where we have a Constitution without the Province of Quebec, which is why we brought in Meech Lake, which is why I hope my honourable friend will support that, too." Mulroney brought forward his own motion, which stated:

> That this House reaffirm its commitment to support, protect, and promote linguistic duality in Canada, *as reflected by this House in the Constitutional Amendment [Act]*, 1987, and the Official Languages Act, 1988.

It was a clever ploy which played to the Quebec nationalists and embarrassed the opposition parties, which now both wavered in their support of Meech. The NDP, under its new leader, now demanded amendments as a condition for supporting the accord. The Liberals, in the midst of a leadership contest, were torn. Candidate Jean Chrétien was a critic of Meech, while candidates Paul Martin and Sheila Copps supported it.

Harper and Grey worked hard on the speech she was to give when Mulroney's motion came up for debate. This would be the opportunity to lay out precisely the Reform Party's position on official languages and on Meech Lake, to explain the Quebec Resolution passed at the Reform Party's 1989 Edmonton assembly, which had caused a scandal in some parts of the country. It would allow Grey to repeat some of the more ringing phrases of Manning's House Divided speech. The resolution before the Commons raised fundamentally the question of what vision of Canada would be vested in the Constitution forever. Fortunately, there was a Reform Party MP in the Commons, and she was prepared to give the most important speech of her career, one in which the voice of the West would speak out loud and clear on the country it wanted.

The debate on the Mulroney motion began after Question Period on the afternoon of Thursday, February 15, 1990. It was expected to last three full days, including prolonged evening sessions, so as to give every MP an opportunity to speak for twenty minutes on the motion. The recorded vote was to come at the end of the third day, late on the following Monday. Just before the debate began, the three party House leaders had an exchange on the timetable. Government House leader Douglas Lewis replied to the questions of his counterparts: "The debate will continue tonight with twenty-minute speeches until such time as the last person speaks. When the last member is finishing speaking, we would simply adjourn until tomorrow. That same arrangement would take place on Monday." Lewis was asked at what time the vote would take place on Monday evening. He replied: "I can be very explicit on when the vote will take place: with enough notice that every member will have an opportunity to be here and vote." Those words, that promise, would be significant later in the light of what was about to happen.

Brian Mulroney spoke, defending Meech Lake and the official languages. Herb Gray, acting leader of the Liberal opposition, spoke next, saying nothing about Meech Lake, but defending language rights and "the two founding peoples," a concept anathema to the Reform Party. Lorne Nystrom then spoke on behalf of the NDP. He, like Herb Gray, said he supported the resolution; he, like Gray, said not one word about Meech Lake. But, surprisingly for an MP from Saskatchewan, he also endorsed the theory of two founding peoples.

In the event, Deborah Grey never spoke. She never gave the great speech Harper and she had prepared. She never gave it because the other parties pulled a fast one on her. After Mulroney, Gray, and Nystrom had spoken, the Speaker called the question and the debate shut down. It was obviously done by pre-arrangement. Despite the promise that every member wishing to speak would be given twenty minutes, despite the promise of ample notice to be given before the vote, the debate was over. The member from Beaver River was deprived of her opportunity to address the Commons and the country.

Instead of her speech, Deborah Grey voiced her indignation: "Unfortunately, what we saw yesterday was a sad display of gamesmanship. I find it appalling that an issue so sensitive, so necessary to be looked at in an objective manner could be so scornfully dismissed by three carefully orchestrated speeches. The real danger to democracy is when legitimate dissent becomes restricted to only extreme groups far removed from legitimate institutions. That, I believe, is a real danger in the country today, as illustrated by the events of yesterday. I want to put on the record that I am displeased with what went on, and I am sure the Canadian public who watched this on television was equally appalled."

Even while the country was approaching a state of crisis over official languages and over the Meech Lake Accord, even while the country was being rent apart and the increasingly strong tensions were there tearing at each of the three parties and causing conflicts within each caucus, a false wall of unanimity was put up. It was intolerable that someone should stand up in the House and speak against the sacred cows of the Meech Lake Accord and the Official Languages Act. And so the three parties found a way to silence the only voice that they could not control by cajoling, bribery, or intimidation: that of Deborah Grey, with Harper as her speechwriter. The established parties had found another way: deception and hypocrisy. Deborah Grey made her final comment: "I want it clearly on the record that the Canadian people are seeing this, expressing frustration, and, in fact, shrugging their shoulders, saying: 'There they go again in the House of Commons.'"

Harper, working in Ottawa, witnessed the separatist threat growing while an unpopular and problematic change to the Constitution was being foisted on the people. But, along with the threat, he saw the opportunity for the Reform Party. A party which would stand up for the people against the elites was needed. The Reform Party was positioned as never before to replace the PCs as the voice of the West, and to offer to the whole country an alternative to the failing vision of the Tory-Grit-NDP consortium. "In the next few years, there will be enormous opportunities for a new political party that is well-led and well-structured," Harper told the press.

Besides his day-to-day work of guiding Deborah Grey in the Commons, Harper spent much of his time preparing for a Reform Party expansion east of the Manitoba border into Ontario. From the start, he had agreed with Manning that Reform must think nationally, even as it concentrated initially on the grievances of the West. But he had been more impatient than Manning for an eastern breakout. After the 1988 elections, in his memo to Preston, he had urged an immediate move to lift the restriction in Reform's constitution against setting up constituencies outside the West. His fear then was that Reform would become captive to its western clientele and embrace a purely regional vision. But Manning feared that an early expansion would strain the party's resources in talent and money. The 1988 election campaign had shown just how puny and inadequate were their means. When the issue of expansion was taken up by the party at its assembly in Edmonton in October 1989, the outcome of the debate was in accordance with Manning's preference: a committee was appointed to study the related issues of launching Reform parties that would contest provincial elections, and of expanding the federal party outside the West. The committee would bring its recommendations to the next convention of the Reform Party to be held in April 1991.

But, meanwhile, despite Mulroney's frantic efforts, the Meech Lake ∠ Accord unravelled. Mulroney promoted a "parallel accord" and sent a committee under Jean Charest to consult across the country. Lucien Bouchard then seized on the Charest report, which proposed to "promote" English and French across the country, as an excuse to break with Mulroney, leave the cabinet, and declare openly for the secession of Quebec. Mulroney decided to "roll all the dice" and convened a week-long meeting of the First Ministers during which the dissidents – Liberal Clyde Wells and Conservative Gary Filmon – were subjected to maximum pressure to cave in. Filmon did, Wells wavered, but an aboriginal member of the Manitoba legislature, Elijah Harper, finally defeated the Meech Lake Accord by raising an eagle feather. Canada faced an uncertain future and the Reform Party prepared to restructure the country.

Chapter 13

CHOOSING ONE'S CANADA

THE YEAR 1991 WAS a dismal year for Canada, but a good one for Stephen Harper and for the Reform Party. At the Reform Party's April assembly in Saskatoon, Stephen was introduced briefly to a strikingly attractive, effervescent blond by the name of Laureen Teskey. He would meet her again in Calgary, but he'd been so concentrated on his public role in Saskatoon that when he met her a second time, he didn't recognize her. He would not make that mistake twice.

Cynthia Williams, his former fiancée, recalls the occasion. "Steve and I kept in touch even after we broke up. We just phoned and talked. We remained friends, and I'm the one who introduced him to Laureen." Cynthia and Laureen knew each other from work. Both were employed by a Calgary firm called GTO Printing, where Laureen was the resident graphic artist and Cynthia was an account executive. As Cynthia remembers, "Laureen had actually heard Steve speak in Saskatoon. She'd gone there to that conference. I remember thinking that Laureen would be the perfect girl for Steve. Steve and I were going for lunch one day, and I said to Laureen, 'Why don't you come for lunch with me? I'm going to go meet Steve.' So that's how they met."

Cynthia and Laureen share some common traits. Both are fair, both are energetic and extroverted, both studied journalism before developing other specialties to earn a living. "Actually, we do have a lot in common," Williams acknowledges. "We are both outgoing personalities. Except that I'm very much *not* that right wing. I'm very much a Red Tory and quite proud of it."

In conversation with me in 2002, Laureen Teskey was torn between her irrepressible spontaneity and the reserve her husband demanded, not only because of his public role as leader of the Opposition, but also because of his own ultra-cautious personality. "I must be good," she interrupted herself when she found herself drawn into revealing confidences.

She spoke about where she was born and spent her early years, in a small town in Turner Valley, an hour's drive southwest of Calgary. She was very much a tomboy and preferred to play hockey rather than play indoors with dolls. Her family was into ranching and the oil industry, but Laureen always loved words. That was what attracted her to take courses in journalism at the Southern Alberta Institute of Technology. When she found she didn't have the gift, she switched to a major in photography. There she discovered she was a natural and soon also became a whiz with computers. She found her passion when she went to work for a printing company: she was fascinated by the printing press and what it could do. She would go early in the morning and stay until late at night. "I couldn't get over being paid for working at something I loved." Some years later she would establish her own consulting business in computerized graphics.

The impression she left was that of an outgoing woman, confident, with an unusually high energy level, candid, just as spontaneous as Stephen was reflective and introverted – someone who loved to laugh and to provoke by sallies that could sometimes be politically incorrect. Asked how she came to meet Stephen, she rejected the saying, "If you want to meet a man, join a church." Instead, she offered: "If you want to meet a man, join a political party." Then she cautioned herself, "I must be good." But she added that it was not love at first sight between her and Stephen. Love came gradually. Shortly after that first lunch with Stephen and Cynthia, Laureen offered to help him with the charts and graphs that he needed for his master's thesis. She noticed that he often came by to ask her for inconsequential changes and then stayed for dinner.

Indeed, Stephen Harper's thesis had been dragging on. He had received his first degree in 1985, but the completion of his master's degree had been constantly interrupted by politics. Apart from the two years in Ottawa as assistant to Jim Hawkes, then, as a Reformer, to Deborah Grey, he'd been absorbed with the formulation of party policy, with making speeches to groups large and small, with campaigning in the

1988 elections and, on top of that, with teaching part-time. He was still living the spartan life of a graduate student, sharing an apartment with his brother Grant. Laureen recalled that, when she met him, all he had to wear day in and day out were the same two suits. He had had to receive extensions from the economics department as he requested more time to complete the thesis. But, at last, in September 1991, it was finished.

His topic sprang from his combination of interest in the economy and in politics, and in their intersection. As a disciple of Hayek, he was skeptical of the Keynesian policy of government intervention in the economy to counter economic cycles. Furthermore, he suspected that the fiscal decisions of Canadian governments after 1945 would reflect the cycle of their electoral interests more than the cycle of economic growth and recession.

In perfect theory, if Keynes were consistently and effectively applied, each annual federal budget would show a surplus corresponding in size to the growth of the economy, and show an equivalent deficit each time the economy contracted. In the long run, the national debt would remain more or less constant, at a relatively low percentage of the gross national product. In fact, in charting the rise and fall of federal budget surpluses and deficits against the growth and contraction of the economy, he found a rather feeble relationship between them. Keynes's counter-cyclical policies were more preached than practised. Or, if there had been attempts to practise them, they'd missed their target. "The record indicates that particularly activist Keynesian policy has been rare in the post-war period. The results indicate that it should remain so."

But what about the prediction that federal spending would correspond more to the timing of elections than to the swings in the economy? Harper found some evidence of it, but not such that he could demonstrate it over the entire post-war period. And so he reached this conclusion: "While the electoral factor represents a major constraint upon the practice of appropriate fiscal policy, the results tend not to support the premise of deliberate electoral engineering predicted by theory." In other words, governments had not, in general, manipulated their pre-election spending as crassly for electoral gain as his theory had predicted. That was a setback for his theory. But he did learn powerful lessons about how governments made their budget decisions, and how that related to the performance of the economy. This knowledge might serve him in the future in the real world of politics. He was now not only an economist, but a political economist.

His attitude toward a career in politics gradually changed. The Reform Party was increasingly calling on him to go out and give speeches. Some of his speeches were taped and sent to meetings of Reformers across the province. He came to realize that his speaking style was too academic and he set about improving his delivery. He accepted the now frequent invitations for him to act as master of ceremonies at public events. He was soon in demand at weddings, notably the marriage of his close friend and confidant, John Weissenberger, to Angela Tu. It was, in fact, through Stephen that John met Angela while all three were graduate students at the University of Calgary. "There was a dearth of eligible women in Geology," recalls Weissenberger. "Angela shared an office with Stephen. They were both doing their master's degree in economics, and Stephen thought that Angela and I might be compatible because we both had travelled extensively in Europe and liked to listen to classical music. So, in the summer of 1987, he set up a coffee date for the three of us and then bowed out at the last minute." They were married on May 12, 1990, with Harper their master of ceremonies for the reception.

These were exhilarating times for the Reform Party, even as Canada went through the most dangerous challenge ever to its existence as one country. On that evening of Friday, June 22, 1990, when the Meech Lake Accord collapsed, Quebec entered into a pre-revolutionary state of anger, defiance, nationalist exaltation, and a fierce determination to define and pursue its own future outside the trammels of the Constitution of Canada. On that historic night, in Quebec's National Assembly, the separatist leader of the Opposition, Jacques Parizeau, held out his hand to Premier Bourassa, offering to join him in a sacred national union, excluding *les autres*, to decide Quebec's future: "Since, tonight, we find ourselves *entre nous* [within the family], let's simply accept that we are able to meet together *entre nous*, and discuss *entre nous*, not with all kinds of other people, *entre nous*, about our future and about what we must do." Premier Bourassa had answered with an echo of Charles de Gaulle's call from the balcony of Montreal's city hall, in 1967, "English Canada must understand very clearly that, no matter what anyone else says or does, Quebec is today and forever a distinct society, free and able to take on its destiny and its development."

The premier's defiant statement sounded like the prelude to a declaration of independence. And, in the streets of Montreal, the crowds, parading on June 24 to celebrate the traditional Saint-Jean-Baptiste holiday, carried a phalanx of Quebec flags and signs with separatist slogans. The old cries that had been silenced after the 1980 referendum were heard again: "*Le Québec aux Québécois!*" and "*On veut notre pays*" and, rhythmically, "*In-dé-pen-dance!*" It was a living, shouting paradox. Both Robert Bourassa and Brian Mulroney had claimed that Meech Lake was the answer to the old question, "What does Quebec want?" But the crowds demonstrating in the streets showed no sign of sadness, grievous loss, or disappointment. On the contrary, the mood was one of exultation and defiance. Out with the tedious, endless, inconclusive constitutional negotiations of the past thirty years. Now was the time, now the opportunity, for decisive action – "*Le Québec aux Québécois!*"

Premier Bourassa followed up by establishing a Commission on the Political and Constitutional Future of Quebec, popularly called the Bélanger-Campeau Commission after its two co-chairs, banker Marcel Bélanger and Jean Campeau, a former civil servant who headed the province's pension fund. At its first public meeting, Bélanger spoke as though Quebec were no longer bound by the Constitution of Canada: "Following the failure of the Meech Lake Accord, the political and constitutional status of Quebec will be determined by Quebeckers. Quebec will decide its own future."

Even before Meech failed, Bourassa had requested his party's policy committee, chaired by lawyer Jean Allaire, to begin preparing a constitutional policy to be submitted to the party convention in March 1991. By early 1991, both bodies had submitted their reports and both recommended that Quebec hold a referendum on secession no later than the following year. And so in May 1991, the Bourassa government introduced the legislation recommended by both the Allaire committee and the Bélanger-Campeau Commission. Bill 150 stated: "The Government of Quebec will hold a referendum on Quebec's sovereignty between June 8 and June 22, 1992, or between Oct. 12 and October 26, 1992. The result of the referendum will have the effect, if it is favourable to sovereignty, of proposing that Quebec acquire the status of a sovereign state exactly one year from the date that it is held." The bill assumed that Quebec was free to make whatever choice of a future it wanted, irrespective of the Constitution of Canada. "Quebeckers are free to choose their own destiny, to determine their political status, and to ensure their economic, social, and cultural development." The bill prescribed setting up two committees of the National Assembly, one to explore all facets of Quebec's accession to sovereignty, the other to study any offers that might come from the government of Canada for "a new partnership of a constitutional nature."

Quebec was aggressively making plans for a future of its own while the government of Canada seemed paralyzed. Prime Minister Mulroney was now a hostage to the separatists he had recruited to run for his party in 1984. If he took a strong stand against secession, many of his Quebec MPs would surely defect to Lucien Bouchard's recently founded Bloc Québécois. His government would fall. And so he played for time and appointed several study groups rather than take action.

The Reform Party, while secessionist fever raged in Quebec, carried an unusual responsibility to speak for Canada. It was a call that Manning had long been anticipating, especially as the Meech Lake Accord approached its fate. Frank Dabbs, Manning's biographer, recorded his concerns: "It was now clear that if the Meech Lake Constitutional Amendment was enacted, it could destroy the country in terms of the West. B.C. certainly and Alberta probably were just one charismatic leader away from a secessionist movement, Manning began to tell others." But the approaching crisis also presented opportunities. Manning had embarked on the venture of founding Reform in 1987 because the West was mistreated and because the federal government, under both Liberals and PCs, had been profligate. Three years later, the stakes were much higher. This was the time and place for Manning to fulfill the destiny which he had long felt awaited him. "Throughout much of my life, I have found myself 'preparing' for something that lies ahead, something my personal intuition anticipates," Manning wrote in his autobiography of 2002, *Think Big: My Adventures in Life and Democracy*. "For example, I became convinced many years ago that the West would generate another new federal political party, and thus began to prepare for that eventuality. I also became convinced that coping with secession threats to national unity would be the greatest challenge facing federal politicians in Canada in the latter part of the twentieth century, and I became a lifelong student of that subject."

Now, with tensions mounting across the country almost by the day, the central issue facing the party was no longer defending the West, it was saving the country. That imperative displaced Reform's former priorities. Policy development, Harper's first responsibility as chief policy officer, had to be concentrated now on formulating a clear, workable alternative to the establishment's disastrous venture into nation-building. The new policy must be consistent with Reform's founding principles, but it must also be national in vision; it must be a policy that could be defended credibly in every part of the country. And there was a natural deadline for such a policy: the next biennial assembly of the Reform Party, scheduled for April 1991, in Saskatoon.

———————

The Reformers arrived in Saskatoon with a sense of mission. The three established political parties had discredited themselves by a leadership that had brought the nation to the brink. Only Reform, on the federal scene, had retained, even much increased, its credibility. Its perceived pertinence was attested by the flock of journalists from across the country who, for the first time, converged on Saskatoon to cover a Reform convention. The Reform Party now mattered nationally. It had, in this sense arrived.

The second day was devoted to policy and Stephen Harper opened the morning session with a major speech. He titled it "The Reform Vision of Canada." His tone was sombre. "As you review the policy and other business of this assembly, you should keep in mind at all times the political situation in which we find ourselves," he began, to a hushed hall. "It is not necessary to tell you that Canada is today in a state of crisis. There is a crisis in the economy, a crisis of public confidence in our political institutions, and a crisis in the finances and operations of government itself. Of all the crises we face, however, the one most likely to be the focus of the next election concerns the very viability of Canada as a nation and, specifically, the constitutional arrangements under which Canadians live, and by which they govern themselves."

Harper's speech was sober, analytical, precise. He took for granted that there must be substantial change in the near future in the constitutional structure of the federation. He attempted to define what was possible and desirable, what was impossible or unacceptable. Whereas Manning's speech to the convention would be radical – he would invite his audience to define and help create "New Canada," which had the latent resonance of "New Canaan," the Promised Land of the Bible – Harper's speech was fundamentally conservative. He did not evoke "New Canada" but rather sought to locate, given the crisis and the need for action, the inner and outer limits of desirable change to the existing Canada. "In outlining our approach, it is first necessary to look at those positions that Canadians do not want us to take," Harper said as he began his analysis of the situation. "These are positions that, in our view, simply do not carry the judgment of the mass of ordinary Canadians in large parts of the country and for good reason."

He rejected the constitutional status quo, and maintained that the West, like Quebec, wanted change. But he rejected any form of special status for Quebec, or the alternative of a massive devolution of powers to all the provinces. He also rejected trying to build Canada on the foundations of two official languages: "These are the pet projects of a political priesthood. Will all three major parties admit that their linguistic and cultural policies are not the essence of Canada?" He warned against inserting in the Constitution all the pet projects and transient partisan visions of the politicians. The Constitution must be beyond the *plat du jour*. "Canadians do not want a Constitution built around the ideology of the Left or the Right. Issues of free enterprise as opposed to socialism, or big government as opposed to small government, should be decided by elections and by the normal legislative process." And finally, he rejected any process of executive federalism like that which produced the Meech Lake Accord: "Will the three major federal parties agree that no major change in the terms of Confederation should take place without the consent of the public?"

After defining what he found unacceptable, Harper then presented the principles on which, he proposed, the country's future should be built. His first principle brought the Reformers to their feet, cheering: "*Reformers want a strong country built by those who want in.*" Yes! Yes! Harper had articulated in eleven words what most Reformers rejected:

the persistent policy of rewarding those who threatened to break up the country. Manning, in *The New Canada*, noted: "At this point [Harper] was interrupted by such strong applause that it took several minutes to restore order."

Then Harper went on, "For nearly thirty years, political elites have pursued constitutional change on the premise that Canada must accommodate those who wish to divide it in order to stay together. Canadians are rejecting that premise. A country must be built on its strengths. At this point in our history, that means starting to build a constitutional consensus among the nine provinces and the two territories that have a deep commitment to Canada as one nation. The government of Quebec says it wants to know what the rest of Canada wants. This request must be answered."

At the previous assembly in Edmonton in 1989, Harper and Stan Waters had pushed Manning to take a firmer stand on appeasing Quebec. Quebec must accept some fundamental shared values if it were to function as an integral part of the federation. Manning's "House Divided" speech had shocked many. But now, given the Allaire and the Bélanger-Campeau reports, a great number of Canadians had reached the same conclusion. Quebec's price for remaining in the federation, as proposed in those reports, was simply beyond what the country should be willing to pay.

"Reformers want a genuinely federal system, including a strong national government with strong regional representation, and strong provinces to protect cultural identity and regional character," Harper articulated as his second fundamental principle. Strong provinces should appeal to Quebec's conservatism. Strong regional representation meant something like the Triple-E Senate, which would appeal to the West. "At the same time, it is the proper role of the provinces to protect those things that make them distinct. All provinces must control their own jurisdictions without federal interference, and all provinces must have equal legislative authority."

From the start, Harper had opposed the invasion of provincial jurisdiction by federal governments using the spending power to bribe or bully the provinces into a forced consent to these intrusions. Harper extended the principle to matters of language and culture. "Most importantly, we would propose that, subject to the Charter of Rights, jurisdiction for matters of language and culture should rest with the provinces. This could be extended to include provincial jurisdiction even in the language of federal administration in the provinces."

He pleaded for a division of power in a reformed Constitution that was based on functional criteria rather than the demands of Quebec: "Reformers want a division of powers designed to fulfill the needs that Canadians share, including the need for a competitive economy, a responsible community, and a sustainable environment. The mission of Canada is not to create a nation built on divisive issues like ethnicity or ideology."

His final principle, indispensable for a true Reformer, called for democratic reform, including reform of the House of Commons to give all legislators more authority, and greater use of direct democracy to elicit popular consent. "Canadians want legislative federalism, not executive federalism, as an essential element of any genuinely national government," Harper went on. He asked for a return to the original intent of the federation, which was for the legislators to make the laws, not for the prime minister to impose them by fiat. And the people must also have their say. "No new constitutional deal and no new arrangement with the government of Quebec will be accepted by us but by demonstrated popular consent, either by an election or, preferably, by a constitutional referendum law requiring the popular ratification of constitutional change."

It was a big speech, very substantial. If one were to search for the most accurate expression of Harper's fundamental political vision for Canada, it is to be found in this speech, along with his memo to Manning of March 10, 1989. The speech demonstrated the thoughtful, cautious, complex, conservative but still moderate cast of his approach to politics in a situation of crisis. He did not indulge in flights of oratory; he did not let himself be carried away into demagogy. On the contrary, he warned that Reformers, at this critical stage for the country and with federal elections expected in the following year, must exercise self-discipline, moderation, and solidarity once policies had been voted on by the party. "We will be asked whether the Reform Party's agenda is free from extremism, especially on issues like language and immigration. . . . We must oppose not only the Trudeau–Mulroney version of legislated national bilingualism, but also so-called English rights groups that advocate legislating one national language. Likewise, when we say we need major reforms to the criteria, the levels and abuse in immigration, as we do, we must also distance ourselves from those who are really focused on the race or ethnic background of immigrants. Do not allow the Party to be shot in the foot on these issues by radical elements, as has happened far too often to new parties." His words would prove prophetic.

There was one moment during the assembly that the delegates were to remember with particular emotion. On the last day, they debated a proposal to expand the Reform Party east of the Manitoba border by creating constituency associations and running candidates there in federal elections. Harper seconded the motion and it carried, subject only to ratification by the membership. In these circumstances of a national crisis, the move east into Ontario and the Atlantic provinces took on a special meaning. It was a form of national reconciliation for the Reformers; they were creating new bonds of solidarity with Canadians from other provinces. John Weissenberger remembers that moment. "I can get very emotional about it even today. It was an incident that I'll never forget for the rest of my life. We came down to the vote, the vote carried, and the mood of the room was just buoyant and positive. We were very idealistic and thought that things could change for the better. And someone spontaneously started singing "O Canada," and within seconds everyone was on their feet singing "O Canada." It signalled that we were not a party of division; we wanted to build across the country. It wasn't forced; it was absolutely spontaneous. It meant, give Canada a chance."

Such was the euphoria of Reform's senior strategists, coming off the highly successful convention, that they began planning to form a minority government in Ottawa within about five years. Key to the new optimism was the party's very rapid expansion in Ontario, which had already begun under Harper's auspices before the enabling policy was officially adopted.

The party's new stature meant that Harper was now much more often in the public eye, kept busy responding to the many attacks directed against Reform now that it could no longer be ignored. At the Saskatoon assembly, the party had adopted a new policy with respect to aboriginals. It immediately came under attack as racist or worse. An Alberta aboriginal who had previously been president of the Indian Association of Alberta, Roy Louis, warned of what would happen if Reform formed the

government: "I think the native people should be in fear," he told the
Red Deer Advocate. "I think we would see apartheid." Harper countered: "I think it's just rubbish." At their convention, the Reformers
voted that "The Reform Party supports the establishment of a new relationship with aboriginal peoples beginning with a constitutional convention of aboriginal representatives to consider their position on such
matters as the nature of aboriginal rights, the relationship between aboriginal peoples and the various levels of government, and how to reduce
the economic dependence of aboriginal peoples on the federal government and the Department of Indian Affairs." The policy supported a
transfer of responsibility for aboriginals from the Department of Indian
Affairs to "accountable agencies run by and responsible to aboriginal
peoples and the replacement of the current economic state of aboriginal peoples by their full participation in Canada's economic life and
achievement of a state of self-reliance." It was rather the opposite of
apartheid. The Reform policy also supported "the early and mutually
satisfactory conclusion of outstanding land-claim negotiations." But it
did not propose native self-government that would mean sovereignty.
Harper explained that Reform would not advocate Indian self-rule until
there was a widely accepted definition of its meaning. "One of our concerns is it would raise problems similar to apartheid by having a racially
segregated government."

A similar attack was made a few months later by Sheila Copps, deputy
leader of the Liberal Party of Canada. Speaking in Edmonton, she accused
the Reform Party of preaching an "Anglo-Saxon, single integrated
culture" which she compared to "Aryan philosophies." She said that
Preston Manning was "as insidious and devastating" as Lucien Bouchard.
Harper again was called to the rescue. "I find it funny that she criticizes
us for promoting separatism," he replied. "When the party says we want
to find things that bind Canadians together, she accuses us of promoting
too much unity in some kind of hidden Anglo-Saxon, racist agenda. The
party is against political agendas based on race, language, and culture,
which [are promoted] through the current multiculturalism program."

In May 1992, Harper was called on to reply to a slur from the prime
minister himself. Mulroney, in speaking to a group of high-school students in Williams Lake, B.C., told them to remember the recent Los
Angeles riots when "people talk to you in code, trying to convey messages

of hate, trying to convey messages of division, trying to ask you to hate when you should be asked to love one another as fellow Canadians." In Los Angeles, there had been looting and widespread fires after four policemen were acquitted even after being videotaped beating a black man, Rodney King. According to the *Calgary Herald*, "Mulroney said the Conservatives are appealing to good nature while others have policies promoting bigotry. Although he didn't name the Reform Party during his three-day visit to the B.C. interior, some critics have described Reform's stance on immigration as racist." The *Herald* recorded Harper's reaction. "For any Canadian politician to try to score political points from racial violence, particularly in another country, is really disgusting. These people are so out of touch that they ignore legitimate concerns while just dismissing the Reform Party as being socially abhorrent."

The Quebec government had set an ultimatum: the rest of Canada must make acceptable guaranteed "offers" to Quebec on restructuring the federation, otherwise Quebec would hold a referendum on secession in 1992. Mulroney put Joe Clark in charge of travelling the country to see what "offers" could be worked out. Clark went to meet Premier Bourassa, who had refused since the failure of Meech to take part in any negotiations on the Constitution. He wanted the offers delivered on a platter. But they did talk, and Clark emerged to say: "I think the great challenge that we're facing is to try to find a way to express the reality that Quebec is a distinct society in a fashion that is acceptable to others in the country." Meech is dead, long live Meech!

Joe Clark clearly thought that the way to get a good constitutional agreement was to flatter Quebec nationalism. In Quebec City, Clark said: "I'm trying to find a way to establish a Canadian pride similar to Québécois pride." The week before, speaking to the Empire Club in Toronto, Clark held up Quebec as the model for Canada. "Part of the challenge for all of us is to achieve in the whole of Canada the kind of transformation that was triggered in Quebec by the Quiet Revolution."

On September 24, 1991, Joe Clark's committee made public the government's package of draft suggestions – for discussion – which had the title *Shaping Canada's Future Together: Proposals*. Mulroney appointed a peripatetic body, the Special Joint Committee on a Renewed Canada, to shop the proposals around the country and then produce a report. But since too few members of the public answered the invitation to appear before the committee, it held five huge televised conferences, a kind of travelling circus of Canadian political performers, who struck their tent in different cities across the country, from Halifax to Vancouver, with stops in Calgary, Toronto, and Montreal. A different theme of constitutional renewal was discussed in each. In addition to politicians and the swarm of the media, most of those attending represented well-known interest groups. There were also a few "ordinary Canadians" selected randomly from among all those who applied. Never in the history of Canada had such a witch's brew of politics, showmanship, and concern for the future of one's country been concocted.

Harper went to all five of the meetings, representing the Reform Party. But, apart from constantly defending the Triple-E Senate as an essential ingredient in any new Constitution, Harper and Reform played a relatively minor role. These were the elites gathering together to articulate out loud all the pieties of the elite consensus – one that left out in the cold the Reform Party and most Canadians.

The committee reported in February 1992. This became the starting point for another travelling round of consultations and negotiations. Quebec continued its boycott, waiting for the "offers" to be made in due time, before the referendum scheduled to be held on October 26, 1992.

Joe Clark met for the better part of five days with nine premiers in the attempt to reach an agreement on the package. The deal breaker had been the issue of reforming the Senate. Finally on July 7 came the breakthrough: Clark and the nine premiers agreed on what was considered something like a two and one-half–E Senate: the senators would be elected, and there would be an equal eight senators from each province. A super-majority in the Senate would be required to block a bill from the Commons. A simple majority vote would not be enough, because the bigger provinces feared that the smaller provinces could muster a majority in the Senate that represented only 17 per cent of Canada's population. For Quebec, the agreement meant its historic twenty-four senators would fall in number to eight: quite a loss of power. Quebec, with almost 25 per cent of the population, would hold 9 per cent of the Senate's voting power.

According to the agreement, Quebec would be recognized as a distinct society, with a mandate to promote its distinct identity. But this would be balanced by the vested requirement that English minorities in

Gov't under MULRONY 1992.

Quebec and French in the rest of Canada would also be promoted – something Quebec had refused in 1990. In the wording of the agreement, the Charter of Rights and Freedoms was to be interpreted "in a manner consistent with the preservation and promotion of Quebec as a distinct society within Canada and the vitality and development of the language and culture of French-speaking and English-speaking minority communities throughout Canada."

And Quebec would get a veto over any constitutional change to Canada's central institutions of government, a guarantee of three judges on the Supreme Court of Canada, and guaranteed control over future immigration to Quebec. Aboriginal people were to have a right to self-government declared "inherent." And the agreement contained the NDP's cherished "Social Charter" of rights.

When the announcement of Clark's breakthrough agreement was made late in the evening of July 7, there was a sense at Reform headquarters that the party's reaction would be critical for the party's future. This was a time when the country must make a momentous choice. Reform must get it right. But Preston Manning was nowhere to be found. He had disappeared, as he did periodically, was incommunicado. His staff didn't know where to reach him, and he did not phone in. What was to be done?

By the standard of Harper's speech in Saskatoon, the agreement was unacceptable. It recognized Quebec as a distinct society; it conferred distinct rights on some languages and cultures but not others; it recognized an undefined aboriginal self-government. And the Senate proposal was not an unqualified Triple-E. But Harper nevertheless drew up a news release on Wednesday, July 8, that expressed his qualified encouragement for what had been accomplished so far – with more remaining to be done before the agreement was final. "Reform Party Encouraged by Premiers' Agreement" was the headline of the communiqué. And it began on a positive note: "The Reform Party today expressed cautious optimism for a constitutional agreement negotiated late Tuesday night by Canada's premiers, but reiterated that no constitutional reform plan should pass without a binding national referendum. 'The provisions for a reformed Senate appear to be a significant step in the right direction. Although there is not quite a Triple-E Senate – elected, effective and equal – the premiers have gone much of the distance toward such an institution. We think the majority of Canadians will agree with that,' said Stephen Harper, the party's chief policy advisor."

According to George Koch, who had been Ottawa correspondent for *Alberta Report* but was now back in Calgary headquarters working as Manning's speechwriter, "Harper, showing his smarts, sensed that this would never stand. So he thought, 'It had a two and a half–E Senate that was very, very close. It was the closest anybody ever came to what Alberta wanted on the Senate. It was almost there.' And so he decided to say some really positive things about it. I think he realized it was a no-lose approach because, if it went through, at least you've signed on to something that's pretty good; and if it doesn't go through, then your criticisms later will sound more credible and more reasonable. One of the things that irritated him at the time was that Manning was nowhere to be found. He was somewhere off in the hills riding a horse and fishing and would not respond. So Harper had to carry the ball on that one."

The communiqué ended with the hope that the prime minister would accept the terms negotiated and put the package to the people in a referendum. " 'What we're asking for is a democratic, yes or no, binding, nationwide vote on the actual content of the agreement,' Harper said. 'It's our sincere hope that what we see in the final agreement is good for Canada. This will allow us to get on with other things,' Harper said. 'The big tests will be whether the Quebec government and the Quebec federal Conservatives endorse the package and whether the federal government submits the deal to a binding referendum,' Harper said."

Harper had certainly gone out on a limb, taking a strongly articulated position in the name of the party. As chief policy officer, he was one of two people authorized to speak for the party. But this was a critical moment. Harper judged that the need to give an early signal to Reform followers and to the public required that he act and not wait for the leader to reappear – no one knew when that would be. He sometimes disappeared for weeks.

Harper left himself one opening for a change of posture if Manning were to be unhappy with the communiqué after his return, or if new developments occurred. The communiqué stated: "Harper said the Reform Party has not yet seen the details of the package, and will offer a fuller assessment once party officials have viewed the fine print. The party will also consult its membership, Harper added."

Mulroney, who was travelling in Europe, wasted no time to show that he was more taken by surprise than impressed with the agreement. He understood immediately that Quebec – which clung to every scrap of power and always reached for more – would not accept such a drastic loss of influence in the Senate. Bourassa's reaction was noncommittal: he would study the package. But in Quebec, the deal announced triumphantly on July 7 remained an orphan. No one claimed the child.

And so the travelling across the country resumed. The negotiations in all the capitals were on again, this time out of the public eye. Twice Mulroney summoned the premiers to meet with him at Harrington Lake for less formal discussions. Premier Bourassa had now joined the talks at last. An official First Ministers' conference was held in Ottawa from August 18 to 21. Then they all met again for two days in Charlottetown and there, pressed by Bourassa's ultimatum that a referendum would be held on October 26, and that two months' notice were required to study the proposals, the First Ministers finally announced an agreement on August 28.

The Charlottetown agreement precipitated a crisis in the leadership of the Reform Party. It was much less satisfactory than had been the tentative agreement of July 7. In fact, the proposed powers of the reformed Senate had already been watered down when the First Ministers met in Ottawa from August 18 to 21. And Reform had issued a communiqué on August 20 in which both Manning and Harper were quoted, although it seems to have been written by Harper: "Senate Deal Is No Deal: Reform Party" was the headline. " 'This Senate could defeat a bill pertaining to natural resource taxation by a vote of 50 per cent plus one senator,' said Manning. 'But if the Senate defeats any other bill, no matter how offensive that bill may be to the regions, that decision can be simply overridden by a joint session of the Senate and the House of Commons, in which Quebec and Ontario each have more votes than the entire Senate.'

"Stephen Harper, chief of policy for the Reform Party of Canada, said in Calgary that . . . the tradeoffs made by premiers during the First Ministers' conference were unacceptable. 'Essentially what we have is equality of representation in a Senate that has power over natural resources taxation. The tradeoff for that is a Senate that lacks powers over anything else,' Harper said."

The final deal struck in Charlottetown would have guaranteed to Quebec in perpetuity 25 per cent of all seats in the Commons. The fast growing provinces of Alberta and British Columbia would be deprived forever of a political weight even approaching the number of their citizens. So, from the start, it seemed evident to Harper that Reform must denounce the deal and fight it in the forthcoming national referendum. But Manning was hesitant. He was holding back.

The meeting to discuss the party's strategy involved Manning, Stephen Harper, Tom Flanagan, Ron Wood – a former journalist who had become a Manning adviser – George Koch, and Koch's companion, Laurie Watson, whose title was manager of communications. As Koch recalls, the discussion soon became heated. "Our underlying assumption is that it's obvious that we're going to be against the deal. So Manning starts musing in this kind of technocratic, abstract way, 'Well, what if we endorsed it? What if there was a Two-E Senate and we used that to block Mulroney's legislation?' and so on. And gradually, it's dawning on us that this isn't just a little preamble to get warmed up, he actually wants to seriously talk about whether or not we should even oppose this thing. And I could see Ron Wood: he was just shaking his head and was puzzled and maybe dismayed. Flanagan, he also keeps his emotions pretty close to his vest, but it threw him for a loop. And Harper – I can't really remember the look on his face, but I just remember Laurie and I were both sort of apoplectic. And so a big argument ensued, and it really was Manning against everyone else. He really dug in his heels, and the meeting ended without Manning's committing to oppose Charlottetown." Then Manning left with his family for a planned week of holidays.

That meeting left a rift between Manning and Harper that would become wider in the course of the referendum campaign. As Tom Flanagan describes the meeting in *Waiting for the Wave*, "Manning did not actually favour the Charlottetown Accord, but neither was he interested in leading a struggle against it. At that stage, he wanted the party to remain neutral, to run an information campaign and comment critically on some features of the deal, but not to oppose it as such."

There he parted company with all his staff, including especially Harper. They all felt that their past policy resolutions, as set down in the Blue Book of "Principles and Policies" required the same position that the party had taken toward Meech Lake: unqualified opposition. And so they were upset at Manning's obvious ambivalence. Tom Flanagan described the scene: "Watson and Koch were visibly upset at what they saw as a betrayal of Reform. Harper was calmer but equally opposed, and made it clear that he would oppose the accord no matter what happened. In the end, Manning agreed that we would take steps to consult members of the Reform Party and postpone any decision until he returned from holidays."

What had happened? At the Saskatoon assembly, Manning had given one of his great speeches in which he insisted that, like Quebec, the rest of Canada had to define its own constitutional future through a series of constitutional conventions. He had positioned himself as the voice of English-speaking Canada, able to negotiate with a secessionist Quebec because, unlike the parties of Brian Mulroney and Jean Chrétien, he had no stake in Quebec and so no conflict of interest. For them to be the negotiators, it would be "Quebec negotiating with Quebec."

But in 1992, as Flanagan observed, Manning had been backing away from that position. "What happened that morning [at the meeting] capped a trend in Manning's thinking on the Constitution that had been growing for almost a year. He had said surprisingly little in public about the Constitution during 1992. At least since April of that year, Rick Anderson had been advising him not to fight a constitutional agreement but rather 'to move the agenda along quickly' to the rest of the 'New Canada' agenda of parliamentary, fiscal, and economic reform."

Rick Anderson had appeared and was the new major influence on Manning's thinking and strategy. A long-time political strategist with the Liberal Party of Canada and the Liberal Party of Ontario, at the time of his first encounter with Manning Anderson was manager of the Ottawa office of the public relations consulting firm Hill & Knowlton. Anderson had broken with the federal Liberals and joined the Reform Party. But his views were very different from those of Harper. As Flanagan explained: "Perhaps because he had grown up in Montreal, keeping Quebec happy has a priority for him that it does not have for most Reformers. As early as April 1992, he advised Manning not to oppose any constitutional deal that might be forthcoming because, he said, 'the country is bone-tired of the constitutional process.' Anderson also has little objection to official bilingualism in its present form, and he advised Manning to dissociate himself from the criticism of bilingualism that Alberta premier Don

Getty made in January 1991. Most importantly, Anderson rejected the strategy of The Party of the Right. In his view, 'Canadian voters are ideological only in the broadest sense; they eschew ideological purity and prefer practicality on virtually all specific issues.'"

Rick Anderson was the antithesis of Stephen Harper. He was, above all, an expert at playing the game of politics and advising political clients. His growing influence over Manning went back to a debate within the party: Should they become more professional in their approach to politics? As early as the November 12, 1990, issue of *Alberta Report*, a major story by Kenneth Whyte had been titled: "Filling a vacuum: The RPC is short of organizational expertise." Whatever appeared in *Alberta Report* had great influence on Manning and the other leaders, because *Alberta Report* was enthusiastically supportive, almost alone in that category.

"Reform's upper echelon is conspicuously short on professional political experience; none of its chief organizers has held public office and none has experience in national campaigns aside from the RPC's run in 1988," Whyte wrote. "It has been operating without first-rate polling, public relations, and fundraising services – the professionals who tell candidates how to speak, dress, deliver a line, avoid or address an issue, seize a photo opportunity, and plead for money. Nor does it have access to the extensive research budgets and parliamentary resources enjoyed by its established competitors."

Whyte had interviewed Harper for his article, and he quoted Harper's response to the criticism. "While acknowledging some organizational shortcomings, Mr. Harper says the strength of the RPC membership makes up for a lot of them. As for help at higher levels, Mr. Harper says the RPC is loath to start staffing itself with talent from other parties for fear of becoming indistinguishable from them. A party that professes to stand for political integrity and systemic reform, he says, doesn't want to pick up a bunch of slick 'old-line political hacks.'"

In 1991, after the breakthrough in Ontario, the Reform Party had started taking on political pros. Rick Anderson, engaged as a consultant in September 1991, was the one who emerged over time as Manning's chief strategist, displacing Stephen Harper.

This provides some background to the strategy meeting on the Charlottetown Accord. At headquarters, while Manning went off on vacation, preparatory work continued, as Koch relates. "One of Stephen's jobs was to do a detailed analysis of the deal, of what it actually meant. So he literally went off and he just thought for three days, like some Buddhist. He wouldn't talk to anyone on the phone. He just isolated himself and just spent the time thinking. And when he emerged, he emerged with what became the counter-strategy, which was that *this is no deal*. There are more than fifty things that still had to be negotiated. And some of them included things that would have to be altered in the Constitution. Others included multi-billion-dollar spending programs that would have to be agreed to by everyone, from interest groups to provincial governments. So basically, what he did was twofold. One was, by arguing that this wasn't actually a deal, he obviously made the parties to the deal look terribly incompetent and dishonest. And also, the Constitution fatigue factor – those people who would have signed on to it just because this was the end, thank God, those people would now become doubters. Because if this really isn't the end, if this is just the beginning of thirty more rounds of negotiations, then what's the point?"

Koch was assigned to poll members on their attitude to the Accord, and the response was overwhelmingly negative. Meanwhile, as the days and then more than two weeks went by, the news media and members wondered why it took so long for Reform to state where it stood on the Charlottetown Accord. Harper, though, did not wait for a signal from Manning before giving a strong indication to the news media of where he stood. In a Canadian Press story of August 23, the day after the announcement in Ottawa that the First Ministers and aboriginal leaders had reached an agreement in principle, Harper gave his initial reaction, criticizing it and predicting that Albertans would ultimately vote against it in a referendum.

A Canadian Press story on September 7, ten days after the announcement of agreement in Charlottetown, commented on the silence of Preston Manning: "The Reform Party, the only major political party that has yet to take a stand on the constitutional deal, is coming under increasing pressure from its members to mount a campaign to scuttle it. 'We continue to get a strong feeling that the vast majority of our people don't like the deal and feel it's worth fighting,' said Reform policy chief Stephen Harper. He acknowledged 'it would be difficult' to endorse the pact after such opposition. Leader Preston Manning, who has shown no reluctance in the past in commenting on Canada's constitutional malaise, is refusing to announce the party's position until next Thursday. 'We have grave reservations about it,' he said Friday. 'We are endeavouring to see if other people share those convictions and how can one communicate that in a way that is constructive and positive.'"

The article referred to explanations being mooted for Reform's delay in taking a stand. "Political observers say the party is being cautious because the constitutional deal has put Manning in a quandary. If he backs it, he risks alienating those attracted by the Reform's pro-English Canadian policies. If he opposes it, he will be labelled as anti-Canadian at a time he is trying to expand the Reform's national base. 'For many people, this will be seen as a vote for Canada,' said political scientist Keith Archer from the University of Calgary. 'It will be very difficult to oppose this on substantive grounds and at the same time say you're in favour of the country.'"

When the party finally went public with its stand, it followed the line of attack sketched out by Harper. He was interviewed extensively in English and French by news media from all parts of Canada. The party ran off tapes with an interview of Harper on one side and of Manning on the other. "If people believe that the deal is a step forward, they should vote for it. They should not expect perfection," Harper tells his interviewer. "But what we will argue is that this deal is worse than the status quo. It creates an economy that is weaker, it gives the regions less clout in Confederation, it creates a Parliament that is less democratic, it creates an amending formula that is more rigid, and, more than anything, it isn't even a final package. We have here something that is essentially an agreement to discuss constitutional matters in more than fifty areas. It enshrines a process of further constitutional negotiation. Well, our Constitution today may be flawed, but surely this is no reason to dump it for something that is completely undefined, and to start negotiating the Constitution for years to come. That's exactly what Canadians don't want. There are people who don't like it and are going to vote No, and there are people who don't like it and are going to vote Yes, because they think that Yes means that negotiations are over. And it's important to point out for that very reason that a Yes does not mean negotiations are over at all. If you read the agreement, a Yes means negotiations are beginning."

Premier Don Getty became incensed at one attack by Harper and Tom Flanagan against the deal he had negotiated and signed. Getty claimed that the deal on the Senate would prevent forever another National Energy Program because the deal would give the Senate a veto over taxing natural resources. Harper and Flanagan claimed that the veto of the Senate could be bypassed if a Commons bill put a tax on coal, natural gas, or oil to help pay for environmental protection. The Senate could prove to be toothless. A nettled Premier Getty accused the Reform Party of dragging the constitutional campaign into the mud. In his attack, he singled out Stephen Harper: "I mean, I was fighting for Alberta while he was still learning how to blow-dry his hair," said Getty, the former macho football player.

When the initial announcement of the Charlottetown deal was made, it was greeted with relief across the country, and polls taken soon afterward showed a majority in favour, even in Alberta and Quebec. Initially, the Reformers felt they were fighting in a losing cause. Angus Reid/Southam News published the first poll of the campaign on September 2. The poll found 61 per cent of Canadians outside Quebec would vote to accept the deal with only 20 per cent prepared to reject it and 18 per cent undecided. Even in Quebec, the Yes side led by 49 per cent to 38, with 13 per cent undecided. Columnist Geoffrey Stevens waxed enthusiastic in the *Gazette* on September 6 over the Yes side's "Dream Team" – the high-powered organizers from each of the three major parties who had combined. With them, Stevens said, the Yes side could hardly fail. "The Yes team does not have to defend the agreement as the best or most permanent of all possible constitutional deals," he enthused. "It has simply to invite the public to compare the Dream Team in Yes colours to the ragtag bunch on the No side and to conclude that the good guys' agreement is better than anything the bad guys can offer." And indeed, the Yes side, outside Quebec, had all the established political parties, all the beautiful people, the literati and the cognoscenti, the rich and the powerful. Almost every newspaper endorsed the Yes. Only the ragtags – Preston Manning, Stephen Harper, Judy Rebick, Bill VanderZalm – were for the No. The contrast of the two sides was on display on CTV's Question Period when Clark, a former prime minister, faced off against Deborah Coyne, a never-elected, thirty-seven-year-old

[handwritten annotation: TRUDEAU should reason in speaking out against the Charlottetown Accord]

constitutional lawyer, Clyde Wells's former adviser, who had organized the "ragtag bunch" for the No. And she wiped the floor with him.

But as time went on, as with Meech Lake, where Reform had taken an initially scorned position, support for the Yes softened. A turning point occurred on October 1 when Pierre Trudeau came out of retirement to attack the constitutional deal in a dinner-meeting speech at an incongruously named restaurant, *La maison du egg-roll*, in one of Montreal's slums. He began his dissection with the same theme that Harper had chosen. His message was that the Charlottetown agreement was not so much an agreement as a rough draft. It left a great number of questions unsettled. It featured twenty-six asterisks at different clauses to signal that this clause would require further discussion and a political solution.

But, above all, Trudeau's message was that the Charlottetown agreement placed collective rights above individual rights, weakened the Canadian Charter of Rights and Freedoms, and created a hierarchy of six different categories of citizen, with the lowest class encompassing most Canadians. It was a devastating demonstration of logic and legal analysis. Trudeau very effectively showed what kind of vision of society was projected in the Charlottetown agreement. It was one in which individuals were not equal, rights were not equal, and freedoms were subordinated to governments. His speech resonated across the country.

In early September, Manning made a decision to create a steering committee of six people to run both the referendum campaign and the election campaign expected to follow in 1993. It included Manning himself and Rick Anderson – but not Harper. As Flanagan relates. "Ostensibly, Manning had created the steering committee for reasons of efficiency, but the real reason obviously had more to do with his perceptions of loyalty and political orientation. By excluding Watson and me and not inviting Stephen Harper to participate, Manning was marginalizing the people who had really wanted to fight the referendum campaign and had helped develop the strategy for doing so. Now, the only strategist on the committee was Rick Anderson, who was in fact a Yes supporter."

Indeed, it became known in October that Rick Anderson, now Manning's chief strategist, was in favour of a Yes vote in the referendum, when he announced it to a journalist. Here is Flanagan's account of the impact: "The news hit the Reform Party's staff and activists like a mortar round, for all of us thought that Anderson was on our side as an active member of the steering committee. . . . Tempers flared as Manning, Fryers, and Shaw clung to Anderson. The few who knew the truth about Manning's early wavering on the referendum saw the Anderson affair as further evidence that Manning's populism, combined with Anderson's advice, was leading him to depart from the Reform agenda. This was the last straw for Stephen Harper. Although he decided to continue with his candidacy in Calgary West and not to raise a public challenge against Manning, he withdrew from national office activities. The whole affair, combined with the other events of the campaign, had a similar effect upon me. On October 14, I asked my department head at the university to arrange a return to full-time teaching effective January 1993."

Koch recalls the shock on the Reform staff when Rick Anderson came out publicly for the Charlottetown Accord. "Rick went public with his decision. And he talked about how his conscience wouldn't let him be against it. No one in the Reform Party would have cared if he had said, 'Preston, look, I can't fight this thing, I have a career to protect.' We wanted him out of the way. We didn't want his involvement one way or the other. Without a doubt, we didn't feel that he was a true Reformer. But it was Preston who kept thinking we needed his professionalism and his Ottawa experience."

Koch corroborates Flanagan's account that Harper was disillusioned by the entire experience of those weeks. He ceased taking part in the national campaign and concentrated instead on his own riding of Calgary West, where it was anticipated that he would again be a candidate. "I know that he seriously considered not even running. He was just giving up, just getting out altogether. So, at some point, he did resign as chief policy adviser and said, 'I'm just going to concentrate on my riding and becoming an MP.'"

Preston Manning, in his memoir *Think Big*, had a different perception of the event. He had, of course, read Flanagan's account of the meeting on the Constitutional Accord of 1992. Both accounts agree that Harper and others were from the start opposed to the Accord. Manning maintains that he was as well, but felt that a party of the grassroots owed it to the members to consult them before taking a public position. "In the end, this consultative approach stood us in good stead. Unfortunately, it also created tensions with two of my key policy advisers, Tom Flanagan and Stephen Harper. Tom and Stephen interpreted 'the delay' in attacking the Charlottetown Accord as a personal reluctance on my part to oppose it. This was not the case, but it would not be the first time that Tom and Stephen and I would differ on the extent to which we should involve the grassroots of the party in strategic decision making. At this point, I did not fully appreciate that, while Stephen was a strong Reformer with respect to our economic, fiscal, and constitutional positions, he had serious reservations about Reform's and my belief in the value of grassroots consultation and participation in key decisions and my conviction that the adjective to distinguish our particular brand of conservatism should be 'democratic.' "

On October 26, the Dream Team in Yes colours lost the referendum on the Charlottetown Accord. The Reform Party was on the winning side as the No side won 68.0 per cent of the referendum vote in British Columbia, 60.1 per cent in Alberta, 55.2 per cent in Saskatchewan, and 61.6 per cent in Manitoba. Clearly the West wanted out of that deal. In Quebec, the No vote was 55.4 per cent. It was 51.1 per cent in Nova Scotia. So six provinces – including Quebec – voted No.

The Yes vote was 62.4 per cent in Newfoundland, 73.6 per cent in Prince Edward Island, 61.3 per cent in New Brunswick. In Ontario, 49.8 per cent voted Yes and 49.6 per cent voted No. Ontario was evenly divided. Across the country, the Yes vote was 44.6 per cent, the No vote 54.4 per cent. Once again, against all early expectations, Reform was on the winning side. But now Reform had some internal battle scars.

Chapter 14

THE 1993 ELECTIONS

[handwritten margin notes: LIBERALS seats Oct 25 / 177 of the 295 seats / PROGRESSIVE Conservatives were virtually annihilated / 169 PC elected in 1988 / ONLY 2 were voted back in]

THE ELECTIONS OF October 25, 1993, were unprecedented. Never before had one of the two great parties governing Canada since 1867 been so crushed, discredited, humiliated, virtually annihilated. Of the 169 Progressive Conservatives who had been elected to Parliament in 1988, only one – Jean Charest – survived the hecatomb. A second member, Elsie Wayne, was a newcomer from Saint John, New Brunswick, where she was already a local celebrity. These two ghostly survivors of what had been a government were ten members short of the twelve required by the rules of the Commons to be recognized as a political party.

The New Democratic Party had elected forty-three members of Parliament in 1988, with 20.4 per cent of the national vote. As recently as January 1991, it had surged in the polls ahead of all the other parties under its new leader, Audrey McLaughlin. But on this fatal October 25, the NDP vote fell to 6.9 per cent, and it elected only nine MPs, three short of the requirement for recognition.

Quebec, through most of its history, had plumped for the party likely to form the government. Its MPs had governed with John A. Macdonald, Wilfrid Laurier, Mackenzie King, Louis Saint-Laurent, John Diefenbaker, Lester Pearson, Pierre Trudeau, and Brian Mulroney. But now Quebec had repudiated Jean Chrétien, her son who was about to become prime minister, to plump for Lucien Bouchard, her son who wanted to break Quebec away from Canada. The Bloc Québécois took fifty-four of Quebec's seventy-five seats, the Liberals nineteen, and there was one independent. As for the Progressive Conservatives, who had won sixty-three seats in 1988, they were cut down to one seat – that of Charest.

Chrétien would become prime minister with a comfortable majority, as the Liberals took 177 of the House's 295 seats. But the big news of that election day, along with the surge of the Bloc, was the breakthrough of the Reform Party. It had failed to capture a single seat in 1988. Now there would be fifty-two Reformers in Parliament, including one from Ontario. Reform had received 18.7 per cent of the national vote, compared to 41.3 per cent for the Liberals, 16 per cent for the PCs, and only 13.5 per cent for the Bloc. But the Bloc ended up with two more seats than Reform and so it formed the Official Opposition. The West was now in, but the Bloc Québécois was in further.

What this unprecedented Parliament would hold, no one could tell. Brian Mulroney had sown the wind; he had reaped the hurricane. And yet, as recently as the previous March, it seemed as though Mulroney would pass on the succession to Kim Campbell, who would restore Tory fortunes to their past glory. The country had grown profoundly distrustful of politicians. Campbell, like Preston Manning and Lucien Bouchard, seemed like an anti-politician's politician, and that was what the disillusioned country wanted. She suddenly burst into public consciousness as a fresh face, irreverent, bubbling with humour and candour. In a much-noted photograph, she held up before her the black lawyer's robe, behind which appeared her naked shoulders. It seemed to say: You see, the professional person is out front, but behind it lives a vulnerable, genuine woman. She'd been minister of justice, now she was minister of national defence – the first woman to occupy that post.

Few outside of her own circle knew where she stood on any of the great issues affecting the country. Yet she won the leadership in June and became at age forty-six the country's first female prime minister. There followed a summer's honeymoon with the public that made likely her victory in the coming election against the politician's politician, shopworn Jean Chrétien. In the Liberal caucus, many MPs predicted an imminent disaster and agitated for Chrétien to step down in favour of the rising Liberal star, Paul Martin. Chrétien called them "nervous nellies."

In the Reform Party the prospects were bleak. After the referendum on Charlottetown, the party went into decline in the opinion polls and its membership fell back for the first time. The earlier years of Reform had coincided with the great struggle over Canada's very identity, and the Reform Party had been almost alone in the epic battle against the Meech Lake and Charlottetown accords. But now, by a common consent, changing the Constitution seemed off the public agenda. Even Reform's fight for a Triple-E Senate to redress the balance of the federation had fallen into the background as, in 1992, the party called for a five-year moratorium on constitutional negotiations. Stephen Harper had explained it this way in an interview of September 1992, during the anti-Charlottetown campaign: "I think that the reality here is that the Reform Party is making a real concession, in adopting the policy of a constitutional moratorium. We're making that concession because the public is making clear to us that they'll not support further constitutional negotiations at this time. . . . It is a matter, I think, of bending to the public will. But we've made a sacrifice, and what we'll say to all politicians is, 'You have to be prepared to make the same sacrifice. You're going to have to give up your pet constitutional projects because the public is absolutely sick to death of this.'"

Early in the summer of 1993, Kim Campbell promised to eliminate the deficit in five years and proposed policies for curbing immigration. She left language policy largely to the provinces and, more generally, brought the Tory government to the right of the political spectrum. The need for a Reform Party was not as evident. Besides, Campbell was also from the West, and she offered a more scintillating personality than did the earnest Preston Manning.

The big policy thrust for Reform in anticipation of the elections was no longer the Triple-E Senate, it was the objective of curbing government spending and eliminating the deficit. As Manning recounts in *Think Big*: "On March 29, 1993, in Toronto, I unveiled our 'Zero in Three' plan. I began with the bad news. This year, the federal Conservatives would run a deficit of about $36 billion, their eighth in a row. Accumulated federal deficits had created a 'debt hole' $460 billion deep. If you wanted to get out of a hole, the first thing to do was to Stop Digging!"

He then described the plan to bring the deficit down to zero in three years, which was to prove Reform's salvation during the 1993 election campaign. What Manning did not acknowledge was the debt he owed to others in its construction. Herbert Grubel, one of the country's most distinguished economists, would be elected to the Commons as a Reform candidate in 1993. Seven years later, after having served one term in Parliament, he would publish his political memoirs under the title *A Professor in Parliament: Experiencing a Turbulent Parliament and Reform Party Caucus*. He, the economist with an international reputation, said this about Zero in Three: "One of the meetings of candidates in Calgary devoted considerable time to the discussion of the election platform. The economic policies had been worked out in some detail by a team under the leadership of Stephen Harper and the direction of Manning and Cliff Fryers, the Reform Party chairman. Harper has a strong background in economics and was studying for a master's when he entered politics a few years earlier. He was ably assisted by Dimitri Pantazopoulos, a young economist who, after the election, worked in the Reform Party research department for a year or so before leaving for greener pastures in Washington, D.C. The fiscal plans had obviously been given much thought and I found little to disagree with."

Harper, more than Manning, shaped the electoral platform, titled Zero in Three. It is significant that he had been secretly assisted by a group of officials in the Department of Finance in Ottawa, whom Harper had consulted when he was researching his thesis on federal budgets in the post–World War II period. Some finance officials, appalled at the Tory government's heedlessness in the face of spiralling debt, were only too happy to give him professional advice.

The federal budget of April 26, 1993, brought down by Don Mazankowski in the middle of the Tory leadership campaign, was the swan song of Brian Mulroney's nine years of government. If you looked past the rhetoric, the facts were chilling. Through seven years of steady economic growth, Mulroney had failed to eliminate the towering budget deficit. It was $35.5 billion in the year just ended, 1992–93. "Relative to the size of the economy, Canada is now by far the most indebted of the major industrial countries," the Department of Finance stated. "Further, Canada's net foreign liabilities reached a post-war record in 1992 – 43.8 per cent of gross domestic product. Its previous peak was 42 per cent in 1961." The federal debt had now reached $458.6 billion – more than twice what it was when Mulroney took office. The projection in the budget was that, by 1998, it would have ballooned to $563.2 billion. And that was the optimistic scenario, based on projections of good growth over the following five years.

The Tory budget offered the best possible contrast to Reform's Zero in Three plan. Reform put on a public relations blitz, sending a précis of Zero in Three to all its members and printing out the plan in bulk to be distributed by the Reform constituency associations. The plan received a respectful reception in the news media and among financial specialists in the private sector. For example, the *Calgary Herald* on May 9, 1993, ran this typical comment: " 'What the Reform Party is saying is what a lot of us have been saying for years. We expected the Tories to do all or some of these things eight years ago. When they tried, there was a great public outcry. Now there seems to be a mood that it's time to make tough decisions,' says Gordon Currie, president of the Calgary Society of Financial Analysts."

And so the stage was set for the 1993 elections. Manning relates that there was a disagreement over strategy: "Tom Flanagan was conscious of our low standing in the polls. Both he and Stephen Harper wanted us to focus most of our campaign revenues and activity in the West. The rest of us felt it was imperative that we run a bigger, more national campaign, in particular, one that included Ontario. . . . In the end, we decided to run a national campaign, which meant we needed a campaign director with national experience. Rick Anderson was the natural choice."

Harper would not agree. He did not consider Anderson a Reformer, and feared that Manning's populism combined with Anderson's pragmatism would move the party to the centre and away from the right. But Flanagan and Harper were both categorically conservative, and they saw the party's future as requiring it to establish itself clearly and permanently on the right.

Harper and Flanagan would have accepted Anderson in the role of expert adviser, but not as the party's top strategist. His appointment as campaign director caused a coolness between the party leaders. "I faxed Manning a letter saying that I strongly disapproved of the Anderson appointment and I would not refrain from criticism in the media," Flanagan wrote. "He responded by doing what he had to do if he was going to appoint Anderson: he fired me from my position as policy adviser." Manning had wanted Harper to be a policy adviser for the election campaign, a role Harper had played in all previous campaigns but which he had withdrawn from during the No campaign in the Charlottetown referendum. Flanagan writes, "Harper declined to serve. He had not wanted to be involved anyway, but the final straw for him was a written pledge sent out by Cliff Fryers to be signed by everyone in the campaign organization, which required them to refrain from publicly criticizing Campaign Management Committee decisions. The pledge was heavy-handed at best, and especially inappropriate for a nominated candidate, who has independent responsibilities to the constituency association and voters of his riding."

Manning referred to these conflicts in *Think Big*, but he placed them in the context of personalities rather than ideologies. "Stephen and Tom had never forgiven Rick for being on the 'wrong side' of Charlottetown. But the problem with getting Stephen to accept Rick and the challenges of a national campaign went deeper. Stephen had difficulty accepting that there might be a few other people (not many, perhaps, but a few) who were as smart as he was with respect to policy and strategy. And Stephen, at this point, was not really prepared to be a team player or team builder. In any event, in the summer of 1993 Stephen was adamant that Rick Anderson not be our campaign director, and he was prepared to air his objections in the media. We discussed the situation with our candidate representatives across the country. They unanimously endorsed the national campaign organization as proposed, with Rick Anderson as director. They suggested that a group of Alberta candidates appeal to Stephen to reconcile his differences with Rick. In due course, a group including Jim Silye, Bob Mills, Ian McClelland, Diane Ablonczy, and Ray Speaker met with Stephen. Their message was, 'We want Rick on the team. We want you on the team.' But Stephen refused to budge. He withdrew from the national campaign effort to work almost exclusively on his personal campaign for election in Calgary West. This was a blow to our overall campaign effort, and it put more of a burden on those who had to fill the gap left by his withdrawal."

The rift at the top would never really be reconciled. The public would not know that Preston Manning was at odds with the person widely considered as his likely successor, Stephen Harper. But the impact would be felt for years to come, even past Manning's retirement from politics and in Harper's later career as leader.

In the run-up to the election, Kim Campbell began mending fences and tried to counter criticisms of the PC government. In July, she announced some tightening of immigration policies and, as part of a reorganization of government, moved responsibility for immigration to the new super-ministry of Public Security, which also encompassed prisons, police, and the parole system. Harper responded that the Tories had constantly criticized Reform policies as racist. "Yet, over the past year, they've adopted all the major planks of Reform's immigration program, restricting family-class immigrants, tightening refugee screening, and putting more emphasis on attracting immigrants who can contribute to the Canadian economy. While Reform applauds those measures, the Tories are now adding a potentially dangerous negative spin to immigration policy, emphasizing security and control and implying that immigrants are a threat that must be kept out. I am surprised they'd go a step further and link immigration as a law and order issue."

On August 9, Campbell announced in Vancouver that, under legislation she would be bringing in, members of Parliament would no longer be eligible to collect their pensions before age fifty-five. The "gold-plated" pensions of MPs had been a favourite target of the Reform Party. She also announced her intention to curtail lobbying and reduce patronage. But Harper, unimpressed, put out a press release: "The Conservatives have wallowed in pensions and patronage for nine years, so this sudden change of tune is hard to take seriously." And he added: "The tactic of the Conservative Party in this election is to run on the Reform Party agenda against the Liberals."

Finally, on September 8, 1993, Kim Campbell called the election, and no sooner had she emerged from speaking to the Governor General than she made a serious blunder when she spoke to reporters on the grounds of Rideau Hall. Her most defining promise during her leadership campaign had been to eliminate the $35-billion deficit in five years. How would she do it, she was now asked? She replied that she would not reveal her deficit-cutting plan until after the election, she would only make public the "principles that will surround that process." They were:

"No increase in tax burden. Increasing revenues only through the growth of the economy and getting to the goal through the reduction of government expenditures." That meant huge cuts in government spending. But Campbell wouldn't tell Canadians how and where she would cut. Why? Because, she said, she must first consult the provinces and she must consult the people. Only after the election would she unveil her "new program." It would certainly come as a surprise package.

The next day, while campaigning in Utica, Ontario, she said in reply to a question: "It is obvious, and Canadian men and Canadian women know very well that, in the end, there are going to have to be cuts in the social programs." Then she caught herself and added the word *maybe*. Her staff, appalled, whispered in her ear, and she then tried to take it back and blame the Reform Party for wanting to cut social programs. No, she did not plan to cut social programs. It was those others, "People who have their head in the sand on that issue are writing the recipe, I think, for the destruction of Canada's social programs." But she had outed her duplicity, and it would follow her throughout the campaign. She made her worst blunder when, pressed again to reveal her plans for the social programs, she replied that an election campaign is "the worst possible time to have such a dialogue." The reply was stunning in its arrogance. The election campaign was the only time the voters could hold their leaders accountable – were they not even then to be let in on their secrets? The answer played into the hands of Reformers, confirming all the Reform denunciations of "top-down leadership." Campbell had become Manning's best electoral weapon. When, finally, she would give in to public pressure and reveal some numbers, it would turn out that they didn't add up, and that she didn't even understand them. Her campaign was perfectly designed to show the Reform Party off to best advantage. The Zero, in Campbell's campaign, was herself.

On his first day of the election campaign, Preston Manning, speaking from Calgary, berated the other leaders for coming into the campaign with platforms already drawn up. They should have first gone out and listened to the people, Manning claimed, and then put forward a program inspired by the people. The people were saying, he claimed, "We don't trust you and we don't believe you." Manning himself set out on a "Let the People Speak" tour. He and his candidates were to spend more than a week giving the microphone to "the people" to let them vent their preoccupations and concerns. The candidates would listen and learn, and this phase was then to be followed by a second phase, "Now You Have a Choice," when the candidates would announce Reform policies. As Flanagan noted, "For some reason, opponents never picked up on the contradiction implicit in the fact that party positions had already been set and literature had already been printed in preparing for this phase, even though it was supposed to follow and depend on 'Let the People Speak.'" The Reform Party was punctilious about adopting its policies at its biennial convention. It certainly couldn't accept that the leader and the candidates should make them up on the fly because of what a few people might say during the campaign.

In Calgary West, Stephen Harper had been nominated as the Reform candidate as far back as mid-1992, just before the campaign against the Charlottetown Accord. The meeting, well attended, had been held in Calgary's Ernest Manning High School and Preston Manning, whose home was in the riding, moved Harper's nomination, praising him to the skies. That was just before they had their dispute over the Charlottetown Accord. Now, going into the election campaign, the two again disagreed on strategy. Harper proposed that the campaign be conducted as an all-out attack against the Tory government. Manning, always reluctant to engage in confrontation, always inclined to the reconciliation of opposites, chose instead to campaign positively on the Reform platform.

For Harper, the campaign in Calgary West was a rematch against Jim Hawkes, who had defeated him easily in 1988. But the course of their contest was very different this time, as Hawkes recalls with some bitterness: "I remember '93 because it came as such a shock. We went into that campaign with 72 per cent of the vote when the election started, and we came out with 15.3 per cent."

Harper appointed John Weissenberger as his campaign manager. His brother Grant was put in charge of organizing the fabrication and distribution of campaign signs. The youngest brother, Robert Harper, was in charge of the organization at the level of the polls. Their mother, Margaret, spent hours every day at campaign headquarters answering phones and attending to whatever needed doing. Stephen's father, Joe Harper, a chartered accountant now retired and living in Calgary, was in charge of keeping the financial records, along with another retired accountant, Bill Kobes. They ran a tight control over expenditures and the campaign ended with a comfortable surplus: the donations were in the order of sixty-five thousand dollars, which was well above the approximately fifty-thousand-dollar maximum that the law allowed to be spent.

The inflow of money was only one sign of a campaign that was generating excitement. Another was the flow of volunteers, with close to one thousand people walking in off the street. There was a telephone team assigned to promote Harper and pinpoint his supporters. Another team went door to door, distributing Harper's personal pamphlet and a broadsheet containing the Zero in Three platform. Another team was assigned to the poll organization, acting as scrutineers on election day, striking off the names of those who had voted, and passing on the information to those who were assigned to get out the vote.

The core team organizing the campaign was made up of battle-hardened veterans. They had worked on Harper's 1988 election campaign, then on Stan Waters's 1989 senatorial campaign, then on the No campaign in the 1992 referendum. At mid-campaign, they sensed that the whole broad middle of the community was swinging to Reform. Meanwhile, Harper was out every day knocking on doors and greeting people. Jim Hawkes was equally assiduous in campaigning on the streets and in the malls. He had been an attentive MP, but he could not resist the ebb tide of public opinion that had swung away from the Tories. His campaign sent out his literature by mail because it did not have the volunteers to saturate the riding's households with personally delivered drops.

Hawkes and Harper met again at all-candidates meetings during the campaign. There were eight candidates in the running, including a Natural Law Party candidate who proposed to cure the country's ills by the application of "yogic flying." His campaign did not take off. This time, unlike 1988, Harper was not deferential to his former mentor, nor was he hoping or expecting to be defeated. Now, he wanted to win and become a member of Parliament.

One all-candidates meeting was held at Bowness High School on October 5. Despite Harper's interest in pushing Zero in Three, the other candidates were more interested in controversial issues like homosexuals' rights and the prohibition of marijuana. The Liberal candidate, prominent Calgary lawyer Karen Gainer, defended the right of homosexuals to marry. "I think same-sex marriages should be recognized by the Canadian government," she said. "It's an issue of all people having equal rights, and the Liberals favour those rights." Harper, in response, replied that issues of conscience should not be defined as a matter of partisan policy by political parties. Then he turned aside a question by a joke: "I've been on my own for a long time and I have never been asked about my sexual orientation." Hawkes, to attack the Reform Party, kept comparing its policies to those of Social Credit under former Alberta premier Ernest Manning. Harper parried: "I think Mr. Hawkes wants to fight the 1935 election all over again." The *Calgary Herald*, reporting on the meeting, observed: "The confidence of the Reform Party was oozing from Harper: 'I wouldn't be surprised if we swept Alberta and British Columbia. Or at least win the vast majority of seats.'"

Hawkes worked all out, knocking on doors and talking to his constituents from morning till night. But he was encumbered, as were all the Tory MPs in Alberta, by the Mulroney legacy. In addition, he had been the member to sponsor Bill C-114, the amendment to the Elections Act that sharply limited financial expenditures by third parties during an election campaign. The National Citizens Coalition, fighting what it called the "election gag bill," had chosen Hawkes as a special target. It ran an advertising campaign against him, spending a reported fifty thousand dollars to ensure his defeat. Hawkes was bitter, claiming that they distorted the facts. He was also bitter over the reporting on the election campaign by the *Calgary Herald*. "They had presented Kim Campbell in an unfavourable light consistently. They had Preston Manning prominently and positively on the front page of the *Calgary Herald* forty-seven days in a fifty-six-day period."

Manning came by once to speak in support of Harper, just outside Harper's campaign headquarters in a small strip mall. His speech, though brief, was punchy and laudatory. Manning spoke again toward the end of the campaign in the Stampede Corral, where a rally assembled a huge crowd of Reform supporters from all the Calgary ridings. There was a sense that a great breakthrough was imminent and Manning rose to the occasion.

The big story of the 1993 election campaign was the fall of Kim Campbell, and the simultaneous rise of Preston Manning and Lucien Bouchard. As the vanishing support for the Tories created a vacuum, it was filled by the Liberals in the Atlantic region and Ontario, by the

Bloc in Quebec, and by the Reform Party in the West and some parts of Ontario.

In a campaign with enough turning points to make all the leaders dizzy, perhaps the most decisive was the incident of the ad that offered an unflattering photo of Jean Chrétien, with such voiceover comments as, "I would be embarrassed to have this man as prime minister," and "Does this man look like a prime minister?" It gave Chrétien a priceless opportunity to pitch for sympathy over the congenital deformity that twisted his mouth: "It's true that I have a physical defect. When I was a kid, people were laughing at me. But I accepted that because God gave me other qualities, and I am grateful." There was an immediate outburst of indignation over the ads, with even Tories going public with their disapproval. Campbell decided to pull the ads. But the harm was already done, and her decision merely confirmed the growing public impression of the incompetence of the Tory campaign.

The misfortunes of Kim Campbell made the fortune of the Reformers. History moves in mysterious ways. In the early months of 1993, it seemed that the Reform Party might have lost its appeal to the people with the constitutional struggle now in abeyance. But the collapse of the credibility of the new Tory leader, coming after the years of economic and political mismanagement by the Mulroney government, restored a recognized mission to the party of Preston Manning. Now, the Reformers must go to the Parliament to restore the public finances. On past evidence, the Liberals could not be trusted to do it – they were proposing a target deficit of 3 per cent of GNP – and the Tories had proven they lacked the will.

1993 And so on October 25 the Reform Party won 22 of Alberta's 26 seats, losing 4 to the Liberals and wiping out the PC Party that had dominated Alberta since 1958. In British Columbia, Reform won 24 of the 32 seats, with 6 going to the Liberals and 2 to the NDP. Saskatchewan was divided three ways: Reform took 4 seats, with the Liberals and the NDP each taking 5. In Manitoba, Reform took only 1 seat, while the Liberals took 12, the NDP 1. In Ontario, Reform won a single seat, while the Liberals swept the other 98.

In Calgary West, Stephen Harper defeated his first political mentor, receiving 39,139 votes – 52.1 per cent of the total cast. Jim Hawkes came in third, behind Liberal Karen Gainer. Despite his years of service since 1979 he received a mere 15.7 per cent.

With fifty-two Reform members elected to Parliament, the party and its leaders would have the opportunity to show the whole country what Reformers could do as they brought their different approach. Preston Manning was already talking of expanding into Quebec before the next elections and planning a two-election strategy that would sweep him into power in four years. For Stephen Harper, now would be his opportunity, working with fifty-one other MPs, to press for the creation of a permanent, explicitly conservative Reform Party, rather than the populist party due to expire in the year 2000. And, before the year was out, he would marry Laureen Teskey and dream of a family of his own.

——◦——

Chapter 15

THE REFORMER IN PARLIAMENT

ON THE NIGHT OF the October 25 elections, when the extent of the Reform Party's breakthrough had been confirmed, Preston Manning went before the television cameras and exulted: "Reformers, we are on our way! This is what our dream has done." Now was the time to turn those dreams into reality. Manning was confident that the reality would mean Reform forming the government before very long. "One of these times, the West is going to produce a genuine national party that's going to go all the way," he told a news conference.

As the posse of fifty-two Reformers descended on the federal Parliament, Manning was determined that they would not be captured by the culture of Ottawa, but would instead impose their own culture of frugality and rectitude. His objective was to act as "Her Majesty's Constructive Alternative" with a "higher standard of behaviour" than traditional opposition parties had exhibited. Reformers would not reflexively attack every proposal put forward by the Liberal government. They would reflect, graciously support measures compatible with Reform policies, and propose "constructive alternatives where there is disagreement."

This would indeed be a different "opposition." But when it came to the test, would Reformers change Ottawa, or would Ottawa change the Reformers? Deborah Grey offered the testimony of her own past four years: "I think I have been able to maintain the ideals and the vision I had when I came to Parliament Hill. But my personal experience was very difficult because, as the other parties started to see us as a threat, I was treated with absolute contempt." Diane Ablonczy, a founder of Reform

and now the MP for Calgary North, was confident that she would not go
native: "I have worked for over six years to bring change to our federal
system and I'm not giving up now. Deborah Grey wasn't changed and
she was all by herself. Fifty of us are going to be even less susceptible to
the system." Another newcomer, Dr. Grant Hill, MP for the Alberta
riding of Macleod, expressed the new view of politics as practised by
non-politicians like himself. "What truly we're going to try to do is have
a more democratic Parliament with co-operative views of legislation,
rather than argumentative views." Until he had joined the Reform Party
in 1990, he said, the last thing he ever expected to be was a politician.

Stephen Harper, now the MP for Calgary West, insisted that Reform
would not, like other parties, impose party discipline on the MPs when
it was to the detriment of their own constituents. Their MPs would represent their constituents to Ottawa, not represent Ottawa to their constituents. "If there is a conflict between my party's view, my personal
view, and the wishes of a clear majority of my constituents, it is the latter
that ultimately must prevail." But he recognized that a procedure must
ensure the caucus spoke with one voice in important matters, except
when an MP could demonstrate that his constituency opposed the
common position.

Harper was appointed chair of a committee to look into how the
caucus would handle the tension between caucus solidarity, freedom to
represent constituents, and the need to protect the image of the party
from damaging extremist statements. Deborah Grey, as an experienced
MP, also sat on the committee. Harper told journalists that Reformers
must walk "a fine line by sticking to the right-of-centre policies of small,
fiscally responsible government and free enterprise, that allowed them to
vacuum up the Tories' support – without sounding uncaring or eccentric.
Obviously, you want to avoid extremists and you want to avoid what you
would call yahoos. The party has to have people who are presentable, but
at the same time those people have to articulate the party's message. The
party's objective in the election was to displace the Tories. If we stick to
the kind of policies and perspectives on which we ran the campaign,
there is very little chance the Conservatives will ever come back."

Harper, though only thirty-four, was the only one, with Deborah
Grey, who was familiar with the hallways and byways of Parliament Hill.
Even Manning, the prophetic leader, had only penetrated the sanctum

behind the Peace Tower as a visitor. He was to discover the marked difference between the consensual political culture of Alberta (where his father, Premier Manning, had been unassailable), and the naked aggressive partisanship that characterized Ottawa. From the start Harper was realistic about Reform's prospects, unlike some of the starry-eyed new MPs: "With a majority government, we're back to a situation where the government can govern the way it always has, if it wants. We can only attempt to establish some rules for our own behaviour and maybe bring some innovations."

A journalist pointed out to Harper that he, Preston Manning, and Ray Speaker were the only professional politicians in the caucus. "I've never thought of myself as a politician," Harper replied. He referred to his two years as a legislative assistant in Ottawa as "my tortured political past." But he conceded that a new life was starting for him. "Obviously, I am a politician now. It's going to be a real challenge to remain a representative of the people of Calgary in the Parliament of Canada, as opposed to becoming an Ottawa animal. A politician, in dictionary definition, is someone who works in politics. But obviously it has other connotations that we would hope to avoid." Already, Harper was well viewed by journalists. A story by reporter Tim Harper (no relation) in the *Toronto Star* on November 6, 1993, referred to him as "Stephen Harper, sometimes called the 'respectable' Reformer."

The Reform MPs came determined to resist the flesh pots that were commonly known as "perks," such as the highly subsidized Parliamentary Dining Room, closed to the public, with its ornate ceiling, its fluted columns, its waiters in tuxedos, and its lavish buffet tables overflowing with cakes and pies; or the barbershop where the MPs could have their honourable hair cut free of charge and their shoes shined for the same price. Manning, in particular, felt that he must offer "leadership by example." As leader of a recognized party, he commanded a car equipped with a telephone and a driver always at his service. He refused both, seizing the opportunity to teach a lesson on what Reform morality would mean to Ottawa. He summoned the television cameras and ceremoniously handed over the car key to an official, adding a brief homily on the need for frugality. Another privilege of leadership was a spacious suite of rooms in the Centre Bloc of the parliamentary compound. Before October 25, NDP Leader Audrey McLaughlin had occupied one on the fifth floor, one floor down from the Parliamentary Dining Room. But now, in her fallen state, she was considered an independent MP and was evicted. Her suite was given to Preston Manning, who saw another opportunity to practise leadership by example. He explained in *Think Big*: "We decided that we wanted to use Audrey's large corner office for strategy and Question Period planning sessions, so my assistant Jean-Marie Clemenger and I crammed ourselves into the two small offices formerly occupied by Audrey's assistants, and this became our workplace for the next four years. By keeping my own office demands modest, I hoped to minimize turf wars among my own MPs for 'the best' offices."

Between the elections of October 25 and the opening of the new Parliament on January 17, 1994, the new Reform MPs were summoned to Ottawa to reconnoitre the terrain, find lodgings away from home, move into their allotted offices, pick a staff, and receive briefings on what they could expect in their new life. They would begin each caucus meeting by singing "O Canada." As caucus chair to preside over their meetings, Manning appointed Deborah Grey, who was thereafter known as the "den mother." They needed a House leader, someone expert in the intricacies of parliamentary procedure, to keep track of the flow of legislation and of committee hearings and who would confer with the other parties' House leader to reach agreements for the orderly conduct of the business of the House. The House leader usually also served as an informal father confessor when the MPs ran into personal problems or disagreements. Manning chose to bypass the highly experienced Ray Speaker, who'd been a member of the Alberta legislature for thirty years and had served as a minister in the governments of Ernest Manning and Donald Getty. Instead, Manning picked a thirty-one-year-old Saskatchewan farmer with no parliamentary experience, Elwin Hermanson. No doubt Manning's intention was pedagogical: his was a grassroots party of citizen legislators rather than professional politicians. It was part of his conception of the new politics for the New Canada that he believed was struggling to be born.

Another important posting was that of the party whip, responsible for maintaining discipline in the caucus and assigning the MPs their hours when they were to be in attendance in the House or on committees. Manning thought that the term *whip*, with its connotation of brutal compulsion, was inappropriate for a grassroots party like Reform. So the post was assigned to the gentle Diane Ablonczy, a lawyer and former teacher who had been the party's founding chair of the executive committee. Rather than "whip," she was given the more collegial title of "caucus coordinator."

Traditionally, an opposition party chose a "shadow cabinet" with one MP, called a "critic," assigned to shadow – that is, keep a constant, severe eye on – a designated cabinet minister. So the leader would be the "critic" of the prime minister, the "finance critic" would be the critic of the finance minister, and so on with each and every minister. But Manning declined to appoint a critic corresponding to each minister. Instead, he assigned different teams of MPs to specialize in different "clusters" of policy areas. This would pre-empt the usual classic duels in the Commons during Question Period between the opposition critic and the corresponding minister, which had made the reputations of rising opposition stars.

An early decision to be taken was what to do about the lavish pensions and other perks which the Reform candidates had criticized so freely before and during the election campaign. Stephen Harper was appointed to chair a committee that would consult the MPs and come up with recommendations. The issue became especially pertinent when the new finance minister, Paul Martin, made an announcement on November 29 that shook the country and inspired the Reform Party. The estimated federal deficit for the fiscal year ending in March would not be the $32.5 billion announced the previous April by the Tory finance minister. The current estimate had it soaring to between $44 and $46 billion. Prime Minister Jean Chrétien immediately wrote the premiers and leaders of the Yukon and Northwest Territories inviting them to a December 21 conference on the economy and job creation. "Difficult economic and fiscal circumstances must be addressed with concrete measures to promote economic renewal," he wrote.

In response to such grievous economic news, Stephen Harper took it on himself to speak for the Reform caucus. "Every member of our caucus is certainly willing to take a cut [in salary] in line with a program to eliminate the national debt and deficit," Harper announced. He and Manning also denounced the fact that the government's projections were so consistently and egregiously wrong. He proposed that outside financial experts should be hired to oversee the government's budget forecasting. "There's an ideological difference of views between ourselves and the Liberals on how to handle the deficit, and we can debate that. But surely we don't have to debate facts and numbers. It's silly. Why not have qualified people do that?" He added that his party's "principal function" in the coming year would be to press constantly for fiscal restraint.

A week later, though, he acknowledged that he had spoken too quickly about all caucus members taking a pay cut. "We found there are still some differences of opinion," he told journalists, who found the retraction amusing. Some MPs were reluctant to receive less than the standard salary of $64,400, plus a tax-free allowance of $21,300. They had made no such commitment during the campaign. "Reform did not run, as a party, by advocating a pay cut for its members," Harper explained. "Some individuals did, but the party as a whole did not. That's where the difference of opinion lies."

Harper's committee had drawn up a fifteen-page questionnaire asking the MPs for their views on different subjects, including salary and pensions. Deborah Grey had been turning over to charity 10 per cent of her salary ever since 1990. For her, it had been a matter of tithing as a Christian duty rather than for deficit reduction, and she said she would continue the practice. Ray Speaker announced that he would give 15 per cent of his salary to charity. Harper himself announced that he would personally take a pay cut. Eventually, about 90 per cent of the caucus would display their frugality by earning less than other MPs. That included Preston Manning.

Another pledge made by many was to opt out of the "gold-plated" pension plan which assured them of a pension payable immediately, regardless of age, after they left the Commons, if they had been MPs for six years. The Reformers considered it excessively generous. They claimed that the retired MPs, over a lifetime, would receive on average six dollars for every one dollar they had paid into the fund. In response to the Reformers' denunciations, Chrétien announced that he would allow those who wanted to opt out of the pension plan to do so. The pension policy was to divide the Reform MPs and lead to grief later, when many would retract their promise to reject the pension.

These were big issues for Reformers in the last two months of 1993, when the newly elected MPs were intent on demonstrating their "differ-ent way of doing things." The publicity they received then turned into a source of embarrassment a year later, in November 1994, when Harper had to announce that Preston Manning and some other MPs were calling for a review of the pay-cut policy. "There will be a few less taking the pay cut," he acknowledged. "A lot of people made commitments during the election to take a pay cut. But there were others who made commitments only on pensions, and they have opted out of the pension plan." Other MPs admitted that their change of heart was because they had not received as much credit for their collective self-abnegation as they had expected. "Some members have indicated it is a hardship and are wondering if the pain is worth the gain," said Calgary MP Jim Silye. Elwin Hermanson offered this explanation: "We certainly haven't got much public play on the fact that many MPs are making sacrifices. But I also think the fact the government has become more fiscally aware is partly due to the approach Reform has taken."

Besides taking a pay cut, Manning had made a helpful suggestion to reduce the federal deficit. Since Lucien Bouchard, the new leader of the Official Opposition, had chosen to live in Hull rather than in Stornoway, the official residence that went with his new job, Manning suggested that Stornoway be sold or turned into a bingo hall. In 1997, Manning would become the leader of the Official Opposition. He promptly moved into Stornoway and accepted the car and driver that he had refused ostentatiously when he first arrived in Ottawa.

Before the close of that momentous year of 1993, Stephen Harper and Laureen Teskey were married on December 11. The marriage was a simple ceremony, in the presence of only a few close friends. It took place in the small house that the couple had bought together in Northwest Calgary, and a justice of the peace presided. Laureen had been briefly married before and Stephen, a very private person, resisted a lavish public wedding. But, being a conservative economist, he made a practical decision with a political twist. "When I was elected, I was married just after that, in 1993," he would recall three years later. "Being an economist by training and watching what was planned in the fiscal policies of the government, my wife and I took out a mortgage. I said, 'Lock that mortgage in today for five years because under the government we will not get interest rates this good for the next five years.' Today, even with the low interest rates the government is talking about, one cannot lock into a mortgage at the interest rate I locked into in late 1993." In

Ottawa, he found a furnished suite in an apartment hotel where he would stay when the Commons was in session.

In January, the Reformers were summoned to Ottawa for the opening of Parliament, which would be in session for the first time in seven months. They were on their best behaviour. Preston Manning announced that, instead of taking a seat in the middle of the front row, as party leaders normally did, he would sit in the second row. Most of the Reform MPs would occupy their seats in the order that their names were randomly drawn, rather than according to the hierarchy of importance to which they were assigned by the leadership. The only exceptions were Reform House Leader Elwin Hermanson, and Deborah Grey, both assigned to the front row. Manning would be flanked by Ray Speaker on one side and Stephen Harper on the other. Diane Ablonczy, the "caucus coordinator," explained to me at the time what it meant: "We want to focus on constructive alternatives rather than simply, you know, jeering and staring. It's our visual message, it's to point out that there is no real hierarchy. Your significance is because you were elected to represent people, not because of your position in the party. It's to enhance the respect and regard that we have for each elected representative." She also explained why she was called caucus coordinator rather than whip: "Whip suggests a top-down, stringent party discipline. We think that isn't appropriate."

When the new Parliament got down to business with the Speech from the Throne on January 18, it inaugurated a new era – that of Jean Chrétien, following the era of Brian Mulroney (Kim Campbell never met Parliament as prime minister). The styles of the two were in conspicuous contrast. After the grandiloquence of the mellifluous Mulroney's first Throne Speech, vintage 1984, Chrétien's first Throne Speech was laconic, unadorned, articulated in simple, down-to-earth language. But equally striking was the similarity of the problems which each proposed that the country must urgently address. Chrétien's Throne Speech, like Mulroney's of November 5, 1984, conveyed a sense of a new beginning, a sharp departure from the style and priorities of the previous government.

Chrétien's first concern was unemployment and the speech made the connection between job creation and reducing the federal deficit. "The government will pursue the fiscal discipline necessary for sustained economic growth. The budget will be tabled in February and will include measures to bring the federal debt and deficit under control in a manner that is compatible with putting Canadians back to work." In summary, Chrétien, without a grand design to make Canada unrecognizable as Mulroney had promised to do, proposed instead a restoration by taking many small steps. But Manning's position would be that the Liberals, like the Tories, made promises, while the Reform Party kept them.

The tone of the Throne Speech would be important for the fortunes of the Reform Party. So much of what the new prime minister was proposing was in keeping with the spirit of Reform's own proposals. Chrétien, like Manning, was more modest in personal style. His first gestures, like Manning's, had been to send a symbolic message of frugality. He had cancelled the contract, signed by Kim Campbell, for purchasing EH-101 helicopters. The Liberals had claimed that would save $2.316 billion over the next four years. Chrétien announced on taking office that he would never use the "Taj Mahal" of a government jet which had been refurbished in the Mulroney era for the travels of the prime minister. And he abolished the position of chief of staff for each minister, a Mulroney innovation, and limited the number of assistants for each minister to five.

Beyond the facts and figures, Chrétien was not the perfect foil for Manning that Mulroney had been. Manning professed populism as a conviction, but he did not have the sensibility or the style of a populist. He was too reserved, too deliberate, too intellectual to come across as a man of the people. It was Chrétien who was earthy and direct. Even his fractured English, inelegant French, and twisted mouth made it easier for him to establish a rapport with ordinary people as one of themselves – only cannier and more experienced.

When the party leaders gave their first speeches, Manning was all sweetness and honey. He laced his speech with humour, gracious compliments toward other members and protestations of his desire to work with the government to make the 35th Parliament serve the citizens of Canada. He even delivered three paragraphs of his speech in laboured French, and he extended a compliment to the prime minister, commenting without irony on his lengthy service to his country in the Commons. "I think it is inspiring for the new MPs in this House to see that experience, knowledge, and devotion are rewarded, and not just ambition." This was, indeed, a different way of doing business for political adversaries.

By contrast, Lucien Bouchard played the Grand Inquisitor. He depicted federal Canada in the most sombre, depressing, even catastrophic terms. Quebeckers were among the most unfortunate people in the entire world. He achieved some of his gloomy effect by employing alarming words such as "crisis," "bitterness," "disappointments," "lost illusions," "endless trials," and a thesaurus' worth of other despairing terms. "For the long ordeal imposed on those of goodwill in Quebec and English Canada, we have nothing to show today except bitterness, suspicion, lack of understanding, and a deep collective disaffection. We are about to lose every kind of courage, even the courage to look reality in the face."

The following day, Manning asked the prime minister for assurance that he wouldn't allow the members of the Bloc "to consume a disproportionate amount of the time and attention of this House" on the question of Quebec's sovereignty. Chrétien replied: "I cannot stop them from talking about separation. They have the freedom to do that. But I know very well that, if the Official Opposition keep talking about separation and constitutional problems, they are not living up to why they are here. Because the people in every riding in Quebec want every member of this House to work together to make sure that we have economic growth and job creation." Manning also asked to be reassured that Marcel Massé, the new minister of intergovernmental relations, would be concerned with the needs of all the provinces, and not just Quebec.

Initially, the stance of the Reformers with respect to Quebec was to ignore the issue. The party was calling for a five-year moratorium on constitutional talks and Chrétien had also campaigned promising to put the Constitution aside indefinitely. The paramount concern for both Reform and the Liberals was the economy. Harper commented: "That's going to colour everything and I think it will colour things far more than the developments on the unity issue and Quebec." Manning initially dismissed impatiently the heated exchanges on the status of Quebec between the Bloc and the government. He called it "an old family quarrel."

The day after the Throne Speech, Stephen Harper rose to make his first statement in the Commons, as Hansard recorded: "Mr. Speaker, in response to the Reform caucus report on parliamentary pay, perks, and pensions, the government has advanced a plan to reduce certain benefits on Parliament Hill. The Gagliano report is a commendable first step that will save the taxpayers of Canada some significant dollars and will be supported on this side of the House. However, there are significant actions that still must be taken. Let me indicate two. Each member of Parliament continues to receive a tax-free, non-receiptable expense allowance starting at $21,300 a year. This must be reformed. Also taxpayers are insisting on real, comprehensive reform to MPs' and senators' pensions, not tinkering. Canadians are demanding reductions to taxpayers' contributions that are at least $10 million in excess per year by private-sector standards and a benefit structure that has created actuarial liabilities of nearly $200 million. The taxpayers will be watching and we will be watching."

The style of his statement was technocratic. But it did conform to Reform's new ways by complimenting the government on making some reductions in expenses, as proposed in the report prepared by Minister Alfonso Gagliano. Then, Harper got down to business, urging the government, in accordance with Reform ethos, to lead by example by cutting the pay and pensions of the members of both Houses of Parliament.

The next day, January 20, Harper got to give his maiden speech. Reading it eleven years later, it seems again more technocratic than memorable. The most interesting part, quoted in an earlier chapter, deplored the federal National Energy Program of 1980, and the devastation it caused to Calgary's economy and to Calgarians. The rest was a plea for the government to get serious about the national debt and the deficit, which were strangling the economy and causing a brain drain. "Today the federal government presents not hopes but obstacles to economic recovery. The obstacles are most clearly represented by the national debt and the deficits adding to it which we are experiencing and have experienced in the past number of years. I am not going to recount the statistics. I am an economist and that would be economics and that is a dangerous combination. Let me talk instead about what these numbers mean.

"In the election campaign my colleagues and I in the Reform Party argued strongly about the need to understand the long-term link between fiscal mismanagement and economic recession and decline. We argued against the view that we should create jobs rather than fix the financial problem, not because we oppose creating jobs but because these are not conflicting objectives. They are the same objective. Countries like companies or households that mismanage their financial affairs do not create jobs. They destroy them. Households, businesses, families, and governments that mismanage their affairs do not fulfill dreams. Those who mismanage their affairs watch their dreams slowly slip away. Many of my generation, young professionals, the backbone of the future of Canada, have left Canada, are leaving Canada, or are thinking of leaving Canada, because they fear the high taxes and the declining services that this mismanagement has brought about and may worsen in the future."

It was a solid, serious maiden speech. Time would prove its pertinence. Before Paul Martin discovered that the federal deficit and the national debt were imminent threats to the well-being of all Canadians and that Canada was well along on the road to catastrophe, before Martin had the blinding revelation on the road to his 1995 budget, Harper was already focused on the country's most serious problem, its out-of-control public finances.

As for Preston Manning, he began his parliamentary career with high expectations. "Preston really thought that we would form the next government," Deborah Grey reveals in her memoirs. So far, the two-election strategy put forward by Manning and Cliff Fryers in 1991, and repeated before Reform candidates in 1993, seemed to be working according to plan. Manning and his party had been extraordinarily lucky. Periodically, just when they seemed about to sink below the level of relevance, events had conspired to raise again their significance and the loyalty of their following. There had been the 1987 Constitutional Accord, which made Reform's fortune for three years as the only party opposing it. Then there was the Charlottetown Accord, which again gave Reform a unique public profile in opposition. Then there was the debt and deficit hole which Kim Campbell handled so disastrously. And Manning had turned each situation to his advantage with brilliant insight. It almost seemed providential, the way he had brought the party from nothing to its present heights in a mere six years.

He judged that the separatist Bloc Québécois's being installed as Her Majesty's Loyal Opposition would work to Reform's advantage. He believed that, in the atmosphere of post-Charlottetown fatigue and the long disenchantment with Quebec politics and with Quebec politicians, who had for so long monopolized the country's agenda, the Bloc and the Liberals would destroy each other. Canadians across the country would be outraged at the sight and turn to the Reform Party as the only alternative to the Liberals. This was also a viewpoint suggested by Harper right after the elections: "Like it or not, we're the only party that can claim to be the alternative government."

Manning did not agree that the Bloc should be accepted as the Official Opposition. The authoritative *Beauchesne's Parliamentary Rules and Forms* had this definition, which Manning quoted: "The political party which has the right to be called the 'Official Opposition' is the largest minority group which is prepared, in the event of the resignation of the government, to assume office." By that definition, clearly the Bloc could never qualify as the Official Opposition because it was not prepared to assume the office of the government of Canada. The Governor General would never have called on the BQ to form a government, because no other party would have considered supporting it to replace the Liberals. Besides, the BQ and its leader were not prepared to fill the essential role of the Official Opposition, that is, to scrutinize all the government's actions in the interest of all Canadians. This was clear in the BQ's election manifesto, *Un nouveau parti pour l'étape décisive*: "The Bloc Québécois MPs will have no other fidelity except towards Québec," the manifesto stated on page fifty-four. And it defined the Bloc MPs as representing only Quebec: "The representatives of English Canada will have before them, in the House of Commons, those of Québec. The thesis of the two founding peoples will be confirmed at last in the daily functioning of the parliamentary institution." But, for reasons never credibly explained, the BQ was in fact recognized as the Official Opposition, with all its privileges. Perhaps Chrétien feared that refusing the Bloc the recognition that normally went to the party with the second largest contingent of MPs would trigger a backlash in a year when provincial elections were expected in Quebec and the Parti Québécois was climbing in the polls.

Once the parliamentary session got underway, Manning and his Reformers found it increasingly difficult to get their message across to the public. The "different way of doing things" drew attention for a brief time. But when it ceased to be a novelty, it became merely ineffective. In Ottawa, extreme partisan politics was the norm and it was centred on the daily Question Period. There Manning was at a distinct disadvantage.

In Question Period, Lucien Bouchard and his party got to ask the first questions. The Bloc rather than Reform became the visible parliamentary antithesis to the government, seated directly opposite, across the aisle. Reform was shuttled to one side, physically and metaphorically, and Chrétien often referred to it derisively as "the third party," as in "third wheel." Bouchard was the reverse image of Manning: fiery, with a rapidity of reaction and delivery that Manning could not match. Bouchard had the sensibility of a populist, not in the sense that he was a man of the people, but he was an orator who could stir the masses, speak with passion, and often went emotionally over the top. Manning's measured words could be most impressive when he delivered a carefully crafted speech. He was the prophet who looked over the hills and beyond the valleys to describe a kind of promised land, New Canada, which others had not seen. But the short bursts of oratory required by the Commons rules were unsuited to Manning's meditative style. And the inevitable contrast between Manning and Bouchard was to Bouchard's advantage. Bouchard also had his vision of a promised land, that of a sovereign Quebec. His was a more targeted audience and he spoke fervently on a narrower range of concerns. He did not aspire to form the government of Canada so he was not limited by having to ensure that his words would still be responsible a few years into the future. He wanted apocalypse now, or at least before 1995 was out. And his constant subject, the secession of Quebec, was inherently more dramatic than Manning's patient construction of a more frugal and democratic government, a more prosperous and just Canada. Bouchard could easily snatch the headlines, especially as Jacques Parizeau came closer to power in Quebec.

No wonder Manning was later to express his dislike for Question Period. "Although I did my duty, I resented the time spent on Question Period. . . . I am not an actor, and I feel dishonest when called upon to 'manufacture' sentiments that I do not really feel. . . . Frankly, on most days I would have preferred to have been answering questions rather than asking them."

The commitment to consulting the grassroots on important questions also weakened the impact of the Reform MPs in an arena that demanded instant reaction to the high moments of the political cycle, such as the Throne Speech, the speech on the budget, or decisions by the Supreme Court of Canada. There are also the inevitable, unpredictable, and sudden crises that strike like an earthquake, when the journalists and the public demand an instant response from the prime minister and from the leaders of the opposition parties. Manning's experience in the previous six years had not prepared him for the demands of politics as instant theatre, with its own imperative rules that can be ignored only at a price. Such was Manning's delay in responding to the budget speech delivered by Finance Minister Paul Martin on February 22, 1994. As Flanagan relates in *Waiting for the Wave*, "Manning chose to ignore media expectations about timeliness. Before making a speech in the House of Commons on Martin's first budget, he spent two weeks consulting the grassroots. By the time he got around to addressing the issue, the media were on to other issues and barely reported his speech."

The new MPs were also frustrated because, by Manning's rules, their respective responsibilities were not precisely defined. In the absence of a precisely designated critic for each minister, the MPs were unable to specialize in the workings of a specific ministry so as to become an expert on the doings and deficiencies of that ministry. And the news media, pressed for time as always, did not like having to shop around to get the right person to respond to developing news. It became easier not to consult the third party.

No doubt the expectations of the MPs and their constituents were too optimistic about what they could do in their first months in Parliament. But the MPs felt, and heard the message from their supporters, that their performances were disappointing, that they weren't getting their message across, that there was much talk but not the expected action. In part, as the second opposition party, the rules and traditions of the Commons gave them little power to effect change. The prime minister, by controlling a majority of the MPs, had sole and almost unlimited power. But the MPs knew that they could do better if they were better organized.

Manning's influence over many members of his caucus weakened. They became critical of his style of leadership. At the same time, Stephen Harper, though one of the youngest MPs, acquired a following. In March 1994, Manning proposed to delegate the House Leader, Elwin Hermanson, as Reform's representative on the Board of Internal Economy, an all-party committee dealing with parliamentary housekeeping. But one MP nominated Stephen Harper, and he won the vote to become the delegate.

A serious confrontation between Harper and his leader occurred after stories ran in the *Globe and Mail* in late March revealing that

"Manning collects $31,000 a year from party." Given the Reformers'
constant criticism of perks, pay, and pensions, the fact that the Reform
leader was collecting a secret subsidy from the party in addition to what
he received as an MP and as leader of a recognized party caused immediate embarrassment. It made Manning look like a hypocrite for all his
holier-than-thou denunciations. How the information was leaked to the
press is still not known. But a reporter for the *Calgary Sun* interviewed
Harper about the matter, and his story was run on April 6 as the lead
story under the headline, "Manning in pay perk storm." Harper was
quoted as saying: "The whole idea of non-accountable expenses is not
acceptable." And he also said: "The compensations are not consistent
with what the party is asking of Parliament." The very next day, a senior
committee of the party's executive council sent a letter of reproof against
Harper to all the members of caucus. The letter was also released to
journalists. "We are appalled," the letter began. "The article indicates
that Mr. Harper is misinformed on how the Leader's accountability for
expenses is handled. We accept that Mr. Harper disagrees with and questions our decisions, however we are disappointed that he did not make
use of the Constitutional mechanisms established by members at the last
Assembly to deal with such issues. Mr. Harper did not even place a
phone call to the appropriate Committee members to get the facts or to
register his concerns prior to expressing himself in the media."

The letter was profoundly misguided from the point of view of
public relations, if nothing else. It simply drew more attention to the
issue of Manning's secret perks. And, by censuring Harper, a member of
Parliament, so publicly and so scornfully, it ensured that bad feelings
would remain. Manning had personally approved the letter. How could his
relations with Harper ever be cordial again after so public a humiliation?

The incident caused much comment in the news media. Kenneth
Whyte, who had reported extensively on the Reform Party as a reporter
for *Alberta Report* in 1991 and 1992, was now editor of *Saturday Night*
and a recurrent columnist in the *Globe and Mail*. He flew to Harper's
defence in the *Globe* on April 9 and revealed that Preston and Sandra
Manning had, between them, received more from the party than had
been revealed so far. "Mr. Harper's alleged transgression was to tell a
reporter Reformers can't criticize the pay and perks of other politicians
without accounting for the $43,000 in allowances that Mr. Manning and

his wife, Sandra, receive from the party for clothes, a car, and other items. They have not been required to provide receipts for these expenses."

The episode discredited Manning's scene on Parliament Hill when he refused a car and driver. It also blew away some of his reputation for frugality, for candour, for bottom-up rather than top-down governance. Manning's overreaction would have seemed high-handed in any political party, but more so for the leader of Reform.

Kenneth Whyte made other revealing comments in his column. "An exceptionally serious young man and a dedicated conservative, Mr. Harper has none of his leader's ease about compromising policy and principle to political ends. This initially produced a creative tension between them. After a while it created trouble. . . . Their relationship cooled. Mr. Harper's first loyalties shifted in a definite way from the person of Mr. Manning to the policies and principles of the party. On a number of occasions since, sometimes publicly but more often in private, Mr. Harper has urged his leader to toe the party line on election strategy and staffing, among other issues. It was that sort of behaviour that earned him this rebuke this week." Kenneth Whyte was much respected in conservative circles. His defence of Harper and rebuke of Manning brought out into the open the tensions that had been building between the two men, and it was not to the advantage of Manning.

Harper also became Reform's prime star for the media. He was invited for many television interviews with Peter Mansbridge, Craig Oliver, and Lloyd Robertson. He was constantly quoted in newspapers. He knew how to speak the journalists' language. A Canadian Press story by Jim Sheppard provided a list of MPs who, in the reporter's judgment, were the best performers in Question Period: "Best questions from opposition MP: Reform's Stephen Harper, for getting straight to the point and handling curveball returns." Linda Goyette, an editorial writer with the *Edmonton Journal*, wrote a column in which she dreamed of a provincial Reform party appearing on the scene in Alberta as a counterpoise to the provincial Conservatives. "I like to think of Deborah Grey or Stephen Harper as the leader – intelligent, outspoken conservatives as opposed to dumb-dumb bigots – with the capacity to express the views of Alberta's far right in rational language."

On June 9, 1994, an event occurred which further shook the confidence of many MPs in their leader. The Commons was debating a bill to

confer self-government on First Nations in the Yukon Territory when MP
Herb Grubel rose to express his reservations, while recognizing the good
intentions that inspired it. "It is my judgment this bill will do a great deal
of harm, much like policies of the past have done an unfortunately large
amount of harm." The subject was touchy. As an economist, Grubel was
convinced that subsidies in perpetuity would not solve the chronic problems of aboriginals. And he uttered these fatal words: "All of us – it is a
human condition – dream about having a rich uncle who pays us a guaranteed, generous income so we can retire somewhere on some South Sea
island and be happy ever after. . . . We understand it is in the human condition that we need an obligation, that we need a job, that we need to
work. We have refused to give in to our children, yet we have been misguided when in the past we have given in to the demands of the native
community to give them more physical goods, to allow them to live on
their South Sea island equivalent."

The outcry was immediate: Grubel was denounced as a racist on
radio, television, and in print. Manning, the next day, dissociated himself
from what Grubel had said, and cut him loose. He maintained that what
Grubel said did not accord with party policy. In fact, it was within the
range of party policy, and certainly not contrary to it. It merely put in
vivid words the concern of many Reformers. The 1991 Blue Book said
this: "The Reform Party believes that native people should have rights
and responsibilities for their lives and destiny within the structure of
Canadian life. The Reform Party is concerned, however, that such innovations not establish or reinforce racially segregated societies or racially
based governmental structures." It was arguable that the Yukon First
Nations Self-Government Act did, in fact, represent a racially based governmental structure and perhaps a racially segregated society. And the
whole insistence of the Reform Party on a policy of equality of rights for
all Canadians would support the legitimacy of what Grubel said.

Some MPs, notably Harper, came to his support, and judged that
Manning had simply let himself be intimidated by political correctness.
As Grubel wrote in his memoirs: "Many caucus members were very supportive of my being in trouble with the media and Manning, knowing
that some day they, too, might say something politically incorrect and
end up 'in the soup,' and were critical of Manning's handling of the
affair. Ray Speaker and Stephen Harper, the promising, bright young

Calgary MP, suggested that Manning should have used the media attention to explain the Reform position on native issues to Canadians. This
could have been done quite simply by having me coached on how to
deflect media questions and turn them to issues of more substance. I am
confident I could have handled such an assignment."

When the time came for summer break, the MPs organized a session
of self-criticism, expressed their disquiet over Manning's conduct of the
party for the first session, and demanded changes. They demanded that
he appoint proper critics for specific ministers. They also complained
that he was running a one-man show and that other MPs must be promoted before the public. Harper said: "It's essential. The party has to
develop more recognized and respected faces. It doesn't need fifty-two,
but it needs more than one." The MPs also demanded that Manning
move to the front row of the Commons, which he agreed to do. They
found that Diane Ablonczy, though well liked by all, was not strong
enough to impose discipline on the caucus.

In July, the new order became evident when Manning announced
changes. "They want me perhaps to be more visible. I'm not anxious to
be invisible," he said, explaining why he would move to the front
bench. He announced his new shadow cabinet. In some instances, a
single Reform MP was the critic of a single ministry. Stephen Harper was
appointed sole critic for intergovernmental affairs, shadowing minister
Marcel Massé. He was also part of a threesome that were critics on
national unity: the other two were Jim Silye and Bob Ringma. Herb
Grubel now became critic for finance, along with Ray Speaker.

The new order was spectacularly on display when the Commons met
in late September. Day after day during Question Period, the Reform
MPs pummelled the prime minister over what was called "the Dupuy
Affair." Out went the respectful courtesies, the "constructive" alternatives, and the new way of doing things. In came the old adversarial ways
with a vengeance. Michel Dupuy, an ex-diplomat who was now Secretary
of State, had written a letter to the Canadian Radio-television and
Telecommunications Commission to ask that the regulatory body give
"due consideration" to the application for a broadcast licence by one of
his constituents. Now, the CRTC was an arms-length tribunal of the government, but it reported to Parliament through the Secretary of State,
Michel Dupuy. Stephen Harper waved in the Commons a "confidential"

copy of ethical guidelines for cabinet ministers which cautioned every minister "to take very special care to avoid intervening, or appearing to intervene in cases under consideration by quasi-judicial bodies." The CRTC was, without the slightest doubt, a quasi-judicial body. The Reformers called for Dupuy's resignation.

But Prime Minister Chrétien replied that Dupuy had committed an "honest mistake," and that the guideline was only a recommendation, not an order. It was his prerogative to judge whether Dupuy had seriously misbehaved and he judged that he had not. "The prime minister is the one fully responsible, and I'm fully responsible of the decision I've taken, and I will stand by it," Chrétien said. The Reformers decided that they smelled blood and, day after day, every question that they were allotted became a charge against Dupuy and against the prime minister for supporting him.

Harper led the attack. "Is it the prime minister's version of responsibility that he has no responsibility for his own guidelines, no responsibility for his ministers, no responsibility for his own statements? Is it the Mulroney version of responsibility – to heck with the facts, we'll wait for the next election?" The sustained attack by the previously "constructive" Reformers became so virulent that Manning was called to order by Speaker Gilbert Parent for charging the prime minister with "gross stupidity or unethical conduct or both." The Speaker ruled that those words were unparliamentary language. Manning changed his accusation to a "gross error in judgment" and "conduct unbecoming a prime minister." Chrétien countered that the Reformers were "out fishing and catching no fish." Harper then went before the television cameras in the lobby outside the Commons and alleged that the facts indicated Chrétien was "lying." That was decidedly unparliamentary, but the Speaker wasn't there to reprove him.

From October 13 to 15, the Reform Party held its biennial assembly in Ottawa and the delegates to the convention adopted more radical positions than they had in the past. This time, unlike at the 1991 assembly in Saskatoon, Harper was not the chief policy officer, he was a member of Parliament. He did not deliver his previous warnings against taking extreme positions that would harm the party's reputation. One of the policies adopted stated: "Resolved, that the Reform Party support the repeal of the Official Languages Act." Reformers also passed a resolution that favoured a California-style, three-strikes policy for convicted criminals. Anyone who committed three "serious" offences would face life in prison. Though more than 79 per cent voted for the measure, it was replaced the next day by a less draconian resolution requiring that "any person who commits on two or more separate occasions a serious personal injury offence be deemed a dangerous offender and subject to an indeterminate period in jail."

The most controversial resolution at the convention touched on same-sex marriage and the attendant benefits such as pensions. It set Manning and Harper against each other on a fundamental issue of policy. The resolution stated: "Resolved, that the Reform Party support limiting the definition of a legal marriage as the union of a woman and a man, and that this definition be used in the provision of spousal benefits for any program funded or administered by the federal government." It was adopted by 87 per cent of the delegates. Stephen Harper was one of the rare Reformers to oppose the resolution. "Those are not partisan issues. Those are moral issues. People have to be able to belong to political parties regardless of their views on those issues." He was opposed both to the convention's coming up with a heterosexual definition of marriage, and also to a movement within the caucus to oppose the inclusion of sexual orientation as a ground for protection under the Human Rights Act. He proposed that if the MPs wanted to take a position on such issues, they should hold a referendum among their constituents and be guided by the results. "I think it's perfectly legitimate to have moral objections as well as moral approval of homosexuality, but I don't think political parties should do that."

On December 6, Preston Manning unveiled a statement from the caucus opposing the inclusion of sexual orientation in the Human Rights Act. Manning said he was against all discrimination, but he disapproved of listing specific prohibited grounds. "We would much rather see prohibited grounds of discrimination being any violation of fundamental rights rather than getting into categories." He added that such rights as the entitlement to life, to liberty, to security of the person, and freedom from discrimination, which were already protected in the Canadian Charter of Rights, should be strictly enforced for everyone, whether a citizen is gay, black, old, or a member of a smaller religious or political group.

Harper spelled out his own position on the subject in a letter to the *Calgary Herald* after a story appeared which he felt portrayed him inaccurately. "My personal views on some of these issues are the following: I do not support the special legal recognition of same-sex relationships, the compulsory provision of marital benefits to same-sex couples, or a number of other possible implications of such legislation. However, I do believe that there should generally be protection from discrimination on the basis of sexual orientation in hiring, promotion, accommodation, and many other areas covered by the Canadian Human Rights Act. I also believe that the definition of sexual orientation may be an issue and should be clarified."

In 2004, he would take a different position, which would be more liberal. Then, he would not only favour personally the protection for homosexuals against discrimination under the Human Rights Act, he would also favour that same-sex couples should be eligible to form recognized civil unions and eligible for the same marital benefits as heterosexual couples. But he would still oppose that such unions be qualified as marriages.

In his letter to the *Calgary Herald*, he explained that, though such were his personal views, they would not necessarily indicate how he would vote if the issue of sexual orientation in the Human Rights Act came to a vote in the Commons. "All households in my constituency of Calgary West will shortly receive my newsletter, *The Calgary West Reflector*, containing a survey with questions on a number of matters relevant to the possible inclusion of sexual orientation in the CHRA. I hope to have the results by mid-January. My eventual vote in the House of Commons on this issue, if and when a bill is tabled by the government, will be determined by the contents of that bill and the results of my constituency survey."

He maintained that his positions, both at the convention and with respect to the caucus position that Manning had made public, did not depart from party policy as the article on him seemed to suggest. "I have in no way broken with Reform Party policy, nor have I expressed support for or against the amendments to the Canadian Human Rights Act. In fact, I would point out that no amendments to this Act have yet been tabled. In the 1993 election campaign, Reform made it clear that matters relating strongly to ethical, moral, and religious views should not be matters of Party policy. This is also contained in the caucus position regarding the Human Rights Act. On such questions, Reform MPs should attempt to ascertain the views of their constituents and vote according to those views where a consensus exists. Reform MPs should also make their personal views known."

Increasingly, Harper felt that he and Manning were moving in divergent directions. The ideological divide that separated them was the same which he had defined in his March 10, 1989, memo: the choice between a principled conservative party of the right on the one hand, or a populist party which, because it claimed to belong simultaneously to the right, the left, and the centre, was, he thought, ideologically unpredictable, inherently unstable, and essentially dependent on the prophetic leader to define which way "the common sense of the common people" pointed.

Manning's view, Harper felt, depended for success on an intuitive grasp of where a popular movement would be heading next. It meant sometimes leaping inconsistently from one passing public mood to the next. Looking back on the Reform's first year in Ottawa, it was obvious that much of what the MPs had taken so seriously in late 1993 and early 1994 had been mere stunts – the virtuous rejection of car, driver, front-bench place in the Commons, Stornoway, pay, perks, and pensions. So much had turned out to be mere posturing and had then been reversed in a way that had made the Reformers look ridiculous.

Harper was convinced there was a better way, and that it meant taking the decision to adopt the principles of conservatism and to build a permanent party on that basis, unlike the intentionally transient party which Reform was meant to be, either attaining power by the year 2000 or going out of existence. Its sunset clause was even inscribed in its constitution.

Harper decided to go public with his sense of the choices that were offered. He wrote a piece that appeared in the *Globe and Mail* on March 21, 1995. It was titled, "Where does the Reform Party go from here? To be credible as the logical alternative to the Liberals, says a

Reform MP, the party can't just fight elections on the popular protests of the day." In that piece, Harper did not name names or make explicit the conflicting nature of the alternatives that he was putting forward. But he was running up a flag to see who would salute.

"The real challenge is the need for Reform to embrace a plausible permanent role for itself in the political system," he wrote. "The party's own constitution calls for its dissolution in the year 2000, and Reform has tended to define itself by contemporary 'populist' protests, such as opposition to the Meech Lake Accord, the GST, or Allan Rock's gun registry. The impression is that the party wants either to form a majority government right away or to pack up and go back to the farm. Indeed, the stated mission of the party has become a simple electoral one: to form a majority government in the next federal election. As a self-described populist movement, its avowed method for achieving this is to respond to a series of popular protests against specific actions of the current government, as well as to a more general sense of dissatisfaction with the political system."

That was a fair summary of the Reform Party as understood by Preston Manning, the Reform Party to which Harper still belonged as a member of Parliament. But, against that mission statement for the party, he sketched out an alternative, his own, the same vision that he had first embraced in 1987 after long reflection and had maintained ever since.

"I suggest, however, that the logical permanent role of the Reform Party is to accept itself as the principal force of the democratic right in Canadian politics, like the Conservatives in Great Britain, the Republicans in the United States, or the Christian Democrats in Germany. Such a party must do what the Progressive Conservatives failed to do: adapt to the contemporary issues of political conflict and to a new conservatism that is populist rather than paternalistic.

"For the Reform Party to transform itself into such a permanent political force requires adaptation in organization more than in policy. It means doing what modern national conservative parties do. It means constructing a coherent coalition in a pluralistic democracy. It means developing a diversity of contacts throughout society and developing channels of influence throughout the party itself. And it means fighting all elections, federal and provincial, from the broad right of centre, not just planning to fight one election around the protests of the day.

[handwritten in left margin: MISSION STATEMENT FOR CS]

"Sectarianism is a possible outcome of a strategy of simple populist protest. But with the right decisions, Reform can emerge as the critical element in the development of a broadly based national alternative to the Liberal government."

It was an important statement. On the response it would receive would depend Stephen Harper's political future.

Chapter 16

THE 1995 REFERENDUM

ON ELECTION NIGHT, October 25, 1993, when the extent of the Bloc Québécois's sweep of the map of Quebec outside Montreal had become clear, a triumphant Lucien Bouchard uttered again the last words that René Lévesque had spoken on May 20, 1980, the night of his bitter referendum defeat: "*À la prochaine!*" Till next time! It had seemed, then, a forlorn hope. Now, thirteen years later, it had the ring of a promise – or a threat, a revenge on history. The next referendum campaign began that night. The propaganda battle would be fought without respite, day after day, by the fifty-four Bloc MPs and all their staff paid by the taxpayers. Deborah Grey remembers, "Exchanges in the House between the Liberals and the Bloc were vitriolic. It was horrible to have to sit and listen to them go after each other."

Preston Manning, Stephen Harper, and the fifty other Reform MPs had arrived in Ottawa determined to talk about their first priorities, which were economic: the debt, the deficit, the Goods and Services Tax, the excesses of government. Harper the economist was especially eager to do battle on these grounds. At first, Manning dismissed the heated exchanges between the Bloc and Liberals as a tedious "family quarrel," and he determined to concentrate on the real issues that preoccupied his own constituents: taxes and the economy. And Harper would never fail to remind the country that Canada needed a Triple-E Senate.

But the Bloc's two-seat advantage in the House over Reform and its title as the Official Opposition gave it the pivotal role during the daily Commons Question Period. Then, on February 26, 1994, barely a month after the new Parliament opened, the Parti Québécois won a by-election in what had been a perennially Liberal riding. The issue of secession immediately took greater relevance. Manning questioned Chrétien about it the following day: "Bonaventure has been considered to be the most federalist riding in Quebec. With a provincial election looming on the horizon, does the prime minister acknowledge the need for a new and more vigorous strategy to increase support for federalism in Quebec?" But Chrétien brushed off the question with what would be his constant response until Jacques Parizeau actually led the Parti Québécois to power the following September: "Mr. Speaker, the best way to sell federalism in Quebec is to have a good, efficient, honest government in Ottawa."

Little by little, as Deborah Grey recounts in her memoirs, the Quebec issue took over the attention of the Commons and the news media: "Most of the focus of the 35th Parliament was the Quebec referendum that was held on October 30, 1995. Reformers constantly asked the Liberals what strategy they had to renew federalism that might ward off the separatist threat. Their cupboard was bare. Chrétien seemed to think that if we kept talking positively, everything would turn out fine."

In the early going, Manning and Harper practised a three-prong approach. First, they would prod Chrétien to show his hand and declare his policy for responding to the growing likelihood of a secession crisis. Secondly, the Reformers would insist that any settlement with Quebec must respect both the rule of law and the equality of the provinces; they would condone no sweetheart deal of the kind that Mulroney had championed. A secession, should it come to that, would require that its terms be negotiated, and Reform would insist that those terms be tough. But, thirdly, Reformers would propose at the same time a fundamental reform of the federation, a New Canada, one that would define more clearly the respective jurisdictions of the federal state and the provinces, and that would assign to the provinces responsibility for many functions now exercised by Ottawa, notably the protection of language and culture. Reform now accepted that there should be a moratorium for several years on attempts to revise the Constitution. But that still left ample room for reforms that could be implemented within the existing Constitution.

Lucien Bouchard, meanwhile, set about trying to trap Chrétien into a commitment that he would recognize as binding the results of a future referendum vote in Quebec on secession. It was a daring move because there was absolutely no basis for it in the Constitution of Canada, and no other country in the world conceded a right to one part of its population to hold a referendum on secession and then actually secede on the strength of a majority vote in that part of its population. Furthermore, in René Lévesque's 1980 referendum, the premier had not claimed that a majority Yes vote would give Quebec a right to secede, nor had Prime Minister Trudeau conceded such a right, quite to the contrary. In August 1977, the Lévesque government had published a white paper on the significance of the Referendum Act that it planned to introduce. The white paper, *La Consultation Populaire au Québec*, made it clear that it announced an instrument for consulting the people, not for determining automatically the future of Quebec. For that reason, it argued, there was no point in designating a threshold of victory.

"The referendums that will be held under the law that the government has the intention of presenting would have a consultative character. Indeed, under the present Constitution, it is impossible to confer a direct legislative power to a referendum process, because that would go against the powers and functions that are reserved for the lieutenant-governor. This means that, to give legal effect to a referendum, it would be necessary to make use of the processes already available to amend laws, whether these be constitutional in nature or ordinary." The impact of a referendum, the white paper said, was "the political value of the referendum process." It claimed no more. "This consultative character of referendums *means it would serve no purpose to include in the law special clauses with respect to the majority required or to the required level of participation.*" When the Referendum Act was actually passed in 1979, it specified no threshold of victory, whether 50 per cent or any other percentage.

But Lucien Bouchard made his move anyway, counting on a bit of revisionist history that Chrétien had perpetrated in his 1985 political autobiography, *Straight from the Heart*, written after he had left public life following his loss of the Liberal leadership to John Turner. Chrétien recalled his pledge of the early 1970s to accept the results of the impending referendum: "'We'll put our faith in democracy,' I said. 'We'll convince the people that they should stay in Canada and we'll win. If we don't win, I'll respect the wishes of Quebeckers and let them separate.'"

That was just bravado. In the early 1970s, Chrétien had no power, no authority to say: "I'll respect the wishes of Quebeckers and let them separate." Pierre Trudeau, the prime minister, never, at any time, recognized that Quebec had a right to secede, referendum or no referendum. But that imprudent boast was on the record and Bouchard prepared to exploit it.

So, on May 24, 1994, Bouchard opened Question Period as follows: "Last week," Bouchard began, "the prime minister stated that since the Canadian Constitution is silent on the matter, the issue of Quebec's sovereignty is, and I quote: 'purely academic.' This statement raised some doubts about the prime minister's position, that is to say, whether or not he recognizes Quebec's right to decide on its own sovereignty. I want to ask the prime minister to remove these doubts as to his position on the subject and to tell this House whether or not he recognizes Quebec's right to self-determination."

Chrétien offered, as usual, an ambiguous reply: "In 1980, we allowed a referendum to be held on the question of Quebec's separation. As I said several times last week, and I say it again today, only 5 per cent of Quebeckers see the issue of separation and the Constitution as a priority. It is my duty to deal with the nation's real problems instead of spreading political and economic uncertainty in this country, and to make sure that Quebec remains in Canada. And I am convinced that Quebec will remain Canadian."

Bouchard returned to the attack: "I asked a fundamental question which requires a clear answer. My question is whether the prime minister of Canada, of this country, respects Quebec democracy. Will the prime minister tell us clearly, and I will repeat my question, as head of state and prime minister, whether or not he recognizes Quebec's right to self-determination?" Chrétien refused again to give a clear answer, so Bouchard returned to the charge a third time: "I want to ask the prime minister whether he realizes that his ambiguous remarks imply that he reserves the right not to recognize the desire for sovereignty democratically expressed by Quebeckers. How can he reconcile this ambiguous attitude with his own behaviour and that of his leader, Pierre Elliott Trudeau, in 1980, when they were both very much involved in the Quebec referendum campaign and they agreed to abide by the outcome of this democratic process? Why don't this party and this government follow the example of the Conservative Party and the New Democratic Party, which adopted resolutions formally recognizing Quebec's right to self-determination?"

In his third response, the prime minister again evaded the question, and he failed to challenge the absolutely false statement that, in 1980, Prime Minister Trudeau had "agreed to abide by the outcome of this democratic process." Chrétien, instead, replied with the same ambiguity: "I want a referendum with a very clear question, not playing on words to try to confuse people, not talking about sovereignty, not talking about sovereignty-association, but talking about the real thing: the separation of Quebec from Canada. I am a democrat but I am not going to spend my time debating that because I know clearly that the preoccupation of the people of Quebec is exactly the same as the preoccupation of all Canadians. They want jobs, job creation, and growth."

At a time when the country was likely to soon face a challenge to the very foundation of the constitutional order on which the Canadian state was built, instead of clarity, credibility, and consistency of vision, the prime minister of Canada offered evasions, ambiguities, and retreats that sent only one clear message: he did not dare defend the constitutional order. *I am a democrat*, the prime minister said. What did he mean, or what was he implying? That exchange gave important intelligence to the separatist camp. Chrétien really believed that the issue was one of "democracy," as the separatists argued, and not one of right – of legality or the rule of law. He was afraid to defend the Constitution. The next day, in the National Assembly, Opposition Leader Jacques Parizeau followed up on Bouchard's challenge: "The highly noted participation of the federal authorities, both financially and personally, notably Messrs Chrétien and Trudeau, at the time of the 1980 referendum, serves as a precedent and establishes the legitimacy of the process." Even the federalist premier Daniel Johnson agreed with Parizeau that day in the National Assembly: "It seems to me perfectly clear that in Quebec . . . we already exercised in 1980 the right to self-determination. And so I don't see why it would suddenly have disappeared."

What all three, Bouchard, Parizeau, and Johnson, claimed was demonstrably false. Trudeau had done the opposite of "agreeing to abide by the outcome." Trudeau had stated clearly that neither he nor the rest of Canada were bound by the outcome of a referendum in Quebec, and he would refuse to recognize a majority vote for sovereignty-association. In his great speech on May 14, 1980, just six days before the referendum, before a massed crowd in Montreal's Paul Sauvé Arena, he said: "Mr. Lévesque has asked me what my attitude would be if the majority of Quebeckers voted Yes. I have already answered this question. . . . Mr. Lévesque will be welcome to come to Ottawa, where I will receive him politely, as he has always received me in Quebec City, and I will tell him that there are two doors. If you knock on the sovereignty-association door, there is no negotiation possible."

Trudeau then confronted directly the argument that democracy rules. He used an analogy that Quebeckers would understand. Newfoundlanders were bitter over the Churchill Falls contract made with Hydro-Quebec in the 1960s, which made no provision for the rising price of power. That contract had earned many billions of dollars for Quebec, and very little revenue went to Newfoundland. So Trudeau said: "It is like saying to Mr. Lévesque, 'The people of Newfoundland have just voted 100 per cent in favour of renegotiating the electricity contract with Quebec. You are obliged, in the name of democracy, to respect the will of Newfoundland, are you not?' It is obvious that this sort of logic does not work. The wishes of Quebeckers may be expressed through a democratic process, but that cannot bind others – those in other provinces who did not vote – to act as Quebec decides."

But, under Chrétien, the Liberal government now spoke as though it recognized a right for Quebec to secede, regardless of the rule of law. On June 6, for the fiftieth anniversary of D-Day, Deputy Prime Minister Sheila Copps had commemorated the landing of Canadian soldiers in Normandy by saying: "Very few of us will have to choose to give our lives for others' liberty. The liberty to speak out; the liberty to separate." The *Toronto Star*, in reporting her speech, noted that Copps stared straight at the Bloc benches when she said: "the liberty to separate." She thereby suggested that secession was a guaranteed right for which Canadian soldiers had died.

Harper and the other Reform MPs witnessed with incredulity the preposterous claims of Bouchard and Parizeau and the spineless response of the government ministers. And so they struck back with a motion of their own, that was debated in the Commons on June 7, 1994. It proposed, in part, "That this House strongly affirm and support the desire of Canadians to remain federally united as one people. . . ." This gave Harper his first opportunity to cross swords with Lucien Bouchard as each put forward their incompatible visions of Canada. Harper contrasted the Reform vision of equality of individuals and provinces with the granting of special rights to some clients of the federal state: "We are suggesting the government of Canada should concentrate its efforts on the responsibility for the promotion of our collective identity as a nation rather than the focus it has had in the past generation on things like official multiculturalism or the promotion of Canada as a federation of two founding peoples: the English and the French. In our view we should be going toward more race-, culture-, language-neutral concepts of our nationhood. Defining a country as a union of founding peoples, English and French, in this day and age, is to Reformers as ridiculous as it would be to define it as a nation of two founding religions: the Protestants and the Catholics."

This vision was certainly different from Bouchard's, and also from that of Brian Mulroney and Jean Chrétien. But the strongest moment of Harper's speech came at the very end. He gave a solemn warning to the prime minister as well as to the separatist leaders: "I remind all members that all serious constitutional change, all constitutional change, anything that would significantly change in our federation the status of any citizen or any province, requires respect for democracy, for the Constitution, and for the rule of law. It is not compatible with unilateral or illegal actions. I expect as we debate our future in the next few months that the expectation of all Canadians will be that we continue to function in the context of a constitutional democracy and we will all respect the rule of law."

Lucien Bouchard had no intention of respecting the rule of law, and Jean Chrétien was doing nothing to uphold it. When Bouchard spoke, he rejected utterly the policies Harper had enunciated. "For Quebeckers, their national government is in Quebec and the doctrine of provincial equality represents a denial of their history and of their aspirations for the future." He reiterated the myth cherished by Quebec's political class that, despite all conclusive refutations, Canada was originally created as two founding peoples. For Bouchard, Canada's problem was that the two peoples were too different to be accommodated in one country: "We have two realities: we have Quebec and we have the rest of Canada.

The Quebec people do not think they are better than any other part of the country, but they think they are different. They have done nothing to destroy anything. We do not intend to destroy Canada. We intend to adapt the political structures to the realities." Bouchard was prone to euphemisms, presenting secession as "adapting the political structures to the realities." Bouchard did not want to destroy Canada, only improve it by removing Quebec.

The debate that day had elicited nothing but banalities from the Liberal government, which avoided any commitment to uphold the Constitution. And so, the next day, Manning sent a letter to Chrétien that expressing his disquiet over the absence of leadership at the top to respond to a dangerous issue: "Prime Minister, we cannot stand by passively and allow Quebec voters to make the decision – separation or Canada – without offering them a vigorous defence of Canada, including a positive federalist alternative to the status quo. And we cannot let them make their decision without disputing the separatist contention that separation will be a relatively uncomplicated and painless process. . . . With millions of Quebeckers indicating their desire to vote for the separatist Parti Québécois in the forthcoming provincial election, it is necessary to prepare for this challenge, and not bury our heads in the sand."

Manning accompanied his letter with a list of twenty questions that raised all the thorny constitutional and practical problems that would be triggered by an attempted secession of Quebec. They suggested that the Reform Party would provide tough answers to those questions. The first question asked, "How would the Government of Canada respond to a formal request from the government of any province to secede from the Canadian federation?" Another question suggested that secession would require an amendment to the Constitution – which neither the Parti Québécois nor the Liberal Party of Quebec accepted. And Manning raised the sensitive issue of partitioning a seceding Quebec: "What principles would guide the Government of Canada with respect to resolving the conflicting claims of the government of a seceding province and of identifiable groups within the province that might want to remain within Canada (for instance, aboriginal groups)?" He even raised the question of whether force would be used in the event of attempted secession.

Manning's questions raised the issues that Chrétien should have raised at the beginning of his mandate, when the Bloc Québécois's success in winning more than two-thirds of Quebec's seats portended a serious secessionist threat in the near future. A provincial election had to be held in Quebec within the coming year, and the Bloc's sweep projected a Parti Québécois victory. But Chrétien never gave a substantive answer to Manning's questions. In the House, he continued to respond with rambling, evasive answers to all questions dealing with the threat of secession. His response was, indeed, to bury his head firmly in the sand. Manning, from his early dismissal of the national unity debate, soon appointed Harper as Reform's point man on the issue, and he gave it increasing priority himself: "Within our caucus I had assigned Stephen Harper, our best mind when it came to strategy and policy, to the unity file. He was also one of the four bilingual members of our caucus," Manning would recall in *Think Big*.

On September 12, 1994, the issue of secession ceased to be "hypothetical" when Jacques Parizeau's PQ won the provincial elections and began to prepare for a referendum. Harper's responsibility suddenly became paramount. Parizeau was a very different leader from René Lévesque, and the state of federalism in Quebec had seriously deteriorated since the referendum of 1980. Above all, Jean Chrétien was no Pierre Trudeau.

Parizeau was determined to turn Quebec into a sovereign state, with or without an association with Canada, with or without the true will of a majority of the people of Quebec. All he required to make the leap to independence was the merest 50 per cent of the vote plus one, in a referendum on a cannily contrived question. For him, that would be final, there would be no turning back. He once compared his imminent referendum to a lobster trap: once in, there was no way out. Though he maintained some public ambiguity about his intentions before the referendum that would be held on October 30, 1995, he made himself crystal clear afterward. He planned to make a unilateral declaration of independence shortly after a winning referendum, as part of his strategy to win recognition from France and from former French colonies: "I never committed myself, either in public or in private, not to make a unilateral declaration of sovereignty," he wrote in his 1997 book *Pour un Québec souverain*. In the year 2000, on the twentieth anniversary of Lévesque's 1980 referendum, he explained the difference between Lévesque's appeal to the people and the one he held: "There are still analysts who have not caught on to the fact that the difference between 1980 and 1995 is that, in 1995, we go for keeps. If it had won by 26,000 votes in the other direction, I was going for it, I would have done it." In 2004, interviewed on CPAC television, he asserted: "Listen, the only reason that I went into politics was the independence of Quebec. If you elect me, I go for it. Not to negotiate sovereignty, to declare it. So we came close, we were short 52,000 votes out of nearly 5 million. With 52,000 more votes, Quebec would be an independent country today – you understand, [independent] for seven years now."

There could be no doubt of the revolutionary determination, not only of Premier Parizeau, but also of Lucien Bouchard. The leader of the Bloc Québécois met with the editorial board of the *Gazette*, with the account published on October 11, 1994. He was asked, "Is 50 per cent plus one enough?" "Yes," he replied. "If we have 51 per cent support – I would like to have more – but if we have 51 per cent, well, we have a democratic mandate to go further. This is democracy." He was asked to explain what he meant by going further: "If the referendum goes Yes and the federal government drags its heels, would you then support a unilateral declaration of independence?" He replied: "Yes, at the date announced in the question. Because the date would be part of the mandate given to the government."

The next day, Chrétien was taping an interview with Anne-Marie Dussault of Radio-Québec. She cited Bouchard's words and asked Chrétien what would happen if the federalist side lost the referendum. His answer: "I don't know. The prime minister has a constitution to respect and there is no mechanism in the Constitution permitting the separation of any part of the Canadian territory." His statement, so different from his usual bromides, caused a shock. "Chrétien calls into question Quebec's right to self-determination," *Le Devoir* blared at the top of its front page.

That same week, the Reform Party was holding in Ottawa its biennial convention. On the Thursday, two days after Bouchard's support for a UDI, Preston Manning held a press conference to discuss the convention opening that day. Instead of a thundering denunciation of Bouchard's threat, Manning was rather supportive. Asked by a reporter if he would recognize a majority Yes vote in the coming referendum, he replied: "I think it is generally conceded that, if any province democratically – a majority of its people – decide that they want to leave, and they've done so through a referendum asking a straight question, then that would be conceded." I asked Manning a follow-up question: "Would a bare majority suffice?" He replied: "My own view is, on referendums generally, any departure from 50 per cent plus one is hard to justify."

At the convention, Manning gave as usual a major address on the Saturday. He won great applause when he raised his voice: "And to the separatist politicians we say, 'We're going to take you on.'" He went on: "Once the Quebec Assembly convenes, it has promised to pass an anti-constitutional act – a solemn declaration to secede. And if the Bloc supports that, it will cross a line in the constitutional sand which will disqualify it once and for all from continuing to masquerade as Canada's Loyal Official Opposition." But he made no suggestion in his speech that he would repudiate a UDI.

Two years earlier, on January 23, 1992, speaking to the Montreal Canadian Club, he had suggested that secession was something outside the purview of the existing Constitution. "In the absence of such law, we tip the scales in favour of the minority who want a New Quebec outside of a New Canada on their own terms, rather than in favour of that vast majority of Canadians who want to see a New Quebec inside a New Canada on mutually agreeable terms." In other words, Manning would allow Quebec to secede if that was what Quebeckers wanted. And even to secede, as he put it, "on their own terms." That suggested his consent to a unilateral process of secession in which the federalists would have little or no say on the conditions.

It was Stephen Harper who took up the defence of the Constitution and of the rule of law. He did not accept, as did Prime Minister Chrétien and Manning, that the Constitution of Canada contained a vacuum with respect to the secession of a province. For him, the Constitution did apply and secession could only be achieved legally by an enabling amendment to the Constitution. And so, the following Monday, when the Commons met for the first time since the statements by Bouchard and Chrétien the previous week, Harper put this question to Marcel Massé, the Minister of Intergovernmental Affairs: "Last week the prime minister was quoted as saying: 'A prime minister of Canada has a Constitution he must respect and there is no mechanism in the Constitution permitting the separation of any part of Canadian territory.' We know that separatism would require substantial constitutional amendment. Will the Minister of Intergovernmental Affairs commit to the House, on behalf of the government, that it is the position of the Government of Canada that any change to the constitutional status of a province would have to be done legally and would require, under the amending formula, the consent of all provinces?" But Massé followed Chrétien's practice of evading the most important question facing the country. "This is a hypothetical question on which the prime minister commented in general. I certainly do not intend to go any further than that."

Two days later, Harper again returned to the subject, and proceeded to disagree with the assumption that "there is no mechanism in the Constitution permitting the separation of any part of the Canadian territory." He countered: "While that is very narrowly true, in fact the Constitution does have provisions relating to amendment of various things that would be required in the event of the separation of a province. These are things as elementary as the transfer of the legitimate powers of the federal government to a province which would, generally speaking, require the consent of two-thirds of the provinces representing 50 per cent of the population. In other cases, where it actually involves institutional change, it would require unanimous consent. These clauses are laid out in Part V, sections 38 through 49, of the Constitution Act, 1982."

Harper was exactly right, as the Supreme Court of Canada would confirm on August 20, 1998, in its decision on the unilateral secession of Quebec. And Harper then drew the appropriate conclusion from his analysis: "My question to the government [on October 17] was merely that it affirm that it is the position of the Government of Canada that the constitutional status of a province could only be changed legally, and would be done through this amending formula. This would of course not apply simply with a separation scenario but to any constitutional change. I would maintain that it is the duty of the federal government which purports that national unity is its highest priority *to recognize that it does have an obligation to uphold the Constitution*."

Harper's was a voice crying in the wilderness. He was considered an extremist, a hard-liner, both then and later, for saying out loud that the government must uphold the constitutional order. "I would also note that politically, there would be considerable advantage for it to make clear to the people of Quebec that, when they are being told that separation can be achieved unilaterally, that this is legally untrue. In fact, it would also be politically untrue, politically unfeasible to pursue in that manner." If Chrétien had taken this advice, he would have spared himself and the country much danger, and changed the course of the political history of Canada over the following years.

But the government's position was spelled out by John English, Parliamentary Secretary to Minister Massé: "The Minister of Inter-governmental Affairs for whom I am answering believes that the Constitution Acts do not provide any rules or procedures for secession of one of the provinces. . . . It seems to us that the premise of the member's question is that we should say: 'You cannot leave unless we let you go.' That does not seem to be a very helpful approach at this time. Our approach is to argue to Quebeckers that the case for secession cannot be sustained. It involves costs and risks that are unnecessary, and that this country is too precious to be destroyed. We want the question to be put fairly and quickly. I do not intend to talk on behalf of the Leader of the Opposition, but I believe he said this morning in Toronto that he is a democrat and we are all democrats. Certainly, we in this Chamber are all democrats and a democratic decision is appropriate and will occur, we hope, promptly and with a clear question."

We are all democrats. And Chrétien had said, "I am a democrat." The naive view prevailed that the constitutional order could be over-turned by a referendum held in one part of the country. The ignorance of international practice, the generalized misunderstanding of liberal democracy among politicians and journalists, was putting the country in peril. Harper was the exception.

On December 6, 1994, any doubt about Jacques Parizeau's revolu-tionary intent vanished when the premier unveiled his strategy for the coming referendum. He made public a draft bill which stated in Section 1: "Quebec is a sovereign country." The intention, he revealed, was to have the bill adopted by the National Assembly before the referendum, but to be promulgated after the referendum, if the vote returned a major-ity Yes. The referendum question was to be: "Are you in favour of the law adopted by the National Assembly declaring the sovereignty of Quebec?" And the bill had a blank first page where normally there would be a pre-amble. Parizeau explained that the people themselves would write the preamble. He invited everyone to send in their suggestions. It could begin, for example, by, "We, the People of Quebec . . ." just as the U.S. Constitution begins: "We, the People of the United States . . ."

To help the people decide what they wanted in the preamble, Parizeau announced that fifteen commissions would be set up, one in each of Quebec's regions, each presided by a local *notable*, and with a Quebec cabinet minister assigned to each. They would hold public hearings in which everyone was invited to come and deliver a personal conception of what should be the future sovereign Quebec. Besides these regional commissions, there would be a commission to hear the advice of elders, and another to hear the testimony of the youth. Finally, a national commission would be held to put it all together and make recommendations.

The entire process was, as Parizeau had announced beforehand, *astucieux*, canny. It brought politics out of the National Assembly and into the four corners of Quebec where people lived. The people would be brought into the loop, mobilized, co-opted to ensure a burst of pride and enthusiasm for an independent Quebec that would produce a Yes majority. Parizeau went on television that same evening to recite the defeats and humiliations of the recent past, the patriation of the Constitution in 1982 over the refusal of the National Assembly, the failed Meech and Charlottetown accords, and the current deadlock. Sovereignty was the solution.

So what was Ottawa's response? In the Commons that afternoon, both Preston Manning and Stephen Harper demanded that the government take a stand on whether the draft bill was constitutional. Manning led off: "Does the Government of Canada agree that the draft act respecting the sovereignty of Quebec is beyond the legal powers of the government and assembly of Quebec?" In the absence of Chrétien, Deputy Prime Minister Sheila Copps replied: "The Government of Canada has every confidence that the people of Quebec, when given the chance to vote on the real question of whether they want to become a part of a separate country or whether they want to stay in Canada, will vote an overwhelming yes to Canada." She avoided addressing whether the draft bill was constitutional, and when Manning and Harper pressed her, she continued evading, and even suggested that both were disloyal: "[Harper] is on very dangerous ground when, at a very crucial point in Canada's history, [Harper] and his leader and other members of his party are more intent on attacking the federal government than on attacking the separatists."

That exchange encapsulated the attitude of the Liberal government, from the prime minister on down, until the last week before the referendum. What Parizeau had set in motion was manifestly unconstitutional. The Liberals' entire riposte was that Parizeau did not frame the referendum question correctly. They thereby suggested that, with the question properly rephrased, Parizeau could proceed without a care in the world. By silence, by omission, by unwarranted concessions, the Liberals consented to Parizeau's proposal to secede unilaterally.

The next day, Manning returned to the crucial issue. Copps now had had a day to absorb the implications of Parizeau's draft bill. Manning asked: "The Charter says that Canada is founded upon the principle that recognizes the supremacy of law. If that principle is to guide federal government reactions, then at least it should be willing to put forward an opinion on the legality or illegality of separatist initiatives. Can the Deputy Prime Minister at least tell the House as a bare minimum what principles will guide federal reactions to separatist initiatives?" Copps was just as evasive as the day before.

On December 8, Chrétien was back in the Commons. Questioned about the legality of Parizeau's draft bill, he, too, was evasive: "I do not want to debate what is in this project of law. We can have a long debate on that. The question is a very simple one. They should have the honesty to ask the Quebec people first: 'Do you want to separate, yes or no?' To play games like that will lead nowhere. It is just a sign that they are afraid to be honest with the people and ask a very simple question: 'Do you want to separate from Canada, yes or no?'"

On that day, the Commons debated a Bloc motion, "That this House enjoins the government to recognize the legitimacy of the democratic process initiated by the Government of Quebec in order to allow Quebeckers to chart their own political and constitutional future." The separatists urged their view that "democracy" gave Quebec a green light to secede on the strength of a majority vote in Quebec. The government never questioned that revolutionary assumption, but only insisted that the question had to deal precisely with separation.

Also on that day, Stephen Harper was on a CBC television news panel with host Pamela Wallin. He insisted that Jacques Parizeau's proposal was entirely unconstitutional and that the federal government must defend the Constitution. "I think in the immediate future our role is really to speak for the Parliament of Canada and for the rights of all Canadians through the Parliament of Canada. The Parliament of Canada and Canadians cannot be stripped of their power, and a province cannot redefine its constitutional status, as Mr. Parizeau asserts, without any reference to the rest of the country or its legal rights and obligations. And that's an important point to make. When a premier gets up and says, 'I will negate all the powers of the federal Parliament, of the courts, I will do so just by passing an act in the Assembly, I'll negotiate it, if I feel like it,' I think it's very important that a clear message be sent out that that will not happen. It is in nobody's interest to allow that kind of fantasy to go on."

Harper was exactly right. But the fantasy did go on, maintained by collusion between the two separatist parties and the government of Canada. For months before and after Parizeau put out his draft bill, Manning and especially Harper tried to get Chrétien to say that he would defend the Constitution against an unconstitutional attempt at secession. But the prime minister, always the artful dodger, evaded and avoided. Giving the people good government was all that was required, and they would vote No. Ask the proper question and they will vote No. He would not even countenance the possibility that they might vote Yes. His answers gave aid and comfort to the separatists by their failure to challenge their proposal to violate the Constitution by taking Quebec out of Canada without an enabling amendment to the Constitution.

The week following Parizeau's announcement, Justice Minister Allan Rock explained before a *Cité libre* dinner crowd his own position on the issue of constitutionality: "Is everyone interested in these technical details? To my mind, it's not constitutional. But that's a technical question. The real question is for Quebeckers, in a referendum. It's possible to have a debate on the constitutionality of the draft legislation – a very interesting one for lawyers – but what matters more is the will of Quebeckers."

On December 15, in a year-end interview with Preston Manning in his office in the Parliament Buildings, I asked him to reconcile his press conference statement of October 13 that a province could secede by voting for secession in response to a clear question, with his strong statements in the Commons in defence of the constitutional order. In reply, Manning defended both statements. "If a group of people – a province – democratically decide, through a clear question, on a clear issue, that they want to get out, then the federal government should be prepared to enter into negotiations. But the central principle is that the rule of law ought to prevail: that as much of this as can be done within the framework of law, the better. You ought to go as far as you can with the rule of law. Then, ultimately, that's why we add this consent of the governed."

I asked, several times, "But what if Quebeckers vote for secession and an amendment to the Constitution cannot be achieved to allow Quebeckers to secede under the rule of law? Which principle will prevail, that of 'democratic legitimacy,' or the rule of law?" For all the words that poured forth, the answer was impenetrable. My conclusion: Manning wanted to have it both ways. His romantic populism and his conservatism were at odds in this instance, so he would not choose. Or, if he chose, "democratic legitimacy" would trump the rule of law. That was quite different from Harper's thinking.

Parizeau's argument for a right to secede relied on the myth of the two founding peoples or two founding nations, a fabrication created in the twentieth century by Henri Bourassa. Since Canada violated the founding contract, Parizeau argued, Quebec was no longer bound by it. His argument could have been easily demolished by the federal government. But the leader of the Quebec Liberals, Daniel Johnson, subscribed to the same myth. Though he was a federalist, he and his party had maintained for a generation that Quebec had the right to choose any constitutional future it wanted, including secession. This had no support in international law or in the Canadian Constitution. But Chrétien was deterred by Johnson, the nominal leader of the No forces in the referendum, from attacking the separatist venture on its illegality.

It took a private citizen to test in court Parizeau's seditious process. Guy Bertrand, a prominent Quebec City lawyer, petitioned the Quebec Superior Court for redress, claiming that his rights under the Canadian Charter of Rights and Freedoms were threatened by Parizeau's revolutionary plan. He wrote the prime minister and the minister of justice, asking for them to intervene on behalf of Canadian unity. Both refused. Chrétien, in his reply to Bertrand of August 14, 1995, refused to defend the Constitution and wrote in part: "I consider that the central question is the will of Quebeckers to be part of Canada. I have the strong conviction that the best strategy towards those advocating the separation of Quebec is to insist that they demonstrate that separation is in the best interests of Quebeckers and to demand that they ask an unambiguous question. I think I understand the reasons why you want to challenge the legality of the draft bill. I don't believe, however, that at the present time, the government of Canada would be well advised to act in the way that you recommend."

Chrétien spoke of the "best strategy," as though strategy determined whether or not to enforce the Constitution. And so Bertrand alone pleaded for the constitutional order before Mr. Justice Robert Lesage. Premier Parizeau's lawyers argued that the court had no jurisdiction over secession because it was essentially a political decision. When the judge ruled against their motion to dismiss, Parizeau ordered his lawyers to withdraw from the case.

On September 8, 1995, Mr. Justice Lesage rendered his declaratory judgment, and it condemned Parizeau's venture. Draft Bill 1 "constitutes a grave threat to the rights and freedoms . . . guaranteed by the Canadian Charter of Rights and Freedoms" and is "manifestly illegal," the judge asserted. "The court cannot condone a violation of the constitutional order. . . . The [Quebec] government is investing enormous means to achieve its end. It is attempting to overthrow the constitutional order by using its political power and public funds. . . . The prejudice is irreparable. With such a scenario, the stability of the legal order is compromised." The Quebec government never appealed. Instead, it denounced the Constitution of Canada. Quebec's justice minister Paul Bégin stated: "We don't feel bound by the 1982 Constitution." Then, on September 10, 1995, Parizeau himself told Jean-François Lépine on Radio-Canada television: "We never signed it. The 1982 Constitution, that the judge reproaches us for I'm not sure what, for not following it in all its terms, that Charter was refused by René Lévesque; then it was refused by Premier Pierre-Marc Johnson; it was refused by Robert Bourassa, it was refused by Daniel Johnson; it was refused by me. . . . You understand that, today, to invoke that Constitution to tell us, 'And why don't you accept it?' Well, we are going to say, 'Listen, we never accepted it, we never signed it.' "

Despite the clear declaratory judgment, years of mythical thinking about secession had so corrupted public opinion that Gilles Lesage, in an editorial in Le Devoir on September 11, 1995, utterly misrepresented what the judge had ruled: "The process is legitimate. . . . The judge recognizes that the case put forward by lawyer Bertrand can ultimately only be settled by the people, and the people alone. It is the court of the people that must decide in the last resort, he says in effect, and no court judgment can go against the will of the people. . . . The will of the people must be sovereign." Lesage enunciated precisely the opposite of what the judge had really found. Nor was *Le Devoir* alone. Alain Dubuc, editorial page editor of *La Presse*, on September 12 described the issue of legality as *"une considération technique,"* a mere technicality, of little significance: "The federalist forces agree with the sovereigntists to recognize the democratic value of the referendum exercise and to wish that the future of Quebec depends on the choice of the people rather than on technical considerations. . . . The principal contribution of this judgment will be that it demonstrates the limits of legality and that it reminds us that the constitutional approach has the unfortunate tendency to lead us nowhere. *Ce sont des coups de toge dans l'eau* – these are pointless legal flourishes."

Now, if ever, the federal government had the duty to defend the constitutional order, so clearly defined by the court, and to uphold the rule of law against a provincial government in open rebellion. The judge had based his decision on the Canadian Charter of Rights, which gave citizens the right to appeal to the court if their rights were violated by the state. Mr. Justice Lesage had found that citizen Bertrand's Charter rights were seriously threatened by Parizeau's referendum venture. If true of Bertrand, it was true of millions of other Canadian citizens. It was the duty of the prime minister and the justice minister to protect all those individuals' rights, as well as the peace, order, and good government of Canada. Instead, both took a dive, kept silent, and stayed out of sight for several days. There was no press conference, no communiqué, not even a scrum. They had no comment on what the court termed attempts "to overthrow the constitutional order." The first reaction from the government came on September 12 from Lucienne Robillard, the minister representing the federal government in the referendum campaign. As she entered a cabinet meeting, she was asked about the Lesage decision. In effect, she repudiated it. The journalist then asked: "Are you saying the federal government must accept the outcome of the referendum, no matter what?" She replied: "We always said that Quebeckers have the right to express themselves about the future of Quebec in Canada – inside or outside Canada – and we are in a democratic country, so we will respect the vote."

When Chrétien was approached, he dismissed the significance of the court ruling. He assured reporters that the No side would win and that questions about recognizing a Yes victory were only hypothetical. "Don't waste your time with the *if*, *if*, and *if*." And Allan Rock also evaded responding to the court decision on the same grounds.

That court decision, and the government's dereliction of duty, should have set up the Reform Party's finest hour. The court had confirmed what Manning, and especially Harper, had insistently repeated. Reform was vindicated; the Liberal government exposed. But when, on September 18, the Commons returned from the summer recess, ten days after the court judgment, the Reformers made a 180 degree turnabout. During the summer, the MPs had heard angry comments from western constituents who demanded an end to squabbling over the Constitution. They wanted the Quebec issue settled once and for all, win or lose.

And so the first Reformer up that day, Ray Speaker, ignored the court decision, but rebuked the government for paying too much attention to the referendum: "As Parliament returns for its fall session, the country faces a number of important challenges: health-care reform, tax reform, pension reform, UI reform. Yet none of these issues are on the government's fall agenda. Why? Because the government has been hijacked by the Quebec referendum. . . . If neither the Liberals nor the Bloc will speak on behalf of all Canadians, the Reform Party will. We have the people, we have the plan, and we have the will to confront the tough issues."

Jan Brown was the Reformer up next: "I would like to congratulate the city of Calgary. After many months of hard work and patience, Calgary has won the competition to host Expo 2005. . . ." Then came the turn of Margaret Bridgman: "I call attention to the need for appropriate sentencing in order to prevent habitual offenders from victimizing communities. . . ." John Duncan began, "The Canadian agenda includes a lot more than the Quebec referendum," before raising the issue of "documented lawlessness" at Camp Ipperwash, under native occupation. Bob Mills prefaced a question on Canadian peacekeepers in Bosnia with this remark: "Today, we have heard a great deal about the October 30 Quebec deadline, but the government has an important September 30 deadline on the future of the Bosnia peacekeeping mission. . . ."

Preston Manning, with his first opportunity in three months to question the prime minister, began: "Canadians want this Quebec referendum to be decisive and conclusive. They do not want any confusion or ambiguity concerning the meaning of the vote, before or after. Yet the leader of the Opposition clouds the issue when he says that he is prepared to accept a Yes vote as binding and conclusive but not a No vote, and the prime minister does not help things when he implies that he is prepared to accept a No vote as binding and conclusive but waffles on the meaning of a Yes vote." This was the old, "A pox on both your houses" gambit. Manning then enunciated Reform's new posture, that he would maintain for the rest of the referendum campaign: "For the benefit of all Canadians, including Quebeckers who want clarity and certainty in interpreting the Quebec referendum, will the prime minister make clear that a Yes vote means Quebec is on its way out, that a No vote means Quebec is in the federation for the long haul, and that 50 per cent plus one is the dividing line between those two positions?"

Chrétien fell back on the refrain he had repeated for a year: "If we had a clear question. They are asking the people of Canada: Do you want sovereignty? At the same time they say they want to stay in Canada. . . . I have been asking them for a long time in this House of Commons to give us a real question, an honest, clear question on separation. They want me on behalf of all Canadians to say that, with a clouded question like that, with one vote, I will help them to destroy Canada. You might, I will not, Mr. Manning."

Manning reiterated his new doctrine: "Will the prime minister state unequivocally that a 50 per cent plus one Yes in the referendum will mean, sadly, an end to Quebec's position in Canada and not a new and better union?" Chrétien stuck to the same old line: "They are not being very frank with the people of Quebec. . . . Six weeks from today the people of Quebec, the people who were here, who opened up this country, when the francophones of this land left the Saint-Maurice Valley to open the prairies, do we think these people will want to let go of the best country in the world? They will not."

When Stephen Harper's turn came, he fell in with the new line. Legality no longer was the issue; what mattered was on which side of 50 per cent the referendum vote fell, and that would decide the issue once and for all. "I have to say that I am extremely disturbed, and I think

Canadians will be disturbed, at the answers the prime minister gave to the leader of the Reform Party. We have the separatists in Quebec telling Quebeckers that they can vote Yes and have this imaginary union. Now we have the prime minister saying that a No vote counts and a Yes vote may not count. I ask the prime minister to reconsider that position carefully. Is he not really telling Quebeckers that it is easy and without risk to vote Yes when that is not the case?"

Chrétien dismissed Harper's question: "I do not know what the real question is the member is asking me. I am always telling Quebeckers that they have a chance to vote again on this. For months and months I have asked the Government of Quebec to ask a clear question. It is asking an ambiguous question. . . . Therefore, do not tell me to tell them that it will be over on October 31. This country will be together on October 31 of this year and on October 31 of next year. As long as I am alive it will be part of Canada. Therefore, I do not want to spend my time talking about separation."

Harper returned to the attack, again insisting that the vote on October 30 must be decisive. "This country is not going to stay together just on the basis of one man's interpretation of a referendum question. It will stay together because the prime minister and others are successful in convincing Quebeckers to vote No. I again ask the prime minister, why he does not simply do what the leader of the Opposition is unwilling to do and tell Quebeckers that their vote counts, Yes or No, and that democracy is on the side of the federalists?" Chrétien, as always the dodger, would neither agree nor deny that a 50 per cent vote would be conclusive and final.

In his memoirs, Manning justified his stance that 50 per cent would be decisive by precedent – his mistaken belief that it had been so accepted in 1980 – and by the dangerous situation that was created for federalism by leaving the consequences of the vote ambiguous. "What was most dangerous to our cause was the ambiguity of his position on the consequences of a 'Yes' vote and the voting threshold at which those consequences would become real. To those Liberal backbenchers and media people who questioned my 'loyalty' because my questions made the prime minister's position look weak and confused, my response was simple. The prime minister's position *was* weak and confused."

Yes, the prime minister's position was weak, confused, and grotesquely irresponsible. But Manning did not explain why an undertaking that he and Harper had denounced as unconstitutional should suddenly bind the whole country and all its citizens. Manning also argued in his memoirs that "raising the percentage to 60 per cent or higher, as some Liberals mused, would play into the hands of the separatists in another way. . . . It would encourage 'strategic voting,' something Quebeckers are intuitively more adept at than any other electorate in Canada, a 'we can have our cake and eat it too' position." Again, Manning could be right in terms of tactics, but was certainly wrong in terms of fundamental principles, which must be upheld regardless of which way the wind blows. Neither Manning nor Harper addressed the question of how to square their new doctrine with the rule of law and the Charter rights of the citizens, as defined by Justice Robert Lesage. The Reform spokesmen, in September and October 1995, took a stand inconsistent with their principles of the year before and made themselves supporters of an attempt to overthrow the Constitution of Canada and the Canadian state by unconstitutional means. That deserves a better explanation.

While the Reformers had abandoned the rule of law, they had not abandoned their conviction that Quebeckers must be given alternatives to the status quo if they were to resist the lure of secession. Manning wrote: "Although Reform's influence in Quebec was marginal, we resolved to do what we could. Stephen Harper and Scott Reid had fleshed out our proposed changes to federalism, our New Confederation proposals. These we released on October 15. . . . At a minimum, we hoped to show that there was support for 'changing federalism' in the part of the country we truly represented – the West – and to invite Quebeckers to vote 'No.'"

The "New Confederation" proposals involved substantial changes. The general thrust was to remove power from Ottawa and transfer it to the provinces. But not entirely. "In this spirit of creating a balanced and unified federal state, there remain important federal powers that the Reform Party will not compromise," the document stated. "These include the powers of maintaining a common economic space, eliminating internal trade barriers, creating and coordinating key areas of economic regulation, and representing Canada effectively in international trade negotiations, defence, and foreign affairs." But, by and large, the twenty proposals for a "New Confederation" buttressed the autonomy of the provinces in such areas as language, culture, social services, manpower training, natural resources, housing, tourism, sports and recreation. This was the proposal on language: "We will introduce legislation to replace the Official Languages Act, with a new law, the Regional Bilingualism Act, that will recognize the demographic and linguistic reality of Canada and the practices of provincial authorities." On culture, Reform offered: "We will recognize, by appropriate legislation, that it is provincial governments rather than the federal government which serve as the primary providers and guardians of cultural services and as the regulators of cultural industries."

Meanwhile, Parizeau had been pressured by Bouchard and Deputy Premier Bernard Landry to change his referendum strategy. Both feared that holding a referendum on sovereignty alone would lead to another defeat. Bouchard insisted that Parizeau bow to the voice of the people and make a "*virage*." The referendum question should be inspired by the European Union and offer Canada a "new partnership." Bouchard wasn't going back to Lévesque's "hyphen" linking sovereignty inextricably with association. "We can no longer have the hyphen. Our proposal excludes the hyphen," he explained. "We are, first and foremost, sovereigntists. We want the sovereignty of Quebec." He argued that offering a form of union with Canada was important chiefly because, otherwise, many Quebeckers would not vote for sovereignty. The "common institutions" that he proposed excluded an elected parliament, even one like the weak European Parliament. It only meant that representatives of the governments of Canada and of Quebec would meet in equal numbers to deal with common interests, such as the St. Lawrence River. And each of the two governments would have a veto over any decisions made at the "parliamentary conference." And what if, after secession, such a "union" proved out of reach? "If English Canada says no, the worst that could happen is that we would be a sovereign country. For me, the referendum has to be about sovereignty. Period. And, at the same time, during the referendum period, we should be able to answer people who ask us: 'Yes, but what's going to happen afterwards? Will economic links be maintained?' We will be able to answer yes." Some cynics might call this bait and switch.

Another bonus was that this new proposal brought on board Mario Dumont, the former Liberal youth leader who broke with his party and formed the Action Démocratique du Québec. And so the name of the draft bill was changed from Act on the Sovereignty of Quebec to Act on the Future of Quebec. Section 1 which had originally declared: "Quebec is a sovereign country," was rewritten with less decisive language, in a move toward ambiguity: "The National Assembly is authorized, within the framework of the present act, to proclaim the sovereignty of Quebec. This proclamation must be preceded by a formal offer of an economic and political partnership with Canada." Many voters, as later polls showed, thought they would be voting for renewed federalism rather than secession. Parizeau made sure, though, that the "offer" of a partnership would not stand in the way of a unilateral declaration of independence if, as he expected, the offer went nowhere. And so an agreement was struck between Parizeau, Bouchard, and Dumont on June 12, and the referendum question was modified to ask:

> Do you agree that Quebec should become sovereign, after having made a formal offer to Canada for a new Economic and Political partnership, within the scope of the bill respecting the future of Quebec and of the agreement signed on June 12, 1995?
>
> YES . . .   NO . . .

With the ducks in place, Parizeau proceeded to Quebec's Grand Théâtre on September 6 for a dramatic reading of the "Preamble" of the Act on the Future of Quebec, the text that had been the supposed reason for public hearings across Quebec. Poets had been recruited, notably Gilles Vigneault, to ensure that the text would resonate down the ages. It was titled, "Declaration of Sovereignty." Perhaps some day it would be recited by schoolchildren in an independent Quebec.

> The time has come to reap the fields of history. The time has come at last to harvest what has been sown for us by four hundred years of men and women and courage, rooted in the soil and now returned to it. The time has come for us, tomorrow's ancestors, to make ready for our descendants harvests that are worthy of the labours of the past. May our toil be worthy of them, may they gather us together at last.

Premier Parizeau, sitting in the audience, had tears running down his cheeks as he listened to the words heralding his creation, an independent Quebec.

———◈———

The beginning of the referendum campaign had been encouraging for the federalists. Chrétien was confident his side would win in a walk. Daniel Johnson, head of the No committee, presented himself, not Parizeau, as the apostle of change. Under him, Quebec would once again lead the charge into the constitutional battleground. This put him at odds with Chrétien when he demanded that Quebec be recognized in the Constitution as a distinct society. On September 11, Chrétien had made light of that demand: "Distinct society? We are distinct, no need to put it in the Constitution. When you look at me and hear me speak English, you know I am distinct." As late as October 16, just two weeks before the referendum, Chrétien was still not receptive. He was questioned by Bouchard: "I want to ask [the prime minister] whether he intends to remind Mr. Johnson that the federal government has no intention of amending the Constitution to recognize the distinct identity of Quebec, as he himself, the prime minister of Canada, said on September 11 this year." Chrétien was no longer flippant. The tide in public opinion had turned, Bouchard was now leading the Yes campaign and he was having astounding success with suddenly reverential crowds. "Twice Canadians have been asked to vote on this. I remember the distinct society was part of the Charlottetown Accord. I voted for the Accord. The leader of the Opposition voted against it. The leader of the Bloc Québécois voted against it. The members of the Parti Québécois voted against it. Jacques Parizeau did. We were in favour of the Accord. They voted against it, but today they want it back. I think that is a little ridiculous. As we said before, today the issue is not the Constitution. Today we have to answer a question put by the leader of the Opposition and his former leader, the premier of Quebec, about whether we should separate. When asked the question: 'Should we separate?' the people of Quebec will say no."

In public opinion polls, support for the Yes side surged, and soon showed the Yes winning a majority. Panic swept the No camp. On the evening of October 24, a shaken Jean Chrétien appeared at a mass rally for the No in Verdun and, in deathbed repentance, promised what he had rejected all through the campaign – a distinct society: "A Quebec recognized in Canada as a distinct society by virtue of its language, culture, and institutions. I have said it before and I say it again: I agree." And a veto for Quebec: "Any changes in the constitutional jurisdiction of Quebec will only be made with the consent of Quebeckers." And openness to further changes of all kinds: "Voting No means rejecting separation. It does not mean that we give up anything regarding the Canadian Constitution. We will keep open all the other paths for change, including the administrative and constitutional ones."

The next morning Chrétien met with a worried Liberal caucus. Now the public opinion polls showed the Yes side well ahead, by several percentage points. Chrétien, usually so cocky, choked up and came to tears. He understood that, five days later, Canada was likely to plunge into the most deadly crisis of its history, because of his failure of leadership. That evening of October 25, 1995, Chrétien went on television in a desperate attempt to rally Quebeckers against a Yes vote. His speech now suggested that a Yes vote in the referendum would lead to secession. Nowhere did he do what Pierre Trudeau had done before in the 1980 referendum – assert that a Yes vote could not give Quebec a right to secede. At a critical moment, the prime minister of Canada totally abandoned the defence of the constitutional order.

> Tonight, in particular, I want to speak to my fellow Quebeckers. Because, at this moment, the future of our whole country is in their hands. . . . What is at stake is our country. What is at stake is our heritage. To break up Canada or build Canada. To remain Canadian or no longer be Canadian. To stay or to leave. This is the issue of the referendum. . . . The fact is that, hidden behind a murky question is a very clear option. It is the separation of Quebec. A Quebec that would no longer be part of Canada. . . . A Yes vote means the destruction of the political and economic union we already enjoy. Nothing more. . . . The end of Canada would be nothing less than the end of a dream. The end of a country that has made us the envy of the world. . . . Do you really think it is worth abandoning the country we have built, and

which our ancestors have left us? Do you really think it makes any sense – any sense at all – to break up Canada?

Now, just five days before the 1995 referendum, Chrétien suggested publicly, clearly, that a Yes vote would mean the destruction of Canada. Now, he didn't talk about a hypothetical question, about good government as the solution. He was pleading with the people. But, by commandeering television time, he gave equal time to the Yes forces, and the far more eloquent Lucien Bouchard spoke passionately, for fifteen minutes. Bouchard pushed all the emotional buttons of Quebec's tribal mythology. He appealed to a people who had been schooled to perceive their history as one of defeat, danger, subjection, and humiliation. He promised them that, at long last, they would be able to deal with the rest of Canada "*d'égal à égal*," as one equal to another. All that was required was to vote Yes. Then inequality would disappear as two sovereign nations met with all the politeness and protocol that govern international relations.

"The time has come to cease asking for permission and begging. Only a Yes can bring change. It is time that we take up our responsibilities. I will vote Yes, because it is the act of a people that has self-respect, that has self-confidence, and that stands tall." Along with Quebec's sovereignty, there would necessarily be an economic and political partnership with Canada, because the interests of each would compel such a coming together and Quebec would come to the table strong. "After a Yes, it is no longer one person alone that will sit down to the negotiating table across from English Canada. The mandate to act as negotiator which Jacques Parizeau entrusted me with, I will have the honour to carry it out from a position of strength because of the backing of the people of Quebec who will have given a mandate for sovereignty to Mr. Parizeau and his government."

Once the negotiations were successfully concluded, the ministers of the two countries would meet in a Partnership Council, each partner having an equal number of ministers and equal power, to make joint decisions together. Each would enjoy a veto over all decisions, and Quebec would, at last, be the equal of Canada. "No more quarrels. At home in Quebec, we will be able to look to our own affairs. . . . Solidarity will be at hand. After the Yes that I hope for, we will all be together, businesspeople, workers, managers, women, men, the young, and the not so young."

It was a powerful performance. The wonder was that, on the day of the referendum, October 30, 1995, the Yes side did not win; the No defenders, Chrétien and Daniel Johnson, had been so pathetically weak. That day, Parizeau taped a televised message in anticipation of a referendum victory that night. It caused a shock among those who heard it, including television producer Benoît Aubin. Parizeau said categorically: "Quebec is standing tall! The people of Quebec, by its majority vote today, has just announced to the world that it exists. That affirmation, serene and democratic, nothing and no one will be able to erase. A simple and strong decision was taken today: Quebec will become sovereign. Let a seat be prepared at the table of the nations."

On that fateful referendum night, Manning and Harper, along with other MPs and staff, met in the Reformers' office on the fifth floor of Parliament's Centre Block to watch the returns on television. It was painful. Early on, the Yes side took a big lead as the reports came in from the Magdalen Islands, then the Gaspé. That lead, though slowly diminishing, was maintained through most of the evening. Finally, after hours of anxiety, the big numbers from Montreal Island began to land, and the Yes lead turned into a slight majority for the No. The result: 50.6 per cent No, 49.4 per cent Yes. It was a harrowing experience for federalists. And it seemed to portend another referendum challenge before long. Next time, the separatists seemed likely to win.

Stephen Harper had learned a lesson. Neither he nor the country could rely on the Liberal government. He prepared a private member's bill of his own, to deal with the situation when and if it recurred. The next time, if he could help it, there would be no question of saying "a Yes vote means Quebec is on its way out, a No vote means Quebec is in the federation for the long haul, and 50 per cent plus one is the dividing line between those two positions." The next time, a referendum on secession should not depend on the improvisation of the prime minister or the pretensions of a secessionist government. It should be framed, in advance, by federal law. And the rules of the game should be known by all beforehand.

So Harper introduced Bill C-341, "An Act to establish the terms and conditions that must apply to a referendum relating to the separation of

Quebec from Canada before it may be recognized as a proper expression of the will of the people of Quebec." Its short title was the "Quebec Contingency Act (Referendum Conditions)." The bill received first reading on October 20, 1996.

Harper had seen the weak federal position always on the defensive, uncertain of its legal justification. His bill would end ambiguities and uncertainties, and it would restore the initiative to the federal government rather than abandon it to the secessionist government. Section 8 stated: "A unilateral declaration of independence by the government of Quebec or the legislature of Quebec, or the refusal of either to submit to any Canadian law that applies in Quebec is unlawful and of no force and effect with respect to the Constitution of Canada and the general laws of Canada and does not affect (a) the jurisdiction of Parliament to pass laws that have effect in Quebec; (b) the ability of the Government of Canada to govern Quebec as a province of Canada; (c) the jurisdiction of the courts to apply the law of Canada in Quebec; or (d) the continuance of Quebec as a part of Canada under Canadian law."

No more shilly-shallying, no more subordinating the rule of law to tactics. The bill asserted that Canadian jurisdiction would continue to apply in Quebec and that the laws and the courts would be enforced. A unilateral declaration of independence, instead of shaking the pillars of the country, was declared in advance null and void.

Quebec could hold a referendum on secession, the bill recognized. But, if the question asked was ambiguous, as it was in 1980 and 1995, Section 2 announced that the referendum would not be recognized as valid. If, in holding the referendum, the Quebec government stated or implied that the results of the referendum would authorize a unilateral declaration of independence, again the referendum would not be recognized. And the non-recognition would not be merely a matter of empty words. Section 4 of the bill spelled out the consequences: "(a) the Minister of Foreign Affairs shall advise the representative in Canada of every State with which Canada has diplomatic relations that Canada does not recognize the referendum or plebiscite as valid." Subsection (b) stated: "the Minister of Intergovernmental Affairs shall inform the Government of Quebec that Canada does not recognize the referendum or plebiscite as valid." In the past, France had interfered shamelessly in Canadian affairs, openly supporting separatism in Quebec. But France could do so because the government of Canada never defined a clear line stating that a unilateral declaration of independence would be resisted and that no foreign country should intervene. Canada's timidity had invited abuse. This bill would draw the line. Within Quebec, many voters voted for secession because they were led to believe that it was an option as valid as voting for a change of government. The federal government, when led by Brian Mulroney and Jean Chrétien, had allowed the secessionists to mislead the people about the true risks and conditions of secession.

Harper's bill did not prohibit secession. If the referendum question was deemed clear and the process was in accordance with the Constitution "the Government is authorized to enter into discussions with the Government of Quebec to conclude an agreement on the terms on which Quebec might separate from Canada." But, once again, all must be done in accordance with the legal requirements for amending the Constitution, as Section 7 made clear: "In any [such] discussion, the Government of Canada must (a) consult with the provinces to seek the consent of each province to the terms; (b) obtain the consent of any province to any matter that requires an amendment to the Constitution of Canada to which the province must consent; (c) require the inclusion of a provision that the agreement will not become effective until it is approved by a majority of voters who reside outside Quebec, decided by a vote in a referendum under the Referendum Act; and (d) permit the inclusion of a provision allowing for the government of Quebec to seek the approval of voters who reside in Quebec, decided by vote in a referendum or plebiscite under Quebec law." These were stringent conditions, far removed from the illusions under which the 1995 referendum campaign was waged. But they accorded with the facts of life. This bill, had it passed, would have brought Canada more in line with the legal systems of most democracies, although it would still be more permissive toward secession than most, including France or the United States. Such a bill would have ensured that the rights of all citizens were protected, both in Quebec and in the rest of Canada. The Parizeau initiative was essentially based on bluff, not law, and the government proved too timorous to stand on principle. Harper's bill was framed to call that bluff.

When Harper resigned from Parliament shortly after the bill was introduced, its sponsorship was taken up by Preston Manning. It died in

April 1997 when the 35th Parliament was prorogued. But throughout the episode of the 1995 referendum, when Canada went through a near-death experience, Harper demonstrated better judgment in addressing the issue of secession than any other politician. Let history record it so.

Chapter 17

—◦‖◦—

NEW HORIZONS –

POLITICS BY OTHER MEANS

ON JANUARY 14, 1997, Stephen Harper announced that he was resigning his seat in Parliament and, at the age of 37, was joining the National Citizens Coalition as vice-president. The NCC's president, former *Toronto Sun* reporter David Somerville, would retire at the end of that year and Harper would then assume the presidency. The parliamentary journalists in Ottawa were stunned. For them, the descent from Parliament Hill to a contentious right-wing advocacy organization like the NCC was a big step down, especially for Preston Manning's heir apparent. Harper's explanation, that he wanted to spend more time with his family, left them skeptical. One reporter asked bluntly if this was a strategic withdrawal till Manning resigned. In reply, Harper ruled out a future run for the Reform Party's leadership. He also hinted at his frustrations as an MP. "I'm looking for an opportunity where I'm not bound by a party line and where I can simply push the kind of public policy matters that are most important to me. I have been an active supporter of the National Citizens Coalition for a number of years. I'm a strong supporter of the things that it stands for – political and economic freedoms."

Now Harper would do politics by other means. At last, for the first time since he took to politics as an undergraduate, he'd be entirely his own man. No need to walk in the shadow of a leader, to talk the themes devised by someone else. He had his own message to deliver. He would be in charge.

In Ottawa, over three years, he'd established a reputation as a moderate amid people considered outside the pale of respectable discourse.

He'd voted on first and second reading *for* a government bill on gun control. That broke with his caucus's stance, but he explained that his urban riding was divided. Eventually, though, he voted against the bill. He'd also protested against the resolution adopted by the Reform assembly to exclude homosexuals from the Canadian Human Rights Act. Reporters had found him thoughtful and articulate on controversial issues.

That he surrendered a seat in the Commons – the prize so many fought so hard to grasp – enhanced his standing. He was now in constant demand for discussions on radio and television, and found himself quoted in newspaper interviews. He also provided a steady stream of commentaries in columns and letters to the editor. He seemed to be everywhere. On January 29, two weeks after his resignation, he was on CBC-TV's *The National*, discussing with Hana Gartner how to fight child poverty. She prompted: "We made a promise to the United Nations in 1989 that we were going to eliminate child poverty by the year 2000." Harper countered with conservative skepticism: "Well, I think the 1989 resolution you talk about probably was the high-water mark of political stupidity in this country; we felt that somehow the Parliament of Canada could just declare child poverty was going to be outlawed and that it was going to throw enough money at it to do it. I think taxpayers feel we're throwing lots of money at social programs. The question is whether they're effective. And I think to do that, you have to start to examine the incentive structure of those social programs. But I think, even more broadly, you have to examine economic policy and whether we have policies that create the jobs that allow parents to provide adequately for low-income children."

On February 9, he was on CBC-TV's *Sunday Report* with Wendy Mesley. The topic was "Protecting Canadian Culture." Harper was skeptical about policies designed to penalize foreign publications in Canada: "It's simply old fashioned industrial protection really disguised as a cultural policy. And I think what the cultural protectionists are increasingly fighting are not Americans, they're fighting other Canadians, they're fighting Canadian consumers and taxpayers who don't want to pay the direct and indirect costs of these policies."

Mordecai Richler wrote: "Quebeckers quite properly take Preston Manning's motley band for a giggle, the latter bunch hopelessly diminished since the departure of Stephen Harper, their one MP of substance." Allan Fotheringham gossiped in a February 11 column: "Harper, the attractive Alberta MP who is as fluently bilingual as Manning is not, announced he was leaving 'to spend more time with my family.' Since then he has taken a high-profile job with a right-wing interest group, which of course will allow him a lot of time with his family. Everyone on the inside generally accepts that he is just waiting until the sincere, but awkward, Manning goes."

Harper and the National Citizens Coalition were a good fit. The NCC had begun as a personal ad campaign against medicare in 1967 by Colin M. Brown of London, Ontario, who had made a fortune in the insurance business. He was incensed at the expansion of federal intervention during the Diefenbaker and Pearson years, with hospital insurance, medicare, and federal-provincial financing of social welfare. That was the same disapproval that had driven Manning, father and son, to publish *Political Realignment*, also in 1967, and Ernest Manning would sit on the NCC's advisory council from its incorporation in 1975 until his death in 1996. Others who also served were John Robarts, the premier of Ontario, and Stan Waters, the Reform candidate in Alberta's 1989 election for the Senate and who was appointed to the Senate in 1990 by Brian Mulroney.

At the start, Colin Brown was aligned with the PC Party against the Liberals. But, disenchanted with Red Tories like Robert Stanfield and William Davis, he quit the party in 1975. Until the Reform Party was founded in 1987 – the year of Brown's death – he was very much on the fringes of political opinion. And yet his NCC managed to survive and thrive, despite (or because of) the fact that his message, "For more freedom through less government," was considered politically incorrect by all the parties in the Commons, by almost all provincial governments, and by the right-thinking sages who pontificated at most newspapers and on television. The NCC had fought the NEP, which gained it Harper's approval and his membership. It had won court victories against "gag laws" that almost eliminated federal election campaign spending by non-politicians. One such victory had made possible the important pro-free-trade campaign by a business coalition in the 1988 elections. It also made possible the NCC's virulent campaign against Jim Hawkes in 1993, to the advantage of Stephen Harper.

The times were changed when Harper went to the NCC. When it first came to public attention, Reform advanced policies that were so far outside the pale of respectable conventional consensus that it was treated as a caricature. By 1993, Reform's campaign to bring the deficit down to zero in three years earned respectful attention from the *Globe and Mail*, but from the Liberals the charge that its "slash and burn" policy would bring the country to ruin. The 1993 Liberal Red Book promised: "Given the current state of the economy, a realistic interim target for a Liberal government is to seek to reduce the federal deficit to 3 per cent of gross domestic product by the end of its third year in office." The Liberals made no promise to bring it down to zero. After they were elected, though, when Harper spoke in the Commons on March 7, 1996, in response to Paul Martin's budget, he was able to wax ironic that the Liberal plan was "to attack the 'slash and burn' policy of the Reform Party while slashing, in particular, social programs far deeper than the Reform Party ever proposed." In a vindication of Reform's prophetic insistence on retrenchment, the Liberal budgets would actually cut $3 billion more than Reform had proposed. *in their budget*

Reform had helped make the Liberal pirouette possible. Harper *et al.* had warned for years that Canada would hit a wall, that investors would flee, and the Canadian dollar would dive in value. In 1994, that doomsday scenario had actually played out in Sweden and in Mexico. It seemed that Canada would be next. To avert disaster, Martin brought down his 1995 budget with severe cuts to federal spending and to transfers to the provinces. The dynamics in the Commons, where the NDP and the Tories had collapsed while the Bloc's economic policies were not credible, meant that the threat to Liberal dominance was on the right, not the left. So they could veer sharply to the right without being attacked for it by their chief opponents, the Reformers. The dynamic was the opposite of what it had been when Mulroney tried to cut spending and the Liberals howled.

Now, at the NCC, Harper pursued the conservative agenda by spending money to promote conservative causes, as had been done previously. He also brought the NCC's support to new causes: he raised money to support the court case of French-speaking parents in Quebec who wanted to be allowed to send their children to an English school. He also raised money to enable lawyer Brent Tyler to challenge Quebec's commercial sign law, which requires that French be twice as prominent on signs as all other languages combined. But Harper also brought a new dimension by his frequent appearances in all the news media, and that usually cost the NCC nothing. Because of the NCC's new respectability, the news media publicized widely, free of charge, all the NCC campaigns on billboards, in newspapers, and on radio or television. The NCC could occasionally garner free publicity in news media right across the country for a paid ad which had appeared in a single city.

The situation was perplexing. On the one hand, conservative ideas were becoming more and more accepted. Harper's own popularity with the media attested to that. More and more publications, more and more foundations, more academics were propagating conservative perspectives against the long liberal ascendancy. The decidedly conservative Conrad Black had taken over the liberal Southam chain of newspapers in May 1996, and soon replaced soft liberal editors with editors of a more conservative cast at several of his publications, such as the *Gazette* and the *Ottawa Citizen*. He now controlled 58 of Canada's 105 daily newspapers, and he soon made good on his statement to the *Globe and Mail*: "We're going to try and recruit the very best people we can and produce the best papers we can, and publish them to the highest standards we can. And that means separating news from comment, assuring a reasonable variety of comment, and not just the overwhelming avalanche of soft, left, bland, envious pap, which has poured like sludge through the centre pages of most of the Southam papers for some time." Black followed that up by founding the *National Post* in the fall of 1998, and the *Post* would provide Harper with an always available platform for airing his views. The Sun Media Newspapers were also receptive, especially the *Calgary Sun*, founded in 1980. The Fraser Institute, no doubt the best known and most influential of the conservative think-tanks, had been founded in 1974. The Donner Canadian Foundation began earlier, in 1967, to provide grants in pursuit of its mission statement, "to encourage individual responsibility and private initiative to help Canadians solve their social and economic problems." Conservative-minded newcomers in unlikely places included the Atlantic Institute for Market Studies, headed in Halifax by Brian Lee Crowley and founded in 1994, and the Montreal Economic Institute, headed by Michel Kelly-Gagnon, founded in 1999. These were among the signs and the stimulators of a conservative revival in Canada.

And yet Reform, the one truly conservative federal party, showed little promise of breaking in any conceivable future the Liberals' hold on power. This paradox was the central focus of a major historical and political analysis that Harper published with Tom Flanagan in the same month that he left Parliament. It immediately attracted considerable attention in the media for its complexity and depth, and it established Harper's reputation as a major thinker on politics. "Public policy reflects the growing conservatism of public opinion," the co-authors wrote. "Canada is not the same country it was ten years ago. Almost everyone in public life now takes balanced budgets, tax reduction, free trade, privatization of public enterprise, and targeting of social welfare programs for granted, while critics on the left bemoan their loss of influence."

Titled "Our Benign Dictatorship," the lengthy article was published in a now defunct conservative review *The Next City*. The central ideas had originally been delivered by Harper as a speech to the Winds of Change conference held in May 1996 at the instigation of columnists David Frum and Ezra Levant. These two had invited conservatives from different walks of life to Calgary to discuss how to unite the right – in effect, how to bring about the fusion of the Reform and PC parties. Harper, the contrarian, had argued that this was impossible, and not necessarily even desirable, because of the three quite different political cultures, which, historically, had come together on a few occasions in the Conservative Party since 1896 to enable the party to take power. Harper warned that this conjunction of the three cultures had happened only rarely, when the electors were angry at the Liberals, and had always proven unstable. This marked a fundamental difference between the Conservative Party and the Liberals, who constituted the only truly permanent national party. As a result, Harper had concluded, "The Liberals and the Conservatives don't alternate in their control of the Canadian Parliament. For a hundred years since 1896, Liberal government has been the rule, their opposition habitually weak, and alternative governments short-lived. Although we like to think of ourselves as living in a mature democracy, we live, instead, in something little better than a benign dictatorship, not under a strict one-party rule, but under a one-party-plus system beset by the factionalism, regionalism, and cronyism that accompany any such system."

The three cultures that had come together to form PC majorities under Robert Borden, John Diefenbaker, and Brian Mulroney were respectively the old Tory strain in Ontario and the Atlantic provinces, the nationalist tradition in Quebec, and the populist tradition of western Canada. In many ways, these three were incompatible and so, rather than try to unite them in one party, Harper suggested that there was more promise in creating a coalition of three "sister parties" that would agree to each occupy a different region of the country at election time, while working together to defeat the Liberals and form a coalition government.

"If co-operation is ever to work, the fragments of Canadian conservatism must recognize that each represents an authentic aspect of a larger conservative philosophy. Reformers will have to realize that there is something genuinely conservative in the Tory penchant for compromise and incrementalism. Tories will have to admit that compromise, to be honourable, must be guided by underlying principles, and that Reformers are not extremists for openly advocating smaller government, free markets, traditional values, and equality before the law. And both will have to recognize that Quebec nationalism, while not in itself a conservative movement, appeals to the kinds of voters who in other provinces support conservative parties. The Bloc Québécois is strongest in rural Quebec, among voters who would not be out of place in Red Deer, except that they speak French rather than English. They are nationalist for much the same reason that Albertans are populist – they care about their local identity and the culture that nourishes it, and they see the federal government as a threat to their way of life."

Flanagan, Harper's co-author for this article and also a like-minded supporter in his past disagreements with Preston Manning, was a distinguished political scientist who had been invited to Harvard University to deliver a lecture on Canadian politics. He took Harper's speech at the Winds of Change conference as the first draft of his lecture and developed it further for his American audience. It was then published under both their names.

Harper had prophesied that, with Jean Charest as PC leader, the Quebec question would form an obstacle to uniting Reform and the PC Party. Charest supported entrenching Quebec's "distinct society," while western culture insisted on equality of provinces. Similarly, Harper suggested, Manning's populism, as opposed to conservatism, would prove an obstacle to a union of Reform with the "Blue Tories" of Ontario. This analysis was soon proven correct.

When, in April, Chrétien called elections for June 2, 1997, Harper and the NCC were ready. They launched an in-your-face campaign against the MPs' "gold-plated" pension plans that Harper had denounced in 1994. In Edmonton, where two of the three Liberals had won election in 1993 with tiny pluralities, the NCC ran a newspaper ad featuring MPs Anne McLellan and Judy Bethel, their heads topping caricatures of two pigs guzzling champagne while lolling in a trough overflowing with dollars. The caption read: "On June 2nd . . . chop the pork! Re-electing these MPs will cost you $1.7 million." The ads named the ten MPs likely to garner the largest sums over a lifetime. They were called "pension porkers." Bethel would go down to defeat on June 2, McLellan would barely survive. Other ads were run on radio. One of the targeted MPs was British Columbia Reform MP John Cummins, who, unlike the other Reformers, had signed on to the Commons' pension plan. Despite the attack, Cummins would be re-elected in 1997 – and in 2000 and 2004.

This $200,000 ad campaign was only possible because, in 1996, the NCC had won in the Alberta Court of Appeal a judgment of unconstitutionality against the Elections Act which limited to $1,000 the total that could be spent by a third party. Explaining that the ads were run in twenty-three ridings and targeted mostly MPs elected in 1993 who would become eligible for their parliamentary pensions after six years as MPs, Harper conceded that the ads were hard-hitting: "We're obviously attacking people." But he defended their message as a "positive agenda" against parliamentary self-indulgent excess when Canadians were being hit with a $10-billion increase in Canada Pension Plan premiums.

In April, just before the elections were called, an Environics poll showed the Liberals solidly ahead of Reform in western Canada, by 40 to 25 per cent, while the NDP and Tories were tied at 17 per cent. And yet, on June 2, the Liberals would get only fifteen seats in the West. Reform consolidated its western base, taking sixty of the West's eighty-eight seats, nine more than in 1993. But in Ontario, where Manning had concentrated so much effort, Reform lost its only seat. Its share of the Ontario vote fell from 20.1 per cent to 19.1 per cent.

On election night, Harper was part of a panel of commentators on CBC-TV, hosted by Hana Gartner. He noted how the first-past-the-post electoral system wreaked havoc in a large, regionally diverse country like Canada. The Liberals, with only 38.5 per cent of the ballots, would again form a majority government with 155 seats.

Five days after the election, Harper and Flanagan published their analysis of the campaign in the *Calgary Herald*. They emphasized the polarizing effect the Quebec question had exercised, in the expectation that another referendum on secession would soon be called by Premier Bouchard. As part of his platform, Chrétien had promised to amend the Constitution to recognize Quebec as a distinct society. Charest went even further, widening the gap between Reform and PCs.

"The conventional political spectrum of left to right is now crosscut by a dimension of conflict over national identity, which was highlighted in the election campaign," Harper and Flanagan wrote. "Reform, with its slogan of equality of provinces and citizens, espouses the long-standing view of most western Canadians – and many other English Canadians – which John Diefenbaker called 'One Canada.' The Liberals and, even more so, the Progressive Conservatives, have embraced 'distinct society' as a covert way of defining Canada as two nations. And the Bloc Québécois, taking matters to their logical conclusion, wants two sovereign nations. For the past thirty years, the Liberals and PCs have taken turns playing what the journalist Peter Brimelow called the 'patriot game.' The patriot game has created the Reform Party as its antithesis and nemesis. Summoned into life by the Mulroney cabinet's decision to award the CF-18 maintenance contract to Montreal 'in the national interest,' the Reform Party rejects the premise of the patriot game – that the highest purpose of federal politics is to ward off separatism by making ever more accommodations for Quebec."

Harper had been concerned in 1986–87, as he thought through his political vision with John Weissenberger, about how the Quebec question had pre-empted a conservative revival in Canadian politics. Now, writing with Flanagan, he saw the same dynamic at work in the recent election when Reform had been treated with contempt by all the other parties. "Up to this point, Reform has triumphed in the West, but not elsewhere, because the West loses the most from the patriot game. The dynamic economies of Alberta and British Columbia disproportionately bear the

cost of the regional transfers that are supposed to keep Quebec and
Atlantic Canada happy. Meanwhile, the West's agenda of constitutional
reform is put perpetually on hold because central Canadian elites see it as
a threat to their domination of the system. As time runs out on the patriot
game, the Liberals, Progressive Conservatives, and New Democrats have
entered into a rhetorical alliance with the Bloc Québécois. They all
agree that the Reform Party is the real threat to national unity, and they
vie with one another to heap abuse on Manning. Epithets fill the air –
'bigot,' 'civil war,' 'party of division,' and much more. This intensifies
the original line of the three old 'national parties,' that the Bloc
Québécois and the Reform Party, as 'regional parties,' were evil twins,
equal threats to Confederation."

There was bitterness in their analysis. The election had made Reform
the Official Opposition, displacing the Bloc, which had fallen to forty-
four seats from fifty-four in 1993. Reform had also increased its share of
the national vote, but only marginally, with 19.4 per cent compared to
18.7 per cent. The election had made a united opposition to the Liberals
now less likely. Charest, whose election platform was conservative as it
was first announced, and echoed Mike Harris's Common Sense Revolution, soon abandoned that platform completely to run a Progressive
Conservative campaign to the left of the Liberals. Charest rebuked the
Liberals for having tightened up the unemployment insurance program,
thereby winning for his party thirteen of thirty-two seats in Atlantic
Canada, and five in Quebec. His twenty PC seats meant the party was
again recognized in the Commons and safe from being absorbed by
Reform. But Charest further widened the gulf between the two anti-
Liberal parties by packing his roster of Quebec candidates with separatists. He even denounced Chrétien for having referred the legality of
secession to the Supreme Court of Canada. In mid-campaign, on
May 22, when questioned on Radio-Canada's newsmagazine Le Point,
he accepted that the National Assembly alone should set the referendum
question on secession. At most, leaders from outside Quebec could make
a "political" statement as to how they interpreted it. When asked if he
would recognize a referendum victory for the Yes with "a majority of 50
per cent plus one," Charest acquiesced: "With a very clear question, yes,
I think so." Asked whether Quebeckers alone had the right to determine
their future, he agreed. "Let's be clear about one thing, the right of

Quebec to determine itself, its future was settled in 1980." He claimed that Trudeau's participation in the 1980 referendum campaign implied recognition of that right. Harper and Flanagan commented: "The Reform Party's taken a hard line with Quebec, and the PCs have taken, really, something that's categorized as pure appeasement."

Charest's position dovetailed with that expressed on April 16 by Premier Bouchard in a speech to the National Assembly. Bouchard denounced the patriation of the Constitution on April 17, 1982, and developing a claim for a right to secede unilaterally, orated: "Fifteen years ago, Canada committed the irreparable." Canada had "destroyed irremediably the compact that had linked the Quebec nation to the Canadian nation for 115 years." Quebec had the right to secede because "Canada" had persecuted "*le peuple québécois*" when Prime Minister Trudeau "tore up the compact between two nations." Bouchard's outrage knew no bounds. "It was the imposition of an assault by a majority against a minority. In no democracy in the world was anything ever done that was so iniquitous, so unacceptable, as this fundamentally reprehensible act. These events are serious. That is why today the cabinet has adopted a decision reiterating, in the name of the people and the government of Quebec, the unacceptable character of the Constitution Act of 1982, and reasserting the right of Quebec to determine alone and democratically its political status." On that same day, Liberal leader Daniel Johnson repeated his support for "our right to take charge, ourselves, of our development and our destiny." He even taunted Bouchard for having been only a recent convert to that view. The previous December, an official Liberal Party document on the Constitution claimed: "The Quebec Liberal Party recognized explicitly the right of the Quebec people freely to determine its future during a General Council meeting in 1980, and it has many times reiterated it since."

The Quebec issue, which had become prominent during the election campaign, deepened the split between the West and the rest of the country. During the debate of the party leaders, Chrétien was asked by Bloc leader Gilles Duceppe whether he would recognize a majority vote for secession; his only answer was to ask Duceppe what the question would be. He made no statement about the rule of law or the Charter rights of Canadians. The Reform Party broadcast a campaign television ad that demanded "a voice for all Canadians, not just Quebec politicians." It featured the faces of Chrétien, Charest, Duceppe, and Bouchard, each circled in red with a diagonal slash across the face. Given the Quebec-centred vision of Canada displayed by each, it was fair comment, and recalled how Quebec had monopolized national attention for almost four decades, to the detriment of the West. But the ad provoked shrieks of outrage: it was a rejection of Quebec, divisive, undemocratic, and bigoted.

In the aftermath of the elections, Manning recognized that power was eluding him, that Reform and the PCs were killing each other in Ontario, and that something must be done before the next elections. He commissioned a former Ontario Tory, Nancy Branscombe, who had been defeated as a Reform candidate in Peterborough, to approach Tories at the constituency level across Ontario to see if there was support for running joint Reform–PC candidates in the next elections. From the start, Harper held out little hope for this approach. "I don't think a proposal by one party to take over another is going to go anywhere." This initiative would eventually grow into the project that Manning would announce in 1998, to transform the Reform Party into a United Alternative, meant to attract people from all other parties. Manning insisted that this was not a "unite the right" movement, because right and left in politics were obsolete. But it would mean changing Reform's predominantly conservative ideology to something more mainstream. And it meant softening Reform's stance against special recognition for Quebec.

Manning's renunciation of 1994's ostentatious parsimony was signalled by his decision to move into Stornoway, the official residence of the leader of the Opposition; Manning no longer proposed that it should be turned into a bingo hall. He acquired an official car and driver. More substantially, his policy shift was demonstrated when, just before the premiers held their annual meeting, the Business Council on National Issues asked them publicly to adopt a declaration recognizing Quebec's "unique" culture and language, while also recognizing the equality of the provinces. At first, this would be done outside the Constitution, but with the intention that the recognition would eventually be vested. Manning wrote the premiers urging them to adopt the powerful business lobby's recommendation.

Harper was skeptical. He remembered that the BCNI had fervently supported the Charlottetown Accord. The premiers, minus the premier of Quebec, after their regular annual meeting in New Brunswick, then convened a special two-day meeting in Calgary on September 14 and 15, where they signed "the Calgary Declaration." Its declared objective was "strengthening the Canadian federation." They enunciated seven maple-syrup principles, supporting equality before the law, diversity and toler-ance, the recognition of aboriginals as part of Canada's diversity, the vitality of English, French, and multiculturalism. But their real objective was principle five: "In Canada's federal system, where respect for diver-sity and equality underlies unity, the unique character of Quebec society, including its French-speaking majority, its culture, and its tradition of civil law, is fundamental to the well-being of Canada. Consequently, the legislature and government of Quebec have a role to protect and develop the unique character of Quebec society within Canada." And, to counter any objections, principle two declared: "All provinces, while diverse in their characteristics, have equality of status." And there was principle six: "If any constitutional amendment confers powers on one province, these powers must be available to all provinces."

As with Meech and Charlottetown – initially – reaction to the Calgary Declaration was favourable at first. An Angus Reid poll pub-lished October 1 found that 70 per cent of Canadians considered the dec-laration a step in the right direction. Support was found in all regions. The lowest support, which was found in Quebec, was at 62 per cent. But Harper, both before and after the premiers met, campaigned against the declaration, in letters to the editor, in op-ed pieces, in NCC ads. In November, the NCC commissioned its own poll. As Harper reported, only 33 per cent of the sample agreed that "recognizing Quebec as a 'unique society' will make Quebeckers feel more loyal to Canada and diminish the chance of Quebec's seceding." Even in Quebec, only 39 per cent agreed, while 49 per cent thought it would either do nothing to diminish the chance of secession or would actually encourage it. Harper commented, "Obviously, Canadians have some serious doubts about both the unique society concept and the premiers' underlying strategy."

Harper and Flanagan together signed a piece that appeared in the *Calgary Herald* the day before the premiers' meeting. Their powerfully argued piece was titled, "Dear premiers, It's time to oppose – not appease – separatism." They argued that to recognize Quebec's uniqueness in law would have the opposite effect from that intended. "The French language and culture in Quebec are stronger today than ever. Declarations about

Quebec's uniqueness, no matter how well intentioned, simply create the impression that Canada's recognition of Quebec has been inadequate and that Quebec is somehow threatened by being part of Canada. In fact, the reverse is true." They pointed out that Quebec's uniqueness had in fact been recognized by the Quebec Act of 1774 and the Constitution Act of 1867. But it was not such a declaration that nationalists were really after, it was special status and more powers for Quebec. "As recently as August 21, Daniel Johnson proclaimed that distinct society must be nothing short of 'a new legal framework for Quebec.' That means power – and a lot more – and you all should know it by now. . . . Even today, Johnson – besides advocating an omnipotent distinct society clause – still refuses to sign the Constitution, insists on Quebec's right to sovereign self-determination, and resists federal efforts to make any referendum process abide by Canadian law and the Constitution."

Daniel Johnson soon proved their point that "unique character" would merely be an opener, an appetizer. He stated: "The front door for discussions among the provinces, including Quebec, on the division of powers, is the recognition of Quebec and the role of the National Assembly with respect to our specificity. This is what is in the Calgary agreement. Everything else will follow."

Premier Bouchard called the declaration "an insult." It was a telling argument that Flanagan and Harper made. In interviews, Harper insisted that the premiers missed the country's real priority: "If you're seriously worried about the next referendum, then have a direct plan to deal with the threat of a unilateral declaration of independence. I think monkeying around with declarations and anything other than a straight agenda for governing the country is looking for trouble." Harper understood the key logic of Quebec's myth of two founding peoples, shared by both the Quebec Liberals and Péquistes: that its dynamic drove a quest for powers without any logical resting point short of independence. The two parties competed against each other, each striving to prove itself more national-ist than the other. And a fundamental factor in that dynamic was the unfounded assumption that the French language and culture were under constant threat from English and needed the protection of constantly bolstered Quebec powers.

Later, in the *Calgary Herald* and the *Financial Post*, Harper attacked Manning's justification for defending the Calgary Declaration on the grounds that it affirmed the equality of the provinces. That would remain in practice a dead letter, Harper argued. "Manning depicted the Calgary deal as a trade-off between Quebeckers desiring recognition of their unique language, civil law, and culture, and others – particularly Albertans – desiring recognition of the equality of provinces and citizens. The depiction is simply untrue. The Calgary deal was agreed to by the nine premiers and two territorial leaders from outside Quebec, but not by anyone inside Quebec. The Quebec government is not party to the declaration. Quebec's opposition Liberals are not party to the declaration. Just as significantly, the federal government is not party to the declaration. In other words, the Calgary Declaration is not a trade-off between Quebeckers and non-Quebeckers. It is an offer made to Quebec by the rest of Canada. As with any negotiation, Quebec politicians can be expected to make a counter-offer to the Calgary Declaration. That counter-offer will invariably propose strengthening the special Quebec uniqueness provisions and further weakening the equality provisions." He insisted that, before the declaration be vested in the Constitution, it must be approved by a referendum.

In the event, the Calgary Declaration was approved by nine provincial legislatures, but not by Quebec. When Premier Bouchard proposed in May 1998 to hold hearings on it, manifestly to ridicule it by comparing it to Quebec's past demands, the Liberal leader, now Jean Charest, refused to attend. The Calgary Declaration simply faded away. Harper's definitive judgment on it: "I think Meech was tragedy, Charlottetown was farce, and Calgary is something less than farce."

When the new Parliament opened with the Throne Speech on September 23, 1997, it offered a nod to the Calgary Declaration: "The government will work closely with provincial and territorial governments to further advance the progress made by nine premiers and the territorial leaders last week in Calgary toward the full recognition of the diversity inherent in the federation, including the unique character of Quebec society." This was the positive salute to Quebec's aspirations. But it was coupled with a warning: "Our future as a country is too precious for us to risk losing it through misunderstanding. Therefore, the government will bring frankness and clarity to any debate that puts into question the future existence or unity of Canada. It will create a better understanding of the true complexity and difficulty for all of us in severing ties that have developed in building a nation together."

This double message corresponded to Plan A and Plan B of Intergovernmental Affairs Minister Stéphane Dion, who had been recruited by Chrétien in January 1996, three months after the fright of the 1995 referendum. Dion was a professor of political science at the Université de Montréal, and as a rare federalist in academe, he had defended the federalist cause during the referendum campaign in weekly televised debates broadcast by Radio-Canada. Dion had regularly bested the separatist spokesman, Laval University political scientist Guy Laforest. Dion had supported Meech and even maintained that opposing Meech meant being anti-Quebec. But he had also rebuked the Quebec Liberal Party for denigrating the federation and flirting with secession. "A separation declared unilaterally, by a small majority, would have no legal basis, either in Canadian law or international law," he had written in *Cité libre*. "To those who will say that the majority of a people have the right to secede, others will reply that if Canada is divisible, Quebec is also, that if a Canadian minority has the right to withdraw from Canada, then a Quebec minority has the right to withdraw from a secession which it does not accept."

With Dion in the cabinet, the government pursued both plans simultaneously. Dion gave rapturous speeches across the country proposing that recognition of Quebec's uniqueness might save Canada. Harper countered them in newspaper columns. Dion and Chrétien convinced the premiers to make their Calgary Declaration. But it meant nothing without Quebec's support, and that support never came.

At the same time, the Chrétien government shifted toward Plan B, sending a reference to the Supreme Court of Canada on the legality of a unilateral secession. This was a still tentative move in the direction that Harper had laid down in his Bill C-341. But, in their "Dear Premiers" letter, Flanagan and Harper noted the shift: "The federal government has been slowly drifting to an unprecedentedly firm line – emphasizing the rule of law, demanding to approve any referendum question, refusing to recognize a simple majority vote in a referendum, and threatening to partition Quebec if all else fails. Some of these positions are not fully developed or thought out, but at least they show a determination to act from a position of strength. The expectations of Canadians have also changed. Loyal Canadians from across the country will be directly involved in the next referendum, notwithstanding Quebec's referendum laws. They will send a strong message that this is a Canadian, not a Québécois issue. As a consequence neither Chrétien nor his successor will dare repeat the mistake of letting Johnson and the PLQ run the show. The premiers need to orient themselves in this new environment. They need to discuss the implications of Canadians' new assertiveness and Ottawa's new position."

Harper and Flanagan were way ahead of the premiers, of the federal government, and of elite opinion, which all were still submissive before the claim of Quebec's political class to have an unfettered right to choose whatever constitutional future Quebeckers wanted. Any denial, such as that of the Reformers, was considered *lèse-Québec*. This bowing to Quebec's autarchy was shared not only by the Péquistes and Quebec Liberals, but by almost every last journalist and by the Quebec population in general, as shown by opinion polls. Those who did place conditions on Quebec's secession, such as the rule of law and the rights of aboriginals, were denounced as weirdos, extremists, as the lunatic fringe. Lise Bissonnette, publisher of *Le Devoir*, cautioned her readers that these extremists were no more representative of Quebec's English-speaking community than Raymond Villeneuve, a convicted FLQ killer, was representative of French Quebec.

The advisory opinion of the Supreme Court on secession was rendered on August 20, 1998. It stated that Quebec did not have a right to secede unilaterally, either under Canadian law or international law. To be lawful, secession must be carried out through an amendment, in accordance with the terms of the Constitution Act, 1982. The terms must be arrived at by negotiations carried out so as to respect four fundamental principles: the federal principle, democracy, the rule of law, and the rights of minorities. If a referendum on a clear question showed a clear will to secede – or to carry out any other amendment to the Constitution – the Parliament and the provincial governments would have to meet and negotiate. The outcome was not foreordained, as any agreement had to respect the four principles. If, after negotiations in good faith, such an agreement could not be reached, Quebec would not have the right to secede.

The court's answer was complex and subtle, but clear and coherent. It rejected secession as a right, but asserted it as a possibility. It recognized the importance of a clear preference expressed in a referendum vote, but the democratic vote was not decisive: it had to take into account the rights of other provinces and of the federal government (the federal principle), the rights of all minorities – especially the official language minorities and aboriginals. It must respect the Constitution.

The court's unanimous decision made a mockery of Justice Minister Allan Rock's promise to Quebec on September 26, 1996, when he announced the reference: "It is terribly important to remember that in the Canadian context there is no political justification to argue for a unilateral declaration of independence by the Quebec National Assembly. . . . There have been two referenda in Quebec. The leading political figures of all the provinces and indeed the Canadian public have long agreed that this country will not be held together against the will of Quebeckers clearly expressed. And this government agrees with that statement." It was a promise, made with the sole condition of clarity, that Rock had no authority to make. It was an elitist promise, like the Meech and Charlottetown accords. But the Charter had established the supremacy of the Constitution over Parliament, and the Charter established the rights of the people, which Parliament could not legally surrender to the Quebec government except by an amendment to the Constitution which involved strict conditions, including the consent of the provinces. Allan Rock, who had not defended the Constitution before the 1995 referendum, had made a promise the following year that went against Justice Robert Lesage's decision of 1995 and that would be discredited again by the Supreme Court.

Harper's response on that day of Rock's 1996 promise was much closer to what the court would say two years later: "Clearly the vagueness and unpreparedness of the country on this profound question of the rule of law cannot be allowed to continue. . . . We view this as only a first step. To the extent that the government is increasingly prepared to look at plan B options, it must be prepared to table a legislative framework for such a contingency and also to take greater efforts to inform the Quebec population of not just the possible cost but the consequences and possible conditions of their secession." And he pointed out that the position the government was now coming to was what he had argued in 1994 – before the referendum. "I would point out that our position is not new and is not the result of the referendum campaign. Indeed, we made our position on these issues clear a very long time ago."

The decision of the court was rejected by Premier Lucien Bouchard who had always said in advance that he would not be bound by it, and by Jean Charest, still leader of the PCs, who spoke as though the court had said nothing, meant nothing: it was all still "a dark hole."

In the event, at the end of 1999, Prime Minister Chrétien overruled his own caucus and announced that he would be bringing in a Clarity Bill to define under what conditions the federal government would accept to negotiate secession. Premier Bouchard expressed his shock in a special statement on television and launched an immense advertising campaign to rouse Quebeckers against the federal outrage. The campaign was a failure. Most Quebeckers rather liked the proposal for clarity. So, in the year 2000, two bills were making their way through the legislative process, Bill C-20, the Clarity Act in Ottawa, and in Quebec, Bill 99, "An Act respecting the exercise of the fundamental rights and prerogatives of the Quebec people and the Quebec State." The two were at opposite poles. Quebec's Bill 99 summarized all the assumptions and myths that had accompanied the separatist movement since 1960: that unilateral secession was a right, that a 50 per cent plus one Yes vote triggered that right in a referendum where the question and all the rules were set by Quebec, that the territory of Quebec was inviolable, and that no federal referendum held on these subjects would have any validity. The act totally ignored the Supreme Court's unanimous advisory opinion.

The Clarity Act, like the Supreme Court's decision, has been commonly misunderstood and the federal government has done little to enlighten public opinion. For instance, on December 9, 2000, the *Globe* stated in a lead editorial: "Under the Clarity Act, Quebec has the right to secede providing it does not try to baffle Quebeckers with another muddy referendum question or bolt from Confederation with a razor-thin referendum win, as it was about to do in 1995. . . . Yes, Quebec has the right to secede. Both the Supreme Court and Parliament have affirmed that." The *Globe*, five years later, has still never corrected that utterly false interpretation of the Supreme Court's clear statement and of the Clarity Act. The same error was conveyed on December 11, 2000, in a *Le Devoir* editorial by Michel Venne: "By adopting this year Bill C-20 [the Clarity Act], the two houses of Parliament recognized a right to self-determination which can lead to the secession of any province – Quebec, obviously – which holds on its territory a referendum on a clear question and which gets the approval of a clear majority." There was, in fact, absolutely no question of a right to self-determination justifying secession, in either the court decision or in the Clarity Act.

The Clarity Act followed closely the Supreme Court's advice. It recognized that "The Supreme Court of Canada has confirmed that, in Canada, the secession of a province, to be lawful, would require an amendment to the Constitution of Canada, that such an amendment would perforce require negotiations in relation to secession involving at least the governments of all of the provinces and the government of Canada." By the rules for amendment laid down in the Constitution, such an amendment would require the consent of every provincial legislature as well as the consent of both Houses of Parliament.

Such an amendment to permit secession would not be easily attained, no matter what the score was for secession in a referendum. The test for secession in the Clarity Act, as in the Supreme Court's answer, was that the rights of all parties be respected, and not just the desires of the Quebec electorate. And so, the Clarity Act mentioned some of the issues that would have to be settled before an amendment could be passed to authorize secession: "No minister of the Crown shall propose a constitutional amendment to effect the secession of a province from Canada unless the government of Canada has addressed, in its negotiations, the terms of secession that are relevant in the circumstances, including the division of assets and liabilities, any changes to the borders of the province, the rights, interests, and territorial claims of the aboriginal peoples of Canada, and the protection of minority rights."

At last, Stephen Harper's position, first sketched out publicly in 1994, then explicitly and comprehensively spelled out in 1996 through Bill C-341, was triumphantly vindicated. His views at the time were dismissed and denounced by the prime minister, by Lucien Bouchard, by Quebec's news media. But the Supreme Court raised precisely the issues treated in Harper's bill: the rule of law, the clarity of the question, the rights of the provinces, and the rights of minorities. But Harper's bill went further. The federal government asked the court to pronounce on the legality of unilateral secession, but it asked the court *not* to answer other pertinent questions, such as what were the rights of aboriginals whose lands were in Quebec, if Quebec attempted to secede. And yet, in the event of an attempted secession, the rights of aboriginals and their territories would be the single most contentious issue to be settled. Why did Ottawa ask the court not to define the rights of aboriginals? It remains a mystery.

The great weakness of the Clarity Act, unlike Harper's Bill C-341, is that it does not deal with the most likely outcome, that is, a unilateral declaration of independence. It states under what conditions the federal government would negotiate secession – but not what it would do if the Quebec government declared independence without negotiations. And yet that is precisely the most likely scenario, to judge by the past statements of premiers Parizeau and Bouchard. Harper's bill indicated precisely what the federal government would do: domestically, it would enforce all its laws and maintain the Constitution before the courts; internationally, it would advise all other countries that Canada did not recognize the independence of Quebec.

Harper's bill was superior in another way as well: it laid down that the federal government would not recognize any referendum result as valid if the Quebec government had in any way implied that a positive vote would confer a right to secede unilaterally, that is, without being authorized by an amendment to the Constitution. Harper's bill would have removed all ambiguity, and it is ambiguity that could some day lead to a majority Yes vote in a referendum, if the people of Quebec were to vote under the illusion that they were not bound by the Constitution, or that Canada would not enforce the Constitution. Yet both are now common suppositions in Quebec.

On the issue of secession, Harper was prophetic.

Chapter 18

SAVING THE VISION

[handwritten: After the Fed elections of Nov. 27. 2000]

[handwritten: MAR 25. 2000 Reform died]

[handwritten: election Nov 2000]

NOW WAS THE SEASON of his discontent. After the federal elections of November 27, 2000, Stephen Harper began to despair of his country. Those elections confirmed almost everything he had fought against. Jean Chrétien, increasingly arrogant, despite the evidence of corruption, *[handwritten: to April]* cronyism, mismanagement, and reckless spending, emerged triumphant. He increased the Liberal caucus by 17, to 172. Unobstructed Liberal victories loomed far into the future.

Reform, the party Harper had helped create, no longer existed. In its place, an uncertain "United Alternative" had been ponderously constructed. From his post at the National Citizens Coalition, he had called it, with conscious irony, "a house divided against itself" – an echo of Manning's great "House Divided" speech of 1989 in Edmonton. When, on March 25, 2000, Reform died, to be replaced by the Canadian Alliance, Harper confided that Reform had long ago died in his heart. "I am not very emotional about it in that the tears I cried, or the loss I felt, happened a long time ago. I could see what was happening long before most people became aware that it had happened. . . . It's like when a relative dies who has actually been ill or out of it for some time."

Now, led by Stockwell Day, the Alberta provincial Tory who had supported the Charlottetown Accord, the Canadian Alliance had gone down to defeat. What vision it would project was unknown. Harper expressed in writing the disarray of his soul. This private man was not given to self-analysis, but he was a compulsive analyst of public affairs. He once told a friend: "I think about strategy twenty-four hours a day."

His way was to conduct a constant analysis of Canada publicly, in the form of essays, memoranda, speeches, statements, columns, and letters. He did so now. Always critical, he was now disenchanted. His first words had the taste of lemon. "The latest dribblings from the mouth of Canada's prime minister suggest Alberta's wealth can be attributed to the federal government. While there is clearly no merit to the claim, we must not ignore the implied threat: If Ottawa giveth, then Ottawa can taketh away," he wrote in the *National Post*, eleven days after the election.

In the past, he'd decried the West's exploitation and demanded fair treatment. Now, exasperation permeated his complaint. "After sober reflection, Albertans should decide that it is time to seek a new relationship with Canada. Obviously, I come to this conclusion after long watching the Reform movement and witnessing its most recent rejection by the very electorate that, in creating the Canadian Alliance, it had twisted itself into a pretzel to please."

"The West wants in" was no longer his call. Nor was he saying that Alberta wanted out, as some surmised. He concluded from Canada's rejection of the West that Alberta should recover all its constitutional powers to build, within Canada, a society expressing Alberta's values rather than those imposed by Ottawa. Alberta should do what Quebec had done – without brandishing the threat of secession.

"The Alliance was devastated by a shrewd and sinister Liberal attack plan. The strategy – sometimes subtle, but sometimes blatant – was to pull up every prejudice about the West and every myth about Alberta that could be dredged. . . . For many of us, this federal election has stripped away any veneer of openness to reforming Canada. Those who conceived the Reform Party, and helped nurture it through its transformation to the Alliance, have not discovered a path to power; they have hit a wall."

Chrétien had called the elections on October 22, only forty months into his 1997 mandate. He caught the new party and its new leader, Stockwell Day, unprepared, disorganized, and exhausted by the two years of travail it took for Reform to give birth to the Canadian Alliance. Manning, the founder, had been ousted by Day. The provincial Tory would not be allowed time to assimilate the culture of his new party nor to heal the wounds of the campaign. No time, as an outsider, to establish his authority over a caucus that revered Manning. Chrétien used the system to his advantage, making sure that Day would have no opportunity to become known to Canadians. Chrétien's hatchetman, Warren Kinsella, clutched Barney the Dinosaur to mock Day's fundamentalist religious beliefs. Instead of being punished for manipulations that again marginalized the West, Chrétien gained in all three regions east of Manitoba.

Early in the campaign, government television ads trumpeted an agreement on health-care funding reached by Chrétien and the premiers. Chrétien launched his campaign by saying the election was a choice between "two visions." They soon became a Manichean choice between good and evil. Chrétien, addressing the 50th Congress of Liberal International, meeting that year in Ottawa, declared that he was in the midst of an election campaign. Then, as reported by the *National Post*'s Robert Fife, "Mr. Chrétien portrayed Canada as an ideal 'liberal' nation with no discrimination on the basis of sex, race, or handicaps. He then implied that those values are at risk in the current election. 'We have to keep working on that because we never know when there will not be a force that will come and appeal to the dark side that exists in human beings.'" Later, in his first campaign TV ad, Chrétien presented himself as defending Canada against a heartless Alliance: "The Reform Alliance party would have a country where the interest of the few will take priority over the well-being of the majority. With your help, I will not let this happen. In our Canada everybody must win." He went further on November 11, saying in French, "The proposition of Stockwell Day is to destroy Canada." Immigration Minister Elinor Caplan, running in a heavily Jewish riding, claimed that the Alliance was supported by "Holocaust deniers, prominent bigots, and racists." Harper had responded angrily: "They think they are the party of Canada and that anyone running against them is therefore running against the country on some moral level. Liberals and leftists of various shades have for the last decade constantly invoked fascism whenever faced with right-of-centre opponents."

Chrétien suddenly attacked Alberta's Ralph Klein for supposedly violating the Canada Health Act by permitting some private delivery of health care. He'd said nothing about that before, and still said nothing of Quebec's broader private medical services, or its refusal to refund the full medical bills of travelling Quebeckers, thereby violating the Canada

Health Act's principle of portability. Then, mid-campaign, the *Globe and Mail* turned musings by MP Jason Kenney about some private delivery of health care into a screaming headline that the Alliance favoured "two-tier" health care. Chrétien followed up this misinformation with his own: "Stockwell Day cannot cover up his 'hidden agenda' to impose two-tier U.S.–style health care on Canadians." Since Chrétien had prevented Day from becoming properly known, the charge of "a hidden agenda" stuck.

Harper, in his post-campaign analysis in the *National Post*, admitted that Day's campaign had not been stellar. "The CA did indeed run a weak campaign by any measure. It lacked any clear strategy, policy focus, or coordinated rebuttal to predictable attacks." But Harper saw the Liberal campaign as confirming the cleavage between Alberta's political culture and the cultures of central and eastern Canada. "Alberta and much of the rest of Canada have embarked on divergent and potentially hostile paths to defining their country. Alberta has opted for the best of Canada's heritage – a combination of American enterprise and individualism with the British traditions of order and co-operation. We have created an open, dynamic, and prosperous society in spite of a continuously hostile federal government. Canada appears content to become a second-tier socialistic country, boasting ever more loudly about its economy and social services to mask its second-rate status, led by a second-world strongman appropriately suited for the task."

Those harsh words would be spat back at him later. The campaign again confirmed the breach between Alberta's culture, which put a high priority on freedom of political speech, and the Quebec-inspired state *dirigisme* of Canada's central institutions. In May 2000, Ottawa had amended the Elections Act to reinstate restrictions on third-party spending, previously struck down by western courts. The new act prohibited interveners outside recognized political parties from spending more than $152,550 nationally or $3,051 in any riding. Harper, as NCC president, applied for an injunction against the restrictions and won. The federal government appealed; the Alberta Court of Appeals unanimously upheld the injunction. As Harper commented in the *Calgary Herald*, "This is the law that would restrict Canadians from spending their own money on political advertising during elections, making it illegal to do so without the permission of federal officials." The act required that anyone spending more than five hundred dollars must register with Elections Canada. Ottawa appealed to the Supreme Court of Canada and won, in an 8 to 1 decision. The sole dissenter was Justice John Major – from Alberta.

The defeat devastated Harper. The NCC had won all its previous court battles against such restrictions. Harper found the law iniquitous because it favoured established political parties over individual citizens. The government could spend without limit before elections in spuriously "non-partisan" advertising, as Chrétien had done just before the writ was dropped. Newspapers, pundits, unions, could argue their views at will before the national citizenry – but not the ordinary citizen. Advocacy groups, like the NCC or Campaign Life were prevented from waging an effective campaign. Harper pointed out the inconsistencies: "The gag law does not prevent someone from 'buying' a political party or candidate. That remains perfectly legal in Canada. It only prevents you from buying an ad to express your opinion. In fact, under Canadian law, wealthy individuals or interests can remain completely anonymous when they make contributions through a leadership campaign or through a constituency association." He refuted the charge that the NCC proposed "U.S.-style" election laws. "It is gag laws that will actually make Canada more like the United States with its highly regulated electoral regime. Interestingly, those American regulations, imposed in the name of electoral fairness, have ended up enhancing the power of larger parties and incumbents at the expense of smaller parties and ordinary voters." In the event, prevented from attacking MPs for their gold-plated pensions, he announced that the NCC would spend fifty thousand dollars to attack the "gag law."

One flippant campaign statement by Chrétien confirmed for Harper that Alberta-baiting paid off in Canadian politics. "I like to do politics with people from the East. Joe Clark and Stockwell Day are from Alberta. They are a different type. I'm joking. I'm serious." Harper responded. "Albertans would be fatally ill-advised to view this situation as amusing or benign. Any country with Canada's insecure smugness and resentment can be dangerous. It can revel in calling its American neighbours names because they are too big and powerful to care. But the attitudes toward Alberta so successfully exploited in this election will have inevitable consequences the next time Canada enters a recession or needs an internal enemy. Having hit a wall, the next logical step is not to bang our heads against it. It is to take the bricks and begin building another home – a stronger and much more autonomous Alberta. It is time to look at Quebec and to learn. What Albertans should take from this example is to become 'maîtres chez nous.' In one policy area after another, the province of Quebec, with much less financial independence than Alberta, has taken initiatives to ensure it is controlled by its own culture and its own majority. Such a strategy across a range of policy areas will quickly put Alberta on the cutting edge of a world where the region, the continent, and the globe are becoming more important than the nation-state."

He repeated the slogan of Quebec's Quiet Revolution, but repudiated its separatist accompaniment: "We should not mimic Quebec by lunging from rejection into the arms of an argument about separation. As that province has shown, separation will simply divide our population in a symbolic debate while, still part of the country, it isolates us from any allies." His manifesto ended with a call to rally around the province: "Westerners, but especially Albertans, founded the Reform/Alliance to get 'in' to Canada. The rest of the country has responded by telling us in no uncertain terms that we do not share their 'Canadian values.' Fine. Let us build a society on Alberta values."

In January 2001, Harper wrote the notorious "Firewall" open letter to Premier Klein in the *National Post*. It was also signed by other prominent conservatives, such as University of Calgary political scientists Tom Flanagan and Ted Morton. Titled "The Alberta Agenda," it gave specific examples of what Albertans should do. "We believe the time has come for Albertans to take greater charge of our own future. This means resuming control of the powers that we possess under the Constitution of Canada but that we have allowed the federal government to exercise. Intelligent use of these powers will help Alberta build a prosperous future despite a misguided and increasingly hostile government in Ottawa." It designated the Canada Pension Plan, the collection of income tax by Ottawa for all provinces but Quebec, the RCMP as provincial police, the financing of health care and welfare. A fifth proposal was to hold a referendum in Alberta on the Triple-E Senate.

The most significant proposals dealt with public pensions and health care: "Withdraw from the Canada Pension Plan to create an Alberta Pension Plan offering the same benefits at lower cost while giving Alberta control over the investment fund. Pensions are a provincial responsibility

under Section 94A of the Constitution Act, 1867; and the legislation
setting up the Canada Pension Plan permits a province to run its own
plan, as Quebec has done from the beginning. If Quebec can do it, why
not Alberta?" The letter also proposed withdrawal from the Canada
Health Act, which sets five conditions for federal funding. "Resume
provincial responsibility for health-care policy. If Ottawa objects to
provincial policy, fight in the courts. If we lose, we can afford the financial penalties Ottawa might try to impose under the Canada Health Act.
Albertans deserve better than the long waiting periods and technological
backwardness that are rapidly coming to characterize Canadian medicine. Alberta should also argue that each province should raise its own
revenue for health care – i.e., replace Canada Health and Social Transfer
cash with tax points, as Quebec has argued for many years."

Everything proposed fell within provincial jurisdiction, with no suggestion of breaking the law or flirting with secession. But what remained
in the public mind was a vivid metaphor – that of a firewall. "It is imperative to take the initiative, to *build firewalls around Alberta*, to limit
the extent to which an aggressive and hostile federal government can
encroach upon legitimate provincial jurisdiction."

Ken Boessenkool, an economist who worked with Stockwell Day in
the Alberta government, was also a signatory to the open letter. He
recalls: "Within days after the election, Stephen called and said, 'This is
preposterous. What are we going to say, what are we going to do about
this?' The prime minister basically said, 'Western Canada is a bunch of
different folks, I don't like dealing with them, and we don't like the
West.' We had been a direct object of ridicule from the prime minister in
a national campaign, and he was not punished for that. And a lot of us
started to think, you know, we've been fighting this federal agenda for a
long time, I wonder if there is something we can do provincially? If we
wanted to answer his campaign with a provincial focus, what would
we do? And I immediately said, 'We can opt out of the pension plan. I
thought of this two years ago. It's in the Alberta budget.'" As for the
word *firewall*, Boessenkool says it was not in the early drafts. "The word
firewall has been both the greatest blessing and the greatest curse. It was
a blessing because it was an easy moniker that actually, in a computer
sense, represented what we were saying. But most people who heard the
word *firewall* didn't understand the computer sense in which we meant

it – to keep the regular communication going between Ottawa and the province, but to stop the bad things from getting in. It was a word inserted later on; it was not the core idea that we were trying to get across. The words we were hoping for in the headline were 'An agenda for Alberta – within Canada.'"

Boessenkool, while in high school, had campaigned for Reform in the 1988 elections. He went to Ottawa with Reform MP Ray Speaker after the elections of 1993, and there he had got to know and admire Stephen Harper. "There were a number of people in the party who had become uneasy with Manning's populism and we all developed a deep respect for Stephen," he recalls. After two years in Ottawa, he left to obtain a master's degree in economics at the University of Toronto and do research for the C.D. Howe Institute. He wrote thirteen papers published by the institute and one, on a family-friendly tax system, drew the attention of Alberta's treasurer, Stockwell Day. Day called, said he wanted major changes to Alberta's tax system, and asked if Boessenkool would be his policy adviser. He accepted conditionally – if Day was serious about bringing in a single tax rate, commonly called a flat tax. And so he was off to Edmonton. The proposal for a single tax rate appeared in Alberta's budget of February 28, 1999. "Stock is a major salesman, he could sell ice to Eskimos, and he sold that single rate tax to Alberta." The audacity of it brought Day immense national publicity. Boessenkool also had another audacious plan in mind – to have Alberta withdraw from the Canada Pension Plan: "If you look in the 1999 and the 2000 budgets, there's a whole section at the back of the budget which was not widely reported, about what an Alberta Pension Plan would look like."

But Day left the Alberta government in 2000 to run for the leadership of the Canadian Alliance. Alberta's exploration of a withdrawal from the Canada Pension Plan was dropped. Boessenkool had asked Harper whether he had considered running for the leadership, and Harper replied that he could not win against Manning. Boessenkool agreed; he maintains that only Day could have beaten Manning. His reputation as treasurer of Alberta attracted economic conservatives, while his reputation as an evangelical who acted on his beliefs attracted religious conservatives who felt betrayed by Manning. Day had led the campaign to prevent Alberta's health system from paying for abortions, which, he argued, were not a medically necessary treatment. In 1989, he had fought extending human-rights protection to homosexuals.

Harper was often mentioned as a possible contender for the Alliance leadership, but he chose to support Ontario's Tom Long, strategist of Mike Harris's Common Sense Revolution. Long was a conservative in Harper's own style. He believed in policy as the key to power and in pressing conservative wedge issues rather than competing for the centre. Harper explained why he endorsed Long: "As one whose own name has been bandied about as a candidate, let me make it clear that I believe the best person to be prime minister of all Canadians, regardless of region, is Tom Long. Thirteen years ago, some of us decided the best route to being more at home in Confederation was to leave the federal Tories and found a new party. Tom Long as leader of the Alliance is not a threat to that vision, but a promise to take it to power."

Day won the leadership on July 8, 2000, against a bitter Manning who had warned: "Stock is the Alliance's Kim Campbell." With his youthfulness – he would turn fifty in August – his onstage karate kicks, and his theme of "an agenda of respect," he received good press reviews. In the election campaign that followed, he gained on the Chrétien Liberals during the early weeks. His campaign manager, Rod Love, had previously steered Klein's career to the premiership. Boessenkool had meanwhile left government to work as senior economist in the private sector. He recalls, "Rod Love called me during the 2000 campaign when his tracking poll clocked Day at 33 per cent. He said, 'Ken, we're going to start doing some transition planning, and you're going to be part of that team.' We were going up by one or two percentage points a day, and we could have won – we could have got 38 per cent in that election, there certainly could have been a minority government. So we started putting together a transition team – and two days later Stockwell held up that 'no two-tier' sign in the debate. Rod Love called me back and said, 'Forget it,' so we dropped it."

When the votes were counted on November 27, the Canadian Alliance won 25.5 per cent of the vote, six points better than in 1997, and raised its roster of MPs from sixty to sixty-six. In crucial Ontario, two MPs were elected, and the percentage of the Ontario vote eased upwards from 19.1 to 23.6. But Day had done himself harm within the party by failing to reach out to Manning and Long. Worse, he violated the populist tradition of Reform by running a campaign centred on himself rather than policy. On some policies he improvised, such as putting off to a fifth year the proposed 17 per cent single tax rate. He wavered on Alliance policies such as the encouragement of private enterprise within the publicly supported health system, retreating instead to repudiating "two-tier health care" – whatever that meant. And he repudiated what he had previously endorsed, a referendum on abortion if 3 per cent of the electors petitioned for it. He suggested it might require 25 per cent.

After the elections, serious blunders came to light. Day had secretly authorized a payment of fifty thousand dollars to convince Jim Hart, an MP from British Columbia, to liberate his seat on July 19 so Day could run for it. When Hart later sued to get paid, Day tried to evade responsibility. Then, it became known that Day had libelled Red Deer lawyer and school trustee Lorne Goddard, who had defended a man charged with possession of child pornography by claiming that the courts had established his legal right to it. Day wrote the *Red Deer Advocate* that Goddard "must also believe it is fine for a teacher to possess child porn. Perhaps even pictures of one of his own students, as long as he got the photos or video from somebody else." He threatened Goddard with defeat at the next school-board elections. Goddard filed a suit against Day, whose expenses were paid by a provincial fund. Rather than settle and apologize, Day insisted on fighting on in his lost cause until provincial authorities gave an ultimatum: settle or pay your own expenses. He then conceded, and the settlement cost the province a total of $792,064.40. Premier Klein called the cost "obscene" and suggested that Day should pay part of it. Belatedly, he contributed sixty thousand dollars but the damage was done. Day had let his religious principles cloud his judgment as an MLA. Worse, his refusal to settle confirmed his bad judgment. The cost of his folly subverted his credibility when he criticized the Liberals for prodigal spending.

More blunders followed, all to be documented lovingly by Manning in *Think Big*. There was the case of the secret agent, James Leigh, whom Day had met and unmet within twenty-four hours, who was and wasn't promised a job to investigate Chrétien's murky dealings in Shawinigan. On March 31, 2001, an Ipsos poll for the *Globe and Mail* showed Day's approval rating had fallen to 32 per cent. Worse was to come. He appeared to be adrift, unaware of the danger, on the wrong side of

Niagara Falls. A parade of staff members resigned or were fired: chief of
staff Rod Love; deputy chief Hal Danchilla, director of communications
Phil von Finkenstein, director of research Paul Wilson, director of operations Chris Froggatt, press secretary Renée Fairweather.

April was the cruellest month. On April 23, Day's chief of staff, Ian
Todd, resigned. He'd been Manning's executive. MP Art Hanger called
on Day to resign. The caucus mutiny was open. The next day, the caucus
leaders resigned from their positions: Deborah Grey, deputy Opposition
leader, Chuck Strahl, House leader, and his deputy House leader, Grant
McNally. Two MPs, Val Meredith and Bob Mills, called on Day to resign.
Deborah Grey wrote in her memoirs: "It was heartbreaking for everyone. So many of us had worked for so many years to get to this point. It
seemed that the whole thing might slip through our fingers."

The caucus split into angry factions. Rather than fight the Liberals,
they provided a continuing news story by fighting each other. A poll in
April showed Alliance support down to 13 per cent. On May 15, eight
"dissidents," led by Chuck Strahl, declared publicly, knowing it would
mean suspension: "It is in the best interests of the Canadian Alliance that
Mr. Day resign." Their suspension and resignations followed. The dissidents soon numbered thirteen, and they took a name: the Democratic
Representative Caucus. They began meeting with Joe Clark's Tories,
exploring a tactical alliance in the Commons.

Harper disapproved of the DRC, but realized that, under Day, the
Alliance was foundering. It seemed that the movement was shattering
into fragments, with the pieces to be picked up by the Red Tories. In
April, Harper and his closest advisers met with Day and his wife at the
house of Ted Morton, who had signed the "Firewall" letter. They offered
to help Day in any way they could to stabilize his leadership. Harper was
in touch with members of the caucus as they went through their anguish.
Eventually, he confided to an intimate: "If this party didn't exist, we'd
need to create it. The party must not be allowed to implode. And if
keeping the party alive requires me to run for the leadership, that's what
I will do. Because the party must survive." There needed to be a "principal force of the democratic right in Canada."

In June, Harper was invited to a dinner at the home of Gerry Chipeur,
a politically active Calgary lawyer who had supported Day. Chipeur's
firm, Chipeur Advocates, had hired Ezra Levant after his firing as

Day's director of communications for denouncing a Montreal judge and suggesting "corruption of the judiciary." Levant, the self-proclaimed "Stockaholic," was at the dinner, as were Sean McKinsley, Day's deputy campaign manager in the leadership contest, Ken Boessenkool, Day's former adviser, and Tom Flanagan, who had supported Day against Manning. One of them recalled: "The attitude of these people who had been close to Stock was that the jig was really up for him. He just couldn't be saved any more. Their big fear was that the DRC would succeed in overthrowing Stock and there would be a Prestonian counter-revolution. So they were proposing that Stephen become the anointed successor. They evoked a scenario in which Gerry would go to Ottawa and become Day's chief of staff, and they would prepare the way for Stephen. Stock would resign at a certain point and Stephen would become the next leader."

In July, there was a big barbecue outside Calgary to raise funds for Ted Morton and Bert Brown, Alberta's "Senators-in-Waiting." Day was to attend, as was Harper. Boessenkool had arranged that Day and Harper would meet, and he was the only other person present. "Stephen indicated to Stock that he was getting increasing pressure to announce interest in the leadership, and he wanted to do that in a way that mini-mized antagonism between Stock and himself," Boessenkool recalls.

Harper was already preparing by laying out publicly, in a series of speeches, his political vision and an implicit platform. But he avoided interviews. He chose to be seen by the public through his own words rather than be interpreted by others. His most ambitious speech was given – incongruously – to the Canadian Institute of Plumbing and Heating at its annual convention, held in Charlottetown. He spoke on June 27, as the schism inside the Alliance neared its climax. He treated his audience of plumbers – quite familiar with leaks – to a complex analysis of the current political scene. He decried the factionalism rending the Alliance. "Canadians are losing interest because this fighting is all about power, not about vision. In this game of power, each of the two sides is trying to outflank the other for the affection of the Clark Tories. It is having a similar policy effect on both sides, requiring them to increasingly avoid any position that would make Mr. Clark uncomfortable. In other words, both wings of the Alliance are gradu-ally eschewing any real philosophical differences with the Liberals. The distinctive political values and policies that brought most 'Reform conservatives' into the political process are advanced with less and less earnestness." The result, Harper said, was that the Liberals were getting a free ride with their perverse policies of "state corporatism," devaluing the Canadian dollar, preventing the provinces from experimenting in the delivery of health care, and trying to counter Quebec separatism by buying loyalty. These policies led to an inefficient economy, political corruption and cronyism, a limping health-care system unsustainable in the long run, and a Quebec chronically dependent on subsidies from the rest of Canada. And what did the opposition parties offer by contrast? More of the same.

"The so-called 'conservative' parties need to figure out, and quickly, where they fit in this world. It frankly matters less whether there are one, two, or three such parties than whether one of them articulates an alternative vision. And in the machinations between their various camps, no alternative vision to the Liberals is being advanced. Without the articulation of a serious alternative vision, the Liberal Party is where a large number of their followers will soon begin to go anyway. And it will not matter whether or not the Liberal one-party state is desirable. People will cross any bridge they find."

It was a master class in political analysis – probably not the plumbers' usual convention fare. The speech was excerpted in several newspapers. It added to speculation about his return to politics to replace Day. A month earlier, Harper had sent a message to old Reformers through a *Calgary Sun* column that attacked federal official languages policy as a state religion, with criticism treated as heresy. His provocative heading: "Official bilingualism: the god that failed." He attacked the policy on two grounds: it was untrue to the real country, and Quebec rendered it inequitable by repressing English. "Real bilingualism in Canada is quite geographically isolated. Most Francophones actually live in French unilingual regions of Canada – mainly in Quebec – and most Anglophones live in English unilingual regions outside the province. Areas with significant numbers of both linguistic groups are almost all narrowly concentrated near the New Brunswick–Quebec and Quebec-Ontario borders, where most genuinely bilingual Canadians also reside." He judged that a truly bilingual Canada was a utopian fantasy. He also faulted a double standard for undermining the policy's legitimacy. "While there have been ongoing and unsuccessful attempts to promote French outside of Quebec, the federal government has increasingly surrendered to Quebec's activist policies of official *unilingualism*. And now the double standard has reached new heights with the appointment of Stéphane Dion as minister of official languages. Dion is an unabashed supporter of the French-only Bill 101 inside Quebec and official bilingualism elsewhere. As minister, he immediately declared his view of national bilingualism as being 'to promote French.'" Harper's conclusion: "As a religion, bilingualism is the god that failed. It has led to no fairness, produced no unity, and cost Canadian taxpayers untold millions."

While Harper was putting his own views on public display, within the embattled Alliance party, several negotiations failed to convince Day he should resign. By July, the party was deeply in debt, contributions had dried up, and Day's approval rating was down to 13 per cent. On July 3, the popular Deborah Grey challenged Day publicly: "Stock, there is no shame in admitting you're not a leader. For the good of the party and the good of the country, resign and call a leadership review." More than once, Day did suggest he might resign or take "a leave of absence." But he always repudiated such scenarios in the end and insisted that he was duty-bound to defend party democracy by staying. At a July 17 meeting of the Alliance caucus in Calgary, a motion of non-confidence had been signed in advance by a majority of the MPs. But Day pre-empted them by announcing that, because "We have become a house divided," (a now familiar phrase) he was calling for a leadership contest and would resign ninety days before the date for the vote that would be set by the National Council. That short-circuited the plan for the massive declaration of non-confidence. But many, inside and outside the party, judged that it might not survive until the election of a new leader. Boessenkool went to Harper: "Stephen, you have to send a signal that you might be available to lead this party. That might prevent a collapse. You don't have to do anything except put out a statement saying that, at the end of the year, you will no longer be running the NCC." The message went out on Canada NewsWire on August 13: "Stephen Harper has informed National Citizens Coalition Chairman Colin Brown that he intends to leave the presidency of the NCC no later than December 31." Boessenkool adds, "My own view is that, had he not done that, the Alliance might have simply ceased to exist."

DRC — Democratic
Representative Caucus

On August 10, a meeting was held over drinks at the 400 Club in Calgary. In attendance were Harper, Tom Flanagan, John Weissenberger, Ken Boessenkool, George Koch, the journalist who had worked as Manning's speechwriter, Mark Kihn, the western vice-president of the NCC, and Eric Hughes, Harper's friend from University of Calgary days. They discussed the situation. Joe Clark had invited the dissidents and other Alliance MPs to meet with him and senior members of his party on August 17 and 18 in the resort of Mont-Tremblant, to discuss working together in the Commons. The invitation did not extend to Alliance's leader Stockwell Day, a clear sign that Clark's intention was to split the party and absorb whatever MPs he could. Preston Manning approved publicly of the meeting, a clear repudiation of Day and endorsement of the DRC. In Calgary, the consensus was that the party's situation was getting desperate and only Harper could save it.

Harper
interested
in
leaving
leader

The August 10 meeting concluded with Harper saying, "I'm interested in running." On August 18, the same group, plus Harper's brothers Robert and Grant, met at the home of Flanagan. This time, the decision was taken: Harper would go for it. And they began preliminary planning, with Tom Flanagan and John Weissenberger in charge. Their first decision: they would take the high road with Day and turn their fire on Clark. The mood was hardly euphoric: their quest was not to fulfill an ambition but to launch a rescue operation. As one participant recalled, "We had a sense of foreboding that, if we didn't get involved, the party was just going to fall apart. This was our last chance to save the party and we all believed in the mission of the party and we didn't want it to die."

They planned a first-stage draft-Harper movement. During the summer, Harper had contacted people asking if they would support him if he ran for the leadership. He had commitments from about ten MPs including Scott Reid, James Rajotte, Charles Penson, and Dave Chatters, and from ex-MP Herb Grubel. Flanagan or Weissenberger contacted these people as well as others, to confirm that they would indeed support Harper's candidacy. Early on, they put out a blue flyer, deliberately frugal, a single 8.5 x 11–inch sheet, folded twice, with writing and a photo of Harper on both sides. The slogan was: "Draft Stephen Harper – True Reformer . . . True Conservative." It laid out his platform: "SMALLER GOVERNMENT . . . LOWER TAXES . . . EQUALITY OF CITIZENS . . . RULE OF LAW . . . NATIONAL UNITY." His pre-campaign button had his name printed in green, the colour of Reform, with the words: "Stephen Harper – True Reformer . . . True Conservative."

Harper wanted a truly national campaign, run by a professional manager, with experienced campaigners from different parts of the country. Preliminary polling from a few lists of constituency members found that Harper evoked a positive response, though Day kept important support at the grassroots level. In September Harper hired a campaign manager, Brian Mulakwa, who had worked for James Rajotte and managed Deborah Grey's last campaign. He had a firm in Edmonton, now called First Past the Post Strategic Communications. Others were hired in Toronto and Ottawa. They began planning an ambitious official launch, intended to be a major news event.

In October, a fundraising lunch was held in Calgary which brought in about $20,000. Over the summer, Harper had also picked up commitments which also totalled about $20,000. Yet late November brought a shattering moment of truth that almost aborted the unborn campaign. From the start, Harper had set the condition that his campaign must not go into debt. But the structure he had set up for a national campaign, with a staff operating in four cities, with people who had never been colleagues, was simply not working out. There wasn't the budget to bring them together and put them up until they had created an efficiently operating structure. All their efforts had concentrated on the grand launch, which would have cost $60,000 on the first day. But the campaign had a total of $40,000. In the meantime, very little had got done and time was running out. Harper fired all the paid people and withdrew, frustrated and depressed, to consider whether to continue.

A crisis meeting without Harper was held by his closest loyalists: Tom Flanagan, John Weissenberger, Ken Boessenkool, Mark Kihn, and George Koch. "These were desperate times. Stephen was seriously thinking of pulling the plug," remembers one participant. They decided they must go on. "We all made the commitment that we were going to do whatever we could to get Stephen through because we were loyal to him. It wasn't up to political professionals any more. We said, 'Now, the people in this room are going to have to do the rest of the campaign. How are we going to do that?' And we thrashed it around five or six hours. A lot of the parts were put together as we were just bouncing ideas. And finally we had a plan." Flanagan was dispatched to meet

Harper at his home and say, "Look, you've got a group of people in
Calgary that are absolutely committed to seeing you win. We know
you're going to win, and we're going to stick with you through this
whole thing." Harper's wife, Laureen, also urged him on.

So the amateurs took over. Flanagan became campaign manager,
Weissenberger the deputy manager, running the organization in the field.
Kihn, a former magazine publisher, raised the funds through direct mail,
Koch and Flanagan provided writing for a brochure, Laurie Watson –
Koch's partner – worked on production through her communications
firm, Boessenkool wrote major speeches, while Devin Iversen, a young
staffer for MP Rob Anders, took charge of the database and phoning.

There was no grand launch after all. On December 2, Harper simply
flew to Ottawa where he spoke to an audience of two hundred Alliance
fans brought together by MP Scott Reid and announced that he was a
candidate. He called for the party to resist the lure of Joe Clark's Red
Tories and urged instead a return to clear conservative principles. He
called for those who had built Reform but since given up to return and
build for the future. Then, back in Calgary, on December 6 he filed leadership nomination papers, deposited the required twenty-five thousand
dollars with the party and obtained the all-important list of members.
He then went on a speaking tour of Alberta during the week of
December 10, with a ten-dollar admission fee charged at each event. His
campaign was off and rolling.

How was he perceived in the media? Shawn Ohler, after attending
one meeting, wrote in the *Edmonton Journal*: "Who's Harper? He's like
that nice economics prof you had in first year, supernova-smart but
almost entirely charisma-free. More compelling orators can be seen
nightly on the Home Shopping Network." Susan Riley, a left-leaning
columnist with the *Ottawa Citizen*: "He is a visionary, a believer in
caucus discipline, and a policy wonk – but with better hair [than
Manning] and a voice that doesn't grate. He faces the same challenge that
undid Manning, too: How to turn a catalogue of complaint – a portrait
of Canada as an international laggard, a slow student, a familiar sad
story of failed potential – into an attractive package for voters. But he is
an intelligent and serious new player in the national debate." *Edmonton
Journal* columnist Paula Simons marked the contrast between Day and
Harper: "They are the opposite faces of the conservative movement.

Stockwell Day is the charismatic, casual social conservative, the pastor-turned-politician who wants to save your soul, while he saves the country from moral decay. Stephen Harper is the reserved, formal, fiscal conservative, the professorial policy wonk, who's happy to keep the state out of your bedroom, as long as you'll agree to keep the state out of every other part of Canadian life. Call it Low Church versus High Church, Dionysian versus Apollonian."

Stockwell Day stepped down as leader on December 12. The next day, by a vote of fourteen to thirteen, a bitterly divided National Council expelled from the party the DRC dissident MPs, including Chuck Strahl, Deborah Grey, Jay Hill, Grant McNally, Val Meredith, and Jim Pankiw. Inky Mark had let his membership lapse. Gary Lunn, who had joined the DRC, had applied to return, but the caucus had so far refused him re-entry.

The other leadership candidates soon declared. Grant Hill, the mild-spoken, gentlemanly physician from Okotoks announced on December 17 that he would be the "candidate of co-operation," between the Alliance and the Tories. Diane Ablonczy had declared that she would be working to bring the parties together; she filed her candidacy papers on December 21. Stockwell Day kicked off his campaign in Montreal on January 7, 2002, by portraying himself as the man of the people beleaguered by the powers that be. "Once again, the elites are saying that this campaign cannot succeed," he claimed. "But we have proved them wrong before, and we will prove them wrong again. Let's prove them wrong again and show that we still stand for strong conservative principles and grassroots democracy, and that we will not let them tell us how to think, speak, and vote." He was the victim of dissidents without respect for party democracy who were abetted by "pundit panelists on the CBC." He put a populist question: "Have you had enough of being continuously scolded by the elites for not thinking properly or voting correctly?"

The issue of working with the Tories dominated the first month of the campaign. "We cannot allow our party's future to be held hostage by Joe Clark and other Tories," Day pronounced. But Day played on both sides of the question. He favoured running joint Alliance–Tory candidates in the next elections, while insisting, "We'll discuss things with the Tories, but it will be from our position of strength." Harper steadily repudiated any overtures as long as Clark led the Tories. He insisted it was a waste of time and a distraction from advancing a truly conservative agenda and holding the Liberals responsible for their damaging actions. "Joe Clark and the Tories don't agree with a single thing this party stands for."

Hill, with his platform of reconciling the two parties, was backed by Conrad Black's associate Peter White, who had resigned in July as the Alliance's co-treasurer, along with party president Ken Kalopsis. Hill was also supported on and off by Ralph Klein, by the four other Tory premiers, by ex-Tory Senator Gerry St. Germain, and by Rod Love, Day's former campaign manager. He had a half-dozen MPs supporting him, notably Vic Toews. But his campaign, like that of Ablonczy, went nowhere, with Alliance members polarized between Harper and Day. Harper was associated with Reform's best days, the early idealistic struggles in the wilderness and the early breakthroughs, before Reform and the Alliance lost their innocence. It was his good fortune that the Manning loyalists, by joining the DRC, had taken themselves out of the contest, and so Harper, ironically, was seen as Manning's heir. Harper's campaign focused on mobilizing current members of the Alliance and past members of Reform, while Day's concentrated on recruiting new members. ← *Harper starts to campaign*

Harper's first solicitation letter, dated December 4, 2001, went to fifty-seven thousand households and reached seventy-five thousand current members. It carried at the heading his new slogan: GETTING IT RIGHT / Stephen Harper / *For Leader of the Canadian Alliance*. It began: "Dear Canadian Alliance Supporter: Imagine the Canadian Alliance didn't exist. Imagine no political party spoke for Canadians like you who cherish conservative principles and values. Imagine the only alternative to Jean Chrétien's arrogant, spend-happy Liberals were Joe Clark's arrogant, spend-happy Red Tories. Not a pretty picture, is it? Of course, I know you don't want the Alliance and its principles to disappear. That's why you stayed loyal when others deserted the party. When the left-wing media declared the Alliance was dead, you still believed. When some argued it was time to dilute our principles, you held firm. I know it hasn't been easy. But here's the good news. You've finally got somebody fighting on your side!" The letter went on to introduce Stephen Harper and enumerate his virtues. It ended: "Stephen has consistently fought for what's right." A separate cut-out section at the bottom was a form for making a contribution. It began: "Dear Tom [Flanagan]: I'm with Stephen in 'Getting it Right' in the fight to save the soul of the Canadian Alliance."

The letter astonished Harper's team by bringing in four hundred thousand dollars. From then on, the earlier dread of a deficit vanished. In the end, with subsequent letters targeted to various constituencies such as lapsed Alliance members and even the list of Quebec's Equality Party, the campaign raised $1.1 million and ended with a surplus.

Day was associated with the failures of the past year, but he also championed an important number of Canadians who felt aggrieved and unrepresented in the political system – the social conservatives. They were outraged that Canada had no law regulating abortion, they opposed special protection for homosexuals, they favoured the death penalty, and a less lenient system of justice. Many were offended that religious principles were marginalized in public life. Day targeted evangelical churches to recruit new members, with notable success. In early February, the Harper campaign lodged a complaint about the way that Day was promoted by the anti-abortion lobby, Campaign Life Coalition, which bills itself as the political arm of the Canadian Pro-Life movement. It used its Web site to sign up new members, with applications to be forwarded to Campaign Life, rather than to the party or to the candidates. This, Alliance officials agreed, broke the rules. By going public with this complaint, Harper focused attention on Day's semi-underground campaign and the danger of a single-interest lobby seizing control of the party. When Harper met the editorial board of the *Ottawa Citizen*, he explained: "My view is that the purpose of a Christian church is to promote the message and the life of Christ. It is not to promote a particular political party or candidacy. I don't think this is good religion, besides being bad politics at the same time." His position rallied a significant number of people who feared that "single issue" social conservatives could capture the Alliance.

On January 19, Harper gave perhaps his most important speech. He titled it "Federalism and all Canadians," in conscious contrast to Pierre Trudeau's book titled *Federalism and the French Canadians*. Harper articulated his own vision of the country. His central principle was that the federal government should not intrude in areas of provincial jurisdiction, but should concentrate on those areas assigned to it by the Constitution, notably by enforcing a free market within the entire territory of Canada. "Under such a pan-Canadian federalism, the provinces should be autonomous in areas of provincial jurisdiction. Canada is a

JAN 2002 provincial autonomy (handwritten)

country of regions with widely differing geography, cultures, and economic interests. Those differences are best served and reconciled by allowing differences to exist among provinces in a wide array of policy areas." He proposed "a strict division of powers between provinces and the federal government" and offered provincial autonomy as a better alternative for protecting Quebec's language and culture than the "special status" proposed at Meech Lake, Charlottetown, and Calgary. "The core assertion of its proponents – that special status is needed to protect the French language in Quebec – is simply false. The French language is not imperilled in the province of Quebec." On language policy, even though Harper expressed regret over the excesses of Bill 101, he stated clearly: "I support Quebec's right to legislate in the area of language. Having said that, I also support the Charter rights to freedom of expression and language choice. As a federal political leader, I would not intervene in Quebec language legislation and I would leave the courts to deal with constitutional challenges." In a glaring omission, though, he failed to state his policy for the official languages at the federal level. There wasn't a word, now, about "the god that failed."

Harper was clear on one other controversial topic: the conditions for Quebec's secession. "Any act of secession on the part of any part of the country must be done within the confines of the current Constitution, which includes the rule of law and clear democratic consent." He noted in his speech that conservative parties had generally sought power by appealing to Quebec nationalists. This was a mistake, because such alliances had always proved temporary and destructive. Brian Mulroney's Quebec adventure was an example. "The broad lesson of history is that Canada's natural governing coalition always includes the federalist option in Quebec, not the nationalist one. . . . It would therefore be a mistake, in my judgment, for the Canadian Alliance to focus on simply grabbing the anti-Liberal vote in order to build a beachhead in Quebec. The party must undertake the long-run work necessary to become a federalist option in Quebec acceptable to a significant number of Liberal as well as anti-Liberal voters."

Of the four candidates, Harper stood out as the one having the clear, coherent, and comprehensive vision. He had been meditating on the state of Canada through his entire adult life. His adversaries accused him of being doctrinaire, extremist, of wanting to return to the past. Day

accused him of being "a quitter" for having resigned from Parliament in
1997. But, ultimately, the contest between Day and Harper would be
decided by who could sign up and mobilize the most members. Harper's
campaign had set up a phone bank in Calgary and, later, a second phone
bank in Ottawa. Under the direction of Devin Iversen, the campaign
acquired on the cheap a stripped down predictive dialler, linked to a
computer, which automatically dialled the numbers on the membership
list, while volunteers with head sets delivered the pitch for Harper and,
using a code, classified the members as supportive or not, the entry going
into the computer. Eventually, as more money materialized, people were
hired, especially in Ottawa, to relieve the volunteers. The phone banks,
with ten head sets, operated ten hours a day, six days a week.

Suddenly, at the end of January, with the deadline for signing up new
members only weeks away, the Harper campaign was struck by worry:
while concentrating on reaching current and lapsed members, while
having great success at fundraising and clearly winning the policy
debates, the amateurs running the campaign had neglected to mount a
big, systematic push to recruit new members. There was no one appointed
as director of membership sales. There was no team assigned to the task.
"We began to hear these rumours that Stock was selling enormous
numbers of memberships through the church basement thing. I said, jeez,
we might lose this thing after all. I had a lot of sleepless nights," said one
of the senior organizers. So, in February, the campaign hired at the cost
of twenty thousand dollars an automatic dialler with one thousand lines
that could do a whole city in a day: they had it make ninety thousand
phone calls with a message recorded by Harper: "Now, this is a serious
fight, and I need your support. Will you join?" It gave the telephone
number of the campaign office, which received 1,500 responses, with
about 650 actually taking out memberships. They also recorded a later
message from Harper: "This is a close fight. I need your help. Can you
go out and sell just two more memberships?" They then hired a tele-
marketing company to make thirty thousand calls. That brought in
about two thousand new members. And the twenty-eight MPs supporting Harper were pressed to have their organizers get out and sell memberships. They came through, notably Scott Reid and Art Hanger. One
of the campaign organizers recalls, "It was frantic. In the last three weeks
of the campaign we had people in the campaign office making calls from

seven in the morning till ten at night." In the end, they estimated that
they brought in about sixteen thousand new members. The problem then
was to get them processed in time. In the last weeks, their polling indicated that they were clearly ahead. But, with Day claiming the lead, they
downplayed Harper's chances in order to keep their supporters motivated to vote, so as to defeat Day and save the party.

In Calgary, a battered and diminished Canadian Alliance gathered in
convention on March 20 to announce the result of the vote. Harper surprised almost everyone, including Stockwell Day, by winning on the first
ballot, with 48,561 votes to Day's 33,074, a score of 55 per cent. Diane
Ablonczy received 3.8 per cent and Grant Hill 3.7. It was a clear victory
after a hard-fought campaign, but to many observers it seemed like a
Pyrrhic victory, given the state of the party. Now there was little to
compare with the atmosphere of euphoria in July 2000 when a new
party acquired a dynamic new leader and everything seemed possible,
even power in the coming federal elections. Then, there were 276,000
members. By March 2002 the number had fallen to 124,000. A poll that
month showed the Alliance, despite all the publicity surrounding the
leadership campaign, with the support of only 10 per cent of Canadians.
The party was nearly $3 million in debt and contributions had dried up.

Harper's victory speech was appropriately modest. Its most important sentence was a cry of defiance: "The Canadian Alliance is a permanent political institution that is here to stay."

Chapter 19

LEADER OF THE CANADIAN ALLIANCE

NO HONEYMOON AWAITED Stephen Harper. No sooner was he elected leader of the Canadian Alliance than a media chorus wrote him off. Much of the mainstream punditocracy declared him too dogmatic, not charismatic, cold, lacking a sense of humour, an ideologue unwilling to compromise, manifestly too conservative for Canadian values. Besides, he wouldn't dance with Joe Clark.

In the *Toronto Star*, columnist Richard Gwyn dismissed Harper as "yesterday's man." Edward Greenspon's column in the *Globe and Mail* fancied him a displaced person: "Stephen Harper: a neo-con in a land of liberals." For the *Globe*'s Hugh Winsor, Harper's election replayed the cycle of western protest parties that briefly blossom, "then shrink back to those regional roots." The new leader "is destined to lead a western Canadian rump rather than a national party." The *Globe*'s editorial board faulted Harper for rejecting the premiers' stillborn 1997 Calgary Declaration. The editorial, titled "Mr. Harper risks a hermetic Alliance," also chided him for rejecting a deal with Joe Clark. "He is a principled man who seems prepared to let the Alliance become the NDP of the right – influential, without a hope of rising to power nationally – rather than bend to circumstance."

The *Vancouver Sun* agreed that Harper's Alliance just might influence Liberal government policy. "Beyond this limited goal, however, we haven't seen anything to suggest that Mr. Harper is the man to build the kind of coalition necessary to win power. He presents himself as unbending, unwilling to make the compromises to appeal to the middle-of-the-road voters and traditional supporters of the Progressive Conservatives." For *Vancouver Sun* columnist Barbara Yaffe, "The fact is, Mr. Harper inherited the reins of a party recovering from a near-death experience, a party that has used up all its political capital with the public." Yaffe saw no hope for the Alliance except in joining with the Tories. And she glimpsed goodwill on the Tory side because Joe Clark "has already made an overture to Mr. Harper. He phoned the new leader even before he made it to the podium to deliver his victory speech."

A leadership campaign usually gives a major party and its new leader a bounce in opinion polls. A week after Harper's victory, Ipsos-Reid asked what effect Harper's leadership of the Canadian Alliance would have on voting intentions. The great majority of respondents – 75 per cent – said Harper would make no difference. Only 16 per cent were more likely to vote CA, while 7 per cent were "less likely." The Alliance did get a slight bounce, with 15 per cent saying they would vote CA. But that was far from the 25.5 per cent the party had won in the 2000 elections. It put the Alliance on a par with Joe Clark's Tories, while the ruling Chrétien Liberals were favoured by 45 per cent, the NDP by 10.

The coolness of journalists and public contrasted with the enthusiasm of the 1,000 delegates who came to the Alliance's convention in Edmonton on April 4. They met in an atmosphere of restoration following a civil war. The year-long nightmare of warring factions was replaced by order, purpose, calm, confidence, and the resolve to banish factionalism. As Diane Ablonczy remarked: "The delegates are absolutely determined that this will not go off the rails again. I would not want to be the first person to cause problems. Whoever did would be tarred and feathered."

Stockwell Day, the deposed leader, looked pinched, uncomfortable, and isolated. But Harper treated him graciously, granting him his first choice in the new shadow cabinet as critic of foreign affairs. Day's name was never mentioned by other delegates. The other previous leader, the party's founder Preston Manning, received an evening tribute during which he was showered with praise. But the event had a bittersweet undertone. Manning was recognized for creating the party and changing the political culture of Canada. But Manning, as everyone present knew, had also encouraged the rebels against Day, supported the Mont-Tremblant meeting convened by Joe Clark with the breakaway

Democratic Representative Caucus, and had called for a joint Alliance-Tory candidate for the riding he had vacated, contrary to the new direction of the party. Harper's victory meant more than merely taking up Manning's succession after an unfortunate interlude: it supplanted Manning's moral leadership. Harper would restore a conservative vision without Manning's ideological populism, and Harper would attempt to reach the promised land of government that Manning had prophesied but never entered.

In his major address to the convention, the new leader ignored the past to reassure the delegates of their future as a party. "Tonight I want to talk to you about the rebirth of our party," he announced to cheers. "The Canadian Alliance is strong, and the Canadian Alliance is here to stay." The faithful understood: no more vacillating over the party's identity, no more compromises on fundamentals. Ontario MP Scott Reid expressed it: "One of the mistakes we made during the United Alternative process was to water down our policies in the hope that, somehow, being less specific would make our support broader. We're now reverting to the policy orientation that Reform had in the past."

Yet the Alliance was under pressure to strike a deal with the Tories. The moneyed people who had financed Stockwell Day before the 2000 elections turned away when the Alliance then imploded. Now they made clear that neither Alliance nor Tories would get their money until the two united. Clark, however, was an unlikely peacemaker; from the start he had treated Reform and the Alliance as ill-bred upstarts. Peter C. Newman quoted Clark after the 2000 elections: "The Alliance party is fundamentally offensive. It's an alliance of people who don't like other people, the very opposite of the inclusion that characterizes our party. In those parts of the country that are a base for us, any kind of association with the Reform/Alliance would give those seats to the Liberals." But now Clark, with his party in debt, was also being pressured by the seven DRC MPs who had joined his caucus in a working coalition. They had demanded that the Tories not run candidates against them in the coming elections, while Clark insisted on running a PC candidate in every riding. After a tense six-hour meeting in Ottawa the day before the Alliance convention, Clark understood he had to move. He called Harper and requested a meeting after the convention.

Harper told the convention about the Tory approach. "Joe Clark made a point of calling me as soon as possible after my election as leader to request a meeting to discuss co-operation – an invitation that, for over four years, he never bothered to extend to my predecessors. Next week I will meet with Mr. Clark to hear what he has to propose. But as I promised you over and over during the leadership race, my priority is to rebuild this party for the next election and there is no time to waste. If we receive serious proposals that would lead to real co-operation in a timely manner, those will be submitted to you, the members of our party, for a democratic mandate. But make no mistake, we will receive such proposals only if Joe Clark continues to move toward the realization that the Canadian Alliance is strong and the Canadian Alliance is here to stay."

He spoke of the party's financial situation, with a debt at the bank of $2.3 million. Before Day's tenure, only 20 per cent of the party's budget came from corporations. But, in the election year of 2000, business interests contributed most of the $19 million raised. Afterward, contributions from direct-mail solicitation fell. A party in debt was for Harper a scandalous incongruity. "Indebtedness is inconsistent with the values of our party, inconsistent with the spirit that saw this party in the 1990s lead the charge for a balanced budget. We will pay down this debt as part of our preparations for the next election. We will run this party the way we should be running the country – and that's debt free." The bank debt would be paid off by borrowing from the constituency associations. The Alliance must not be dependent on a bank. "I have requested that an aggressive fundraising campaign to our members be launched in order to take advantage of the renewed energy in our party. Meanwhile our managers have dramatically cut costs and our fundraisers will continue to aggressively pursue broadly based national fundraising initiatives." In fact, Harper had laid off several Alliance employees.

The DRC dissidents had symbolized the Alliance's earlier failure. Harper had condemned their schism, but spared the MPs personally. Now, having remained outside the party's civil war, he was in a position to invite the rebels to return: "The dissident members have been given a clear and unequivocal opportunity to return and fulfill the obligation to serve with the party under which they were elected."

The convention's energy and harmony sent a message to the DRC, to Clark, and to the public at large, of the Alliance's restored spirit and Harper's firm leadership. Always self-assured, he called on the core members to concentrate on policies rather than personalities, on rebuilding the party and debating how to defeat the Liberals, rather than spending time plotting coups and counter-coups. And the delegates responded.

Journalists used to reporting on the party with ironic condescension were impressed. *La Presse* columnist Lysiane Gagnon described the assiduousness of the delegates in the policy sessions, which reminded her of the early fervent conventions of the Parti Québécois. The more moderate voices made themselves heard over the extremists. A resolution to abolish the Charter of Rights and Freedoms was defeated, one to outlaw research on stem cells was tabled. A delegate employed by Campaign Life Coalition walked out in disgust and went shopping, missing Harper's speech. On issues which had damaged Alliance during the 2000 campaign, more cautious stands were adopted. The "flat tax" was sent back for further study. The number of petitioners required to trigger a citizens' initiative, on abortion for instance, would be the average adopted by jurisdictions recognizing citizens' initiatives: about 5 per cent of the voters in the previous election. On health care, the delegates voted to expand the choices available for medical services by allowing the use of privately owned medical facilities, as was already practised in Alberta with the consent of federal health minister Anne McLellan. But they avoided endorsing a policy allowing private payments for publicly insured medical services.

This new image of the party would give Harper a stronger negotiating hand the following Tuesday when he met Joe Clark in Ottawa. The official reason for their meeting was to find ways to work together. But also at stake was public image: which of the two would appear reasonable, which would be blamed for obstructing. As long as the two parties ran candidates against each other, it seemed that the Liberals would rule forever. The pundits, the public, and many within each party, all wanted the internecine warfare to cease. But was the desirable also attainable?

The United Alternative episode had made reunification more difficult. As Harper had written at the time, it amounted to the attempted takeover of the smaller PC Party by the more robust Reform. It attracted mostly Blue Tories from the PC's right wing. But those who remained with Clark's party were predominantly Red Tories, precisely those most opposed to Reform's policies and image. Clark further complicated reunion by his constant attempts to win the Quebec nationalists, to grant Quebec a special status, to appease separatism. Clark had been the chief architect of the Charlottetown Accord, which Reform so vehemently opposed. A month before that 1992 referendum, when the opinion polls were turning against the accord, Clark warned: "If we lose this, we lose the country." He evoked the fifteen-year civil war in Lebanon to project what might await Canada: "We should recognize that, once, Beirut was one of the best places in the world to live, and it gave in to anger. . . . That could happen here." In 1994, he published a book summarizing his wisdom, ominously titled *A Nation Too Good to Lose*. "There is no doubt that separation could come about," he warned. And he gave separation his blessing: "Canadians would respect the right of Quebec to leave." His solution was to remake the federation to Quebec's specifications: "Quebec cannot accept the status quo in Canada, and, indeed, the changes proposed in both the Meech Lake and the Charlottetown accords will not now be enough to give Quebec reasonable confidence that it can flourish in Canada."

The two parties' political cultures were mismatched. The convention had reaffirmed the Alliance members' paramount role in formulating policy. Clark, the autocratic leader, had opposed the reference to the Supreme Court on the legality of secession and, without consulting his caucus, later decreed PC opposition to the Clarity Act, which Harper had pioneered. During the 2000 campaign, *clark* he promised to scrap the Clarity Act. "I have said it was a mistake, and I would not keep it on the books." At the convention, Harper had declared that the party must patiently build its support in Quebec among federalists – and not among ultra- ⟩ nationalists, as Clark and Brian Mulroney had done. "There's been a debate in Quebec about whether this party should be a fundamentally nationalist or crypto-separatist party, and appeal to that part of the electorate, fundamentally, or whether it should be a party that starts from a strong commitment to federalism – one that is going to compete with the Liberals for the federalist vote. My position on this is clear: We have to be a federalist alternative and that's the direction where I intend to take this party." He would work with "soft nationalists," but repudiated the "knife-at-the-throat nationalism" practised by Robert Bourassa's Liberals.

Though Harper didn't say so, he was also distancing himself from Day's approach, which, like Clark's, was to appeal to the nationalists. Day had chosen as his spokesman Éric Duhaime, previously the spokesman for the Bloc Québécois. He had also hired as chief organizer in Quebec Michel Rivard, a former PQ member of the National Assembly. These two denounced Harper during the leadership campaign as anti-Quebec and Harper's victory almost annihilated Alliance support in Quebec; at the Edmonton convention, a mere eight delegates represented Quebec's seventy-five ridings, and that included Rivard and his wife.

When Harper and Clark finally got together on April 9, their meeting lasted ninety minutes. Afterward, Clark was all injured innocence. Why, he had offered written, detailed proposals for working together on the basis of "the principle of equality." For instance, "We would launch this week a joint examination of the practical options to prevent vote-splitting in each riding." But Harper wouldn't accept "equality" between twelve Tory MPs and the sixty-six Alliance MPs. Not without irony, he offered Clark the mirror image of Clark's "coalition" with the DRC with himself as the leader, that Clark had trumpeted for seven months as the model for uniting the two parties. This proposal, Clark now protested, would make his party "the junior partner." He'd have none of it. And Harper went further, calling for double or nothing: Clark must agree that their parties would not run candidates against each other, or all bets were off. Clark offered process, a series of meetings. Harper demanded results. Clark lost the game of chicken he had provoked. The next day, six of the seven DRC announced that they wanted to return to the Alliance caucus.

They had been feeling pressure from their constituents since the night of Harper's victory, and they heard his speech as an invitation to reconciliation. He had said that founding the Alliance had "refounded" Reform as a coalition, and he urged: "Now I ask you to embark on that hard work once again, to join me in rebuilding this party and to bring together all who share our values and our vision – Reformers, right-minded PCs, and others regardless of their previous political affiliation." He followed up with his explicit invitation to them at the convention.

There had also been negotiations behind the scenes. Jay Hill was the first to put out feelers. Members of his constituency association spoke with Harper during the convention and told him that their MP wanted back. The day before he met Clark, Harper conferred with Hill, Chuck Strahl, and Deborah Grey and set three conditions for their return: they must obtain a supportive letter from their constituency association, pledge permanent loyalty to leader and caucus, and meet with him for a one-on-one discussion. The morning after the Harper–Clark meeting, at the weekly Alliance caucus, Harper announced the prodigals' wish to return. The caucus voted to accept them back. Four returned on April 17: Grey, Chuck Strahl, Jay Hill, and Val Meredith. A fifth, Grant McNally, was still awaiting his letter from his constituency association. Inky Mark chose to remain with the Tories. Jim Pankiw, MP for Saskatoon-Humboldt, had had an altercation in a bar with an aboriginal lawyer who claimed that a drunk Pankiw had challenged him to a fight. Pankiw, refused re-entry, would sit as an independent until his defeat in the 2004 elections.

Ending the Alliance's schism proved a diplomatic coup. Harper had meanwhile resolved the thorny issue posed by Ezra Levant. Manning's resignation had opened up the seat of Calgary Southwest. For Harper to inherit the riding vacated by the founder would serve symbolic and practical purposes, and he would not require a sitting member to resign as Day had done. But Levant, after embarrassing Day by indiscretions as his director of communications, now wanted to return triumphantly to Ottawa as MP for Calgary Southwest. He'd signed up new members, taken control of the riding association, been nominated as candidate, put up billboards vaunting his virtues, and even sent a letter to the thousands of Alberta's Alliance members to endorse his chosen candidates for the three Alberta positions on the National Council. Levant had invested heavily in these campaigns and now resisted every suggestion to step aside for his new leader. Harper announced his preference for Calgary Southwest, without making an issue of it. But privately, he told a friend: "Ezra simply has no idea of the kind of pressure that's going to be brought to bear on him." Indeed, despite his public defiance, Levant was soon deluged by messages from indignant party members. Denunciatory letters to the editor appeared in newspapers. The *National Post* and others published lampooning cartoons. His financial backers withdrew their support. He was in debt – he claimed to have spent $200,000 campaigning – and now was dangerously exposed. The constituency association was broke. Harper, with the surplus from his leadership race, promised to help. Finally, Levant folded.

Edward Greenspon commented in the *Globe and Mail*: "So Stephen Harper has vanquished Stockwell Day, smitten Ezra Levant, stoned Joe Clark, and corralled Chuck Strahl and Deb Grey. In the grapefruit league of Canadian politics, he's putting up impressive numbers. But can he play ball with the Liberals – that's the real test." The test wouldn't be long in coming. By-elections were called for May 13 in seven ridings, including Calgary Southwest. The Liberals and PCs gave Harper a pass. The NDP, Green Party, and Christian Heritage Party ran candidates and there was an independent. Harper caused a stir when he was quoted as saying he "despised" Bill Phipps, the NDP candidate who had been moderator of the United Church of Canada. "Obviously, I don't subscribe to anything he believes politically," Harper explained afterward. He also refused to take part in an all-candidates debate, claiming it was an NDP front. On election day, he received 71.7 per cent of the vote – a foregone conclusion. Elsewhere, the Liberals were jolted by losing to the Tories Gander-Grand Falls, a riding held by Liberal George Baker for twenty-eight years, and in Windsor West, fiefdom of Herb Gray for thirty-nine years, they lost to the NDP's Brian Masse, a popular city councillor.

On a very cool May 21 with occasional showers, Stephen Harper took the oath of loyalty to the Queen, signed the official register, and became the MP for Calgary Southwest. A modest ceremony held in the Commonwealth Room contrasted with the sumptuous reception when Stockwell Day took the oath in 2000. Then, a crowd occupied the much larger Railway Committee Room and refreshments were served. This time, coffee and muffins were available at the back of the room, but only the journalists helped themselves. Harper entered with his picture-perfect family, Laureen, Ben and Rachel, all three fair-haired and blue-eyed. Harper signed the book, patted Ben on the head, then offered him the pen: "Sign it?" Everyone laughed. Harper added: "We'll worry about the dynasty later."

As Harper made his entry to the Commons for Question Period, flanked by John Reynolds and Art Hanger, Jean Chrétien welcomed him graciously, with only a hint of mock partisanship: "On behalf of all the members of Parliament I would like to welcome the new leader of the

Opposition. Perhaps, in terms of security, a seat belt should be put on his seat because it is called the ejection seat. I am delighted to be facing my eighth opposition leader. . . . He is a man of strong convictions who expresses himself very well. He wants to serve the country well. His views are well known and well documented. In fact, I took a refresher course over the weekend. I hope it will not be used too often." Then, in French: "I want to congratulate him. He understood what Canada is all about at a very early age. He also learned French when he was very young and he speaks Canada's other official language well. We wish him a very good and a very long stay as leader of the Official Opposition." Harper responded in the same ironic spirit: "I would like to say to all members that it is wonderful to be back and to see all the familiar faces, and even a few friends. I have been asked many times why I would come back after all these years. I have explained that with statements by members, long debates over the estimates, committee meetings, and the debate over the Mace, it has all been too much to stay away from."

In the spirit of the occasion, he then poked fun at his chief adversary. "There is one reason I came back. Some members will know it has been reported that I was four years old when the prime minister first took his seat in the House of Commons. What is not known is that of course I was an avid reader of Hansard at the time. I recall reading some of the early speeches of the prime minister and turning to my mother, who is here today, and saying 'Mom, someone has to do something to stop that guy.'" Harper also made a playful reference to the rivalry for the Liberal leadership that was soon to force the prime minister to announce his resignation: "I am his eighth leader of the Opposition. However, I am in a privileged position in that besides myself and my party, the Deputy Prime Minister [John Manley], the Minister of Canadian Heritage [Sheila Copps], the Minister of Industry [Brian Tobin], and of course the Minister of Finance [Paul Martin] are all wishing that I will be his last opposition leader."

It was all in good fun. But the atmosphere turned deadly serious when Harper asked his first question. A new era in Canadian politics had begun thirteen days earlier, when Auditor General Sheila Fraser had released a report on three federal contracts, worth $1,625,000, awarded to the Montreal advertising agency Groupaction Marketing Inc. "Senior public servants broke just about every rule in the book," Fraser told a

press conference. "It's quite appalling what we saw." In her report she
stated: "The government files on the three contracts are so poorly documented that many key questions remain unanswered surrounding the
election of the contractor and the basis for establishing the price and
scope of work for the contracts. In our opinion, the government did not
receive much of what it contracted for and paid for." She immediately
referred the transactions to the RCMP and announced that she had
decided to investigate all the sponsorship and advertising programs,
going back several years. Fraser's report kindled concern about a host of
other deals with ad agencies, and all through the month of May, news
reports spotlighted other apparently scandalous transactions.

Harper began his career as leader of the Opposition by raising questions about scandals. That first exchange with the prime minister is
worth reproducing: it would be the paradigm of innumerable exchanges
to come. "The media is reporting today yet another scandal involving
federal advertising contracts. After examining a Public Works audit, it
has been estimated that Public Works paid at least ten times too much to
Groupe Polygone for sponsoring a Montreal hunting and fishing show.
Given the growing evidence of widespread waste and mismanagement of
government advertising business and the fact that the government's
incompetent handling of its advertising and sponsorship is already under
review, will the prime minister stop the waste and abuse right now and
order a freeze of all discretionary government advertising?"

Chrétien responded: "At the request of the Minister of Public Works,
the Auditor General looked into these files, recommended some action,
and is looking at the program as such. The sponsorship program has
existed in Canada for a long time. It is useful in every riding, in every part
of Canada. It is a good program. If there are some problems with the
management of some elements of it, of course we will look at the report
of the Auditor General and remedy the faults. However, I think that
many organizations in Canada need this program to be carried out for
the good of all Canadians."

In the light of what Canadians learned later, that was hardly a satisfactory answer. Harper returned to the subject: "It is great to say that
there are auditor general's examinations going on and of course there
may be a police investigation, but what I think the people of Canada are
looking for is action now from the government. All the government's

advertising activities are under review because of waste, abuse, and mismanagement. The government appears to react only when the Opposition or the media draw attention to its actions. Will the prime minister provide a list of all the discretionary advertising and sponsorship contracts so that we can immediately get to the bottom of things –"

Chrétien replied: "There is a system that allows members to obtain all the information they wish. It is all available. In fact, the government has acted. In 1999, when auditors pointed out a problem to the then minister, we took steps to improve the program. Some of the charges date from then. The current minister of public works has added new reforms to ensure that the errors of the past are not repeated."

Harper came back again: "I think we are all tired of getting this information through access to information and through the media, through all these other channels. We would hope the prime minister would do the right thing and make this information immediately available. Today's reports on Groupe Polygone deal with an internal audit that found problems two years ago. This is the same outfit that hugely overspent tax dollars on *l'Almanach du peuple*. Now it seems that this audit found the government paid a grossly inflated amount to sponsor a hunting and fishing show. Could the prime minister explain why this mismanagement was kept quiet for two years and why it always takes an access to information request or an auditor general's report –"

Chrétien's reply: "This is exactly why we have auditors: to look at the books. In the past the auditor reported to the House of Commons only once a year. In order to make sure that we were more up to date about the problems of administration, the Auditor General can now report four times a year. In terms of all the information the new leader of the Opposition is asking for, he should know that all the information is already available."

All the information was available? During Question Period the next day, Harper again asked that all the contracts for sponsorships and advertising be tabled. "We expect open and honest information here, not to have to make 58,000 access to information requests." Later reports from the Auditor General and investigations to come would demonstrate that getting all the information was like finding thousands of needles in hundreds of haystacks. The surge of sponsorship funding that began after the 1995 referendum would not be financed or declared according to established practices, nor would it be approved or verified according to existing rules. It would take years of determined digging by the media, the opposition parties, the Auditor General, and, eventually, a commission of inquiry, to approach a full accounting. But Chrétien's response to the developing scandal was to stonewall.

CORRUPTION

This was a very different Parliament in a much-changed country that Harper returned to in 2002. When he was first elected in 1993, the country faced financial collapse and Quebec's secession seemed imminent. Harper and Manning asserted themselves forcefully on both issues and proved far more visionary than the new Chrétien government. Now, in 2002, the budget was in comfortable surplus and Quebec separatism was in remission. The most urgent problem now was the abandonment of integrity by government: the abuse of public money for partisan ends, the absence of transparency, the impediments to disclosure, the cronyism, and the reckless subversion of oversight to control spending, as evidenced in the $1 billion that the Auditor General found improperly accounted for in the Department of Human Resources Development Canada. The government's slap-happy stewardship of the public purse was an affront to Harper's upbringing, convictions, and character. His father and two brothers were chartered accountants. Frugality and financial rectitude were bred in the bone. When he became head of the NCC, he reduced the president's salary by 15 per cent. When, in March, he became Alliance leader, he cut the support provided by party statute for the leader until he won a seat. He viewed government from the perspective of the taxpayer and threw himself into the struggle to hold the government to account.

Two days after his swearing-in, the Alliance moved a harsh resolution, "That, in the opinion of this House, the reason why 69 per cent of Canadians polled in a recent survey viewed the 'federal political system' as corrupt is because Ministers of this government have failed to make public their secret Code of Conduct, have broken their own Liberal Red Book promises such as the one to appoint an independent Ethics Counsellor who reports directly to Parliament, and have failed to clear the air over allegations of abusing their positions to further their own interests and those of their friends."

Chrétien, in his speech, acknowledged no fault, confessed no regret, made no apology. "In an organization as large as the government of Canada, mistakes are made every day. . . . Governments should be judged not on whether mistakes are made but on how problems and mistakes are identified and how they are corrected. We on this side of the House have every reason to be proud of our record. I am proud that we gave the Auditor General the ability to issue four reports a year rather than one. I am proud that we expanded the role of internal departmental audits, that we publicize them and put them on Web sites. I am proud that we publicly identify and correct administrative errors." Congratulations! Congratulations!

Harper countered: "The prime minister stood today and defended [the sponsorships] in the interest of national unity. The prime minister is the only person in the country who believes federalist corruption in Quebec somehow enhances the image of Canada in that province. Wrapping himself in the flag is not enough." And he threw back at Chrétien his own words: "On June 16, 1994, the prime minister said in the House: 'There can be no substitute for responsibility at the top. The prime minister sets the moral tone for the government and must make the ultimate decisions when issues of trust or integrity are raised.'"

When he gave his maiden speech on May 28, he chose to emphasize his second-greatest preoccupation, Canada's relations with the United States. Like Mulroney, Harper thought that cordial relations with the U.S. president were essential to shield Canadian trade against protectionism in the Congress. A condition of good relations since 9/11 was a strong defence capability and secure borders against infiltration by terrorists. On both counts, he found the government wanting, and attributed to the government responsibility for George Bush's lack of interest in solving the softwood lumber dispute and in lifting the restrictions on Canadian agricultural imports. "I do not believe the Liberal government really understands the magnitude of these industries. Entire regions depend on these industries. Millions are directly and indirectly employed. We face in some of these trade disputes the potential wiping out of entire regional economies."

Before the 2000 U.S. elections, Chrétien had expressed a preference for Al Gore over Bush. Earlier, he had opposed the Free Trade Agreement with the U.S. and then the North American Free Trade Agreement.

Anti-Americanism occasionally spouted from the Liberal caucus and the cabinet, and Chrétien's own director of communications, Françoise Ducros, had called Bush a "moron." According to Harper, Canada's defence posture was shameful. "For nine years the government has systematically neglected the Canadian forces and undermined our ability to contribute to peace enforcement and even peacekeeping operations, including recently our premature withdrawal from Afghanistan. Most recently we have been inclined to offer knee-jerk resistance to the United States on national missile defence despite the fact that Canada is confronted by the same threats from rogue nations equipped with ballistic missiles and weapons of mass destruction as is the United States." Harper praised Brian Mulroney because "he understood a fundamental truth. He understood that mature and intelligent Canadian leaders must share the following perspective: the United States is our closest neighbour, our best ally, our biggest customer, and our most consistent friend."

Two days later, Harper paid for his first misstep since returning to Parliament. In an interview with the New Brunswick *Telegraph-Journal*, he was asked why Atlantic Canadians didn't vote for the Alliance. He replied that the Alliance had a "can-do attitude," while "I think in Atlantic Canada, because of what happened in the decades following Confederation, there is a culture of defeat that we have to overcome. It's the idea that we just have to go along, we can't change it, things won't change." His comment, though valid, provoked a storm of denunciations. In the Nova Scotia legislature, the parties passed a unanimous motion that denounced Harper and contrasted the Alliance's electoral defeats with the achievements and optimism of Atlantic Canadians. In the Commons, Halifax Liberal Geoff Regan noted: "The media is reporting that certain members with national aspirations are still showing very regional biases. These members tend to make derogatory comments about Atlantic Canada based upon outdated stereotypes." He then enumerated the glories of Atlantic Canada. Sackville NDP member Peter Stoffer was more biting: "This is the third time in two years that Atlantic Canadians have been slandered by a member of the Alliance Party. What is worse, it comes from the leader of the Alliance Party." He, too, seized the opportunity to vaunt the signal merits of Atlantic Canada. Then, "I say shame on the leader of the Alliance Party. He should resign." The prime minister also got in a jab before he was cut off by the

Speaker: "I understand that the leader of the Opposition does not like Atlantic Canada very much. His record as the leader of the Opposition in two weeks is pretty good. He has managed to insult Quebeckers on bilingualism and –"

Chrétien himself faced a severe crisis that weekend. Paul Martin's faction had systematically taken control of the Liberal Party at all levels, and had conducted a whisper campaign against Chrétien for months. Martin's supporters were preparing to defeat the Liberal leader in a vote of confidence at the party's convention scheduled for the following *2002* February. So on Friday, May 31, Chrétien laid down the law, telling his cabinet he intended to serve out his term, and he ordered his ministers to *<* stop fundraising and campaigning for his position or he would fire them. "They will have plenty of time to organize because they will not be ministers any more," he warned. Martin knew the message was for him and announced that he was considering resigning: "I obviously have to reflect on my options." Immediately, his supporters in the caucus raised an outcry about what a catastrophe it would be if Martin resigned.

That evening, Martin disobeyed the prime minister when he addressed the Canadian Federation of Municipalities. His prepared speech promised a new tax deal for the cities, a policy the *Toronto Star* had been pushing. Chrétien was opposed because it would invade the provinces' constitutional responsibility for cities. Martin's office was asked for an advance copy of the speech and he was ordered to delete the promise to the cities. He went ahead and delivered the promise anyway, in a breach of cabinet solidarity that was tantamount to resigning – or forcing the prime minister to fire him. Over the weekend, after inconclusive exchanges, Chrétien put out a statement saying that Martin had resigned and John Manley had replaced him as minister of finance. *2002* Martin denied that he had resigned and presented himself as the victim *Martin* of Chrétien's vindictiveness. His exit from cabinet now left him free to cultivate his popularity, raise money, and prepare to destroy Chrétien in the February leadership review. Chrétien did not yet realize that, even leading over Harper by thirty points in the polls, he was in a fight he could not win. Soon he would announce his future departure. The prospect of a very popular Paul Martin becoming prime minister would eventually put such pressure on both the Alliance and the PCs that it would transform them both.

2002

> Then, on August 6, Joe Clark unexpectedly announced that he would be stepping down from the PC leadership. It came as a surprise: on February 9, speaking to Nova Scotia Tories, Clark had said, "You will have the opportunity in August at our convention in Edmonton to tell me whether you want me to remain as your leader. I am telling you that I want that responsibility and need your active support." But he came to recognize that the support was not forthcoming. He had gambled on the coalition with the DRC and given DRC members prominent positions in the caucus. He'd even agreed to a tentative new joint policy that espoused much of the direct democracy favoured by the Alliance. Such Tory stalwarts as Elsie Wayne were dismayed. When the DRC then flew back home, Clark lost face and support. Clearly his party, deeply in debt, was going nowhere, stuck at 15 per cent in the polls. The demand for new leadership convinced him to announce his withdrawal rather than face humiliation at the August 22–24 convention.

Clark had never concealed his contempt for the Alliance. Just before Harper won the leadership, Clark had said: "As for Stephen Harper, if you want to form a debating club, go with Stephen. They will be exciting, wonderful debates, but they won't elect anyone." The announcement of his departure opened new possibilities. That same day, Harper

> proposed that his party and Clark's unite by holding a joint leadership contest. In the event, the Tory convention reaffirmed the commitment to run a PC candidate in every riding. The meeting also offered the Tories the opportunity to recognize a new star. New Brunswick premier Bernard Lord wowed the delegates with a rousing speech; immediately he was seen as the best prospective PC leader. Perfectly bilingual, Lord had become premier in 1999, winning forty-four of the fifty-five seats. But he resisted entreaties to lure him into federal politics. The PC Party had fallen too low to attract a top-rated proven leader. Ralph Klein also rejected a move to Ottawa, as did Mike Harris, who had announced his resignation on October 16, 2001. Harris explained that he would not be interested as long as the Tories and the Alliance formed separate parties. The refusal of the Tory heavy hitters meant that only little-known and unproven candidates would run, further diminishing the party's chances of making a comeback.

Meanwhile, Harper and the news media had a cultural clash. The media expected Harper to perform almost daily for their benefit. Harper resolved to spend the summer of 2002 rebuilding his party, restoring its finances, and then taking three weeks' holiday. He kept out of public sight. The media couldn't fathom a leader who wouldn't feed the hungry beast. As Tonda MacCharles wrote in the *Toronto Star* on March 21: "Harper is not one to identify personal moments of clarity. Not one to reveal much at all about himself personally. Not one to schmooze. Certainly, not one to stage anything resembling a 'photo op.'" He was not the classic politician. As the summer advanced, Paul Wells declared in the *National Post* that Harper had "disappeared into a witness protection program." There was hardly a pundit who failed to criticize Harper's disappearance. And he had even confessed before vanishing that he was "tired." Meanwhile Martin scored a big media hit flipping hamburgers at a well-attended barbecue during the Calgary Stampede. Harper, meanwhile, was also there with his two children, but he passed unnoticed.

When the Commons returned with a Throne Speech on September 30, 2002, one issue loomed above all others for the Leader of the Opposition: the prospect of war in the Middle East. The 9/11 attacks a year earlier occurred as Harper prepared for the leadership campaign. Later that month, Chrétien visited George Bush in Washington, and said afterward: "If they need us, we'll be there." But the UN's annual Register of Conventional Weapons published that month demonstrated the crippled state of Canada's military. With territory larger than Europe, Canada had less than one-tenth the number of missiles and missile launchers stocked by a country as tiny as the Netherlands; its few tanks and fighter planes were old; its troops down to 50,684 in number. Even if the will were there, Canada's capacity to participate in a war was just a grade above token. Canada did send some troops to Afghanistan after the U.S. launched air strikes there beginning October 7, 2001. But, a year later, George Bush was preparing to invade Iraq – a military operation on a much vaster scale – and Harper supported him entirely, while Chrétien dodged.

For Harper, Canada's response to the Iraq crisis was a test of its values, vision, reliability as an ally, and its sense of international responsibility. He explained himself on October 1 during a Commons debate: "The question is whether Canada would support a multilateral allied action to neutralize the capacity of Iraq to manufacture and deploy weapons of mass destruction should – and, I repeat should – Saddam

Hussein fail to comply with new or existing resolutions of the United Nations. When asked that question yesterday, the foreign minister [Bill Graham] said that the government 'would judge that when it comes.' For three reasons, those being international law, the threat of weapons of mass destruction, and the integrity of Canadian foreign policy, the government's approach is inadequate. Let me be very clear here. The Canadian Alliance position is that it does not want to encourage or urge war. We hope that war may be avoided. Our position states the following: The time has come for Canada to pledge support to the developing coalition of nations, including Britain, Australia, and the United States, determined to send a clear signal to Saddam Hussein that failure to comply with an unconditional program of inspection, as spelled out in either new or existing UN resolutions, would justify action to ensure the safety of millions of people in the region from Iraq's suspected weapons of mass destruction."

Negotiations were underway at the UN Security Council over how to deal with the Iraqi dictator. The previous weekend, the United States and the United Kingdom had submitted a joint draft resolution to the five permanent members of the Security Council, proposing to give Iraq seven days to accept unconditionally inspections of its entire territory by a UN team headed by Hans Blix. But Harper's position was clear: whether diplomacy succeeded or not, nothing should be allowed to stand in the way of a verified disarmament. "Whether or not the Security Council passes a new resolution, a clear and unmistakable message must be sent to Saddam Hussein that his failure to comply completely with not only the UN weapons inspection, but also with the removal of any and all weapons of mass destruction and their components, constitutes legitimate ground for direct action to remove the threat of those weapons."

Harper judged that a resolute show of force by united allies was the best prospect for avoiding war. But it could not be a bluff: the allies, including Canada, had to be prepared to follow through with force if the ultimatum failed to elicit full compliance. In 2004, Harper would minimize his previous commitment for Canada to go to war, citing the fact that our military was so bereft that our contribution to war could only be minimal. But there was no doubt about his meaning in October 2002: "What I am suggesting is that these steps and, frankly, the efficacy of these steps, cannot end in mere diplomacy. There must be a willingness to apply real capabilities to ensure and to make sure Saddam Hussein understands that our desires and the resolutions previously adopted by the United Nations will be adopted." Did this include war? He cited with approval Mulroney's action in 1991, when he led Canada into the first Gulf War: "The situation we have today is a continuation of the Gulf War and the ceasefire situation that was left over from that war. Brian Mulroney, the then prime minister and leader of his party, did not hesitate to do the right thing. He did not quibble about cost. He did not quibble about diplomacy. . . . The position Mr. Mulroney took in 1991 was correct. This party is prepared to pursue and fulfill the conditions of that position through today."

Liberal MP John Bryden challenged Harper: "Biological warfare weapons will not be confined to the Middle East or Iraq. . . . In advocating this very strong stand on the part of Canada toward Iraq and possible unilateral action with our allies, is the member prepared to pay the cost in tens of thousands of casualties by a retaliatory biological warfare attack on a Canadian city?" Harper did not respond that he was misunderstood, that he did not really mean war. On the contrary: "Doing nothing will not exempt us from the possibility of those kinds of actions in the future. . . . We cannot, through the morally neutralist positions of the Liberal Party, exempt ourselves from potentially being hit with those kinds of attacks. Obviously, I would repeat that we should pursue every means possible with obviously minimal violence to achieve our objectives, but *we cannot rule out any measures necessary to achieve what was sought in the Gulf War and what is being sought in existing United Nations resolutions.*"

He judged that war would be legitimate, consistent with previous resolutions of the Security Council: "Our position is that current United Nations resolutions provide sufficient international justification for action." And he had no confidence in the Chrétien government, which already was delinquent by not having joined the coalition in pressing for decisive action after so many years when the Security Council waffled. "The government undermines Canada's reputation with its allies and does nothing to uphold the credibility of the United Nations by not joining in sending a clear message to Hussein that failure to comply will bring consequences. It is a great shame of course that while Canada may eventually help to send that message to Saddam Hussein, Canada's forces lack the basic capacities to contribute to any meaningful solution in a significant way."

Harper considered the question of war and peace as one of transcendent importance. Between October 1, 2002, and May 5, 2003, he spoke in the Commons on the issue of Iraq no less than thirty-seven times, more than on any other subject. He did not have a jingoist enthusiasm or a romantic illusion of war as the ultimate heroic adventure. He rather saw war as a tragic duty assumed by recurrent generations of Canadians. He expressed this in a second debate on Iraq in the Commons, on January 29, 2003. "This party will not take its position based on public opinion polls. We will not take a stand based on focus groups. We will not take a stand based on phone-in shows or householder surveys or any other vagaries of public opinion. We will take our position the way real leaders and great nations make decisions at such moments in history. Real leaders – and I do not mean brutal psychopaths like Saddam Hussein – real leaders, like ordinary Canadians, do not want war. They never have. My parents and my grandparents and their many friends and relatives of their generation have always told me that war is at worst horrific and at best a terribly inadequate way of dealing with the problems of humanity. They also told me that Canadians have nevertheless gone to war many times. In fact, they remember when Canadians were among the leaders in war when it became the only option for the long-run security of Canada and the world. In my judgment, Canada will eventually join with the allied coalition if war on Iraq comes to pass. The government will join, notwithstanding its failure to prepare, its neglect in co-operating with its allies, or its inability to contribute. In the end it will join out of the necessity created by a pattern of uncertainty and indecision. It will not join as a leader but unnoticed at the back of the parade. This is wrong. It is not fitting with the greatness of our history or with our standing as a nation. We need to be standing through tough times and taking tough decisions. We in the Canadian Alliance will continue to take tough public positions and urge the necessary military preparations that make the avoidance of war possible. I can only urge and pray that our government will do the same."

He was wrong in assuming that the government would eventually join its closest allies in the war. He underestimated Chrétien's reluctance to go to war under any circumstances. On March 20, 2003, the "coalition of the willing" launched the attack on Iraq, without Canada. Chrétien's explanation was that there had been no new UN resolution for the resumption of the Gulf War. It was not that the government doubted that Saddam Hussein had possessed weapons of mass destruction. On that fateful day, during a debate in the Commons Foreign Minister Graham outlined the government's position. "First, *I would say that Saddam Hussein acquired weapons of mass destruction.* This is clearly what started this and what brought us to where we are."

Chrétien's sibylline utterances had changed from day to day, but if he held a constant position, it was that he awaited an enabling resolution for war from the Security Council. Yet he had evoked a diametrically opposite justification twelve years earlier to oppose the 1991 Gulf War, despite twelve clear and urgent resolutions of the Security Council calling for Saddam Hussein to be removed by all necessary means from Kuwait, which he had invaded on August 2, 1990. The Security Council had imposed an ultimatum of January 15, 1991. When the Iraqi dictator still had not complied, the allies had declared war, and Brian Mulroney had introduced a resolution in the Commons to support the action decided by the Security Council. Chrétien had taken a totally pacifist position then, saying: "Our national interests have been peacekeeping, a voice for stability, and a voice for independence in war, peace, and stability. . . . Even the UN should not be for war. What is the fundamental principle of the United Nations? It is the peaceful resolution of disputes, not the initiation of wars." And Chrétien had even implied that to go to war would only serve U.S. interests: "I say that the national interests of Canada are very different from the national interests of the United States." In 1991, sentiment in Canada, and particularly in Quebec, ran strongly against war. A Gallup poll in December 1990 had indicated that only 36 per cent of Canadians wanted Canada involved in war in the Persian Gulf, with 55 per cent opposed. In Quebec, only 21 per cent supported war. Very much as in 2003.

So Chrétien's justification for not participating in the 2003 Gulf War – that the Security Council had not given its approval – is not to be taken at face value. Chrétien, ever the politician, knew that his decision not to join George W. Bush and Tony Blair would be popular, particularly in

Quebec. It restored his standing in his home province. Harper was bitterly disappointed on that March 20. He rose in the Commons: "I stand today to speak to a matter of the gravest importance that Parliament can address: the matter of war and specifically the resumption of war against the regime of Saddam Hussein." He recapitulated the compelling reasons for being part of the coalition's attack on Iraq that day, reasons he had put forward during two previous debates, and berated the Canadian government. "Since Saddam Hussein came to power in 1979, more than one million have died as a consequence. They have died through killing and torture as individual opponents, real and imagined. They have died from acts of civil war and mass genocide in the north and south of the country. They have died in invasions launched against his neighbours. Now his final bloody chapter is being read. As it is being written, make no mistake, this party will not be with Saddam Hussein. We will not be neutral. We will be with our allies and our friends, not militarily, but in spirit we will be with them in America and in Britain for a short and successful conflict and for the liberation of the people of Iraq. We will not be with our government, for this government, in taking the position it has taken, has betrayed Canada's history and its values. Reading only the polls and indulging in juvenile and insecure anti-Americanism, the government has, for the first time in our history, left us outside our British and American allies in their time of need. However, it has done worse. It has left us standing for nothing, no realistic alternative, no point of principle, and no vision of the future. It has left us standing with no one. Our government is not part of the multilateral coalition in support of this action and it has not been part of any coalition opposing it; just alone, playing irrelevant and contradictory games on both sides of the fence, to the point where we go so far as to leave military personnel in the region without the active and moral support of the government that sent them there."

He ended with an invocation: "We will stand, and I believe most Canadians will quietly stand with us, for these higher values, which shaped our past and which we will need in an uncertain future. In the days that follow may God guide the actions of the president of the United States and the American people; may God save the Queen, her prime minister, and all her subjects; and may God continue to bless Canada."

He was then challenged by Foreign Minister Graham for saying that the government stood for nothing. "I would like to feel that we too on this side of the House, in spite of his comment that we stand for nothing, do stand for one important value at this time, I believe. We stand for the support of and beside the citizens of Canada who in the majority are largely, emphatically, and determinedly opposed to military action at this time and in these circumstances, not under any circumstance, but under these circumstances. To suggest people are cowardly because they choose to work through the multilateral institutions that are the sole possibility we have of avoiding conflicts like this in the future is, in my view, a mistaken approach." Harper replied by invoking history: "I do not know whether the polls the minister cites represent the opinion of the Canadian people or not, but what I do know is that in these matters we judge the national interests of the country, not at this time, not today, and not tomorrow, but we stand by the permanent national interests of the country. This country and many around the world made tragic errors in the 1930s by underestimating the threats that we faced. We on this side will never do that again."

Chapter 20

COMING TOGETHER

⟍ AN UNUSUALLY EMOTIONAL Stephen Harper appeared at a press conference with PC Leader Peter MacKay on October 16, 2003. "It's an historic and, I think, very exciting day," he began. "I – some of you may
know – I have a reputation of not getting excited too often, [he laughs]
but I actually had difficulty sleeping last night. So, it's like Christmastime,
waking up."

Merger The almost impossible had happened. The two leaders were there to
announce that they had reached an agreement to marry their two
parties. What was rent asunder in 1993 was now to be joined together,
and they were there to publish the banns. "Late last night, Mr. MacKay
and I signed an agreement in principle to create a new political party, the
Conservative Party of Canada, to contest the next federal election in
every riding with every asset of both our parties. The Conservative Party
of Canada will combine the institutional history and expertise of the
PC Party with the grassroots democracy and energy of the Canadian
Alliance. In doing so, it will confront a Liberal government which seeks
re-election on little more than the argument that the opposition is divided.
This division of conservatives is ending. Our swords will henceforth be
pointed at the Liberals, not at each other."

This was the consummation so many had yearned for from that night
in October 1993 when the electorate destroyed the PCs as a national
party and sent a regional party named Reform to occupy fifty-two seats
in the Commons. This was the elusive dream of the 1996 Winds of
Change conference in Calgary, when Harper had expressed his skepticism

that union could ever happen. This was the dream of Preston Manning when, in 1998, he initiated the difficult two-year adventure of transforming the Reform Party through a United Alternative into the wistfully named Canadian Conservative Reform Alliance Party – as though the combining of names would make it so. Harper, at the National Citizens Coalition, had been skeptical. This was the unfulfilled prayer of the Democratic Representative Caucus in 2001 when, in despair, they joined a working coalition with the party of Joe Clark.

Harper had believed this merger impossible. And now he had brought it about. He and Peter MacKay had signed the agreement in principle, both taking big risks by committing themselves to union before their parties were consulted. But it was Harper's vision and Harper's determination that had broken through all resistance. MacKay was brought to the altar by the shotgun as much as by the ring. The scene of MacKay and Harper joining hands was all the more remarkable because, not five months earlier, MacKay had clasped the hand of Harper's antithesis, David Orchard, and signed a marriage contract that made any future union with Harper seem preposterous.

It happened on May 31, at the climax of the Progressive Conservative leadership convention to elect the successor of Joe Clark. Between the first and second ballot, front-runner MacKay's per cent of the vote had slipped, suggesting that he would lose if his opponents ganged up against him. After the third ballot, MacKay was still short of a majority and feared that Orchard would team up with second-place Jim Prentice. Orchard offered to throw his support to either man, whoever would promise in writing to reconsider Mulroney's free trade agreement and commit to make no electoral deal or merger with the Alliance.

Jim Prentice had run his campaign on a platform of uniting with the Alliance, and he turned down Orchard's proposal. MacKay himself had shown interest in the possibility of links between the parties; earlier, while Clark was still leader, MacKay had initiated unauthorized, informal talks with Alliance MPs to explore the possibility of mutual co-operation. But, before the fourth ballot, fearing that he was about to lose the leadership, MacKay signed on the dotted line to the terms set down by Orchard, a passionate opponent of free trade and of any truck or trade with the Alliance.

The first clause of their hastily handwritten agreement stated: "No merger, talks, joint candidates with Alliance. Maintain 301." MacKay had crossed out the word "talks." To maintain 301 meant to run a Tory candidate in all 301 ridings, thereby excluding agreements in some ridings which would have one or the other party abstain to give the other party a better chance at winning. The second clause would have set up a review of the North American Free Trade Agreement, with the review panel's members chosen jointly by Orchard and MacKay. The third clause demanded a "cleanup [of] head office"; the party's national director was to be fired, with the replacement to be chosen after consultation with Orchard. Some of Orchard's people were to go on staff. The fourth clause demanded a "commitment to make environmental protection front and centre. . . ."

After he had won the PC leadership with Orchard's support, MacKay at first tried to keep the document secret, which only increased suspicions. Finally, after four days of badgering he released it. Many were outraged that he had acceded to the leadership of an historic party by making commitments that were so clearly opportunistic. The clause requiring the reconsideration of free trade, the proudest achievement of the Mulroney government, shockingly betrayed party and principle. Tories were dismayed and Harper was distressed. For several weeks before the convention, Harper had been planning to approach the new leader to propose co-operating in the next elections so as to minimize splitting the anti-Liberal vote. Now, his initial reaction to the pact excluding the Alliance was to conclude that all bets were off. "I am just shocked by the sweeping terms of this," he said. "Mr. MacKay has not only indicated no interest at this point, he indicated he is not open to discussion." But after some days of reflection, Harper changed his mind and saw an opportunity. He could now urge Tories to choose between David Orchard and Stephen Harper.

In the following days, he twice spoke to MacKay briefly. Then he made a public invitation to the Tories on June 12 when he spoke in Calgary to an Alliance fundraising "Leader's Dinner." To gales of laughter, he warned: "The choice for the Tories is no longer the status quo. The choice is a coalition with the Canadian Alliance or a coalition with the Orchardistas. We must continue to embrace the vision of uniting all conservatives to take on the Liberal Party." Strategically, he was driving a wedge in the PC Party, inviting right-wing Tories to abandon a party where Orchard now held major power. He drove the same message home on June 16 when he spoke at a Leader's Dinner in Toronto. "It is obvious that this country needs the Canadian Alliance and genuine PCs to pursue 'common cause' – a single slate of candidates against the Liberals in the next federal election. Tonight, I am instructing our party to pursue this 'common cause' initiative."

Then MacKay, in his first public speech since winning the leadership, gave a cautious response on June 19: "Mr. Harper has put forward his proposed solution to the challenge of vote-splitting in certain ridings," MacKay told a luncheon of about 130 members of the Confederation Club, a Tory group. "Neither I nor anyone else have seen the details of what he proposes. But I'll say this: I'm open and I'm interested." Harper, in a press release, immediately welcomed the PC leader's "openness to discussing a 'common cause.' I look forward to exploring this idea further with Peter in the future." They were already on first-name terms.

In his speech, MacKay had stated that, if such explorations were to succeed, they should be carried out behind closed doors rather than through the media. The two men met for three hours north of Toronto on June 26 – apparently in the offices of Magna International, through the initiative of CEO Belinda Stronach. MacKay suggested they each appoint two eminent proxies to explore possibilities and negotiate on their behalf. On July 1, MacKay phoned former deputy prime minister Don Mazankowski and former Ontario premier Bill Davis to ask if they would serve. Both accepted. Later, MacKay included the Tory House leader, Loyola Hearn, to be a third "emissary," representing the caucus. Harper chose Ray Speaker and Senator Gerry St. Germain. Speaker had served in the Alberta legislature in both Social Credit and PC governments, and had then served a term in Ottawa as a Reform MP. St. Germain was a former national president of the PC Party who joined the Alliance in 2000 to become the Alliance's only senator. Later, Harper recruited MP Scott Reid to represent the Alliance caucus. The PC emissaries were far more eminent, but they were also busier and did not get around to meeting with their Alliance counterparts until August 21, much later than Harper had hoped.

He felt pressed for time. The new Elections Act, Bill C-24 – a parting legacy from Chrétien – would go into effect on January 1. It would limit sharply what money corporations or individuals could give to political parties, but it would also give substantial government subsidies to each party, in proportion to the number of votes each had won in the preceding elections. In 2000, the Alliance had received 25.5 per cent of the vote, the PCs 12.2 per cent. The Liberals, with their 40.8 per cent, would have more money for campaign spending than the two opposition parties combined. Each, facing the Liberals separately while fighting the other, would likely be crushed. And time was running out.

At that first negotiation, Don Mazankowski made a proposal that went far beyond the electoral coalition that Harper envisaged: he suggested that the two parties become one. When his emissaries reported back with the proposal, Harper was intrigued and the emissaries began exploring on what principles they could unite. They made rapid headway as the Alliance made most of the compromises on policy. Harper accepted that "English and French have equality of status in all institutions of the Parliament and Government of Canada." This was a principle that Reform had opposed. He accepted that the new party would be named the Conservative Party of Canada, with no remembrance of Reform or Alliance in the new name. He accepted the principle that this party would not be a clearly defined right-wing party, but, "We will create a national force that reaches out to all Canadians, not just like-minded conservatives." As another "founding principle," he accepted that "all Canadians should have reasonable access to quality health care regardless of their ability to pay." No qualification was made, no mention of experimenting with private delivery. Harper even accepted this difficult compromise: the new party would be defined by "a balance between fiscal accountability, progressive social policy, and individual rights and responsibilities." A progressive social policy was more congenial to Red Tories than to typical Alliance members. As MacKay correctly stated at a press conference on September 30, "Our principles, to a large degree, prevailed."

There were also statements that echoed Alliance emphasis on free markets and fiscal prudence. A principle asserting individual responsibility "to provide for themselves, their families, and their dependants" was immediately followed by "recognizing that government must respond to those who require assistance and compassion." A cherished Reform–Alliance principle was evoked: "The Conservative Party of Canada will operate in a manner accountable and responsive to its members." But that wording, too, was flexible enough to be fully acceptable to Tories. It

was Reform's hard edge softened to a generality. There was no mention
of referenda to settle contentious issues, of citizens' initiatives to precipitate a referendum, or of recalling an unsatisfactory MP. No mention,
either, of a Triple-E Senate. Because most of the principles agreed to by
the two sides were rather general and vague, they exorcised the fervour
for the radical democratization of politics that had been Reform's trade-
mark. Also, current circumstances had removed from the agenda what
had been previously an insuperable obstacle to a merger: the Tories'
espousal of special status for Quebec, clashing with Reform's insistence
on the equality of the provinces. As Harper explained: "Canada's constitutional disputes have been more divisive for conservatives [than the
tension between 'fiscal conservatives' and 'social conservatives'], but
tend to arise only in certain eras, as they did during the Meech Lake and
Charlottetown debates that raged from 1987 to 1992. That those debates
are now in the past makes it easier for conservatives to get together in
the present."

Indeed, during the Tory leadership convention there had been scant
mention of Quebec. On April 14, 2003, Jean Charest's Quebec Liberals
had come to power. Constitutional negotiations were not on their
agenda. Separatism was in remission. Even the Bloc Québécois seemed
obsolete, given the likelihood that Paul Martin's bulldozer would sweep
Quebec in elections after he became Liberal leader on November 15.

These agreed principles and policies were not intended to bind the
successor party forever. They were transitional agreements, subject to
review at the first policy convention that the party would hold later.
Later, as it turned out, would be after the 2004 elections – on March 17
to 19, 2005. But the negotiations began hitting snags and very nearly
foundered when the emissaries dealt with the mechanics of the merger.

The Alliance, at the time, had sixty-three MPs, the PCs fifteen. The
Alliance had about 110,000 members, the PCs only a small fraction of
that number. Was it fair to bring these two parties together as equals? On
the other hand, if the Reform–Alliance principle of one member, one vote
were adopted, clearly the Tories would be swamped and the merger
would, in fact, be an Alliance takeover. So, once again, Harper gave way.
The first principle of the merger process would be this: "The Canadian
Alliance and Progressive Conservative Party will treat each other as equal
partners." A second principle would give pre-eminence to the PC tradition

of federating provincial parties rather than the Reform–Alliance principle of abstaining from links with provincial parties: "The Conservative Party of Canada will promote and maintain relationships with existing provincial Progressive Conservative parties and will not establish provincial parties." Harper may have had the image of an inflexible, ideologically driven politician; he was proving to be the opposite in these negotiations where he, rather than the Tories, made all the major compromises.

But Harper was impatient with the slow progress of negotiations on the Tory side. After his meeting with MacKay on June 26, he had immediately chosen his "sherpas" or emissaries and instructed them to be ready to meet their Tory counterparts at any time beginning July 1 – but the Tory emissaries were first available on August 21. The negotiators agreed to meet again on August 30, but then the Tory negotiators asked that the meeting be postponed. Rather than simply accept delay, Harper submitted directly to MacKay on that date his own fourteen-point written proposal for a merger and demanded a reply. His offer had a sense of urgency. He proposed that the caucuses of the two parties start operating as one immediately, that they jointly elect an interim leader who would become leader of the Opposition in the House, and that the new party be legally established by October 10. A founding convention would be held in Ottawa on February 19 to 21, 2004.

The proposal had some attractive features for the Tories. They had a substantial debt, while the Alliance was now debt-free. Harper proposed that the new party combine the assets and liabilities of both parties and immediately raise money to retire the PC debt. But clause 11 was totally unacceptable to MacKay: "The leadership vote shall be conducted by mail-in ballots on the basis of one member, one vote." This would really amount to an Alliance takeover. Also, the PC emissaries felt strongly that, as they expressed it, "All ridings would have to be treated equally. The CA model would lead to a concentration of efforts in areas where an organization and membership are already strong and would not lead to the reaching out to Canadians in all parts of the country. We also believe that any leader, and any vision of the party for the country, must appeal to Canadians in all parts of the nation." The Tories counter-proposed an election with a point system in which each riding, regardless of the number of members, be assigned an equal 100 points. The votes in each riding would be tallied, and whatever percentage of the riding vote each candidate had obtained, riding by riding, would be added up to give the candidate's final sum, which would then be divided by the number of ridings. The candidate with the highest percentage, if it exceeded 50 per cent, would be declared the winner.

The negotiations were stalled, deadlocked over the formula for choosing the new leader. MacKay, who had not told his caucus about the secret negotiations, dared not go to his MPs with Harper's proposal. He knew the caucus would be bitterly divided. His position as new leader was already weakened by the "pact with the devil" he had made with Orchard. A COMPAS poll, published on June 28, had shown that among PC voters, only 24 per cent supported running PC candidates in all ridings as the Orchard–MacKay agreement proposed, while 63 per cent supported an arrangement between the PC and CA parties that would end vote splitting. Among Alliance voters, 86 per cent wanted an arrangement, while only 8 per cent were opposed. Besides this issue, contentious in itself, the manner in which he had won the leadership had tainted MacKay from the start. At the same time, the party's independent prospects for the future were dismal. Even with a former prime minister as leader, the party had been relieved to win twelve seats in the 2000 elections, the bare minimum for it to be recognized as a party. The PC percentage of the vote, which had been 18.8 in 1997, had actually dropped to 12.2 in 2000. With MacKay as leader, with Martin as prime minister, it was likely to drop further in the next elections and the party would no longer be recognized.

On September 14, Harper and MacKay, as well as their House leaders, met for supper and discussed co-operating in the Commons when the new session opened the next day. They also agreed, according to Harper, that their emissaries would meet on September 22, when the PC side would present a counter-proposal. The meeting would be a final attempt to find a solution, and the meeting would continue until an agreement in principle was reached or none seemed possible. But, meanwhile, on September 18, there was a leak about the talks and the CBC reported: "The federal Progressive Conservative and Canadian Alliance parties have begun secret meetings in a last-ditch attempt to unite the right and fight the Liberals in the next election, sources have told CBC News." That untimely leak caused predictable havoc in the Tory caucus. When the emissaries met on September 22 and 23, there was no written counter-proposal. Still, the Alliance emissaries reported to Harper that they thought they had a verbal agreement in principle from their Tory counterparts, which would be finalized by a conference call on September 26. It was expected that the two leaders would then meet on September 29 to sign the agreement. But, on the twenty-sixth, there was still no clear counter-proposal and no agreement. The Tory side remained uncertain on several issues. Harper's emissaries told their counterparts that they would not attend any more meetings until there was a specific counter-proposal to discuss. Harper made the same announcement publicly. On September 28, Loyola Hearn reported: "The emissary talks are dead. We have been advised that the Alliance emissaries would not be attending the meeting." "Alliance pulls plug on unity talks," the *National Post* reported on September 29. Scott Reid was quoted on the negotiations: "We were promised three separate times that we would have a firm proposal at our next meeting; every time we went it was like Lucy with the football, pulling it away from Charlie Brown." Meanwhile, MacKay complained that the Alliance side was putting pressure on his side by leaks to the media.

On September 29, Harper turned the screws a little tighter. He made public a memorandum to his caucus and to the Alliance's National Council in which he summarized the course of the negotiations on uniting. "At this point, I do not know whether Mr. MacKay personally supports the formation of the new 'Conservative Party of Canada,' let alone how he believes it could be done within the current timeframe. I have asked, again, for Mr. MacKay's clear commitment and workable counter-proposal. If I receive that, we shall proceed."

There was now enormous pressure on MacKay and the Tory caucus to reach a settlement, from the Tory premiers, from Brian Mulroney, from major figures in the business community such as Belinda Stronach and Peter Munk, chairman of Barrick Gold Corp. Even before the PC leadership convention, Mulroney had given an interview to Brian Laghi and John Ibbitson of the *Globe and Mail*, who reported: "Mulroney is advising the next leader of the PC Party to take another look at uniting conservatives into a governing alternative to the Liberals." The PC's usual fundraisers were all reporting back: if the party wanted money, it had to come to terms with the Alliance.

On September 30, in an attempt to regain the initiative, MacKay held a press conference with his emissaries, Mazankowski, Bill Davis, and Loyola Hearn. MacKay downplayed the significance of Harper's fourteen-point proposal. "It was only one of many" documents submitted, he maintained. Mazankowski outlined the areas of agreement on principles, but said the CA proposal of one member, one vote, was a stumbling block. "Their proposal violated the principle of the equality of the two parties." He declared that the unity talks were not yet a failure. "We stand willing and able to continue the discussions." The Tories then made public their proposal for electing the leader.

Time was getting desperately short if an agreement was to be reached before the end of the year. On October 2, the PC government of Ernie Eves, Harris's successor, was defeated in Ontario. That provided an added stimulus to unite conservatives so as to win on the federal scene. Ray Speaker and Don Mazankowski remained in touch, trying to set up a meeting of the emissaries. Harper then decided on a stratagem to force the issue. On October 8, MacKay was flying to Toronto after the Question Period in the Commons. Harper rushed to the Ottawa airport and boarded the same flight, confronting MacKay and urging that they meet later that evening. MacKay agreed. They discussed the sticking point: the procedure for electing the leader. Harper offered a compromise, to temper the one person, one vote principle by setting a maximum of five hundred votes from any riding. MacKay refused. Harper also proposed a formula for adopting party policies in convention: it would require a majority of delegate votes that also included a majority from a majority of the provinces.

Harper moved again. On October 10, he offered to accept the Tory proposal of equal riding votes for the leadership, on condition that the Tories accept the Alliance formula for the founding-policy convention. MacKay again refused. There were further discussions. By October 15, Harper had accepted the Tory conditions on both of the unresolved issues. MacKay had no further reason to say no. They signed the agreement that day and the next day made their triumphant announcement.

In the news media, it was big news, generally greeted favourably, though with some notable discordance. Former Tory pollster Allan Gregg explained the calculation that made the agreement possible: "The prospect of annihilation – of the PCs being reduced to an Atlantic, rural rump and the Alliance a Western, rural rump – more than anything else pushed aside all past concerns that stood in the way of unification of the right." *Globe and Mail* reporter Drew Fagan offered the same analysis, while putting a name to the dreaded annihilator: "The merger to create the new Conservative Party of Canada was born of desperation. The electoral map has appeared brutal to the Canadian Alliance and the Progressive Conservatives for some time in the face of the Paul Martin onslaught."

David Orchard, understandably, felt double-crossed by the deal. "This new creation – this so-called Conservative Party of Canada – if it goes forward, will be an illegitimate creation, conceived in deception and born in betrayal." He would soon launch a court action to prevent the miscegenation, but it would fail. Joe Clark put out a terse statement of disapproval: "This is about more than a name and a history. It is about a hard-won reputation as a party that is both inclusive and pan-Canadian. Speaking personally, I cannot support a proposal which would close down that [PC] Party, and put at risk that reputation." He would have worse to say in days to come. He refused to sit with the joined caucuses but finished his term as an independent. Senator Lowell Murray vented his indignation: "The political kingmakers who bankrolled Tom Long, Stockwell Day, and Stephen Harper are attempting to buy the Progressive Conservative Party, shut it down, grab its remaining assets and goodwill, and replace it with their own political party, whose role in our parliamentary system will be to ensure that the pressure on a Paul Martin government comes from the hard right." He also would sit as an independent. Quebec MP André Bachand, concerned that there was no special status for Quebec in the agreed principles, decided not to run again. Manitoba MP Rick Borotsik saw the merger as the takeover of the PC Party by a regional party with an unacceptable vision of the country and decided not to contest the next elections. Nova Scotian Scott Brison first said he would run under the new party label, but eventually changed his mind and ran as a Liberal, as did New Brunswick's John Herron. One Alliance MP, Keith Martin, would join the Liberals, Ontario Liberal John Bryden would join the Conservatives, and Bloc Québécois MP Robert Lanctôt would join the Martin Liberals, only to be defeated in the elections. It was a time of political realignment.

The October 16 announcement introduced a new political star. The *Globe and Mail* ran a big picture, front and centre, of heiress and Magna International Corp. CEO Belinda Stronach, thirty-seven, under the caption, "Stronach: The woman who united the right." It was she, reported Greg Keenan, "who started the process that led to the reunion of the right in federal politics. . . . She was sitting in a room with Stephen Harper and Peter MacKay trying to get the Canadian Alliance and the Progressive Conservatives to put aside their differences and, as she puts it, for the good of Canada, marry." She had consulted with Brian Mulroney. "Her first move in bringing together the Alliance and Tory leaders was to talk to Mr. Harper in early June. She had never met him. A few days later, she met with Mr. MacKay. Then all three got together in late June and started the talks that led to three representatives from each of the parties meeting to start negotiations."

An account in the *National Post* by Francine Dubé explained that Stronach had phoned Harper in June, days after MacKay had won the Tory leadership. "She then flew to Ottawa to discuss with him the need to bring together the two political parties" for the sake of democracy in Canada. The *National Post* devoted an entire inside page, together with a big smiling photograph, to "Magna's political matchmaker." Harper was also quoted: "She put quite a few hours into this and, with her clock running, those were pretty expensive hours."

Why was so much attention paid to someone who had served as an intermediary between the two leaders in getting them together, but likely had a marginal effect on the success or failure of their negotiations? The answer is that politics is also show business, journalism is also entertainment, and Belinda Stronach, with long blond hair, full lips, and smiling millions, was a *dea ex machina* – the goddess who suddenly appears on stage from the wings to resolve the plot that mere humans could not untangle. It helped that she headed a multinational, multi-billion-dollar corporation, founded by her father, Frank, with more than seventy thousand employees worldwide. *Fortune* magazine had ranked her as the second most powerful woman in the corporate world. Already a celebrity, she had been linked socially with Bill Clinton, with a hint of scandalous romance. Never mind that she assured both newspapers that "she has no interest in heading a newly merged Conservative Party of Canada." She had recently hired Bonnie Brownlee as her communications adviser. Brownlee had handled communications for Mila Mulroney when Brian was prime minister. Brownlee was married to Bill Fox, the former *Toronto Star* reporter who was Mulroney's director of communications and part of his inner circle. So, amid the backroom manoeuvres and arid clauses of the merger proposal, "Belinda," as she was called, emerged as a figure of pure romance. Intriguingly, she had what Harper lacked: sexiness and warmth.

There were still obstacles on the road to union, particularly on the Tory side. Each party had to hold a referendum to have the agreement ratified by December 12. Both parties would need the consent of their members and, for the PCs, it meant obtaining a two-thirds approval. A campaign to buy Tory memberships by the November 15 cut-off almost doubled the number of PCs eligible to vote. In the end, huge majorities from both parties gave their consent. On December 5, Alliance voted 95.9 per cent Yes. The next day, the PC Yes vote was more than 90 per cent.

The two parties now became one. Who would lead it? The day after the announcement of the agreement, columnist Don Martin, in the *Calgary Herald* and *National Post*, dismissed both Harper and MacKay: "Despite their heroic sacrifice to make this merger a reality, neither Harper nor MacKay can reclaim the leadership without risking a setback to the ultimate goal of making sleepwalking Liberals wet the bed inside their Ontario fortress. A fresh face is needed." Stephen Harper was the obvious choice for most fervent Canadian Alliance voters because of his record in winning the Alliance leadership and his success in restoring party unity and sound finances. But now the new Conservative Party of Canada wanted to reach out from its western regional base to win the support of the rest of the country. Was Harper the right person to lead a new party with a new image? Many doubted it. Harper was now vulnerable, just as Preston Manning had been in 2000 when Reform morphed into the Alliance and Manning was replaced. Harper could suffer a similar fate.

But circumstances played in Harper's favour. Lord, the most prominent potential candidate, had held elections on June 9 and, to everyone's astonishment, his previous huge majority had melted to a single seat. If Lord now left for Ottawa, his caucus, after appointing the speaker, would be dangerously vulnerable. Time was also a deterrent for potential candidates. The last-minute agreement to unite the two parties took

[handwritten annotations: "MAR 20 2004", "vote on leader for 'C'", "Force to have early leadership conven.", "L", "2"]

almost everyone by surprise. No one had based plans on it. And it came just a month before Paul Martin would succeed Jean Chrétien as Liberal leader. Martin, it was expected, would call an early election. So it was urgent to hold an early vote to give the new party a leader. The date chosen was March 20, 2004. That would leave little time for candidates to assemble a team of organizers, raise money, and make themselves known across the vast country. A candidate had first to deposit $100,000 with the party. Few could quickly raise that sort of money, especially when potential donors had been drained that year by the PC leadership campaign and the Ontario elections. Peter MacKay, Chuck Strahl, and Jim Prentice had all indicated an early interest but finally declined to run.

Paul Martin's reputation was also a deterrent. It seemed that fall that he could walk on water. On October 15, the very day the agreement in principle was signed, Martin made public the names and amounts of his leadership campaign contributions: they totalled more than $10 million. Martin was obviously the darling of the business class, and he was popular in western Canada – even Ralph Klein had lauded him. *[handwritten: MARTIN]* It seemed predestined that the new CPC would be mauled in the coming elections. Polls regularly put the Liberal Party at about 50 per cent, regardless of who led the CPC. An Ipsos-Reid poll published December 15 gave the new party 21 per cent of the vote. That was four points less than the Alliance alone managed in 2000.

That expectation of a dark future for the party discouraged the most obvious candidates. In 2003, Mike Harris had explained he would not be interested in leading the PC Party until it was united with the Alliance. Now that it was, the prize still didn't seem worth the effort. So, in the end, there were only three candidates. The *Globe and Mail* groused in an editorial, "The new Conservatives get off to a dismal start. Belinda Stronach has growth potential, though sharply limited by her lack of experience. Stephen Harper is charisma-challenged. Tony Clement is off the radar. None of the three has even a faint hope of beating Prime Minister Paul Martin in a spring election. The Liberals' near-absolute hegemony in Ottawa will endure for some years."

Harper carried negative baggage going into the campaign, as his two opponents were quick to point out. He had spoken out strongly against the Chrétien government's draft bill to extend legal marriage to two people of the same sex. He had intended to make it a wedge campaign issue whenever elections were called. On October 1, before an agreement with MacKay seemed likely, he had written a letter to twenty-six thousand leaders in religious communities requesting their support for a petition opposing same-sex marriage, to be presented to Parliament: "Our goal is to collect the names of as many concerned citizens as possible and present them to the government," he wrote. "If you would like to participate in this project, please circulate and return the petition, postage free." A poll by Environics Research Group, published in the *Globe and Mail* on October 21, showed that 72 per cent of Alliance supporters polled were opposed to recognizing same-sex marriage, with only 27 per cent in favour. Among PC supporters, 67 per cent were in support of recognizing same-sex marriage with 42 per cent opposed. That exposed a conflict between the cultures of the two parties. Peter MacKay, in a *Globe and Mail* column on December 6, invited Tories to swarm into the new party in great numbers so as to impose their own culture. "There will be no room in the Conservative Party for the bigotry and wedge politics that hamstrung the Reform/Canadian Alliance over the past decade. To be successful, the Conservative Party must be welcomed in all regions, English Canada as well as French Canada, urban centres as well as rural areas."

Harper was also remembered unfavourably in Quebec as a prominent opponent of the Meech Lake and Charlottetown accords, and of the Official Languages Act. He had said in Montreal that French was not endangered in Quebec – a heresy for Quebec's political class. In the Atlantic provinces he was remembered for speaking of a "culture of defeat" and for opposing most regional development grants and unemployment insurance for seasonal workers as a form of welfare – he proposed, instead, tax concessions to attract businesses. Newly elected PC premier Danny Williams of Newfoundland was the most outspoken in expressing his reservations about Harper as leader of the united party: "I do have some concerns as to where the party is going. If it becomes a far-right-wing party then that's not where I want to be positioned. In the back of my mind, I have what is at the back of everybody's mind in Atlantic Canada: a comment made by Mr. Harper some time ago, which is the 'culture of defeat,' the defeatist attitude of Atlantic Canadians, the can't-do attitude in Atlantic Canada." Premier Lord, without naming anyone, said it was important that the new party recognize "that we have

MARCH 20. 2004
Pc
Leadership Campaigne.

a country filled with diversity," and that the party must "reflect the tolerance and generosity of the Canadian people, and if it doesn't do that it will fail." PEI premier Pat Binns was also cautious: "I don't rule anybody out, including Stephen Harper, but I think you know my hope is that the person that ends up on top has broad appeal."

Though Harper had restored unity to a faltering Alliance, he had never made a breakthrough with the electorate, never brought voter support back to the 25 per cent obtained in the 2000 elections. In fact, an Ipsos-Reid poll published in the *Globe and Mail* on December 5 showed support for the Alliance at 10 per cent, for the PCs at 14 per cent. The NDP, under Jack Layton, had passed both to reach 15 per cent. That hardly suggested that a Harper-led Conservative Party would scale the electoral heights. Just three days later, Ralph Klein was quoted in the *National Post* as saying that Harper and MacKay were "good Canadians," but he didn't know whether either had "the timbre of what is needed to be a national leader." Klein had earlier endorsed Mike Harris for the leadership. A Léger Marketing poll toward the end of November asked Canadians who would make the best leader of the new party; only 9 per cent named Harper, 8 per cent named MacKay, 10 per cent named Lord, and 15 per cent named Klein.

Joe Clark had aimed a broadside in the *Globe and Mail* on November 11 *2003.* against the assumption that the two parties would gain more votes by uniting than they would reap separately. The opposite would happen, he predicted. "Progressive Conservatives are being asked to vote 'yes' to suicide," he wrote, just as the PCs were about to hold a vote of all its members on the agreement. "Just imagine what the federal Liberals would do with a new party that is ashamed to call itself 'progressive' and is defined by Stephen Harper/Stockwell Day/anti-gay/ anti-feminist/'We can win without Quebec'/'Yes sir, President Bush.' A shotgun marriage, which produces a party too narrow to compete, would be terrible for Canadian democracy. It would seal our fate as a one-party state."

Harper launched his leadership campaign on January 12 *2004* with a speech in Ottawa. He presented himself as a man of the people in contrast to Paul Martin – but, slyly, with words that contrasted him equally with Belinda Stronach: "I warn you that I am no Paul Martin. I have not been packaged by an empire of pollsters and media managers. I have not

LEADER ASPIRATIONS CAMPAIGN

MARTIN LIB LEADER

HARPER BACK GROUND

been groomed by the experts and the influential. I was not born into a family with a seat at the cabinet table. I grew up playing on the streets of Toronto, not playing in the corridors of power. When I left home for Alberta, I had to get a job. I wasn't on loan to the corporate elite. I'll never be able to give my kids a billion-dollar company, but Laureen and I are saving for their education. And I have actually cooked them Kraft dinner – I like to add wieners. When my family goes on vacation, it isn't on a corporate executive jet. I pay for the ticket and we stand in line to get a seat with everyone else." He appealed for the unity of the new party, targeting Martin and the Liberal government, but rarely his immediate opponents, Belinda Stronach or Tony Clement. "With our new Conservative Party we have embarked on an exciting new course. And, if we can speak with one conservative voice, we can win."

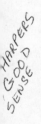

CAUCUS UNITED

Harper ran as the man who had reunited the Alliance and then united two parties. His campaign slogan, "One Conservative Voice," was a reminder of his feat. He dwelt on that in his speech: "Only two years ago I came to our nation's capital as a leadership candidate. Back then we were a caucus divided. Today we are a caucus united. Back then we were heavily in the red. Today we are heavily in the black. Back then we had lost our direction. Today we're working as a team, and facing a prime minister who cannot make a decision." He was, in fact, already acceptable to the right wing of the PC Party. In 1998, he had been courted by the so-called Blue Committee which wanted him to run for the leadership vacated by Jean Charest. He had even been visited by two Tory MPs, John Herron from New Brunswick and Ontario's sole PC MP, Jim Jones, who did their best to persuade him to run. They saw him as the one most likely to head off Joe Clark and bring about a union of the PC and Alliance parties. He had turned down the invitation, saying it would burn bridges to members of his old party. Now, he had achieved that union without ever breaking faith with his Reform antecedents.

HARPERS GOOD SENSE

HARPER FRONT RUNNER

From the start, Harper was the front-runner. He had the advantage of being a sitting MP, with years of experience on the federal scene, and a track record as a successful party leader. He already had a campaign team ready to go. His closest collaborators simply moved off the federal payroll, and left the opposition leader's office to work full-time on the leadership campaign. Tom Flanagan had managed Harper's campaign for the Alliance leadership, had then served for a year in Ottawa as his chief of staff, and then was put in charge of preparing the Alliance for the coming elections. He now dropped that to manage this new leadership campaign. Harper's press secretary since 2001, Carolyn Stewart-Olsen, and his chief policy adviser, Ken Boessenkool, similarly transferred over.

Harper's two opponents had the challenge of proving themselves better suited to lead the new party than Harper. Tony Clement, forty-three, kept reminding his audiences that he, unlike Harper or Stronach, was the candidate who had experience in actual government. During his two terms at Queen's Park, he had been successively minister of transportation, minister of the environment, and minister of municipal affairs and housing; during the 2003 SARS crisis in Toronto, he had acquired national exposure as minister of health. He had also been an early, fervent advocate of the United Alternative process and was the founding *CLEMENT* president of the Alliance party in 2000. He spoke French. His CV was impressive. But Clement also carried some negatives. He was a late starter in the leadership campaign and went in as a loser: he had lost in his own riding during the October 2 election in which Ernie Eves's PCs were defeated by Dalton McGuinty's Liberals. In person, bespectacled, rather undistinguished in appearance, he came across as something of a nerd, even if an intelligent one. But Clement's biggest problem was Stronach, who had instantly become the torchbearer for Ontario PCs who wanted one of their own to lead the new party. She came in as a winner, big time, while Clement had scored in third place two years earlier when he ran for the Ontario party leadership to succeed Mike Harris. He, unlike Stronach, did not spark excitement.

Belinda Stronach had no experience as a practising politician and so she made a virtue of necessity: "Canadians have had enough of political experience, they want leadership," she would repeat. Unlike Harper, *STRONA* who had spent virtually his entire adult life focused on politics, she had run a big international company and would bring that experience, she promised, to growing the Canadian economy. She gave a feminine allure to her commitment by speaking of "baking a bigger economic pie." Nor was she a political illiterate. She had regularly contributed money to various candidates, including fifty-thousand dollars for Peter MacKay's 2003 leadership bid. On the boards of various companies controlled by Magna she encountered Brian Mulroney, Mike Harris, William Davis, Brian Tobin, and former Liberal industry minister Ed Lumley. She had hobnobbed with the best and she could now turn to them for political advice. Her initial impact was impressive. When she spoke to the Calgary Chamber of Commerce on January 23, the turnout of 1,300 people overwhelmed expectations and the event had to be moved. She got a standing ovation for her speech in which she called for an elected Senate, eliminating the tax on capital gains, and, mercifully, killing the gun registry. She was winsome when she explained why a rich lady like her was entering the rough-and-tumble of politics: "My father came to this country with only a few dollars in his pocket. We always learned about the values of hard work and to appreciate what we had. . . . If I can make a contribution to the well-being of Canadians and to the future of Canada, I would like to do that."

She participated in two of the three all-candidates debates, and while she seemed scripted and could not answer questions in French, she avoided disaster, which was not bad for a neophyte. She attacked Harper who could not, she said, expand the party in Ontario and the East. "When you look at the track record of the Alliance, it was a regional party. We must broaden." Clement attacked Harper for his firewall letter. Clement seized on the confusion when Harper's office sent out a letter congratulating some West Indians on the national holiday of India: "You just built another wall," he needled. For her part, Stronach argued: "We must have the lowest taxation rates in the world. . . . We must focus on the economy, the economy, the economy." And who could better run the economy than a Stronach? On her Web site she described Harper as "the person who failed to win 11 by-elections as Canadian Alliance leader" and quoted various contentious statements he had made over the years, including his comment about Atlantic Canada and the "culture of defeat." Stronach was new to public political battles, but she had at her service all the best talent that money could buy, including her campaign manager, John Laschinger, the most experienced and highly reputed political master mechanic in the land.

Harper had taken a personal risk when he accepted that each of the 301 ridings would count equally for the leadership. His support was unmatched in the West. But Quebec represented for him and the new party seventy-five rotten boroughs. Neither the Alliance nor the PC Party had a semblance of constituency organizations after the meltdown of Mulroney's party – even during his days of glory, he had borrowed the

Re: Vote on choosing new leader 6 or "e"

machines of the PQ and the Quebec Liberal Party. In 2000, with the Quebecophile Joe Clark leading the Tories, he had managed to win only 5.6 per cent of the vote. Stockwell Day's pitch to the nationalists had reaped 6.2 per cent. Harper was starting in Quebec almost at ground zero. Stronach, meanwhile, had Brian Mulroney working the phones on her behalf. In Quebec, volunteerism on behalf of Conservatives was almost unknown; there was a cadre of *bleu* organizers who worked for money in every leadership or election campaign and who had prospered since 1993, while the party had not. Stronach had netted almost every last one. Harper hired what he could find; his chief organizer, Richard Décarie, had been a senior aide to Premier Jacques Parizeau and Premier Lucien Bouchard, and he brought in other organizers who had worked for the PQ or the Action Démocratique du Québec. In this campaign, it was not enough simply to pitch a general appeal to the whole province. He had to have an organization in every riding, since every riding counted equally in the final tally and what counted was the percentage of the riding vote, no matter how tiny the actual numbers. Stronach, with Mulroney behind her and deep pockets to draw from, was far ahead in Quebec. An Ipsos-Reid poll published on February 20 showed Harper leading in the country as a whole among Conservative supporters, with 46 per cent support to 26 per cent for Stronach and 17 per cent for Clement. But, in Quebec, Stronach led by 44 per cent to 24 per cent for Harper. That was paradoxical, considering that she could not speak French and he did. She also led Harper in Atlantic Canada, 34 per cent to his 25 per cent.

In the event, when the votes were counted on March 20, Harper led by 55.5 per cent to Stronach's 35.0 and Clement's 9.5 per cent. In Quebec, Harper's 33.4 per cent seemed respectable under the circumstances, though dwarfed by Stronach's 60.5 per cent. Stronach also outclassed Harper in each of the Atlantic provinces. But Ontario was the crucial battleground, and there Harper demonstrated a surprising appeal: he was backed by 56.9 per cent of the weighted vote, winning in ninety-six ridings, while Stronach, with 27.3 per cent of the weighted vote, won in only six constituencies. Clement, who had boasted that he could win Ontario, received 15.8 per cent of the weighted vote and led in only four ridings.

In his victory speech that night, Harper spoke as the heir of John A. Macdonald and Brian Mulroney, and stressed that all Conservatives, not

MAR 20 2004

just those on the right, were welcome in this new-old party. "We need the Red Tory vision of important national institutions and sustainable social programs because the Conservative Party will never leave the vulnerable behind. We need the economic conservative vision of lower taxes, more efficient government, lower debt, and free enterprise, because the best social program is still a job. We need the social conservative vision of strong families and safe communities because our children are our most precious resource and our families are our most cherished institution. And we need the democratic reform vision of a government that is responsible to the people, not a government responsible to [the Prime Minister's Office]." He sent an appeal to all regions of the country, with a special message, in French, for Quebec: "We must pursue our efforts to build this party in Quebec. We must be effective in the founding province of this country and in the founding language of Canada."

He also warned of what to expect in the coming elections. "Fellow Conservatives, if we stand for ideas, if we stand as a team, we will win the next election. But the tired, old, and corrupt Liberal Party is right now cornered like an angry rat. They are going to attack us like we have never been attacked before."

Harsh words. Harper had travelled a long way from the ceremonious politeness that he had brought to Ottawa in 1989 as Deborah Grey's speechwriter or exhibited in 1994 in the Commons under Manning's leadership. The tone of the new leader of the Conservative Party of Canada in dealing with Prime Minister Paul Martin and his Liberal government would be one of unrelenting contempt. That would be his stance as he returned to Parliament for the remaining weeks or months before elections were called.

Chapter 21

———◆———

COMING CLOSE

2002 SPONCERSHIP SCANDAL

MAR 22
2004

WHEN STEPHEN HARPER returned to the Commons for the first time on March 22, 2004, as newly elected leader of the Conservative Party of Canada, his first question was, of course, about the sponsorship scandal. "I have to ask if anything happened while I was away! Two years ago, my first questions as leader of the Opposition were on Liberal waste, mismanagement, and corruption. Two years later, we have no answers. Two years later, we have more Liberal waste, mismanagement, and corruption. My question is simple and it is for the prime minister. How long until Canadians get answers to who is responsible and the truth behind this Liberal sponsorship scandal?"

He did not receive an answer from the prime minister. Paul Martin had chosen Harper's first day in the Commons as CPC leader to absent himself, to travel to western Canada to make an announcement about aid to farmers, an announcement which he could have made on any other day of the week. But he knew that Question Period, on that first day of Harper's new tenure, would receive voluminous coverage by the Parliamentary Press Gallery, anxious to record the first exchanges between Harper and Martin since the latter became prime minister. So Martin preferred to talk about beef in Alberta than scandals in the Commons. That would be the pattern over the next eight weeks until Parliament was dissolved and elections were called for June 28. 2004

In Harper's camp, it was taken for granted that Martin would call elections as quickly as possible in order to catch the new leader unprepared. That was what Jean Chrétien had done to new Bloc leader Gilles

Duceppe in 1997 and to Stockwell Day in 2000. Harper's campaign team, now moved back into the old offices, estimated that the election call could come as little as two weeks after the leadership vote, so they had to be ready in early April. Again under the direction of Tom Flanagan, the preparation for elections resumed, but now on a much bigger scale and at a frantic pace.

It was a much-changed Commons to which Harper now returned, compared with the House before Chrétien prorogued it the previous November 7. Paul Martin officially became the Liberal leader on November 15, and then prime minister, his long-standing obsession, on December 12. The new prime minister chose a cabinet that left out twenty-two of the former ministers, Chrétien loyalists like Sheila Copps, John Manley, Allan Rock, Martin Cauchon, Don Boudria, and Stéphane Dion. Instead of reaching out to his former opponents within the party for the sake of restoring unity after the long internal civil war, he excluded them and even pressured them to leave public life altogether. Clearly, he would allow no rival near the throne. He also wanted to project the image of a brand-new government soliciting its first mandate rather than an old gang going for a fourth. In the first Martin-inspired speech from the Throne on February 2, 2004, the MPs were treated to a grandiloquent Liberal electoral platform voiced by the Governor General in the theatrical splendour of the Red Chamber, after she had been announced by a twenty-one gun cannonade. She read the thematic sentence: "This Speech from the Throne marks the start of a new government; a new agenda; a new way of working." A Throne Speech is meant to announce the government's legislative intentions for the session of Parliament just beginning. This Throne Speech, the prelude to a soon-to-be-aborted session of Parliament as everyone knew, lasted nearly an hour as the senators and commoners were treated to Martin's overarching vision of a Canada to be reconstituted during the next ten years. Martin clearly intended to be around for a good while, and his ambitions were boundless. From cradle to grave, no aspect of the human condition in Canada went unheralded.

But the heady vistas on the future projected that day amid pomp and protocol made way just eight days later, on February 10, to Auditor General Sheila Fraser's nasty return to the past – her comprehensive report on the notorious sponsorship program. After auditing $250 million of expenditures to promote the image of Canada, chiefly in Quebec, she reported: "The federal government ran the sponsorship program in a way that showed little regard for Parliament, the Financial Administration Act, contracting rules and regulations, transparency, and value for money." It was a devastating indictment of governance in the previous regime, when Martin had been the second-most powerful minister. But, in the House that day, Prime Minister Martin depicted himself as the champion of probity to whom a scandal was suddenly revealed and who leaped onto his white charger to chase after the villains: "The situation described by the Auditor General is unacceptable. Canadians deserve better and it is for that reason that the government has acted swiftly. It is for this reason that the government has appointed a commission of inquiry [under Justice John Gomery]. It is for this reason that the government has asked that the Public Accounts Committee be established immediately and that it meet as early as possible, including this afternoon. It is for this reason that the government has appointed a special counsel to recover the funds. We are acting now. . . . The problem described by the Auditor General is that the rules were broken. People did not know that rules were broken. . . . As soon as we formed the government, we cancelled the program. And today, as soon as the report was tabled, we came up with a comprehensive plan to deal with it. We have dealt with it, and we dealt with it as soon as we were able to." But Canadians were not so sure. An Ipsos-Reid poll taken right after Fraser's report and published on February 14 showed that the Liberal support in the polls had plunged nine percentage points to 39 per cent, from 48 per cent in January. Conservative support jumped to 24 per cent from 19. By February 20, exactly a month before the Conservative Party would choose its new leader, an Ipsos-Reid poll showed Liberal support had slipped further to 36 per cent, while support for the Conservatives had risen to 27 per cent, and to 17 per cent for the NDP. The Bloc was now running ahead of the Liberals in Quebec. It was a new political game, so different from what everyone had anticipated just a short time before.

In early February, Martin had scored a coup that promised well for his coming electoral campaign in Quebec: he recruited as both Liberal candidate and as his Quebec lieutenant the popular radio personality Jean Lapierre, who had been a Liberal MP in 1990 when Martin had chosen him to co-chair his campaign for the Liberal leadership. When the

(1991) convention that June chose Chrétien instead, on the same day that the
Meech Lake Accord failed, Lapierre broke with the Liberals and soon
joined Lucien Bouchard to become a co-founder of the Bloc Québécois. *1993*
He left the Commons in 1992 to achieve celebrity as host of a phone-in
program on Montreal's most listened-to radio station, CKAC. Netting
him as his showcase Liberal candidate symbolizing the beginning of a
new era was central to Martin's plan to decimate the Bloc in Quebec and
2004 re-establish the pre-Chrétien Liberal ascendancy. When Lapierre
announced his candidacy on February 5, he proposed that the Bloc was
now past its "best before" date and had no further reason to exist on the
federal scene. He also disparaged the Clarity Act, considered by most
Liberals to be an important Chrétien legacy. He announced that it would
never be applied because he could envisage no referendum in the fore-
seeable future. He added, "And, frankly, if you want my opinion, I think
it is useless – the Act. It's useless because it wouldn't change anything. If
there was a will in Quebec, a clear will to separate, they would not be
able to stop a will like that by trying to have tricks." For Lapierre, the
Clarity Act was nothing but "tricks." What counted was not the rule of
law, but the will of a majority of Quebeckers expressed in a referendum.
When Martin was asked to comment on his Quebec lieutenant's words,
his reply spoke volumes: "It's certainly my intention to be so open, open
to Quebec, that it will never be necessary to apply it." He was asked
directly by Radio-Canada reporter Denis Lessard: "But if there were a
referendum, you would then take it into account?" Martin replied:
"Well, it's the law. But I will tell you something. I think that there never
will be – certainly, while I am prime minister, there will be no referendum, because we will have the kind of country where the Québécois will
want to build a stronger Canada."

   Martin's presumption was an insult to the separatists. It suggested
that their convictions were so shallow that the arrival of a more understanding prime minister would make them abandon their dream of an
independent country. He was also naive. Martin was pursuing the course
that had led Mulroney to grief and that Harper warned against: building
the party by recruiting the nationalists. Martin not only chose a noted
nationalist, but even entrusted him with recruiting the Quebec candidates for the coming elections. Lapierre soon held a press conference to
show off with pride seven candidates who had been prominent in the PQ

or the Bloc. In the event, the candidates recruited by Lapierre were all defeated by the Bloc Québécois.

On March 18, just two days before the vote on the Conservative leadership, Martin touched down in Quebec City to reveal himself as Mr. Clean: "Nothing is more important than integrity," he told the local Chamber of Commerce. "That's why I am going to change the way Ottawa works. This is not a slogan, it's reality. We are going to change the way Ottawa works. And we're going to do it, come hell or high water. We are going to condemn to history the practice and the politics of cronyism. We are going to condemn to history the politics and practice of waste and mismanagement. I am sure that we are at a turning point. Government will never be the same." Come hell or high water was the vivid expression that Martin had used in 1995 when he vowed to defeat the deficit. He was suggesting he would now bring the same determination to uprooting cronyism. It would prove hardier than the deficit.

Martin wanted to turn all eyes toward the future. Instead, Sheila Fraser turned all eyes on the past. At first, Martin claimed that he was not in the know, left out of the loop. Then he claimed that it was a scandal that involved only fourteen civil servants. Then, realizing that the public didn't buy that, he decided to take the lead in denouncing the scandal as a legacy of Jean Chrétien – and, as everyone knew, he and Chrétien were barely on speaking terms. People were outraged? He himself was mad as hell. He was madder than anybody. He would lead the way in the search for the truth. But, despite his conspicuous displays of indignation and resolve, people didn't believe him. A poll published March 19 by Praxicus, pollster for the Conservatives, held that only 23 per cent of Canadians believed that Martin did not know about the shady deals, while 53 per cent believed that he knew.

Martin repeated in the House that he had known nothing about the scandals of the sponsorship program and promised that he would turn over to the Public Accounts Committee all available information so that the public could be fully informed. Did he keep his promise? He was less than candid on the central issue of the so-called Canadian Unity Reserve, which was at the heart of the scandal. Most of the world learned of the reserve's existence for the first time only on March 23, 2004, when Finance Minister Ralph Goodale, delivering his first budget speech, announced its cancellation. Goodale presented this termination of the reserve as just one economy measure among others rather than pointing out that it was the very scene of the crime: "Within our first month in office, we began to tackle the task of identifying the $1 billion in ongoing savings across government which the previous budget had promised and booked. With this budget, we have finished that job through such decisions as cancelling the political history museum, forgoing VIA Rail's capital expansion, *terminating the sponsorship program and the national unity reserve*, reducing advertising programs, and trimming departmental budgets across the board, effective April 1, 2004."

He uttered the words "national unity reserve." What national unity reserve? No one had ever heard of it. Precisely what sponsorship program? In fact, as the Auditor General made clear later, there never was a clearly defined "sponsorship program" identified in the annual estimates of government spending. There was, instead, a $50-million annual reserve available to the prime minister to draw on for unforeseen spending; this is what Jean Chrétien had used – or misused – as the source for the many millions doled out annually to promote the visibility of Canada and the government of Canada – and, not coincidentally, the Liberal Party of Canada. The reserve had been created in 1992 when Brian Mulroney was prime minister. But it automatically lapsed under a sunset clause in 1996 and it had then been specifically renewed, reinstated, and that had required the signature of the finance minister – of Paul Martin. He had, indeed, signed it. In February 2005, he would claim when he appeared as a witness before the Gomery commission that it was just a small amount in a multi-billion-dollar budget, a discretionary fund under the control of the prime minister, and that he had signed his approval routinely, without asking how the money would be spent – it was a reserve, hence supposedly for unforeseen expenditures.

But when Harper questioned Martin about it in the Commons in March 2004, he either refused to answer or evaded every question. On the day after the budget, Harper asked Martin, "What we did learn yesterday from the budget was that the government had been running a secret unity fund of $40 million a year that did not appear in the prime minister's budgets. Apparently, it was kept hidden from Parliament. How many other secret Liberal slush funds has the prime minister had out there?" Martin replied as though there was nothing to it: "In terms of the unity fund, the honourable member ought to know about the fund. In

[handwritten: Re: national UNITY Reserve]

fact it was set up in 1992 by former prime minister Brian Mulroney." He *[handwritten: 1996 NEW RESERVE FUND]*
gave no further explanation. In fact, technically, the reserve fund author-
ized in 1996 was entirely new, not the one started by Mulroney, which
had expired. And how could Harper have known about it? The next day
Harper again asked Martin for an explanation: "In his 1995 budget the
prime minister claimed he was going to 'eliminate waste and abuse.' At
the same time he was converting unity moneys to a private fund dis-
pensed on the signature of the prime minister. Why did the prime minister allow this secret Liberal slush fund to exist under his watch?" Martin
replied in such a way as to imply that the fund was nothing special –
which he knew to be untrue. "As I said yesterday, the unity fund in fact
began in 1992. It was started under the previous Conservative government. At the same time the 1995 budget was the budget that ultimately
led to the elimination of the Tory deficit." His reference to eliminating
the Tory deficit was simply a red herring, a way of evading the question.
It had nothing to do with the real focus of the scandal, the prime minister's reserve. Martin's reply – or evasion – did not satisfy Harper. He
asked for a clear answer: "I would like the prime minister to be clear on
this because Privy Council Office officials have apparently confirmed the
creation of this fund, disbursed on the signature of the prime minister, in
1996, not in 1992, as the prime minister implied yesterday and today.
Can the prime minister be clear? Is he saying Mr. Mulroney also dis-
pensed secret funds on his own signature when he was prime minister?"
Martin again dissembled: "There is nothing secret. All of these moneys
are expensed in the public accounts and in fact there are reserves set up.
There were reserves set up under the Tories. There were reserves set up
under the Liberal government. The problem is that the opposition
members are so full of innuendo and slander that they fail to understand
what is a normal accounting procedure used by the Conservatives and
used by the Liberals." This was using the tactic called, in French, "*noyer
le poisson*," to drown the fish in a cataract of water. You want to know
about reserves? There are lots and lots of reserves. It's simply an accounting procedure. *The* reserve at the heart of the scandal became, in Martin's
answer, just a routine bookkeeping procedure that Harper, to his shame,
was ignorant of. Harper tried again: "It is interesting that, for a fund we
all know about, we have no lists of how the moneys were actually spent.
The PCO mandate was changed in 1996. Since then nearly half a billion

dollars have apparently been authorized on the authority of the prime minister. Why did it take the prime minister nearly ten years to eliminate this practice?" This time Martin refused to answer. Had he been candid and transparent as he claimed to be, he would have admitted that the unity reserve had indeed been used for unorthodox purposes. He might have pleaded that he had signed the authorization to restore the prime minister's reserve, but had been unaware of what Chrétien would do with it. Instead, speaking in the Commons as prime minister, he evaded, misrepresented, and misled the leader of the Opposition, misled the Commons, and so misled the people of Canada about the fund central to the scandal. And that, while claiming that he wanted all the facts to be known.

2004   The atmosphere in the Commons in this new session of Parliament had become bitter since Fraser's February 10 report. The daily Question Period turned into a cacophony of recrimination. Harper rose almost every day like an inquisitor, directing his questions and his scorn at the prime minister – if he was there. When Harper sat down, Peter MacKay, a former prosecutor, rose in turn to point the finger of outrage at the Liberal benches. Almost every day, elsewhere on Parliament Hill, a parade of witnesses appeared before the Public Accounts Committee, gave their conflicting testimonies, and kept the scandal in the widening public eye. This was the theatre of the whodunit, with each day providing a new episode in the search for the villain. Each time Harper rose, the Liberal MPs listened glumly to the barrage of accusations. This wasn't what they had expected when they acclaimed Paul Martin as their leader. Now Parliament was mired in the muck of scandal. To listen to the acrimonious exchanges was depressing, to be their target was pure hell. Martin took to the air, no doubt to escape the constant battering; he quickly became the most travelled prime minister of all time outside of election campaigns. He was, in effect, in one constant campaign, popping up everywhere across the country, desperately trying to reverse the polls that showed his party losing respect in public opinion. On May 12, two days before the last pre-election session, Gilles Duceppe noted sarcastically: "We have a visitor among us today, in the person of the prime minister."

The election campaign of 2004 would be much like Question Period in the Commons, full of charges and counter-charges, demagogy and deceit. Martin clearly intended to rerun the Liberal campaign of 2000 by depicting Harper as an extremist who did not share Canadians' values. To prepare for his campaign, he attacked Harper in the Commons on April 27 by asserting – falsely – that Harper wanted to abolish medicare: "The honourable member [Harper] might want to take a look at some of the speeches he made in the House and some of the policies that he endorsed in the Reform Party, in terms of the drastic scorched-earth policies he recommended in health care and scorched-earth policies in our transfers to the provinces. *If it were up to that member, we would have withdrawn from the entire Canada health policy. That is what he is doing.*" The tactic was similar to Chrétien's attacks against Day in 2000.

But Martin's plan to portray Harper during the election campaign as an enemy of public health care hit a snag on that same day when his own minister of health, Pierre Pettigrew, appeared before the Commons Committee on Health and enunciated exactly Harper's position – that there was room for the provinces to experiment with private delivery of some health services in a publicly funded system. "The Canada Health Act doesn't exclude the offer of services by elements of the private sector insofar as they are paid for by a public regime," Pettigrew told the committee. "I'm saying that some private delivery options, as long as the single payer, the public payer, is there, that's what is in the [Canada Health] Act." Then he told reporters: "If some provinces want to experiment with private delivery options, my view is that as long as they respect the single, public payer, we should be examining these efforts and then compare notes between the provinces. If it doesn't work, they'll stop it. But if it works, we'll all learn something." What Pettigrew said was exactly what the Canada Health Act allowed. But it did not serve Martin's purpose to have his health minister say so. It countered his planned attack on Harper as the would-be exterminator of public health care. So, the next day, a chagrined Pettigrew was sent out to meet the press, read a prepared statement, and then leave without taking one question: "I now realize that I have left the impression that I favour increased private delivery within the public health system. That was in no way my intent, nor is it the intent of the government of Canada. We will be working with provinces collaboratively on a single payer, publicly administered, and publicly delivered health system that is there for Canadians when they need it. The ambition of the federal government is not to encourage private delivery even within the terms of the Canada Health Act. Quite the contrary. Our ambition is to expand public delivery because, as Roy Romanow said it very well, public delivery provides Canadians with the best system possible." His statement nowhere claimed that private delivery of publicly funded health care was illegal. It only went against "our ambition."

That day, Harper raised the issue with Martin in the Commons: "The Liberal government has spent the last four years overseeing the expansion of private health-care delivery within the public system. Yesterday the minister [Pettigrew] said, 'If some provinces want to experiment with the private delivery option . . . we should be examining these efforts.' Today he said it is not his intention to favour private delivery – except that last week he said, 'We know the public administration principle of the Canada Health Act already provides flexibility on private delivery.' Is it not the case that the government is so busy trying to attack this party on health care it does not have a clue on what its own position is?" Martin replied: "The Alliance Conservative position on health care is one that is not acceptable to Canadians and is of very little interest to us. This party, the Liberal Party, brought into being the universal, accessible public health-care system. That was our position at the time it was brought in, that is our position today, and that will be our position tomorrow and for the years to come." Harper commented: "Unlike that prime minister, this leader does not need a press conference every day to clarify his health-care position."

This equivocation over health care was a foretaste of the election campaign. Before it was called, Martin's strategists sent an e-mail from the Prime Minister's Office saying that he was eager for a "head-to-head contest" with the Conservatives' "radical, far-right agenda that is consistently out-of-sync with Canadians." Martin himself told his caucus on April 21 that he planned to centre the election campaign on a choice between Liberal support for health care and proposed Conservative tax cuts – to make them the lowest in the world – that would gut health care and social services. At another caucus meeting on May 5, according to press reports, he even maintained that it would be "the most important election in Canadian history." That was a tall claim, but it suited his demonizing of Stephen Harper. He presented the coming elections as a choice between compassionate Liberal values and policies, and the heartless Conservative policies that would destroy Canadian values, involve Canada in American wars, and eliminate the compassionate dimension of Canadian institutions. On May 4, the *Globe and Mail* ran on its front page – for free – excerpts from attack ads that had been prepared by the Liberals. "If Stephen Harper becomes PM you'll have two health-care options: Be rich. Or don't get sick." Another message: "If Stephen Harper was prime minister last year, Canadian troops would be in Iraq this year." The second message was true. The first, false, demagogic, and cynical.

[handwritten: MARTINS ATTACKS ON 'C']

Martin held his own nomination meeting in Lasalle-Émard on May 20, and again sounded the themes of the campaign that would be launched three days later. He claimed that the combination of tax cuts and increased spending proposed in the Conservative election program would produce a budgetary hole of $50 billion over five years. "Where do they think that money is going to come from? It's going to come from those things that matter the most to Canadians, the vital services on which they rely, the services that single mothers, senior citizens, and students rely on. Provinces will pay. Cities will pay. Families will pay. That's why, when this election is called, it will be about one thing – the kind of Canada that you want, and I can tell you that the kind of Canada we want is not the kind of Canada that Stephen Harper wants." Moreover, Martin maintained, a vote for the Bloc was worse than wasted: it would help elect what Martin persisted in calling "the Conservative Alliance."

In fact, in the following year, data provided by Ralph Goodale's *[handwritten: More Attack Tax Cuts]* February 2005 budget would reveal that there was no "black hole" of $50 billion in the Conservative platform. On the contrary, the Conservatives' estimates in 2004 of current and future revenues were far, far closer to reality than those made by the Liberal government. But, no matter. On May 17, 2004, Finance Minister Ralph Goodale denounced Harper's pledge of tax cuts as "ruthless." He said the cuts would be possible only if the Conservatives cut deeply into government programs, and he declared to reporters with a flourish: "The numbers tell the real story. And they show that any progressive remnant in Mr. Harper's Conservative Party is now well and truly dead." Ever since the 1993 elections, Liberal fortunes had prospered on demagogic depictions of the Reform, the Alliance, and now the Conservative parties as extremist, irresponsible, and intent on trampling on widows, single mothers, the aged, and children.

Events would disprove the charges time after time, but the same charges always worked so well that they would be recycled when the next elections came along. Most reporters in Ontario and Quebec obviously entertained stereotypes of what these right-wing parties represented; come election time, they went looking for candidates who would confirm the stereotypes. They always found what they were looking for.

McGill University economics professor William Watson would look back on the controversies over responsible budgeting that raged during the 2004 election campaign, from the vantage point of the budget of February 23, 2005. "The Liberal platform [in 2004] provided for only $26.3 billion to $28.3 billion of new spending over the next five years," he wrote in the *National Post* on March 3, 2005. "The new and untested Conservatives, by contrast, threatened with their obvious amateurishness to blow up the federal budget. Their platform forecast $57.8 billion of tax cuts and new spending, fully $30 billion more than the Liberals, which would take the country back to the bad old days of Mulroney. Actually, not 'take' but 'plunge.' The Tory program, Liberal analysts wrote, 'would plunge Canada back into deficit.'" Watson then looked at Goodale's 2005 budget. What did he find? "The table shows all federal spending and tax initiatives since last spring's pre-election budget. The five-year total? $82.7 billion." In other words, the five-year forecast was now that the Liberal government would spend $24.9 billion more than the Conservatives had planned to spend – and that Martin had denounced as the height of irresponsibility that would destroy the health system and "the services that single mothers, senior citizens and students rely on." And he got away with it.

On the day before the election was called, the Liberals published a full-page ad in newspapers outside Quebec. Side by side, there were half-page photos of Paul Martin and Stephen Harper. The photos were fair: both men looked businesslike. But the text again suggested that Harper would destroy the existing Canada to replace it by some undefined alien Canada. "It's not which Canadian you choose. It's which Canada," the ad challenged in big red letters. A text in smaller print followed: "Stephen Harper's number-one priority is tax cuts. He has said that Canada's tax levels should be lower than those in the United States. But to accomplish that would mean cutting vital programs and services, at a time when we need to re-invest in health and education, and improve the quality of life in our communities. Paul Martin and the Liberals want to build on the values and institutions we cherish and make them stronger, ensuring equality of health care, education, and opportunity for everyone. Think carefully about what kind of country you want in the coming days. Because, very shortly, you'll be asked to CHOOSE YOUR CANADA."

In Quebec, the same full-page, two-picture format was used, but this time with Martin and Gilles Duceppe juxtaposed. The choice offered was not as apocalyptic as it was in the English ads: "Which of these two Québécois can really make the difference for Quebec?" The answer was not surprising. "Paul Martin wants Canada and Quebec to progress. Gilles Duceppe merely wants Canada not to function." There was no mention of Harper – yet.

When he spoke to reporters on the grounds of Rideau Hall, right after asking the Governor General to dissolve the 37th Parliament, Martin again tried to portray the campaign as a choice between himself, holding high the Maple Leaf, and Harper, draped in the Stars and Stripes. Canadians were called to their patriotic duty: "It's a question of values. It's a question of the kind of country that you want to build. I love the United States. But I love far greater that we are different. I love that we are Canada and we're going to stay that way." He didn't name the presumed unpatriotic Canadian who would move the country south of the border. But the context made it clear. So Harper responded: "My Canada will be as Canadian as any other candidate's. You know, in this country, you can be a Canadian without being a Liberal. The government seems to forget that."

The early Liberal campaign focused on attacking Harper, his supposed policies (much of it fiction), and laying out a string of quotations dredged from his past, including the firewall letter, his "culture of defeat," his criticism of the Official Languages Act, and a comment he had made describing what groups supported the Liberals, which was presented as insulting all immigrants. But, somehow, the salvoes of the early weeks seemed to miss their mark. Harper's counterattack seemed to have more effect as he called for the defeat of a government which had accumulated "a record of waste, mismanagement, and corruption." The Conservative campaign slogan, "Demand better," was a low-key reminder that the Liberals had proved themselves unworthy.

It is a truism that opposition parties don't defeat governments, governments defeat themselves. In the first week of the campaign, it did seem

CAMPAIGN ELECTION JUNE 28 2004

as though the Liberal government was engaged in self-immolation. No matter what Martin said, people didn't believe him. A poll published in *La Presse* on May 22, the day before the election was called, demonstrated the public's skepticism toward him and his government, at least in Quebec. The sample by CROP was asked: "Do you believe the Liberals and Paul Martin when they assert that they were aware of nothing and that only a few individuals are responsible for the sponsorship scandal?" Only 9 per cent believed, while 85 per cent did not. They were saying, in effect, that Martin was a liar. As well, 65 per cent said they were unsatisfied with the federal government and 57 per cent said they were somewhat in favour of changing the Martin government. But still the Quebec public remained ambivalent. Asked in which leader they had most confidence to be in charge of Canada, 35 per cent named Martin, only 12 per cent named Harper. Asked in which leader they had the most confidence to defend the interests of Quebec, 23 per cent named Martin, only 3 per cent named Harper, while 47 per cent named Duceppe. Asked for which party they intended to vote, 42 per cent named the Bloc, 34 per cent named the Liberals, 15 per cent named the NDP, and only 10 per cent named the Conservative Party of Canada.

The momentum in the early weeks of the campaign favoured Harper's Conservatives, and the polls showed him climbing steadily in public acceptance. Martin tried to make health care the wedge issue that would distinguish him from Harper. He would invest an additional $9 billion in health care, reduce waiting times, and create a national home-care program. He would meet with the premiers and keep meeting until they reached a settlement. "I'm going to fight for this reform that is going to give us the fix for a generation," he promised grandly. But, at least at first, his claim that Harper would dismantle the public health-care system had no effect. Harper ostentatiously endorsed the agreement reached the previous year by Chrétien and the premiers, and accused Martin of not living up to that agreement. Surely, if he stood four-square with Chrétien, he could hardly be the extremist destroyer conjured by Martin's fabulation. Besides, Harper proposed devoting more money to health care than did Martin. In addition, contrary to Martin's stereotype of him, Harper proposed a federal plan to cover "catastrophic" drug costs, those in excess of a threshold of $3,500.

Not all was clear sailing for Harper in that first week. On May 27, the Moncton *Times Transcript* published an interview with the Conservative critic for official languages, Scott Reid, under the headline: "Harper government would overhaul bilingualism; requirements for mandatory bilingual services would be eased under Tory government: candidate." The Liberals, the Bloc, and many independent commentators immediately leaped on the interview to trumpet that the Conservatives had a hidden agenda to put the axe to the Official Languages Act. Harper stated that what Reid had said was not party policy and that French was a priority for him right across the country. He quickly accepted Reid's resignation as critic. But the seed of doubt was planted, especially in Quebec.

[handwritten margin note: Scott Reid resigned]

Another event in that first week received less attention. NDP Leader Jack Layton stated in Quebec his position – it was in fact not his party's – which was to recognize Quebec as a nation, to recognize Quebec's right to secede unilaterally, and to rescind the Clarity Act, which set conditions for negotiating Quebec's secession. The statement that he would recognize Quebec's right to secede unilaterally was pure nonsense. At least since the Supreme Court's advisory opinion on secession, no prime minister has the power to set aside the Constitution and the rule of law. But Layton's statement had the effect of reviving interest in the issue of secession, and an enterprising *La Presse* reporter recalled in an above-the-fold, front-page story that Harper favoured the partitioning of Quebec if it seceded from Canada. The headline shouted: "HARPER CAUTIONNERA LA PARTITION DU QUÉBEC. Dans l'éventualité d'un référendum gagnant sur la souveraineté." (Harper will support the partition of Quebec. In the event of a winning referendum on sovereignty.) The reporter asked Harper whether this was still his position. He refused to commit himself, on the grounds that secession was not an issue in the campaign now that a federalist party under Jean Charest formed the government in Quebec. But the reporter quoted unnamed people close to Harper to confirm that it was still his position that parts of Quebec could choose to remain in Canada if Quebec did secede.

But, early in the campaign, these seemed like side issues. As public support for the Conservatives rose, the Liberals pulled out all the stops in their campaign to discredit Harper. On June 3, a joint press conference was held by Martin's Quebec lieutenant, Jean Lapierre, together with Liberal ministers Lucienne Robillard, Liza Frulla, and Denis Coderre.

They had announced that they had a "shocking document" to deliver to the press. In fact, what they had to say was that there was a secret understanding between the Bloc and the Conservative Party to form a government led by Stephen Harper. A vote for the Bloc, they claimed, could bring Harper to power, and that would bring Canada back to the 1950s with respect to the rights of women and of homosexuals. A Conservative government would put an end to a woman's right to an abortion; it would prevent same-sex marriage, take Canada into war, and reduce Quebec's influence in Ottawa.

On June 5, that press conference was followed up by a full-page ad in *Le Devoir*. It stated in a big headline: "TO VOTE FOR THE BLOC IS TO TURN QUEBEC OVER TO HARPER." The ad claimed: "To vote for the Bloc is to allow the rest of the country to choose Stephen Harper. That would mean a Canada that goes backward with respect to abortion, that is ruled by a government without one minister from Quebec, which takes an axe to the official languages, which supports the war in Iraq. Can Quebec afford to open the way to Stephen Harper's Conservative Party? For, to vote for the Bloc is to isolate Quebec."

The Liberals mobilized women's groups to publicize their attack on the Conservatives for having a hidden agenda to ban abortions. Harper tried to counter the charge: "I have no intention of supporting abortion legislation, so there's no way that abortion rights are going to be overridden by my government," he protested on June 9. He was put on the defensive after a Conservative MP from Ontario, Cheryl Gallant, who had once compared abortion to the Holocaust, now compared it to the beheading of an American hostage in Iraq the month before. Immediately, the outcry was raised that the Conservative Party had a hidden agenda on moral issues, such as abortion and the rights of homosexuals. A CPC candidate in Kitchener, Frank Luellau, had gone public with his condemnation of homosexuality from a religious perspective: "I think that the biblical teaching is that it is not a natural kind of relationship. I think it is inappropriate for Christians, especially Christian leaders, to live that lifestyle."

These were not Harper's views. In fact, in November 2003, Harper had fired as critic on family affairs the Alliance MP for Regina–Lumsden–Lake Centre, Larry Spencer, a former Baptist minister who maintained that homosexual acts should be recriminalized. He associated homosexuality with pedophilia and said he would support any bill that proposed to reinstate homosexual acts as criminal. His stance was embarrassing, coming just as the Alliance and PC parties were about to unite. Spencer withdrew from the caucus to sit as an independent and was not re-elected in 2004. But Harper could not disown Gallant's stand, he could only say it was not party policy. His stance for years had been that moral issues should not be a matter of party policy, but each MP should be free to follow his or her conscience and the wishes of the constituents.

Harper was in a delicate position. Because Martin had indicated that he would be calling elections early in the year, the new Conservative Party had to turn directly to election preparation and could not hold a policy convention before the elections. Therefore, Harper had no authoritative corpus of policy formally agreed-to by the party that he could impose on the members. He could not at the same time reject top-down leadership in favour of grassroots authority, and still impose on his party a discipline that it had not authorized. His reluctance to pronounce on social issues was then held up as showing a lack of conviction or, more likely, a hidden agenda. The forty-six-page electoral platform for 2004 listed the nineteen "founding principles" that had been agreed to when the agreement in principle was reached. None dealt with issues like abortion, homosexuality, or the death penalty. The platform spelled out such items as a five-year contribution to health care of $36.8 billion, a program of new spending and tax cuts totalling $57.8 billion. It proposed to reduce the federal tax rate on middle-income Canadians by more than 25 per cent, and to introduce a $2,000 per child deduction to reduce the tax burden on families with children. It proposed to end corporate or union political donations and to end taxpayer subsidies to political parties. It would have required elections to be held on a fixed date every four years, eliminating the prime minister's ability to manipulate this prerogative for partisan advantage. The program also called for ending the power of the leader to appoint candidates without the vote of the constituents they were to represent, as Martin had just done.

But the only stand on a moral issue as such in the program was to advocate closing the "artistic merit" loophole for legalizing child pornography. It also proposed that Parliament, rather than the courts, should decide the definition of marriage – hardly an extremist proposition. Altogether, it was a moderately conservative platform, well within the arc of what is acceptable in a free and democratic society, and not the extremist right-wing horror depicted in Liberal propaganda. It took a stern stance on law and order issues, by proposing that prison sentences should be fully served out: "If you do the crime, you do the time." It would have scrapped the firearms registry and redirected the money saved to law enforcement.

Some of the proposals were controversial, such as one for an elected Senate. The program proposed a plan to reduce air pollution, but would scrap the Kyoto Protocol. It proposed to cut corporate subsidies so as to reduce taxes for all businesses. These were issues on which citizens could legitimately disagree, without one side tarring the other as extremist.

One issue which led Harper to be attacked was that of the war in Iraq, and his proposal for a robust increase in the military budget. By June 9, when polls showed the Conservatives about even with the Liberals, Harper was downplaying his past emphasis on Canadians waging war in Iraq and was claiming that Canadians could have helped prevent war by a resolute show of force in concert with allied countries. "I continue to believe if the allies had acted in a concerted manner to put on Saddam Hussein that kind of pressure, we would have been able to avoid a war, but we didn't do that." It was true that he had urged such a position and such a motivation on the Chrétien government before the start of hostilities, but it was also true that he never limited his support to a show of force, either before or after the actual hostilities were under-way. As for the armed forces, he proposed an immediate increase of $1.2 billion in spending on military equipment. He also proposed increasing the number of troops to 80,000, from about 53,000. Martin, proposing to increase the regular forces by only 5,000, and the reserves by 3,000, decried Harper's proposal as old-fashioned militarism.

A new Liberal TV commercial featured a handgun aimed directly at the spectator, images of soldiers fighting in Iraq, a Canadian flag with-ering, chimneys spewing smoke, and an emergency hospital ward swarm-ing with frantic nurses. All this was supposed to represent what Harper stood for. A voice recited: "Stephen Harper says when he's through with Canada, we won't recognize it. You know what? He's right." Another commercial proved effective by associating Harper with the unpopular former Ontario premier Mike Harris: "Ontarians know too well the damage of Conservative cuts and privatization," said the voice-over. The

commercial did not make the distinction between an Ontario government saddled with a huge deficit, and a federal government enjoying a
huge surplus. Cutting taxes in both cases, the commercial suggested, was
irresponsible and heartless.

By June 9, Harper began suggesting that he was preparing for a
majority Conservative government. He began slipping the words into his
speeches. The explanation, according to someone close to the campaign,
was the expectation that Quebeckers, if they thought that Harper might
well form the next government, would want to jump on the bandwagon
and would take a second look at his proposal for a more decentralized
federation. The tactic backfired. An Ipsos-Reid poll published June 15 in
the *Globe and Mail* showed the Conservatives leading the Liberals by
one percentage point, 32 per cent to 31. Since Liberal support was more
concentrated in the big cities, with more populous ridings, that one point
advantage was expected to translate into many more Conservative seats.
Canadians had wanted to punish the Liberals. But polls also showed that
they considered Martin to be a better prospective prime minister than
Harper. When polls and Harper's rhetoric began to suggest that the
resentment against the Liberals might go beyond punishing them by
reducing them to a minority, and might even bring the Conservatives to
power, the momentum previously evidenced in the polls began to stall.

Then came the leaders' debates, in French on June 14, in English on
June 15. Both were disgraceful ordeals to which the four leaders were
submitted. In the U.S., presidential debates are conducted with dignity.
In Canada, the tradition is to let the leaders fight it out in an undisciplined free-for-all, each man for himself, with only a semblance of order
maintained by the moderator. The format rewards rudeness, brashness,
yelling, and interrupting, which both Gilles Duceppe and Jack Layton
showed themselves adept at, and both saw their poll numbers rise in the
days following. Harper was the most restrained. He often allowed himself to be distracted from what he was trying to say by the shouts, interruptions, and questions thrown at him by his opponents. Still, he came
out of both debates with creditable reviews, mostly on the ground that
he was more gentlemanly than the others. The one clear winner in the
debates was Gilles Duceppe. He was the best prepared, the most targeted
and focused, the most lethal in attack mode. That was bad news for
Martin, because only Martin would lose seats because of Duceppe's

surge. After the French debate, an overnight CROP poll found Gilles Duceppe "the most convincing" in the opinion of 57 per cent, with Martin chosen by 21 per cent, Harper by 8. Still, in rating the leaders' performances, Harper did well: 58 per cent rated him as good or excellent, one point better than Martin's 57 per cent.

On June 15, the morning of the English debate, the *Globe and Mail* reported, "Tories edge ahead in new poll." The Conservatives were one point ahead of the Liberals in an Ipsos-Reid survey. The story went on: "A seat projection based on the new poll suggests the Conservatives would win 123 to 127 ridings if the election were held now, while the Liberals would be limited to 95 to 99. Ontario, which has 106 of the 308 seats in the House of Commons, would be split evenly between Liberal red and Conservative blue."

These were heady times, with the momentum growing in the Conservatives' favour. Would the trend continue until June 28? Anything now seemed possible. After the debates, though, Harper lost the sure footing he had shown before. It seemed as though he was thrown somewhat off stride by his unexpected surge in the polls. Till then, too, the news media and public observed him less critically because he seemed unlikely to form a government. On June 16, Harper made perhaps his biggest mistake of the campaign when he said: "There are no safe seats for the Liberals anywhere, any more. None in Atlantic Canada, none in the West, or in Quebec and in Ontario." And he began talking about the transition of power from the Liberals to the Conservatives. That sent a message to the electorate of over-confidence, of presumption, even of arrogance. It showed a lack of appreciation of the tentative character of his support in Ontario, where Liberals and Conservatives were about on a par. In the polls, voters still rated Martin as the best man to be prime minister.

Harper's boast focused attention on himself, and people were uncertain about who he was. It was in large part his fault. Harper had given no co-operation to journalists who wanted to interview him in depth to establish what kind of man he was, where he came from, what he represented. Naturally aloof, scornful of photo opportunities and of stunts to attract favourable attention, he pushed reserve to something close to paranoia in his reluctance to open himself up to scrutiny. Wanting to control the image of himself that was projected to the public, he would trust no one else to interpret his persona. He now paid the price. Canadians did not feel that they knew who he was. Could he be entrusted with governing the country? Was he a prudent, intelligent leader who would never put the public good at risk, or was he the anti-social extremist that the Liberals constantly depicted? Canadians did not know. And now, when a Conservative government seemed likely, people paid more attention; they wondered and they worried. Now the Liberal attacks began to score.

Two incidents in particular worked against him. One was that Ralph Klein told the world that he would be announcing changes to Alberta's health system two days after the June 28 election. Those changes would include more private delivery of health care and, he said, would probably challenge the Canada Health Act. Immediately, Martin leaped on the announcement to discover a "hidden agenda," a conspiracy where Klein had found in Harper a co-conspirator to undermine the public health system. "He's hoping he'll have a silent partner in Ottawa by the name of Stephen Harper, someone who will not speak up for the Canada Health Act, someone who will be propped up by the separatist Bloc Québécois, and someone who doesn't care. Well, unlike Stephen Harper, I do care. And unlike Stephen Harper, I will look Ralph Klein in the eye and I will say 'no.' Unlike Stephen Harper, I will defend medicare."

Klein was in fact no great admirer of Harper and certainly no intimate. He had called for Mike Harris to lead the new united party and had only expressed doubts that Harper had what it takes. Unlike the four Atlantic Conservative premiers, Klein had not endorsed the Conservatives or actively campaigned for them. But never mind, Klein and Harper were both from Alberta, both Conservatives, and that was enough for Martin. With utter cynicism and hypocrisy, he, a citizen of Montreal, the very capital of private health care, scurried about shouting that Klein and Harper were planning to gut public health care, but they wouldn't reveal the plan until after the election. And it worked.

Klein neg. towards Harper

The second incident occurred when the Conservative war room put out a press release claiming that Martin supported child pornography. It was a subject on which many Conservatives, especially in the West, felt very strongly. They were outraged when, in 2002, the British Columbia Supreme Court supported a defence by John Sharpe against a charge of possession of child pornography on the grounds that written works in his possession had "artistic merit." The Alliance had called on the Liberal government to tighten the law, but without avail. The issue arose during the campaign when, on June 17, Michael Briere, the accused murderer of a ten-year-old Toronto child, Holly Jones, claimed in court that he had abducted and sexually assaulted the little girl after being aroused by viewing child pornography on the Internet. The Conservatives' press release was titled: "Paul Martin supports child pornography?" It cited four occasions when Martin voted against measures to combat child pornography. Harper had not seen the release. It had been faxed to reporters who questioned him about it. Taken by surprise, Harper looked at it, said the headline went too far, and ordered it changed. It was then re-released with a new headline: "How tough is Paul Martin on child pornography?" But Harper defended the substance of the release. "I'm not going to, in any way, give the Liberal Party any break on its record on child pornography. It is disgraceful. They have had multiple opportunities to do something about it and they have systematically refused, and if they want to make the election campaign about that, the next ten days, I'd love to fight that one."

The reaction in the media and in the public was that the release was unfair, grievously insulting, and that Harper should have apologized. He might have, had he not been so contemptuous of the Martin Liberals. For the past four months he had been in a constant, aggressive standoff with them. Their attack ads had been grossly unfair to him. This was for Harper just another episode in a fight to the finish. But the public did not see it that way. Martin struck a note of injured dignity: "This is personal. I am a father and I am a husband. And he has crossed the line and he should apologize." True, Harper had crossed the line. True, Martin had also crossed the line in accusing Harper of guilt by association with Klein. But Harper's excess changed the public perception of Harper. Martin's excess also changed the public perception – but again of Harper, not Martin.

From then on, Harper's campaign was constantly blindsided. He could no longer get across his intended daily message. He was, instead, constantly questioned by reporters about child pornography and his refusal to apologize, about abortion, homosexuality, and use of the notwithstanding clause. What his team called the "bimbo outbreaks" by some of his candidates were seized on by reporters. The issue of bilingualism arose again when a letter surfaced, signed by a member of Harper's staff, which stated the party's policy with respect to Air Canada, then struggling under court protection. Air Canada alone was subject to more extensive bilingual requirements than other airlines. The Air Canada Public Participation Act, passed in 1988 to authorize the privatization of what had been a Crown corporation, required Air Canada to retain its head office in Montreal and to retain the same obli- gation for bilingual services to the public as before. The letter expressed the hope that Air Canada would come under "the same rules of the game concerning regulations" as the other airlines. It stated that a Conservative government's policy would be to "create a competitive environment in the airline industry and leave airlines alone in their fight to attract customers." Martin found that scandalous: "I would never have thought that I would see a leader of a political party, like Stephen Harper, express ambiguity on official languages, express ambiguity on minority languages. And yesterday, when he refused to say that Air Canada would continue to be bilingual, it's terrible, it's unacceptable, and we will never accept it." Martin accused him of having a hidden agenda on bilingualism.

That accusation was much taken up in Quebec's French language press. Harper replied by promising to extend the same obligation for bilingualism to the other airlines, by placing that obligation in the Official Languages Act. But, again, he was placed on the defensive and suspicions were stirred about a hidden agenda.

On Friday, June 25, going into the last weekend before the Monday election, the Liberals dropped the biggest bomb of the entire campaign. Martin held a press conference that was broadcast live across the country. He played a clip from a forty-five-minute video documentary on same-sex marriage, titled *Let No One Put Asunder*. The video, produced and directed by Vancouver filmmaker Alexis Fosse Mackintosh, followed three same-sex couples who got married, and aired interviews with people for and against same-sex marriage, as well as footage of demonstrations for either side. The net effect was distinctly pro gay marriage.

On May 19, just four days before the 2004 election was called, Conservative MP Randy White had been interviewed by the film crew. He was asked whether the Conservative Party would repeal Bill C-250, the private member's bill proposed by NDP MP Svend Robinson, which included sexual orientation as a ground for protection against hate propaganda. The bill received royal assent just the month before, on April 29, 2004. "Well, C-250, I'd repeal it in a minute," White said, according to a transcript provided by the filmmaker. He was also asked what his party's position was on the legal recognition of same-sex marriage.

"Well, my position and the Conservative Party's position are identical. I guess there are two things. On the definition of marriage, we should never allow the courts to usurp the laws of the nation and that's exactly what they've done in this case . . . they've decided that the definition of marriage should change. I think it's absurd, ridiculous, and irresponsible. It's the politicians who should make the laws, not the courts, not the judges." He was asked if the Conservative Party would use the "notwithstanding" clause. His reply was enthusiastically affirmative. "If the Charter of Rights and Freedoms is going to be used as the crutch to carry forward all of the issues that social libertarians want, then there's got to be for us conservatives out there a way to put checks and balances in there. So the 'notwithstanding' clause, which that was meant for when it was originally designed, should be used, and I would think that not just the definition of marriage, but I think you'll see more uses for the 'notwithstanding' clause in the future. And I sincerely hope it is, because the Charter of Rights and Freedoms, I think, you'll even see that redefined as the Charter of Rights and Freedoms and Responsibilities, which is really needed for an amendment."

White was expressing his own opinion, not the new party's, except when he said that the party favoured laws made by Parliament rather than by courts. But he claimed to speak for the party, and displaying a total lack of political judgment, he went way beyond party policy in suggesting the transformation of the Charter and the free use of the notwithstanding clause to serve a social conservative agenda. He played into the hands of Martin who seized on the interview to confirm his worst predictions about the Conservatives: not only did they have a hidden agenda to strike down all kinds of Charter rights, but they were going to attack the Charter itself and twist it into the opposite of what it was intended to do: protect individual rights.

This rant, made public just three days before the vote, had an enormous impact, especially in volatile Ontario and in British Columbia. It was played over and over again on television in those last days. For many, it summed up the essence of the Conservative vision. It seemed to confirm the worst fears about what a government run by Conservative extremists and barbarians would do. White was even quoted as saying: "To heck with the courts!" Had he actually wanted to destroy his party's chances in Ontario, he could hardly have done better. Harper replied that White's statements did not reflect party policy. But the attack, coming in the last days of the campaign, could not be effectively parried.

Michael Marzolini, president of Pollara, the firm that provided polling and strategic advice for Jean Chrétien's three electoral victories, recounts that, mid-campaign, the strategists for Martin's campaign began to panic and sought advice from former Chrétien counsellors, including Pollara. "Pollara prepared a strategy memo based on their private polling from the third week of the campaign. It urged the campaign to 'drag out the dinosaurs' among the Conservative caucus, to highlight and explore their positions on social issues, like abortion, gay rights, immigration, bilingualism, and gun control. Of special significance was the 'hidden agenda' abortion issue, which in the 2000 election had been the Achilles heel of former leader Stockwell Day. It wouldn't have the same potential against Stephen Harper, wrote the pollsters, but it would serve to make the ballot question 'Does Harper think like I do?' Rather than 'Should I punish the Liberals?'"

Obviously the Liberals took Pollara's advice, which Marzolini described in a chapter titled "Public Opinion Polling and the 2004 Election," in a book edited by Jon Pammett and Christopher Dornan titled *The Canadian General Election of 2004*. Marzolini relates that, by the last week of the campaign, "The Liberals did not look any better to Canadians than they had throughout the campaign, but the Conservatives looked a lot worse. It would be a vote based on who people did not like, rather than who they liked the best."

Opinions were wavering in the last days and hours before the vote. But, instead of becoming more outgoing, Harper seemed to reporters to withdraw within himself, to be less available to their questions, and to have a decreased level of energy. Martin, on the other hand, showed he cared, desperately, and spoke of being in "the fight of my life." He put out a frantic burst of energy. On the final day of campaigning, Martin travelled in one day from dipping his feet in the Atlantic in the morning to closing the day with his toes in the Pacific, with several stops and

[handwritten: JUNE 28 L - 135 / C 99 / B 54 / NDP 19]

speeches in between. He called on those tempted to vote NDP or for the Green Party to vote Liberal instead, so as to stop Harper from forming the government. Harper followed a campaign plan made earlier when he was surging in the polls, and returned to Alberta as its champion, vindicating its long frustrated aspirations for recognition and power. "We're going to bring this part of the country into power in Ottawa," he told a rally in Edmonton. "To all Edmontonians, Albertans, and the West, to all of you, I've known all along I can count on you, now I tell you, never forget, you can count on me," he vowed. The day before, he told a crowd in Surrey, B.C.: "I urge you on Monday to say loudly and clearly that old battle cry: 'We want change and we want in.'"

Instead of ending the campaign in Ontario, where he was born, showing that he wanted to represent the central province and all of Canada as a national leader, showing that he understood, showing that he cared, he made the mistake of returning to Alberta and sounding like a regional chieftain with regional priorities, just as the election campaign reached its climax. "For more than a decade, the West and Alberta, in particular, have been demanding change. This is where it all started, and I've come here to tell you today, change is on the way in this country. You can be pioneers again, you can give the new Conservative Party that you've done so much to create, you can give it every single seat in the province of Alberta." He then rode in a triumphant motorcade from Edmonton back home to Calgary.

That night, as he watched the returns come in, Harper's feelings must have been bittersweet. After the heady prospect of forming the government, the actual outcome was a letdown. The Conservatives won 99 seats, compared to 135 for the Liberals, 54 for the Bloc, and 19 for the NDP. There was one independent. On the brighter side, in terms of seats, the Conservative Party had done much better than the 66 seats the Canadian Alliance had won in 2000, and considerably better than 78 seats, which was the sum of the seats won by the two predecessor parties.

But there was much to worry about. The Conservative share of the vote, 29.6 per cent, was better than the 25.5 per cent won by the Alliance in 2000, but far from the 37.7 per cent received in 2000 by the two parties combined. In fact, in every single province, the Conservative Party won a smaller share of the vote than the two parties combined had

won in 2000. In Quebec, the 8.8 per cent vote won by the Conservative
Party was a continuing disaster.

The outcome seemed disappointing only because hopes had risen so
high during the election campaign. But no one, six months earlier, could
have believed that the Liberals would be held to a minority, and with
only 36.7 per cent of the national vote. Helped by the sponsorship
scandal, but also by a solid performance, the Conservatives overcame
most of the disadvantages with which they began existence as a single
party. They had been allowed little time to get ready to face elections,
they had not had a founding policy convention, their policies were still
in flux, the marrying of two cultures, two traditions, two networks of
feudal loyalties, had not had time to become organically integrated. Their
leader, Stephen Harper, was still basically unknown and misunderstood.
And yet they were able to compete credibly in the competition to form
the government, not merely survive, in their first great trial.

Chapter 22

POSITIONING THE PARTY

FOR DECISIVE ELECTIONS

WHEN WOULD THE boot drop? The voters, in their wisdom, created a jittery, unpredictable Parliament by the elections of June 28, 2004. They not only returned a minority Liberal government, they also put Paul Martin in a fix not faced by past minority leaders. Martin's Liberals, with 135 MPs, were initially 20 short of the magic majority of 155 in the 308-seat House. The NDP had only 19 MPs, so it alone could not stabilize the Martin minority. The Bloc Québécois could, with its 54 MPs, but that was out of the question: the Liberals and the Bloc, ideological antagonists on the issue of secession, were each others' only rivals for dominance in Quebec. As for Stephen Harper, as Opposition leader he had no interest in keeping the Liberals in power. But, with 99 Conservatives, he would need more than the Bloc's MPs to defeat the Liberal government.

Right after the elections, Harper announced that he would be considering his future. But he soon found that his position as party leader was secure – until the next elections – and so he announced that he would stay on. And then he disconcerted the journalists once again by disappearing for the summer. He was not inactive. He met several times with Gilles Duceppe and Jack Layton to establish a kind of common front facing the Liberals. The three party leaders signed a joint letter to Governor General Adrienne Clarkson asking that she not dissolve Parliament at the request of the prime minister without first consulting them. Presumably, Harper envisaged attempting to form a government long enough to get some legislation passed before elections that were agreed to by the three opposition parties. Harper also feared that Martin wanted to precipitate an early election to regain a majority.

He was also determined that the Liberals, elected with a minority of the seats as well as a minority of the vote, would not have the moral or political authority to govern as though their program had received the assent of the voters. He would change the way of doing things in the Commons. The Liberals would be forced to recognize that a majority of the elected members were not Liberals, and that the majority's views and interests must be taken into account in the legislation that would be passed in the coming session. The Liberals, as government, would have the initiative for introducing public bills. But when the bills were studied in committee before being returned to the Commons, the opposition MPs would have a majority on the committees; that meant that whenever the three opposition parties could agree by advance negotiation, they could shape legislation in a way that Paul Martin had never anticipated when he made "fixing the democratic deficit" his major plank for winning Liberal backbenchers to his standard against Jean Chrétien. Then, he was promising power in the Commons to the Liberal peons. Now, he would be delivering it in large measure to the opposition MPs. The new Parliament promised to be an interesting place.

Before the new Parliament was even summoned, the new reality appeared when Martin announced that the newly elected MPs were to receive a 10 per cent increase in remuneration, following a previously approved formula that tied the members' raises to that of judges. Harper denounced the impending raise and promised to fight it. The prime minister soon agreed to drop it.

The political atmosphere began to change on September 7, 2004, when the commission of inquiry into the sponsorship scandal, headed by Mr. Justice John Gomery of Quebec Superior Court, began public hearings in Ottawa. Witnesses, beginning with Auditor General Sheila Fraser, were questioned and gave their testimony. The hearings were thereafter in constant counterpoint to everything the government then did or said, constantly recalling, day after day, in a persistent, damning slow drip, all the actors and actions of the scandal that had unfolded underground over several years.

In mid-September, Paul Martin faced his first big political test. He was meeting the provincial and territorial First Ministers to conclude an

[handwritten margin note: Humorous — LIB had to give double to Province in health care allowance]

agreement on health care. Initially, he offered an agreement worth $12.2 billion over six years. But he had made health care the central issue of his *[handwritten margin note: Prov + Health Care]* election campaign, promised "a fix for a generation," and promised to meet with the premiers until such an agreement was concluded. It had provided good campaign rhetoric, but now that he actually had to deliver, he had put himself at a disadvantage. The premiers, by withholding consent, could force the ante upward. He would be there, he had promised, until they all agreed. And he had placed no condition, no upper limit, to his commitment. And now, not only was the burden of proof on Martin to deliver an agreement, but he was further weakened by heading a minority government, which could be forced into new elections almost at any time. He needed as much support as he could get from the provinces, and he needed it immediately, not four years later. So the premiers played the script accordingly, complaining loudly and often about the bad deal that he was offering. They even used the theatre of public embarrassment to shake more money out of their host: one morning, they simply refused to show up for the meeting at the designated time. The television cameras focused on the empty chairs. And so it was that Martin eventually settled for about double what he had promised during the campaign: for an additional $41 billion over ten years. The premiers returned, inwardly rejoicing, to sign the agreement. No doubt the prime minister set a new record: many party leaders had made promises that they failed to keep, but to pay out double what was promised constituted a Martin innovation.

[handwritten margin note: Quebec special clause] There was more. A special side agreement was signed that recognized, in the name of "asymmetrical federalism," that Quebec, while committing itself to the general principles endorsed in the main agreement, was authorized to establish its own measures for reducing waiting times for medical procedures and measuring results and services to citizens. In other words, Quebec could spend the new money as it chose, and report only to its own citizens. Charest even spoke of using the new money for lowering taxes.

Martin and the other provincial premiers praised the side deal as proving the flexibility of federalism in recognizing Quebec's special needs. "The nine other premiers – as well as the three territorial leaders – all agreed with asymmetrical federalism," the prime minister said. "And, in fact, that reflects the reality in Canada." But Premier Charest, triumphant, trumpeted the agreement as an extraordinarily important precedent that would lead to new instances of recognizing Quebec's distinctiveness. He seemed significantly more elated by the recognition of the principle of asymmetrical federalism than by the new millions that would come to Quebec: "This is the first time in history that the federal government has signed an agreement in which they recognize asymmetrical federalism, which is a precedent. For Quebec this sets a precedent that will be helpful to all of us as we go ahead and develop programs in ways that reflect our priorities."

Quote from Premier Charest

Stéphane Dion, now federal environment minister, but previously the point man on federal-provincial relations in the Chrétien government, said the deal gave explicit recognition to what was already done. "We gave an explicit legitimacy to a practice that was not always admitted in words. It will ease relations between the government of Canada and provinces, notably Quebec." Mr. Dion had supported the Meech Lake Accord and recognizing Quebec in the Constitution as a distinct society.

As for Harper, he gave his approval to both the main agreement and the side deal. The main agreement, he maintained, was much closer to what the Conservatives had proposed during the election campaign than the Liberal proposal. As for the side deal, "I have always defended the right of Quebec and others to have primary control in their areas of jurisdiction; that's what federalism is all about," Harper said.

Yet when the Speech from the Throne raised the curtain on the new Parliament on October 5, there was no mention of "asymmetrical federalism," or of the special deal for Quebec. At most, the speech spoke of "respect for the diversity of Canada," which could mean anything or nothing. There had been an outcry within the Liberal Party about recognizing a special status or distinct identity for Quebec, of which this seemed an example. For Trudeau, that had been the first step toward sovereignty-association.

Re side deal for Que.

It was Stephen Harper, speaking during the Throne Speech debate the next day, who most defended asymmetrical federalism. He congratulated the government because it "recognized that Canadian federalism need not be a one-size-fits-all framework, particularly when it comes to provincial jurisdictions." And he went on, speaking in French, to defend asymmetry by precedent: "The principle of asymmetrical federalism, as it has been called, is not new. Our successive constitutions and our history include several examples of formulas that take into consideration the different realities of the various regions of our country." Then he applied the general observation specifically to Quebec: "Quebec in particular, through its elected representatives, has chosen to help create the Canadian federation, precisely because its distinctiveness would be respected and protected there."

This was remarkable. Harper, who had been Reform's most persistent opponent of recognizing Quebec in the Constitution as a distinct society, who had damned the Calgary Declaration for that reason, was now deliberately obscuring the difference between federalism itself, which recognizes symmetrically the distinctiveness of each province or state, and "asymmetrical federalism," which goes beyond the federal principle to make special deals for some. This was the very confusion which Jean Charest propagated in his rhetoric, and which he used to justify the pursuit of a special status for Quebec. It was not innocent or innocuous.

But Harper, trying to overcome the exclusion of his party from the minds and hearts of Quebeckers – the single greatest impediment to his winning power in the next elections – was willing to go a long way to curry favour. He would even distance himself from the Reform Party's past history, to recall only the older tradition of nineteenth-century accommodation in the party of John A. Macdonald: "The new Conservative Party which I have the honour of leading is a young party: it will turn one later this month. However, we are very proud to be the heirs of John A. Macdonald and George Étienne Cartier, two Conservatives who managed to unite English and French Canadians in a federal system that became one of the major achievements of the twenty-first century. I therefore urge the prime minister and all his ministers to respect the will of the provinces that want to sign specific agreements with the federal government when they decide to co-operate with it in jurisdictions granted to them under the Constitution."

The qualification was important: he praised asymmetrical federalism only in areas of provincial jurisdiction. He had explained to the CBC's Evan Solomon in an interview three days earlier why he could support the deal: "Mr. Charest called me before the deal was signed a couple of times and I said, 'Would this deal be something where every province can have its own rights respected and its own deal, is it equal for everybody?' Mr. Charest said yes, and that's what's in the deal. It says that every province has a right to exercise its own jurisdictions, to ask for its own side deal. Only Quebec chose to do that. I can't blame Quebec for doing that. Remember also that this is provincial jurisdiction. The nature of our Constitution is that everyone is supposed to be able to do their own thing in their own area of jurisdiction. I don't consider that special status – but obviously Quebec got a side deal. I think the only question in Alberta people have, is why the Alberta government didn't ask for its own deal. Because it could have done so. And I can't blame Quebec for that."

True, the deal was theoretically open to any province, and within provincial jurisdiction. But it would have been more consistent with Harper's conservative commitments to denounce the federal intrusion into provincial jurisdiction and demand that Ottawa liberate tax room to allow the provinces to take up the slack, without a special side deal for Quebec. It is true that different provinces came into the federation after negotiating different terms, just as it is true that, in 1867, there were different arrangements for women and for men, for the propertied and the propertyless, for white people and aboriginals, for Catholics, Protestants, and all others. In a modern state, specific, ad hoc, and variable relations between a federal government and the members of the federation tend to be replaced by rules which are the same for all, while allowing each to develop its own way within its areas of jurisdiction. Otherwise, each member will be fighting for special advantages, and the other members will angrily fight for equity, which is exactly what has happened since the 2004 elections. Asymmetrical federalism, in practice, is calculated to tear a federation apart, not keep all its members happy.

Paul Martin, meeting with the First Ministers, redefined the principle of equalization payments, which were meant to compensate poorer provinces to the extent of their relative poverty. By negotiating automatic increases in equalization based on population, he undercut the very principle on which equalization was founded and, incidentally, placed a greater burden on the populations of the provinces supporting the equalization payments, notably Alberta and Ontario. He had also redefined equalization on the fly during the 2004 election campaign when, fearing defeat, he phoned Premier Danny Williams to promise that, for Newfoundland and Labrador, revenues from non-renewable resources would not count for equalization. And it precipitated angry demands for corresponding additional payments from Quebec, Saskatchewan, and

New Brunswick, while Ontario premier Dalton McGuinty, in open revolt, launched a campaign claiming that Ontario paid $23 billion more to the federal government than it received in goods and services. This was asymmetrical federalism in practice.

Paul Martin had based his 2004 election campaign on three promises, all within provincial jurisdiction: health care, child care, and money for municipalities. In so doing, he transformed federal-provincial relations into a free-for-all for more money. He exacerbated what Charest called "*le déséquilibre fiscal*" by choosing to dole out federal money rather than vacate tax room. He set the stage for federal-provincial quarrels for years to come. And Harper, instead of denouncing the side deal which was a symptom of Martin's approach, called instead for more side deals.

Harper renewed his appeal to Quebec's distinctiveness when he spoke at a dinner in Quebec City on October 15, 2004. There, as part of what he called a "federalism of openness," he made a startling proposal. "Over the past several years, we have seen innovations in the federalism that is practised elsewhere in the world. In Belgium, for example, the federal authority is shared not only with geographic regions, but also with the language communities. I hope that my party will examine how this idea could be adapted to Canadian reality. Instead of devolving more authority to the provinces in areas like culture and international relations, the federal government could, perhaps, in concert with the provinces and Quebec in particular, establish francophone and anglophone community institutions in such telecommunications and broadcasting jurisdictions as the CRTC, Radio-Canada or the Francophonie, the Commonwealth, and UNESCO."

The proposal was a non-starter for many reasons. The choice of Belgium as a model was catastrophic: in Belgium, the Flemish have a long history of resentment toward the Walloons, who had done their best for a century to eliminate the Flemish language from public life. No comparable resentment can be found in Canada. The suggestion of devolving jurisdiction to language communities would have no appeal to Quebec nationalists, who focus their ambition on more power for the Quebec government, and countenance no competing centre of power, even one vested in a francophone community. Moreover, as the Quebec government proved in the *Mahé* case that went to the Supreme Court, it would prefer to sacrifice the rights of francophones to French schooling in the rest of Canada than to recognize new school rights for English-speaking Quebeckers. In the rest of the country, Harper's suggestion was received as just another doomed attempt to solve the unsolvable.

Harper had also made an overture toward Mario Dumont's Action démocratique du Québec, which had, in September, announced its new policy on the Constitution, which was to press for a maximum of autonomy for the Quebec government. The ADQ proposed to rename the province "the Autonomous State of Quebec," to establish a Quebec citizenship alongside Canadian citizenship, to draw up a Quebec Constitution, to have Quebec join international institutions, and to deliberately carry out actions that were known to be unconstitutional so as to create precedents and acquire more autonomy. The ADQ was radically nationalistic – it had been founded as a breakaway from the Quebec Liberal Party in 1992 when Robert Bourassa accepted to hold a referendum on the Charlottetown Accord. It had joined the PQ and the Bloc to support the Yes side in the 1995 referendum on secession. After a few years of rejecting a new referendum on secession after 1995, it now returned to its original muscular nationalism. But the ADQ was also conservative in wanting a smaller government and more scope for the private sector. Harper had met Dumont several times, had chosen as a Conservative candidate and then his Quebec lieutenant Josée Verner, who had been an ADQ candidate, and as policy adviser Michel Lalonde, who had been a principal policy adviser to Mario Dumont. And so, looking for a foothold in Quebec, Harper counted on the ADQ. In consequence, when the ADQ announced its new policy of *autonomisme*, Harper refrained from criticizing and made sympathetic noises, short of actually endorsing the new policy.

Harper's dilemma of how to gain support in Quebec was exasperating. But he was playing a dangerous game. Much of his appeal had rested on the clarity of his thinking and his unwillingness to compromise fundamental principles when all about him were selling out principle for short-term political advantage. In particular, the rule of law was a non-negotiable principle that Mario Dumont openly proclaimed his intention to violate. The equality of the provinces was also a principle that Harper's supporters considered non-negotiable. While not violating it explicitly, Harper had supported Martin, an ardent promoter of the

Meech Lake Accord, in blessing a principle of asymmetrical federalism that was proclaimed by Charest as a precedent for other asymmetrical arrangements not limited to provincial jurisdiction as usually understood. Quebec had its own definition of provincial jurisdiction.

An Environics poll, published in the *Toronto Star* on October 16, demonstrated how unpopular special status was, except in Quebec. The side deal with Quebec was viewed negatively by 69 per cent of the respondents. Outside Quebec, 79 per cent disapproved, while in Quebec 55 per cent approved. It was a polarizing event, just as the Meech Lake Accord had been. The sample had been unusually large: 1,960 respondents.

When the prime minister spoke during the debate on the Throne Speech, he was far more subdued than Harper on the subject of asymmetrical federalism. He had only two brief sentences on the subject, and neither mentioned Quebec nor federalism, but only an "approach": "The health accord sets out common objectives, but recognizes the different needs and circumstances that exist among the provinces and territories. By recognizing these, by pursuing an asymmetrical approach, we find strength in our diversity."

Harper seized the occasion of the Throne Speech to force changes on the minority government. The Liberal government had not consulted the other parties before constructing the Throne Speech, but Harper did consult the other minority leaders and they came up with five amendments, which offered something for each of the three parties without outraging the Liberals. They included reducing taxes for "low and modest income families"; establishing a citizens' assembly to consider changing the electoral system, perhaps even including proportional representation; holding a vote in the House on any ballistic missile defence treaty with the United States; establishing a commission to reform the employment insurance system so it would no longer subsidize the government; and creating a budget office, independent of the government, so that the forecasting of budget surpluses or deficits no longer would be manipulated for political purposes as it had for the past twenty years.

The Bloc also had an amendment that Harper intended to back. It asked for assurances that the bills to be adopted "fully respect the provinces' areas of jurisdiction and that the financial pressures the provinces are suffering as a consequence of the fiscal imbalance be alleviated, as demanded by the Premier of Quebec." After negotiations back and forth and the threat by the government of precipitating elections, Martin finally agreed to meet with Harper and Duceppe and a deal was struck making minor changes to the amendments, which were mostly then accepted as part of the approval of the Throne Speech. What wasn't incorporated, Harper proposed to impose when the legislation came before the appropriate committee. So Harper had won his point that the minority government would have to take into account the demands of the opposition parties. Jack Layton, meanwhile, who had been a partner in the opposition trio, now announced that he would back the government rather than join the opposition.

It soon made little difference. On November 18, Martin announced that MP Carolyn Parrish was excluded from caucus for her "unacceptable" anti-American and anti-Martin remarks. The Liberals were down to 134. Then, on December 16, Lawrence O'Brien, the MP for Labrador, died of cancer. The Liberals were down to 133. On April 12, 2005, MP David Kilgour abandoned the Liberals to sit as an independent, because of several disappointments, including the sponsorship scandals that made his constituents "want to vomit," and also because of his opposition to same-sex marriage. The Liberals were down to 132. Harper's original attitude had been, as he told one interviewer, "What we've got here is an extended election period. The electorate will have a longer time to make a fuller assessment of who tells the truth to the Canadian people: Stephen Harper and the Conservative Party or Paul Martin and the Liberal Party." But, as anger at the Liberals over the scandal grew, Harper's attitude of wanting to make the minority government work began to change to one of making the Liberal government go. Meanwhile, politics were far more interesting than they had been before the elections, when the Liberals had a secure majority. Now, every day brought its own uncertainties and expectations.

An issue which clearly distinguished the Conservatives from the other parties was that of same-sex marriage. When lower courts had judged that the equality clause of the Charter of Rights demanded that same-sex couples be given the same access to marriage as heterosexual couples, the Chrétien government and its minister of justice, Martin Cauchon, decided not to appeal. Instead, the government prepared legislation to redefine marriage as the exclusive union "of two people" rather than the common-law definition accepted previously by the courts as the exclusive union "of a man and a woman." Meanwhile, to ensure that the proposed bill was constitutional, on July 17, 2003, Cauchon sent a referral to the Supreme Court of Canada with three questions: Is the draft bill within the exclusive legislative authority of the Parliament of Canada? Does the draft bill conform to the Canadian Charter of Rights and Freedoms? Does the Charter protect religious officials from performing marriages between two persons of the same sex if it is contrary to their religious beliefs?

After Paul Martin became prime minister, his government sent a fourth question to the court, thus ensuring that any action would be put off until after elections. The fourth question asked whether the traditional requirement that spouses be of opposite sex was constitutional. Martin clearly expected that the answer would be no, and that the onus of recognizing same-sex marriages would be borne by the Supreme Court rather than by his government. "The Court made me do it," he would be entitled to say. But the Court, rendering its advisory opinion on December 9, 2004, while answering the first three questions, refused to answer the fourth. Yes, the federal government had exclusive jurisdiction to define marriage. Yes, the draft bill recognizing same-sex marriages would be in accordance with the Canadian Charter. Yes, the Charter would protect officials refusing to officiate at a same-sex marriage for reasons of conscience, but legislating on the performance of marriage ceremonies fell under the jurisdiction of the provinces, not Ottawa. As to whether the traditional definition of marriage was constitutional, the court withheld any opinion. The result was that, because the federal government had refused to appeal the decisions of lower courts, the decisions stood in a total of eight of the thirteen provinces and territories, and same-sex marriages there were legal. But they were not in the remaining five jurisdictions.

Martin proceeded to act just as though the court had given him the answer he expected. He maintained that the Charter required that the definition of marriage be changed to include partners of the same sex, and he accused Harper of wanting to violate the Charter rights of Canadians by insisting on maintaining the traditional definition of marriage, while offering every other right of marriage except the name to "civil unions" between partners of the same sex.

Bill C-38, called the Civil Marriage Act, was introduced on February 1, 2005. The short title was misleading. The act dealt with all marriages, including same-sex marriages that were carried out in a religious institution. But the title was meant to assuage the concerns of people who might object to same-sex marriage on religious grounds. When Prime Minister Martin rose to speak on the bill on February 16, 2005, he wrapped himself in the Canadian Charter of Rights: "This bill affirms the charter guarantee of religious freedom. It is that straightforward and it is that important. That is why I stand before members here today and before the people of our country to say that I believe in and I will fight for the Charter of Rights. I believe in and I will fight for a Canada that respects the foresight and the vision of those who created and entrenched the charter. I believe in and I will fight for a future in which generations of Canadians to come, Canadians born here and abroad, have the opportunity to value the charter as we do today, as an essential pillar of our democratic freedom."

He seemed to suggest that voting against Bill C-38 would somehow abolish the charter for future generations. He left backbenchers the freedom to vote for or against the bill, but members of the cabinet were required to vote for the bill or resign. Similarly, the Bloc and NDP MPs were required to vote for the bill. Harper, while vigorously opposing the bill, allowed all his MPs to follow their consciences.

In his own speech, Harper refuted Martin's presumption that the Charter of Rights required that the definition of marriage be changed. The existing definition, he pointed out, had never been adopted by Parliament but was simply a definition adopted and enforced by the courts. He quoted former chief justice Antonio Lamer, in *R. v. Swain* (1991), to the effect that the courts do not extend the same deference to a common-law definition as they do to a statute passed by Parliament: "There is no room for judicial deference, however, where a common law, judge-made rule is challenged under the Charter." The cases decided in lower courts on same-sex marriage had all dealt with the common law, judge-made definition. Harper argued that it was plausible that the highest court would rule differently from the lower courts if faced with

Same Sex Marriage (con't

a definition of marriage that had been adopted by Parliament. Harper added, "There are several precedents of Parliament passing statutes without using the notwithstanding clause to reverse decisions made by the courts, including the Supreme Court, under common law, and the courts have accepted these exercises of parliamentary sovereignty."

He cited one case that made precisely his point: "In 1996, Parliament passed Bill C-46 reversing the Supreme Court's decision in *O'Connor*, which allowed the accused to access medical records of the victims in sexual assault cases. When this new law was challenged in the subsequent Mills case, the Supreme Court ruled in a decision by Justices Beverly McLachlin and Frank Iacobucci: 'It does not follow from the fact that a law passed by Parliament differs from a regime envisaged by the Court in the absence of a statutory scheme, that Parliament's law is unconstitutional. Parliament may build on the Court's decision, and develop a different scheme as long as it remains constitutional. Just as Parliament must respect the Court's rulings, so the Court must respect Parliament's determination that the judicial scheme be improved. To insist on slavish conformity would belie the mutual respect that underpins the relationship between the courts and legislature that is so essential to our constitutional democracy.'" And Harper drew his own conclusion: "We have every reason to believe that the Supreme Court, if it were eventually asked to rule on a new statutory definition of marriage combined with full and equal recognition of legal rights and benefits for same-sex couples, might well choose to act in a much more deferential manner toward the Canadian Parliament than lower courts showed toward ancient, British-made, common-law definitions."

It was, surely, a strong legal argument. And he supported it by an appeal to the common sense of the people, in the form of a question: "Will this be a country in which Parliament will rule on behalf of the people or one where a self-selected group of lawyers or experts will define the parameters of right and wrong?" He then moved an amendment proposing that Bill C-38 not receive second reading. When the vote was held on April 12, 2005, thirty-four Liberals voted for the amendment, as did two Bloc MPs, while Bev Desjarlais of the NDP, known to be against same-sex marriage, abstained. All the Conservative MPs but four voted for the amendment. The exceptions included Belinda Stronach and Jim Prentice, both former PCs.

As winter was turning into spring, the Gomery commission moved its hearings to Montreal, where ad executives replaced politicians and civil servants at the witness table, and their testimony brought the sponsorship scandal ever closer to the Liberal Party of Canada and senior associates of Jean Chrétien. The hearings, now broadcast live to a large audience by Radio-Canada's continuous news channel, RDI, began to capture serious attention and to move politics to the centre of the national agenda, especially in Quebec. People in the street and at the office water cooler talked about the latest revelations, or at least the latest sworn assertions, of payoffs to influence peddlers, of an envelope stuffed with money left on a restaurant table, of people on the payroll of ad companies who were really working for the Liberal Party of Canada. The testimony was shocking, and Stephen Harper began to talk seriously with Gilles Duceppe of voting non-confidence in the government and precipitating elections in the spring or early summer. But first, the Conservatives had to hold their first *policy* convention so as to establish an official platform, one approved by the members, and so close off the line of attack that Paul Martin had used against them in the 2004 election campaign – that they had a sinister "hidden agenda." *MARCH 17/05*

And so the stakes were high on March 17, 2005, when Conservatives from across the country converged on Montreal for the party's convention. Only two weeks before, the Liberal Party of Canada had held its own biennial convention in Ottawa. It had been poorly attended, but the Liberals had closed ranks around their leader, Paul Martin. They had set aside, or at least hidden from public scrutiny, the internal divisions that lay below the surface: the resentments over Martin's long power struggle with Jean Chrétien and his shabby treatment of former Chrétien loyalists when he took over as prime minister; the ambitions of would-be Liberal leaders sensing Martin's vulnerability now that he had brought the Liberals down to a minority government; the dissatisfaction over his now legendary title of "Mr. Dithers" – even the internationally respected *The Economist* used the nickname in the heading of an article focusing on his chronic hesitation to act. But, most important of all, was the festering sense in the minds of many Liberals that Paul Martin had discredited the Liberal Party by calling the Gomery inquiry, had destroyed the reputations of people who had been prominent in the regime of Jean Chrétien. There was a consensus that, in a minority government situation, Martin must not be challenged until after the next elections, which could come almost at any time. And so the Liberal Party had managed an impressive show of unity.

In Martin's climactic speech at the convention, he had clearly positioned himself and his party for the coming elections. He would do a repeat of his 2004 campaign – and Chrétien's campaigns of 1997 and 2000 – in which the Liberals were presented as the party of Canadian values, of compassion, of the Canadian Charter of Rights, while their opponents had alien values, secret agendas to destroy health care, and no respect for the Charter of Rights. "Our most important commitment to the Canadian people was our pledge to protect and defend the values that define who we are. Liberal values. Canadian values. Fairness and justice. Dedication to equality of opportunity. An unflinching allegiance to the freedoms enshrined in the Charter of Rights. The Charter is the heartbeat of our Constitution. It embodies the Liberal view of respect for the dignity of every individual. It protects us. In many ways, it defines us. . . . Now, there are those in another political party who hold a different set of values. They too will be gathering for a convention this month. And Canadians will again be reminded, as they were during the election campaign, that the government and the opposition in Parliament – that the prime minister and the leader of the Opposition – present two starkly different visions of what this country can be and where this country must go. The choice was clear during the election. The choice is clear today."

Without closely defining the differences between himself and the leader of the Opposition, Martin suggested that he defended Canadian values, Harper did not; he defended the Charter of Rights, Harper did not. And he took as his proof positive the fact that he proposed to legislate the legality of same-sex marriage, while Harper opposes that redefinition, offering instead "civil unions."

In these circumstances, how the Conservative delegates behaved at their first convention would be decisive for the future prospects of the party. Would they behave as the extremists of Martin's warnings? Would the "hidden agenda" become explicit – or would the party define itself as moderate? These were the stakes as the party gathered in convention for the first time. For the site, Stephen Harper had chosen Montreal. This was a long distance from the party's demographic centre in western Canada, and Montreal was equally distant in terms of politics and ideology. Quebec had long been a graveyard for the hopes of generations of Conservatives. When the unification of the Canadian Alliance and the Progressive Conservatives was announced in the fall of 2003, Quebec's sole PC survivor in the Commons, André Bachand, repudiated the new party because he considered its Alliance component unacceptable in Quebec. He refused to run in the 2004 elections and his seat was then seized by the Bloc Québécois. On election day, the new party took only 8.8 per cent of the Quebec vote. That was about par compared to the past, except when the party was led by a Quebecker, which Stephen Harper was definitely not. In the elections of 2000, Stockwell Day's Canadian Alliance had won 6.2 per cent of Quebec's vote, Joe Clark's PCs 5.6 per cent.

In addition to all the other ghosts from the past, Harper carried with him the taint – for Quebec – of moral and social conservatism. His most publicized policy was his opposition to redefining "marriage" as the exclusive union of two people, rather than the exclusive union of a man and a woman. It was his wedge issue in the 2004 elections that most distinguished him from the other three parties, and then also the issue which had provoked the most attention in the news media in the nine months leading up to the convention. His position was most popular in Alberta, least popular in Quebec. A CROP poll published in *L'Actualité* magazine just before the convention showed Quebeckers in favour of same-sex marriage by a proportion of 56 per cent to 36 per cent against. Among Quebec journalists, the overwhelming majority manifestly favoured same-sex marriage and considered Harper's position as reactionary.

Another factor making for a risky convention: for the first time, the actual delegates who had opposed each other when the parent parties were separate would now come together to hammer out policies. There had been no time for a founding policy convention before the elections of 2004; Paul Martin's election call had prevented that. What had been negotiated in the interim agreement of October 15, 2003, by the three negotiators for each side – and then signed by the two leaders – had necessarily sought out grounds of convergence and avoided the most sensitive issues that divided one party from the other. But now, the parties that had joined together to fight the Liberals would have their respective former members facing each other to establish common policies. It was differences over policy that had led to their original split. They would now hold their debates in the Province of Quebec, the heartland of special status and distinct society, of Bombardier and asbestos, of Liberal mores and Liberal unemployment insurance for seasonal workers. A shock was to be expected. Could the new party enter the lion's den and come out alive?

For Harper, it was a case of double or nothing. Quebec was the Conservative Party's outsized Achilles heel. Unless Quebec relented on its rejection of Harper and of the Conservatives, the chances of extending the 2004 breakthrough in Ontario and achieving power in the next elections were unpromising. Ontario, for more than a century, had given top priority to accommodation with Quebec. The failure in 2004 to elect a single Conservative MP in Quebec undermined the party's credibility as a future national alternative to the Liberals. But the CROP poll in *L'Actualité* showed that only one-third of Quebeckers could identify Stephen Harper as the leader of the Conservative Party. Quebec displayed toward Harper and his party a killer lack of interest.

And so, since the elections, Harper had multiplied his visits, and shaped some of his policy pronouncements to minimize friction with Quebec. In a concession to its traditional pacifism, he had softened his past support for the Iraq war and instead of clearly supporting as in the past Canadian participation in the American ballistic missile defence program, he now said he would wait to see the details of any proposal before making a commitment. He recognized the *"déséquilibre fiscal"* claimed by Quebec and other provinces and promised to end it by negotiating an agreement that would recognize financially the provincial responsibilities laid down in the Constitution. He even supported a demand that the land no longer needed for the obsolete Mirabel Airport be transferred back to local farmers. And he supported the controversial radio station CHOI-FM in Quebec when the CRTC ordered that it be closed because of its trash and smash stars such as Jeff Fillion.

After the 2004 elections, Harper bolstered his staff as leader of the Opposition by hiring a half-dozen politically experienced Quebeckers drawn from diverse backgrounds. The most visible was the person he chose as his Quebec lieutenant, Josée Verner, the one-time communications assistant to Robert Bourassa then organizer for the Action démocratique du Québec, who ran as a Conservative candidate in 2004 and took 31 per cent of the vote – the highest score of any of the Quebec candidates. She became a spokesperson on Quebec issues and, exceptionally, attended meetings of the Conservative caucus as critic for Quebec's economic development and for the *francophonie* in the shadow cabinet. Harper appointed as his deputy chief of staff Richard Décarie, who had been an aide to Daniel Johnson until he converted to Quebec's sovereignty and then was an aide to PQ premiers Lucien Bouchard and Jacques Parizeau. Décarie organized Harper's 2004 Quebec campaign for the Conservative Party leadership. In a less public role, Harper hired as senior policy adviser Michel Lalonde, the former ADQ candidate and close adviser to Mario Dumont.

But, so far, there had been no sign of reciprocation of affection from Quebec. In fact, in the days before the convention, it seemed likely that a confrontation was in the making between old Reformers and old Tories, between the western delegates and those from Quebec. A Canadian Press story prophesied: "Quebec Conservatives have set the stage for potential political dynamite at the spring Tory convention, saying their stand on abortion, gay marriage, and bilingualism is the only way to wrest power from Paul Martin's Liberals. A list of their recommendations obtained by the Canadian Press includes positions on bilingualism and abortion that could leave 'blood on the convention floor,' says one western MP."

To head off a confrontation on the divisive moral issues, the caucus of elected Conservative members had proposed, with Harper's approval, a resolution for the convention that affirmed the freedom of the MPs to vote according to their consciences: "On issues of moral conscience, such as abortion, the definition of marriage, and euthanasia, the party acknowledges the diversity of deeply held personal convictions among individual party members and the right of members of Parliament to adopt positions in consultation with their constituents and to vote freely." The caucus announced that the resolution, if passed, would make moot other resolutions on the agenda dealing with such issues as abortion, same-sex marriage, and euthanasia, and so they would not be debated. The caucus also suggested that debates on sensitive issues be held behind closed doors. But the announcement immediately provoked an outcry. It was said that Harper was trying to "muzzle" the delegates at the convention. When the Conservative MPs held their weekly caucus two days later, they realized that they had made a blunder and decided

to back down. Whether the free-vote resolution passed or not, the resolutions on moral issues would still be up for debate. And all debates
would be open to the media.

It was in these rather volatile circumstances that the delegates from
across the country converged on Montreal's Palais des congrès. Don
Martin's column in the *National Post* that day had a skeptical question-
and-answer in its headline: "Will they screw it up? All signs point to
'yes.'" The first day of debate on the resolutions in the workshops lived
up to the sombre forecasts, as the newspaper accounts the next morning
testified. "Tories face new divide. MacKay fuming over a bid to quash
unity provision," the *National Post* shouted at the top of its main story of
the day. "Harper papers over rifts," headlined Montreal's *Gazette*. "Tory
unity falters. Differences surface between country's various regions,
founding parties." Another front-page *Gazette* story had the headline:
"Quebec delegates reeling after policies trashed." The *Globe and Mail*
delivered the same message in fewer words: "Fissures open in Tory
ranks." *Le Devoir* offered that message in French: "The factions of the
Conservative Party tear each other apart. The Alliance and Progressive
Conservative wings spent a good part of the day exchanging blows, pro-
jecting the image of a party that finds it hard to get along."

These were precisely the headlines that Harper wanted to avoid.
What provoked them? There were smaller rifts and one big rift. The big
rift, which polarized the convention and threatened the party's unity and
viability, was provoked by Peter MacKay. He, the deputy Conservative
leader and the leader who had negotiated with Harper the union of their
two parties, now chose to make of one resolution a capital issue, an issue
of good faith versus betrayal, of West versus East, of one former party
against the other. The resolution, proposed by Ontario MP Scott Reid, a
confidant of Stephen Harper, proposed to set the number of delegates
from each of the country's 308 Conservative riding associations for
future party conventions. According to the agreement in principle of
October 15, 2003, which led to the unification of the two parties, each
riding association would have the same voting strength as every other,
regardless of the size of its membership, in choosing the first leader of the
new party and, later, in sending delegates to the first policy convention.
This was a concession to the PC tradition, as opposed to that of Reform–
Alliance, which followed the formula of one person, one vote. Harper

had agreed to this, even though he knew that it would put him at a disadvantage in the subsequent leadership race. The western Alliance constituency associations, with their vast number of members, would each have no more say in choosing the first leader or establishing policies at the first convention, than small or even phantom constituency associations in Quebec or Newfoundland.

But while Harper had signed, that agreement was only meant to be temporary – to govern the new party until it could make its own decisions at a properly constituted convention. The agreement had been negotiated by four people from each party. It did not presume to limit the choices of the 2,500 delegates at the first policy convention.

Scott Reid's resolution retained the spirit of the agreement, which was the equality of representation of riding associations. It did not propose a return to proportional representation, as favoured by the former Alliance. It merely attempted to ensure that riding associations that would receive full representation were not, in effect, rotten boroughs. In a country where the average riding contains 110,000 Canadians, it seemed reasonable that a Conservative constituency association should have at least ninety-one members in order to be entitled to send a full and equal complement of delegates to convention. But Peter MacKay stormed out of the workshop and complained to several media representatives attending the convention, claiming that he felt "betrayed." He insisted that the resolution betrayed the principle of equality of the riding associations, without which "there would not have been a merger." If the resolution was maintained during the following day's plenary session, he threatened, "This party is in real jeopardy, in my view."

MacKay's gambit, with its prophecy of a split in the young party, was big news and wildly successful. The dramatic scene dominated television coverage that day and the newspapers the next day, a Saturday. Most journalists took at face value MacKay's assertion that the resolution betrayed the understanding on which the new party was founded, so Reid was painted as the villain. A furious Stephen Harper twice kicked a chair hard in exasperation at MacKay's coup. Harper had approved in advance of Scott Reid's resolution. Moreover, MacKay's drama had the effect of overshadowing Harper's own carefully prepared speech for that Friday evening, potentially the most important of his career so far. He had come to Montreal above all to deliver this speech to the people of Quebec. He came to speak of a vision of federalism that, contrary to the Liberal vision, was open to Quebec's aspirations for autonomy. Instead, Quebeckers heard that the Conservative Party wanted to discriminate against small Quebec riding associations and that Peter MacKay was their protector against the western bullies. Presumably MacKay was preparing for a future leadership campaign for himself or his love, Belinda Stronach.

Harper's speech was, without doubt, the feistiest of his political career. Unlike his usual style, the sentences were short and punchy. He used a teleprompter so that he did not, as usual, break his rapport with his audience by looking down at a text. To the audience, it seemed that he spoke extemporaneously or had memorized his speech. David Frum had worked on the text and it was crafty. It sustained tension by developing in parallel an attack on the Liberals with a celebration of the Conservatives: "Friends, tonight is a tale of two cities, of two parties, of two conventions. . . . Fellow Conservatives, no spin can change the reality. The old Liberal Party is on its way down and on its way out. The new Conservative Party is on its way up and on its way in."

His delivery was still imperfect. Many words were lost to his hearers when he accented strongly some syllables, and then let his voice drop for final syllables. When he switched recurrently to French, a language that stresses last syllables, much of what he said was unintelligible. And he still had not discovered the art of the pause – of making one pause worth at least a dozen words. But, for all of that, he spoke with strength, with conviction, one would almost dare say, with passion. And his narrative was powerful: his tale of two parties depicted in side-by-side portraits an idealistic, principled new Conservative Party in contrast to an old, cynical, and opportunistic Liberal Party. The sound box that made his words resonate was the always present hearing room of the Gomery commission, with new revelations of corruption every day. Harper constantly evoked some of its more damning moments. "Now, by contrast [with the Conservative volunteers], too many of today's Liberals are in politics for what they can get out of it. A contract. A sponsorship. Or maybe just an autographed golf ball."

The audience hung on the leader's words. They laughed when he was funny. They applauded when he scored a hit. And they swept spontaneously to their feet when he reached a climax. "To know what happens to our money, we need to wait for the verdict of the Auditor General, Justice Gomery, the RCMP, the Sûreté du Québec. We have never seen such a thing in 138 years of Confederation. [Applause] And we must never see that again."

While excoriating the Liberals, Harper offered his own contrasting policies – on Kyoto, on daycare, on defence, on relations with the United States, on the democratic deficit, on the definition of marriage. He chose in his speech to define the new Conservative Party by a few sharply etched statements. No longer would Paul Martin get away with accusing him of a "hidden agenda" to curtail women's access to abortion or imply that he would scrap the Charter of Rights to discriminate against homosexuals. "As prime minister, I will bring forward legislation that, while providing the same rights, benefits, and obligations to all couples, will maintain the traditional definition of marriage as the union of one man and one woman. And, while I'm at it, I will tell you that, as prime minister, I will not bring forth legislation on the issue of abortion. And I will tell you this . . . I will always allow all your MPs to vote freely on matters of conscience."

He made a particular appeal to Quebec, contrasting his own respect for provincial jurisdiction with the Martin government's systematic intrusions: "It is not an accident if the great initiatives announced by Martin's government – assistance to municipalities, a childcare program – affect fields of provincial jurisdiction. This spending power has created a dominating federalism, a paternalist federalism, which seriously threatens the future of our federation. . . . To me, one principle is not negotiable: the fields of jurisdiction stated in our Constitution must be respected. I am strongly determined to practice an open federalism."

Speaking there in Montreal, he made a pledge that, at the same time, reminded Quebeckers of how they had been abused and shamed by Liberals from Quebec: "I will never come here to Quebec, attempt to buy elections with dirty money, and call it 'national unity.' Canada is not a sponsorship – and Quebec is not an advertising contract. It is the *patrie* [homeland] of the Francophones of North America and the cradle of our country, Canada." And he made this appeal: "Today, the Conservative Party needs Quebec. And Quebec needs the Conservative Party."

There was one policy that Harper put forward, though, that was apt to displease Quebeckers: "We must strengthen and deepen our access to the American market. So I tell you that, on our common interests with the United States, including on missile defence, our Conservative government will take Canada back to the table." He did not say that he would sign on to the missile defence program. He stated, more cautiously, that he would go back to the table. But that was enough to provoke many negative comments in Quebec newspapers the next day, including this headline at the top of the front page of *La Presse*: "HARPER PREPARED TO REOPEN THE FILE OF THE SHIELD. The CP leader promises to reverse the decision of the Martin government."

In his speech, Harper did not refer to the major event of the day, Peter MacKay's outburst. In fact, though he was furious at his deputy leader, he celebrated his presence as part of recognizing the dual heritage and ancestry of what was now the united Conservative Party of Canada: "This is the party of Jason Kenney and Jim Prentice; of Belinda Stronach and Stockwell Day; of Peter MacKay and John Reynolds; of Preston Manning and Brian Mulroney." The cheers were especially loud and long when Harper celebrated together Manning and Mulroney. That put finality to an episode of strife.

In the event, during the plenary policy session, the delegates reversed most of the policy resolutions that had been controversial when adopted in the workshops. MacKay won his equality of representation of the ridings – equality even for ridings that were closely held by a clique bent on retaining control without being threatened by an influx of new members. MacKay had effectively removed an incitement to recruit new members. Abortion was no doubt the most divisive issue for the convention. Despite a passionate plea by former MP Elsie Wayne, the convention voted 55 per cent against passing a law governing abortion. The relatively strong vote for the losing side at least maintained the party as the best choice for religious conservatives, for whom abortion is a cardinal issue of conscience. Official languages were another issue that could have ignited dangerous polemics, but the delegates resolutely supported bilingualism and even booed one delegate who spoke against it. Resolutions favouring referendums and recall of MPs were voted down, as was even the resolution calling for a citizens' committee to study electoral reform – despite the amendment to the Throne Speech presented by Harper. What emerged from the convention was a party that had proven its determination to be and to be seen as moderate and mainstream – a party of the centre-right in matters of governance and taxation, but in no respect at all a party of the extreme right.

No wonder that Stephen Harper was unusually relaxed and cheerful when he met with journalists at the close of the convention. For him, it was mission accomplished. Despite the eruptions on the first day, his own speech and most of the policies adopted were received favourably in the news media. He had a policy platform that he could sell in Quebec. The number of delegates from Quebec had much surpassed expectations. And the convention had left him with considerable latitude to frame an electoral platform that could appeal to a plurality of citizens. If the objective was to position the party to defeat the Liberals in the next elections and form the government, the outcome of the convention was almost perfect. It delivered, above all, reassurance; it told Canadians that this party would deliver integrity, a more frugal and less spendthrift government, more concern for the taxpayer, more respect for the provinces, and more concern for economic development. But it would not shock the electorate with post-election surprises, with a hidden agenda suddenly popping up like a jack-in-the-box. Harper is known, above all, as an extraordinarily cautious man. He would not attempt to transform the government radically overnight. He would understand the need to cultivate and to carry the assent of the people in this country, with all its regional, linguistic, ethnic, racial, religious, and class differences.

This does not mean that a government, if led by Harper, would not make a difference. His record shows that he is a politician with deep convictions, and he is convinced that Canada needs to change. But, as a bred in the bone conservative, he also understands that change must be consensual, not radical and not shocking. Change must be prepared and be taken up by the citizens.

The convention came just in time. In that same week, the Gomery commission heard testimony that, for the first time, linked secret payments of thousands of dollars from an advertising firm to Liberal Party operatives. Then, in the weeks immediately following the convention, the testimony at the Gomery commission became more and more incriminating for Liberals. Several were forced to resign, including the chief of staff of Canadian Heritage Minister Liza Frulla. A former executive director of the Quebec wing of the Liberal Party, currently working for a foundation raising money for the Université du Québec à Montréal, was instantly fired from his job. He then came out with public statements acknowledging that he had broken the law by making undeclared payments to people working on a Liberal election campaign. He also named people in high places who were in the know.

In the maelstrom of accusations, support for the Liberals plunged, while support for the Conservatives rose. Soon the Conservatives passed the Liberals in several polls. On April 16, 2005, an Ipsos-Reid poll of 1,000 Canadians reported that the Conservatives were supported by 36 per cent, the Liberals by 27 per cent, the NDP by 15 per cent, and the Green Party by 7 per cent. In Quebec, the Bloc led by 41 per cent to 25 per cent for the Liberals, with the Conservatives at 16 per cent, but climbing. In the key province of Ontario, the Conservatives had taken the lead with 39 per cent.

This was a heady surge for Harper's party. But it came mostly because of the public's anger at the Liberals. In a person-to-person comparison with Martin, Harper did not fare as well. Asked who would make the best prime minister of Canada, 42 per cent chose Martin, only 34 per cent chose Harper. Asked who was better on the economy, the score was 47 to 34 in Martin's favour. Martin did better on foreign issues (53 to 27), on social programs (44 to 35), and on having "values similar to your own" (38 to 34). But Harper did better than Martin as the one Canadians trust more (40 to 35) and, especially, as the one who will clean up the corruption in Ottawa (41 to 26).

Martin, as a measure of his distress and his desperation, made an unusual statement to the nation via the television networks, to plead for people not to jump to conclusions before Justice Gomery made his report, in the fall of 2005. There have been few such appeals in the past: the last occurred in the week before the 1995 referendum, when Jean Chrétien was panicked by polls predicting a victory for the secessionists. But, in the Commons, all respect between the parties was gone as accusations were launched across the floor. The country, it seemed, was soon to be plunged into elections, and they were likely to usher in a new era in the history of Canada.

EPILOGUE

We found out: an autocrat who attempted to dismantle the Canada's institutions, Shame on Harper and his toadies!!

NOW, LET'S GET serious. Stephen Harper has moved up in the public opinion polls to the point where he must be evaluated as a contender to become the next prime minister of Canada. It's time to ask the question: Would he be up to that exacting responsibility? What kind of a leader does his record show him to be?

He's certainly different from all the heads of government that Canada has known since Confederation. An introvert in a profession that rewards extroverts, especially since the age of television, he resists the standard gimmicks of politicians courting support: staged photo opportunities, public displays of instant affection for unknown children and puppies, feigned outrage, false familiarity, and rhetorical grandiloquence. In that respect, he is the polar opposite of Paul Martin and Jack Layton, but more like Gilles Duceppe. Unlike most politicians, he almost always means what he says, because he has thought long and hard about an issue before he speaks. As one who was a public intellectual before he ever aspired to be a politician, he also says what he means. And he is consistent in his thinking and his speaking.

That is why it is important to go back and follow his political development over the years. Like Pierre Trudeau, he thought long and deeply about his society, coming to conclusions and insights that were very different from the views of his contemporaries. He became a conviction politician, which is usually an oxymoron. When he then changed his policies, it was because his situation had changed, not his fundamental convictions. His angle of vision was different when he helped found a party

399

limited to western Canada from when he pushed to extend that party across the country, from when he left partisan politics to be a free advocate for a conservative restoration, from when he became leader of the Canadian Alliance, and finally, leader of a political party that joined two previous parties and two different political cultures. The man and his convictions remained fundamentally the same, but his strategies changed.

He exhibits a cold brilliance and a cold arrogance that are unattractive in a public figure. We like our leaders to come begging for our favour. Harper does not beg, he rarely even goes through the motions. Charismatic he is not. Harper and charisma fit together like porridge and champagne. Nor is he warm and cuddly. Pundits revel in spoofing his aloof personality. Don Martin, in the *National Post* on April 12, 2005, at the height of the embarrassing revelations before the Gomery commission, speculated on probable June elections and wrote: "The warmer weather might give Harper time to defrost that icy personality a bit, which has been inexplicably surly and silent since Gomery turned the Liberal brand name to mud." For better and for worse, as his first political mentor and later his adversary, Jim Hawkes, said of him: "What you see is what you get."

Perhaps because he is so different, throughout his political career he has been constantly underestimated. The morgues of newspapers are littered with the corpses of knowing prophecies announcing, for example, that Harper was not the man to lead the Canadian Alliance, not the man to unite the right, and certainly not the leader who could bring the Conservative Party of Canada up to the level where it could threaten the Liberals. The most reputed pundits in the land pointed to the rigidity of his personality and the extremity of his views as evidence that he could never succeed. They never failed to give him advice, rarely taken, on how he should remodel himself. Barbara Yaffe offered him this counsel on April 9, 2005, in the *Vancouver Sun*: "The trick for Harper is to do nothing and keep quiet. With federal Liberals under a big, black cloud owing to the sponsorship scandal, Stephen Harper's wisest move would be to develop a new persona – the strong, silent type." Reciprocally, Harper has made few concessions to curry favour with journalists. He clearly distrusts them and has a low opinion of their perspicacity. But a man who is obviously arrogant and despises journalists can't be all bad.

An unusual trait for a politician is his conviction that correct policies are more important than tactics for winning support and achieving power. He demonstrated this at key moments in his career. In 1987, barely weeks after the Meech Lake Accord was triumphantly announced and immensely popular right across the country, Harper tried to convince the nascent Reform Party that it must oppose it on principle. Five years later, when it seemed that the very existence of Canada was at stake, the country greeted the announcement of what would be called the Charlottetown Accord with instant, widespread relief. Harper again went against the grain – and against Preston Manning's initial reluctance to fight – to insist immediately that the Reform Party must openly oppose the accord. He similarly opposed on principle the popular Calgary Declaration of 1997, which Manning and the Reform Party embraced.

Politicians usually choose an array of policies crafted to win over specific clienteles. Harper, from 1986, demonstrated a far more serious approach. He put himself through a year-long process of reading, reflecting, discussing, and writing, to arrive at a reasoned political philosophy, a vision of what Canada should be and of what changes would be required to achieve that vision. His vision led him to break with conventional politics and conventional political parties. Had he been personally ambitious for a career in politics, he had it made when he was invited to Ottawa to work as legislative assistant to Jim Hawkes. He was ensconced on Parliament Hill and on the government side. But, instead of revelling in the high-level contacts and the opportunities for a political career, he left Ottawa disillusioned, went back to his studies and to his personal vision quest. He was searching for ways to reform the Progressive Conservative Party when he met Preston Manning and decided to help found the Reform Party. He later admitted to political scientist Trevor Harrison that, initially, he did not think the Reform Party would succeed. But he helped found the party anyway because of his conviction that political reform was needed.

Within the Reform Party, Harper demonstrated the same priority for proper policy over personal relations or career advancement. In 1989, in the aftermath of the 1988 federal elections, Harper wrote a long confidential memo to Manning in which he, in effect, told his leader that he was on the wrong track when he defined the Reform Party by its populism rather than by conservatism. This attacked the heart of Manning's philosophy of history, his conviction that the new party must transcend the ideological spectrum of right, left, and centre. The memo was cheeky coming from a graduate student whom Manning had made his policy chief. If Harper had nurtured ambitions to succeed Manning as leader, this was hardly the way to go. Later, as a Reform MP, Harper would protest publicly when Reform's biennial convention voted by 87 per cent against including homosexuals under the protection of the Canadian Human Rights Act. He insisted that the Reformers were wrong, that a party should not take a stand on such moral issues but leave them to a decision between the MPs and their constituents.

Harper was above all a compulsive thinker, and he followed his thinking to its logical conclusion. He had come to distrust the conventional wisdom of the elites. In his personal evolution, he had drawn the lesson that he could rely on no party, on no leader, on no expert to inspire his political convictions – he had to reach them on his own. Harper not only believed in affirming even unpopular policies that were good for the country, he also believed that such policies would make for good politics in the long run, if the party took the time and the effort to build coalitions around such policies. That meant positioning itself on the conservative side patiently and permanently, not just opportunistically as occasions arose in the daily news. His disagreement with Manning's vision would lead him to resign his seat as a member of Parliament and go his own way, rather than engage in an internal civil war. He would become head of the National Citizens Coalition, where he could spend all his time and energy advocating the policies he favoured and denouncing the practices of which he disapproved. It was a way of life congenial to his personality and his inclinations. Among other advantages, he did not have to answer to a leader or make the policy compromises required of the elected member of a political party.

When he did return to active politics by running for the leadership of the Canadian Alliance, it was not out of personal ambition, but because the Canadian Alliance under Stockwell Day was breaking apart and all the effort invested in creating and nurturing the Reform Party would end in a debacle. The Alliance was by then so rundown that it was hardly a great prize, but he felt it essential that there be a truly conservative party on the Canadian scene. After winning the leadership and then getting elected to Parliament in May 2002, he shocked the journalists by disappearing at the end of June for the summer, without so much as flipping a single hamburger during the Calgary Stampede. He spent most of that time mending fences and rebuilding the party's exhausted finances. But the media could not fathom a party leader who would not surface at least every week for photo ops.

He was helped at turning points in his career by circumstances. But he also displayed the chess master's strategic sense of how circumstances can be turned to advantage, five or six moves into the future. He surrounded himself with unusually intelligent political amateurs, several drawn from the academic world, none a conventional politician. These citizen politicians organized the campaigns that made Harper the leader of the Canadian Alliance, then leader of the Conservative Party of Canada, then, for a time during the 2004 election campaign, a prospective prime minister. He did not win then, in large part because the Canadian people felt that they did not know him and had no reason to trust him. His aloof approach to politics in this case did not help.

But, to evaluate him properly, one must abstract from the man's personality and look at the man's record. During the course of his political career, Canada was in fact very badly served by its political class, which consistently embraced harmful, wrongheaded policies. It took a good portion of arrogance to resist the complacent conventional wisdom of the day and to incur the corresponding contempt for those who dared not to share it. On the big-picture issues that arose during his career, the record shows that Harper was consistently right when almost all around him were wrong. He was right, and from the start, on free trade; right, and from the start, on the democratic deficit and on the chronic federal deficit and debt; right on the Meech Lake and Charlottetown accords and the Calgary Declaration; right on dealing with the "fiscal imbalance" and consequent federal-provincial conflict by reducing federal expenditures, especially in provincial areas of responsibility, and lowering taxes so as to leave tax room for the provinces; he was more nearly right on Canada–U.S. relations, where Martin made a mess. Harper was wrong on official languages, and he has now changed his position by recognizing French as a priority across the country.

———◈———

As I write, the likelihood is that the next federal elections will result in a sweep of Quebec by the Bloc Québécois, regardless of which other party actually forms the government. The Bloc seems likely to take every Quebec seat where the electors mostly speak French, leaving a few seats from non-French fortresses to be divided between the Liberals and the Conservatives. Similarly, the likelihood is that, in the next Quebec elections, the Parti Québécois will return to power in strength, and represent almost every part of Quebec's geography except where the non-French are concentrated. An opinion poll in April 2005 indicated that dissatisfaction with the Liberal government of Jean Charest was at 71 per cent. A COMPAS poll for CanWest Global, published on April 16, 2005, had support for the Bloc Québécois rising to an unprecedented 60 per cent, with the Liberal support in the province down to 16 per cent, the Conservatives at 14 per cent, and the NDP at 8.

The prospect of Quebec being represented politically, both federally and provincially, by elected members dedicated to separating Quebec from Canada, sets the stage for what Harvard University professor Michael Ignatieff described as, constitutionally, a "perfect storm." All the political factors would combine to create the worst possible conditions for the continued integrity of Canada. Alfonso Gagliano, admittedly not an unbiased observer, predicted from the safety of a holiday in Florida: "The next provincial election, unless there is a miracle, the PQ will win and they will call a referendum right away. And, goodbye Canada! This is the end." The next prime minister, the next federal government, would be faced with a powerful separatist movement at a time when federalism in Quebec had been discredited by the scandals brought to light before the Gomery commission. It would be hard to save Canada under the leadership of a prime minister leading a party that had always draped himself in the Canadian flag and presented itself as the great defender of Canada in two referenda, in 1980 and 1995. If and when another referendum is held on secession within the next four years, the Yes forces will not only command an impressive phalanx of separatist elected members, they will also occupy the moral high ground. They will claim that the 1995 referendum campaign, so closely fought, so nearly won by them, was in fact stolen by federal skulduggery. They will have the federalist forces on the defensive, afraid of pouring money into the campaign lest they be accused of replaying the discredited tactics of 1995 and of the following years.

With an election looming because of the daily provocation of testimonies on the scandals, Paul Martin appeared to be preparing to replay
Liberal scenarios of past decades, presenting the Liberal Party alone as
the defender of Canada against Quebec's secession. At a meeting of his
caucus on April 13, 2005, according to Mark Kennedy of the *Ottawa
Citizen*, "Martin told his caucus in a closed-door meeting he will make
national unity a central issue of the election. The prime minister indicated he will portray Conservative leader Stephen Harper as soft on
Quebec separatism and a threat to national cohesion."

Is Martin right? How would Harper rate as a prime minister faced
with the threat of secession? For certain, his approach would be very different from that of Brian Mulroney, Jean Chrétien, and Paul Martin. All
three were and are essentially deal makers. Their approach when pushed
hard in a conflict with a province has been to offer the province a better
deal. All three have tried to buy the loyalty of Quebeckers by making
concessions, mostly of more money, but also of symbolic and jurisdic-
tional transfers, such as recognizing Quebec as a distinct society, giving
to Quebec control over the settlement of immigrants – including disproportionate amounts of money – turning over control of workforce
retraining (again with barrels of money) surrendering control over
parental leave, including the money, and making the Quebec government
responsible for collecting federal as well as provincial income tax.

Harper, it is clear from his past, would take a completely different
approach. He is not primarily a deal maker, but primarily a policy wonk,
a public intellectual. Like Pierre Trudeau, he has a clear sense of the non-
negotiable underlying conditions for a civil society, including above all
the rule of law. If the Parti Québécois were re-elected in two years on a
policy of holding a referendum, Harper, were he prime minister, would
make clear to all parties, in Quebec, in the rest of Canada, and in the
world at large, that he would defend the constitutional order, and that he
would resist any process leading to secession that was not conditional on
achieving an enabling amendment to the Constitution of Canada. He
defended the constitutional order well in advance of the 1995 referendum, then did briefly join his party in declaring that the referendum
would be decisive; but he soon expressed his real thinking in the form
of a comprehensive piece of legislation, Bill C-341, designated as the

"Quebec Contingency Act (Referendum Conditions)." Though it was written in 1996, two years before the Supreme Court delivered its advisory opinion on secession, it remains the most intelligent, the most precise and comprehensive response to attempted secession to be found in Canada. It also is consistent with the Supreme Court's opinion. Its most important contribution would be to remove secession from the location where it has lodged for the past two decades, on cloud nine, and force everyone to face the realities of secession rather than bask in its beguiling illusions. That would be more effective as a response to separatism than all the pleading, blandishing, and buying in the world.

———◦———

These are Harper's strengths. They have been emphasized here because, unlike his weaknesses, they have not been generally recognized. His weaknesses, of course, are equally real. He constantly displays an excess of partisanship. From the time he was elected to the Commons, his attacks on Chrétien, and now on Martin, have often been over the top. There is a harshness, a lack of humour, humanity, and moderation, that disregards the traditions of Parliament where all members have a right to be treated as honourable. His excess of partisanship was revealed in the urgency he demonstrated in April 2005 to bring down the Liberal government and precipitate elections. The supposed justification was the testimony at the Gomery commission affirming Liberal involvement at the highest levels in payoffs, kickbacks, fraudulent contracts, and breaches of the law. But the commission, by its very nature, broadcast the statements of witnesses who, in some cases, were suspected of being liars and cheats, with a self-interest in deflecting responsibility for shady actions to others. So much was said there that no ordinary member of the public could possibly absorb it all and keep all the facts in proper perspective. That could only be done by someone like Justice Gomery himself, who attended every part of every session, had access to all the testimony and documents, and to expert advice. In reason and fairness, Harper should have been content to await the judge's reasoned evaluation of the facts in his report at the end of the year. Harper made a rush to judgment instead of awaiting Gomery's knowledgeable assignment of responsibilities. The people of Canada had a right to be better informed before they were faced with the prospect of new elections.

Another of Harper's failings is his reluctance to reveal himself to the public through journalists as intermediaries. For example, he refused to be interviewed for this biography even though he knew it was a serious undertaking by a serious journalist. He seems to have developed a touch of paranoia with respect to the news media. It may simply be part of a compulsion to control everything he can in his environment. He does not easily delegate responsibility. And he has communicated to people close to him, including his staff, his own reluctance to divulge information about himself. One result is that he has made it very difficult for ordinary Canadians to have a true understanding of Stephen Harper. He has placed unnecessary obstacles in the way of their making an informed evaluation of this man who asks them to make him prime minister. They sense in him the absence of a common touch, of humanity, and for that reason they have not warmed to him or developed trust, despite all his impressive qualities. He is someone you can admire without really liking.

But, in the last resort, what is most important in a prospective prime minister is his demonstrated good judgment, his integrity, his wise policies, his broad experience, his willingness to make hard decisions for the common good even if they are unpopular, and his commitment to work to the best of his ability and his energy to lead the country in peace, justice, and prosperity. In each of these respects, warts and all, Stephen Harper rates better than any other leader on the federal scene since Pierre Trudeau.

INDEX

Aberhart, William, 64–65, 107
Ablonczy, Diane, 132, 201–2, 205, 208, 219, 296, 297, 301, 303
Action Démocratique du Québec, 250, 345, 381, 390
Air Canada, 369
Alberta: and Canada Pension Plan, 286; Chrétien on, 283–84, 285; compared to Quebec, 284; Harper's "Firewall" letter, 284–85; recession in, 19
Alberta Report, 62, 85, 87, 177
Allaire, Jean, 166
Allan, John, xii, xiii
Anders, Rob, 295
Anderson, Rick, 180–81, 185, 186, 192, 193
Andre, Harvie, 16, 56
Archer, Keith, 183
Association for the Protection of English in Canada (APEC), 156, 157
Atlantic Canada: Harper comments on, 316
Atlantic Institute for Market Studies, 262
Atlantic provinces: Harper comments on, 1; oil prices and, 18
Atwood, Margaret, 6
Aubin, Benoît, 254

Bachand, André, 336, 389
Baker, George, 310
Baldwin, Robert, 74
Bégin, Paul, 243
Bélanger, Marcel, 166
Bélanger-Campeau Commission, 166
Bentham, Jeremy, 40
Berger, Peter, 48–49
Bertrand, Guy, 242–43, 244
Bethel, Judy, 265
Beveridge, Sir William, 46, 48
Bill 101, 97, 292
Binns, Pat, 341
Bissonnette, Lise, 274
Black, Conrad, 262, 297
Blair, Tony, 50, 323
Blix, Hans, 320
Bloc Québécois, 199, 210, 233–34, 331, 351, 367, 374, 389, 398; and Charlottetown Accord, 251; and Conservative Party, 362; election (1993), 188, 189, 226; founders of,

167, 350; as Official Opposition, 212; strength in Quebec, 264, 403-4
Blue Book, 87
Blue Tory network, 57
Boessenkool, Ken, 285–86, 286, 287, 290, 292, 293, 294, 343
Borden, Robert, 264
Borotsik, Rick, 336
Bouchard, Benoît, 36
Bouchard, Lucien: and Bloc Québécois, 167, 188, 207, 210, 213; and Calgary Declaration, 271, 272; and Clarity Act, 276; compared to Manning, 173, 189; election (1993), 198, 226; and Harper, 277; and Lapierre, 350; leaves Mulroney government, 161; in Mulroney government, 95, 96, 97, 157; Quebec referendum, 227–28; and Quebec secession, 229–30, 235, 268, 276; referendum, 249, 250, 253; secession debate, 232–33; Secretary of State, 95, 96
Boudria, Don, 348
Bourassa, Henri, 242
Bourassa, Robert, 32, 89, 165–66, 174, 243, 307, 381; constitutional renewal, 178; and Meech Lake Accord, 155; and Quebec, 142, 146
Branscombe, Nancy, 269
Brewer, Carl, 9
Bridgman, Margaret, 245
Briere, Michael, 368
Brimelow, Peter, 51–55, 55, 63, 266
Brison, Scott, 336
Bristol Aerospace, 51
Broadbent, Ed, 27, 56, 124; and "Western Assembly," 62
Brockville, 157
Brown, Bert, 290
Brown, Colin M., 76, 260, 292
Brown, Jan, 245
Brownlee, Bonnie, 337–38
Bryden, John, 321, 336
Buckley, William F., 42, 44, 48
Burke, Edmund, 40, 76
Bush, George, 232, 315, 319
Business Council on National Issues, 269–70
Byfield, Mike, 3, 87
Byfield, Ted, 62, 87, 93

Calgary Declaration (1997), 270-73, 302, 378, 401, 403
Calgary Herald, 174, 222, 266, 270, 338
Calgary Sun, 291
Calgary West Reflector, 222
Calgary West Reform Constituency Association, 72, 107
Campaign Life Coalition, 283, 298, 306
Campbell, Kim, 190, 194-95, 198, 199, 208, 209, 212; compared to Day, 287; election (1993), 189
Campeau, Jean, 166
Canada Health Act, 281, 285, 355, 356, 367
Canadair, 51
Canada Pension Plan, 284-85, 286
Canada West Foundation, 61, 77
Canadian Alliance: Chrétien on, 281; and Clark, 293; Clark attitude to, 318; convention (2002), 303-6; creation of, 279, 280; Day as leader, 286-87; and Democratic Representative Caucus, 308-9; dissension within, 289; finances of, 305; and Harper, 290-91; and Harper leadership, 303, 402; and health care, 282; joint candidates issue, 296; leadership of, 287; leadership race, 292-301; media attention to, 306; membership, 300; political culture, 307; racism accusations, 281; union with PC Party, 296, 304, 308, 318, 326-27, 328-38
Canadian Chamber of Commerce, 61, 77
Canadian Conservative Reform Alliance Party, 327
Canadian Federation of Municipalities, 317
Canadian Human Rights Act, 221, 222, 223, 259, 402
Canadian Petroleum Law Foundation, 62
Canadian Unity Reserve, 351, 353
Caplan, Elinor, 281
Carney, Pat, 27-28, 51
Carr, Emily, 109
Carter, Jimmy, 50
Cartier, George Étienne, 378
Cauchon, Martin, 348, 383
C.D. Howe Institute, 286
CF-18 decision, 28, 51, 64, 84, 94, 105, 136, 149, 266
Charest, Jean, 161, 188, 189, 267-68, 342, 376-77, 380, 387, 404; and Calgary Declaration, 272; defusing secession issue, 361; election (2003),

331; and Quebec, 264; and Quebec secession, 276
Charlottetown Accord, 178-79, 181-82, 184, 186-87, 187, 251, 269-70, 307, 340, 381, 403
Charter of Rights and Freedoms, 136, 176, 185, 242, 243, 306, 370, 384, 388
Chatters, Dave, 293
Chipeur, Gerry, 289, 290
Chrétien, Jean, 158, 188, 189, 205, 206, 208-9, 210, 213, 214, 220, 347, 348; on Alberta, 285; and Bush, 319; election (1993), 199; election (1997), 265; election (2000), 279, 280-81, 283; on Harper, 310-11; integrity of government, 315; and Martin, 317; preference for Gore, 315; and Quebec, 180; Quebec referendum (1970s), 228-29; Quebec secession, 227, 230, 231, 241, 256, 235, 268; referendum, 240, 251-53; secession debate, 233-34, 247, 246; and sponsorship scandal, 313, 351, 352, 387; vision of Canada, 232; war on Iraq, 322-23
Christian Heritage Party, 120, 121, 310
Civil Marriage Act (Bill C-38), 385, 386
Clarity Act (Bill 99), 276-78, 307, 350
Clark, Joe, 174; appeal of PC Party to Quebec, 345; and Canadian Alliance, 293, 295, 296, 318; and Charlottetown Accord, 184; comments on Conservative Party, 336, 341; compared to Mulroney, 21; constitutional renewal, 174-75; and Democratic Representative Caucus, 327; election (1988), 105-6, 110; and Harper, 302, 303, 304-5, 306, 308; and Hawkes, 15, 26; popularity of, 43; and Quebec, 174-75, 306; reliance on youth delegates, 74; replacement as leader of PC Party, 327; resignation as PC Party leader, 318; talks with Social Credit, 78
Clark, John, 10
Clarkson, Adrienne, 374
Clemenger, Jean-Marie, 204
Clement, Tony, 339, 342, 343, 344, 345
Clinton, Bill, 50, 337
Coderre, Denis, 361
Commission of Inquiry on Unemployment Insurance, 32
Commission on the Political and Constitutional Future of Quebec (Bélanger-Campeau), 166

Common Sense Revolution, 267, 287
Confederation of Regions Party (COR), 120, 130
Conservative Party of Canada, 1, 326, 347; abortion policy, 362, 396; and bilingualism, 361; and Bloc Québécois, 362; controversy over riding association representation, 392–94, 396; convention (2005), 387, 388–97; creation of, 326–46; elected Senate policy, 364; election (2004), 355–73; environmental issues policy, 364; founding principles, 330–32, 363; homosexual rights policy, 362; leadership race, 338–46; official languages policy, 396; policy on crime, 364; policy on moral issues, 391–92; popularity in 2005, 398; and provincial PC parties, 332; and Quebec, 344–45; rejection by Quebec, 390; rifts in, 293–393; same-sex marriage policy, 369–70, 383–86; uniting with Canadian Alliance, 318
Constitution: and Quebec, 55
Constitution Act of 1982, 55, 147, 149, 237, 268, 271, 274, 285
Copps, Sheila, 158, 173, 231, 239, 240, 348
Coyne, Deborah, 184–85
Crosbie, John, 31, 74
Cross, James, 42
Crowley, Brian Lee, 262
Cummins, John, 265
Currie, Gordon, 192

Dabbs, Frank, 78, 167
Dahmer, John, 129–30, 135
Danchilla, Hal, 289
Davis, William, 260, 329, 335, 343
Day, Stockwell, 336, 347; abortion policy, 371; as Alberta treasurer, 286; and backers, 304; calls for resignation of, 289; at Canadian Alliance convention (2002), 303; and Canadian Alliance leadership, 279, 286–87, 292, 296–300; and Clark, 293; compared to Harper, 310; election (2000), 280, 287–88; flat tax, 286; and Harper, 289–90; and health care, 282; libel suit against, 288; and Quebec, 345; religious views, 288, 298
Décarie, Richard, 345, 391
de Jong, Simon, 63
Democratic Representative Caucus (DRC), 289, 290, 293, 296, 297, 304, 305, 308–9, 318, 327

Denis, Solange, 31, 36
Desjarlais, Bev, 386
Diefenbaker, John, 25, 78, 100, 125, 264
Dion, Stéphane, 273, 292, 348, 377
Dome Petroleum, 62
Donner Canadian Foundation, 262
Dornan, Christopher, 371
Douglas, Roger, 49
Dubé, Francine, 337
Dubuc, Alain, 244
Duceppe, Gilles, 268, 347–48, 354, 359, 365, 366, 374, 383; and non-confidence vote, 387
Ducros, Françoise, 316
Duhaime, Éric, 308
Dumont, Mario, 249–50, 381
Duncan, John, 245
Duplessis, Maurice, 100
Dupuy, Michel, 219–20
Duranty, Walter, 45
Dussault, Anne-Marie, 235

The Economist, 387
Eddy, Jonathan, xii, xiii
Edmonton Journal, 93, 217, 295
Elections Act (Bill C-24), 329
English, John, 238
Etobicoke, 7
Eves, Ernie, 335, 343

Fagan, Drew, 336
Fairweather, Renée, 289
Family Coalition Party, 121
Fife, Robert, 281
Fillion, Jeff, 390
Filmon, Gary, 161
Financial Post, 141
First Ministers meetings, 30, 83, 93, 139, 155, 161, 178, 182, 375-76, 379
Flanagan, Tom, 121; Charlottetown Accord, 179, 180, 185-87; and Harper, 192, 196, 215, 263, 264, 266, 270, 273, 274, 290, 293, 294–95, 342, 348; Harper and Weissenberger interest in, 117; "Firewall" letter, 284
Foreign Investment Review Agency, 21, 47
Forget, Claude, 32
Forget commission, 32, 33, 34, 60
Fotheringham, Allan, 260
Fox, Bill, 338
Fraser, Graham, 142
Fraser, Sheila, 311–12, 348–49, 375
Fraser Institute, 262
Free Trade Agreement, 94, 108–9, 315

Froggatt, Chris, 289
Front du Libération du Québec, 42
Frulla, Liza, 361, 397
Frum, David, 263, 394
Fryers, Cliff, 191, 193, 212

Gagliano, Alfonso, 211, 404
Gagnon, Lysiane, 306
Gainer, Karen, 197–98, 200
Gallant, Cheryl, 362, 363
Gartner, Hana, 259, 266
Gérin-Lajoie, Paul, 143
Getty, Donald, 93, 139, 180–81, 184, 204
Gibson, Gordon, 92, 93
Globe and Mail, 142, 223, 276, 302, 310, 334, 336, 337, 341, 357, 365
Goar, Carol, 142
Goddard, Lorne, 288
Gomery, Mr. Justice John, 349, 375, 398
Gomery commission, 352, 387, 394, 397, 400, 404
Goodale, Ralph, 351–52, 357
Gore, Al, 315
Goyette, Linda, 217
Graham, Bill, 320, 323, 325
Gray, Herb, 159, 310
Green Party, 121–22, 310, 371, 398
Greenspon, Edward, 302, 310
Gregg, Allan, 335–36
Grey, Deborah, 139, 201, 206, 208, 212, 296, 309, 346; as caucus chair, 204; and Day, 292; election (1989), 126–33; and Harper, 126, 132–33, 134; and Manning, 132–33; and official languages, 158–60; Quebec referendum, 226, 227; responds to Throne Speech, 135; revolt against Day, 289; Senate reform, 141. *See also* Democratic Representative Caucus
Groupaction Marketing Inc., 311
Groupe Polygone, 312, 313
Grubel, Herbert, 191, 217–19, 293
Gwyn, Richard, 302

Hallett, Donna, 71
Hanger, Art, 289, 300, 310
Harper, Ben (son), 310
Harper, Christoper, xi, xii, xiii–xiv, 2, 11,
Harper, Elijah, 161
Harper, Grant (brother), 5, 164, 196, 293
Harper, Harris (grandfather), 2, 3–4
Harper, Joseph (father), 1–7, 196; as accountant, 3, 7; education, 3; interest in politics, 9; love of music, 11; move

to Toronto, 4; personality, 11; publications, 2–3
Harper, Laureen, 295, 310, 342. *See also* Laureen Teskey
Harper, Margaret (mother), 6, 7, 11, 12, 196; interest in politics, 9. *See also* Margaret Johnston
Harper, Rachel (daughter), 310
Harper, Robert (brother), 5, 196, 293
Harper, Stephen: on Trudeau, 8–9, 19; adopts western viewpoint, 17; on Alberta, 283–84; and asymmetrical federalism, 377–79; on Atlantic Canada, 316; attitude to Ottawa, 26–27; Belgium compared to Canada, 380–81; and bilingualism, 81, 96–97, 148, 291–92, 369; Bill C-341, 254-55, 273, 277–78, 405; birth, 5; boyhood friends, 8–10; budget (1996), 261; by-election (2002), 310; and Calgary Declaration, 271–72; on Canada Health Act, 285; on Canada Pension Plan, 284–85; and Canadian Alliance, 280, 290–91; and Canadian Alliance leadership, 292–301, 293, 303; career ambitions, 13, 14, 38; career change, 36; and Charlottetown Accord, 181–82, 182–84; as chief policy officer for Reform, 91; on child poverty, 259; and Clark, 304–5, 306; on coalition government, 264; compared to Manning, 295; compared to Martin, 341–42; conservative views, 59; constitutional renewal, 175, 177; controversy over riding association representation, 392–94, 396; on cultural policy, 259; and Day, 289–90; death of father, 1; and Democratic Representative Caucus, 308–9; differences with Manning, 16–217, 111–25, 177, 179, 186, 192–93, 196, 223, 271–72; disenchantment with PC Party, 56; disenchantment with politics, 35–36, 38; and Dupuy affair, 220; early interest in politics, 8–9, 17; early life, 5, 6–8; education, 10, 12, 13, 24, 37, 38, 39–40, 91, 126, 163–64; election (1988), 104–8, 110; election (1993), 192–200, 196–200; election (1997), 265, 266; election (2000), 279, 280, 282; election (2004), 355–73; on environmental issues, 121–22; errors in 2004 campaign, 366–69; expansion of Reform Party, 160; family background, xi–xii, 2, 4; family values, 5; and

father, 11; on federalism, 298–99; federalism of openness, 380–81; "Firewall" letter, 284–85; first statement in House, 210–11; fiscal policies, 164, 191; formation of political beliefs, 14, 20, 21, 39, 40–41; on fourth-party competitors, 120–21; free enterprise, 35; and free trade, 32, 94–95; French, abilities in, 10; and Grey, 126, 134; and gun control, 259; and Hawkes, 24, 26, 37, 41, 43–44, 60, 106; health care, 355–56, 360; homosexual rights policy, 362–63; intellect, 10, 11–12; interest in Mansell, 59–60; interest in policy, 91; interest in Thatcher, 49; and Iraq, 319–25; Iraq war, 364; joins PC Party, 14; leaders debate (2004), 365; leadership of Conservative Party, 338–46, 347; as legislative assistant, 25–26, 33, 132–33; on Liberal Party, 124, 263; on Maritimes, 1, 3, 316; marriage, 207; and media, 318–19; media assessment of, 259–60, 302–3, 306; and Meech Lake Accord, 68, 85, 143–44; meets future wife, 162–63; and Manning, 57, 61, 91, 126, 127, 132, 160-61; meets Mulroney, 21–22; meets with Clark (2002), 308; memo to Manning (1989), 114–25; moral issues and party policy, 363; as MP, 202–3; MP pension plan, 265; MPs interest in, 215; and Mulroney policies, 25; and National Citizens Coalition, 260–62, 265; and *National Post*, 5, 262, 280, 282, 284; on NDP, 124; and non-confidence vote, 387; and official languages, 96–97, 148, 158–60, 169; on PC Party, 122–24; performance in House, 217; personality, 2, 366–67; political beliefs, 39, 65–68, 72, 114–25; political education, 35, 43, 44–57, 58–59; "Political Reform and the Taxpayer," 72; political vision, 123–24, 169–72, 266; proposed uniting with PC Party, 318; on public and private sectors, 118; and Quebec, 55, 83, 84–85, 95–96, 114, 143–48, 169, 270–71, 273–74, 275, 277–78, 298–99, 306–8, 380–82, 390, 395; in Question Period, 217, 220; quits PC Party, 41; reaction to deficit, 205–6; and referendum (1995), 246–47; Reform candidate (1988), 94; on Reform leadership, 125; on Reform Party, 223–24, 266–67; and Reform

Party founding, 71–87; and Reform's electoral platform (1988), 97–103; and Reform's language policy, 122; rejection of Clark, 295; relationship with father, 1–2; relations with media, 88, 366–67, 400, 407; relations with United States, 315, 396; religious beliefs, 21; resignation from Parliament, 256, 258; resignation from PC Party, 71; responds to Throne Speech (2004), 382–83; returns to Parliament, 310; role in Reform Party, 87, 90; on role of the state, 122; same-sex marriage policy, 221–23, 369–70, 385–86, 389; and secession, 232, 236–37, 237–38, 240–41, 254-56, 266; Senate reform, 67; social policies of Conservative Party, 330; and social programs, 259; on social values, 122; speaking style, 165, 171, 394; speeches, 72, 80–85, 86, 90–91, 95–96, 168–69, 211–12, 290–91, 298–99, 311, 315, 394–96; and sponsorship scandal, 312–14, 347; sports, 10; strengths, 91, 399–406; tax cuts, 358; "Taxpayers Reform Agenda," 65–68; temperament, 7, 9, 11, 39; third-party election spending, 265, 282–83; TV appearances, 259, 262, 266; on unemployment insurance, 32, 33, 103; union of PC Party and Canadian Alliance, 326–27, 328–38; views on Quebec, 51–55, 68; weaknesses, 406–7; meets Weissenberger, 41–43, 43, 45; on welfare state, 82, 83, 103, 118–20, 124; and "Western Assembly," 58–63; work ethic, 16; and Youth Wing of PC Party, 16. *See also* John Weissenberger

Harper, Tom, 203
Harris, Lawren, 109
Harris, Mike, 267, 287, 318, 335, 339, 341, 343, 364, 367
Harrison, Trevor, 401
Hart, Jim, 288
Haultain, Frederick, 74
Hawkes, Jim, 260, 400; election (1984), 17, 20, 22, 23; election (1988), 104, 106, 107, 108, 110; election (1993), 196, 197, 199–200; and Harper, 26, 37, 41, 43–44, 60, 104, 106; on Harper, 38, 40; as Harper opponent, 94; and immigration, 32–33; meets Harper, 14–16; and unemployment insurance, 33–35

Hawkes, Joanne, 16
Hayek, Friedrich, 46–47, 164
Hearn, Loyola, 329, 334, 335
Herd, Catharine Jane (grandmother), 4
Hermanson, Elwin, 204, 207, 208, 215
Herron, John, 336, 342
Hill, Dr. Grant, 202, 296, 297, 301
Hill, Jay, 296, 308, 309
Hill & Knowlton, 180
House, Douglas, 33
House commission, 33–34, 60
House of Commons, reform, 171
Hughes, Eric, 293
Hume, David, 40
Hunter, Ian, 45
Hussein, Saddam, 320, 321, 322, 323, 364

Iacobucci, Justice Frank, 386
Ibbitson, John, 334
Ignatieff, Michael, 404
Imperial Oil, 7, 12, 17, 19
Indian Association of Alberta, 172
Iraq War, 319–25
Iversen, Devin, 295, 300

Jackson, A.Y., 109
Johnson, Daniel, 230, 242, 243, 251,
    268, 271, 391
Johnson, Pierre-Marc, 243
Johnston, Hinman, 4
Johnston, Margaret (mother), 4. See also
    Margaret Harper
Johnston, Rupert, 4
Johnston, William (grandfather), 4
Jones, Holly, 368
Jones, Jim, 342

Kalopsis, Ken, 297
Keenan, Greg, 337
Kelly-Gagnon, Michel, 262
Kennedy, Mark, 405
Kenney, Jason, 282
Keynes, John Maynard, 46, 48
Khomeini, Ayatollah, 50
Kihn, Mark, 293, 294, 295
Kilgour, David, 383
Kindy, Alexander, 63
King, Mackenzie, 25
Kinsella, Warren, 281
Klein, Ralph, 281, 284, 297, 318, 339,
    341, 367, 368; on Day's libel suit, 288
Kobes, Bill, 196
Koch, George, 177, 179, 180, 182, 186,
    293, 294, 295
Kyoto Protocol, 364

Lafontaine, Louis-Hippolyte, 74
Laforest, Guy, 273
Laghi, Brian, 334
Lalonde, Marc, 27
Lalonde, Michel, 381, 391
Lamer, Chief Justice Antonio, 385
Lanctôt, Robert, 336
Landry, Bernard, 249
Lapierre, Jean, 349, 350–51, 361
Laporte, Pierre, 42
La Presse, 244
Laschinger, John, 344
Laurier, Wilfrid, 29, 125
Layton, Jack, 341, 361, 365, 374, 383
Leaside, 5–6
Le Devoir, 155, 243–44, 274, 277
Legge, Francis, xii
Leigh, James, 288
Leitch, Merv, 78
Lépine, Jean-François, 243
Le Point, 267
Lesage, Gilles, 243–44
Lesage, Jean, 143
Lesage, Mr. Justice Robert, 243, 248
Lessard, Denis, 350
Levant, Ezra, 263, 289–90, 309
Lévesque, René, 21, 88–89, 143, 234,
    243; economic summit, 30; Quebec
    secession, 231; referendum (1980),
    228; referendum defeat, 226
Lewis, Douglas, 158–59
Liberal Party of Canada, 52–53, 100,
    109, 124, 263; biennial convention
    (2005), 387–88; election (1997), 265;
    election (2004), 354–73, 374; integrity
    of, 314–15; and Martin, 317; popular-
    ity, 339; relations with United States,
    315–16; sponsorship scandal, 312–14,
    347, 349–54, 352–55, 375, 387
Liberal Party of Quebec, 233
Libertarian Party, 120
Long, Tom, 287, 336
Lord, Bernard, 318, 338, 340
Lougheed, Peter, 19, 78
Louis, Roy, 172–73
Love, Rod, 287, 289, 297
Luellau, Frank, 362
Lumley, Ed, 343
Lunn, Gary, 296

MacCharles, Tonda, 319
MacDill, Marv, 72
Macdonald, Donald, 31
Macdonald, Sir John A., 25, 81, 345, 378
Macdonald Commission, 31, 32, 34, 60

MacKay, Peter, 326, 396; controversy over riding association representation, 392–94, 396; negotiations with Canadian Alliance, 332–41; sponsorship scandal, 354; union of PC Party and Canadian Alliance, 327–29

Mackintosh, Alexis Fosse, 369

Maclean's, 155

Magna International Corp., 329, 337

Major, Justice John, 283

Manitoba, 154

Manley, John, 317, 348

Manning, Ernest, 77, 78–79, 92, 93, 117, 198, 260

Manning, Preston, 401; ability in French, 209; background, 77–79; and Calgary Declaration, 271–72; and Canadian Alliance, 293; at Canadian Alliance convention (2002), 303–4; and Canadian Alliance leadership, 280, 287; and Charlottetown Accord, 182, 184; and Clark, 303–4; compared to Bouchard, 173; compared to Harper, 85; constitutional renewal, 177; creation of Reform Party, 69; on Day, 288–89; on deficit, 190–91; differences with Harper, 111–25, 179, 186, 192–93, 196, 216–17, 223, 271–72; effect on Harper, 71; election (1933), 195, 201; election (1988), 105–6, 110; election (1993), 192–200; first speech in House, 209–10; and Grey, 130, 131, 132–33; and Harper, 91, 116, 126, 127, 132, 160–61; Harper meets, 57; Harper memo to (1989), 114–25; "House Divided" speech (1989), 149–53, 170, 279; interest in Mansell, 60–61; leadership of Reform Party, 76, 77, 86–87; Meech Lake Accord, 113–14, 167; meets Harper, 61; MPs' criticisms of, 215, 218, 219; on Mulroney, 64; pay cut, 207; payments from Reform Party, 216–17; and "perks," 207; personality, 190; policy on MPs seating order, 208; political vision, 123–24; populism of, 66, 101–2, 186–87, 192, 209, 242, 265, 286, 304, 401; proposal to run joint PC–Reform candidates, 269; and Quebec, 142–43, 170, 176, 180; Quebec referendum, 246, 247–48; on Question Period, 214; and Reform Association of Canada, 63–65; on same-sex marriage, 221–22; and secession, 235–36, 241–42; secession bill,

256; Senate reform, 179; two-election strategy, 212; union of right-wing parties, 327; and Vancouver assembly, 99; and welfare state, 82; "Western Assembly," 59–63

Manning, Sandra, 216–17

Manning Consultants Limited, 79

Mansbridge, Peter, 1, 217

Mansell, Robert, 59, 60–61, 68–69, 80

Marchand, Jean, 143

Mark, Inky, 296, 309

Martin, Don, 338, 392, 400

Martin, Keith, 336

Martin, Paul, 158, 189, 205, 212, 215, 331, 333, 336, 346; accusations of supporting child pornography, 367; and asymmetrical federalism, 382; budget (1996), 261; and Chrétien, 317; election (2004), 174, 354–73; equalization payments, 379; First Ministers meeting, 375–76, 379; and Harper, 347; health care issue, 360, 375–76; leaders' debate (2004), 365–66; leadership of Liberal Party, 317, 339, 348; and Liberal Party, 317; minority government, 374; nicknamed "Mr. Dithers," 387; and same-sex marriage, 384–86; sponsorship scandal, 349–54, 352–56; succeeding Chrétien, 339; Throne Speech (2004), 383; unity reserve, 353, 354

Marzolini, Michael, 371

Masse, Brian, 310

Massé, Marcel, 210, 219, 236–37, 238

Mazankowski, Don, 130, 140, 191, 329, 330, 335

McCormick, Peter, 92, 93

McGuinty, Dalton, 343, 380

McKenna, Frank, 154

McKinsley, Sean, 290

McLachlin, Justice Beverly, 386

McLaughlin, Audrey, 157, 188, 203–4

McLellan, Anne, 265, 306

McNally, Grant, 289, 296, 309

Meech Lake Constitutional Accord, 69, 83, 84, 124, 134, 135–37, 139, 340, 377, 382, 401, 403; Bourassa and, 155; collapse, 161, 165; Harper and, 68, 85, 143–44; Manning and, 113–14, 149, 167; Mulroney and, 57, 154–55, 157–58, 161, 166; provincial approval, 154; and Quebec, 68, 93, 100–101, 136, 154–56, 165-66; Reform Party and, 87, 91, 92, 100, 190; support for, 157

Meredith, Val, 289, 296, 309
Mesley, Wendy, 259
Miller, Robert, 23
Mills, Robert, 245, 289
M&M Systems Research Ltd., 79
Moate, Larry, 9–10
Montreal Economic Institute, 262
Montreal Gazette, 262
Morin, Jacques-Yvan, 143
Morton, Ted, 284, 289, 290
Muggeridge, Malcolm, 45
Muir, Robert, 62, 73, 74
Mulakwa, Brian, 294
Mulroney, Brian, 208, 209, 264; and
    Bouchard, 95; budget (1985), 30–31;
    budget (1993), 191–92; compared to
    Clark, 21; compared to Trudeau, 21;
    and Constitution, 55; constitutional
    renewal, 177–78; creation of
    Conservative Party, 334; criticism of
    Reform Party, 173–74; death of
    Lévesque, 88–89; defeats Clark, 15;
    election (1984), 21–23, 53; election
    (1993), 189; federal-provincial rela-
    tions, 29; free trade agreement, 31–32;
    and Grey, 134–35; Gulf War, 323; and
    Harper, 21; Harper attitude to, 23–24,
    49, 96, 316; language policy, 101;
    letters from Weissenberger, 71–72; and
    Lévesque, 21; and Meech Lake Accord,
    57, 154–55, 157–58, 161, 166; on
    National Energy Program, 27; and
    official languages, 157–59; Official
    Languages Act, 156–57; and Parti
    Québécois, 21; policies, 29, 50–51;
    policies, and Harper, 25; premiers'
    meeting (1984), 29; and Quebec, 142,
    146, 154–55, 167, 180, 307; and
    Quebec Liberals, 94; and secession,
    256; Senate reform, 141; Shamrock
    Summit, 32; and Stronach, 337, 343,
    345; and Turner, 17; unemployment
    insurance, 36; unity reserve, 353;
    vision of Canada, 100, 232;
    Weissenberger attraction to policies,
    43; and West, 64; and "Western
    Assembly," 62
Mulroney, Mila, 22, 338
Munk, Peter, 334
Murray, Lowell, 336

The National, 259
National Citizens Coalition, 28, 76, 198,
    258, 260–62, 265, 270, 279, 292,
    314, 327, 402

National Economic Summit, 30
National Energy Program, 17, 18–20, 20,
    25, 27, 48, 67, 136, 184, 211, 260
National Policy of 1879, 81–82, 83, 84,
    85
National Post, 5, 262, 280, 281, 282,
    284, 309, 319, 334, 337, 338, 341,
    358, 392, 400
National Public Affairs Research
    Foundation, 78
New Brunswick, 154
New Confederation proposals, 248–49
New Democratic Party, 56, 100, 109,
    124, 310, 341, 372, 373, 398; election
    (1993), 188; Quebec secession, 361
Newfoundland, 154
Newman, Peter C., 23–24, 304
Newton, Peter, 9
The Next City, 263
Niebuhr, Reinhold, 44
North American Free Trade Agreement,
    315, 328
Nystrom, Lorne, 159

October Crisis (1970), 42
Official Languages Act, 81, 94, 96, 97,
    149, 156, 249, 340, 359, 361, 369;
    debate, 158–59
Ohler, Shawn, 295
Oliver, Craig, 217
Orchard, David, 327, 328, 333, 336
Organization of Petroleum Exporting
    Countries (OPEC), 17
Ottawa Citizen, 262, 295, 298, 405

Pammett, Jon, 371
Pankiw, Jim, 296, 309
Pantazopoulos, Dimitri, 191
Parent, Gilbert, 220
Parizeau, Jacques, 143, 165, 214, 227,
    345, 391; election (1994), 234–35;
    Quebec secession, 230, 242–43; refer-
    endum, 238–39, 240, 249, 250–51,
    253–53
Parrish, Carolyn, 383
Parti Québécois, 8, 77, 124, 233, 234,
    306, 404, 405; by-election win (1994),
    227; and Charlottetown Accord, 251;
    election win (1976), 42; Mulroney on,
    21
PC Youth of Alberta, 16
Peckford, Brian, 33, 154
Penson, Charles, 293
Peterson, David, 95, 156
Petro-Canada, 47

Pettigrew, Pierre, 355
Pezzack, Scott, 9
Phipps, Bill, 310
Poulin, Madeleine, 154
Prentice, Jim, 327, 339; same-sex marriage vote, 386
Progressive Conservative Party, 51, 57, 68, 122–24, 263; and Canadian Alliance, 304; Clark resignation as leader, 318; competition to, 63; election (1993), 188, 189; free trade, 108; Harper quits, 41; joint candidates issue, 269, 296; leadership, 318, 327; political culture, 307; talks with Social Credit, 78; union with Canadian Alliance, 308, 326–27, 328–38

Quebec: Alberta compared to, 284; and asymmetrical federalism, 376–79, 380, 381, 382; Bloc Québécois in, 403–4; "Calgary Declaration," 269–70, 271–72; and Charlottetown Accord, 178–79, 184; Clark's appeasement of, 306; and Conservative Party, 344–45; and Constitution, 155–56; and constitutional change, 176; as distinct society, 175–76, 251; election (1994), 234; and English Canada, 157; and federal election (1997), 268; Harper and, 51–55, 83, 84–85, 114, 306–8, 389, 390; Harper's views on bilingualism, 291–92; influence in Ottawa, 362; language laws, 42; Manning on, 180; Manning's "House Divided" speech, 149–53; medical services, 281–82; and Meech Lake Accord, 68, 93, 100–101, 136, 154–55, 165–66; as model for Canada, 174; and Mulroney, 307; NDP in, 124; oil prices and, 18; place in Canada, 141–53; Quiet Revolution, 54, 74, 143, 174; referendum, 174–79; referendum (1992), 175; referendum (1995), 226–57; Reform Party expansion into, 200; Reform Party policy on, 143–53, 269; secession, 42, 144, 145–46, 266, 267–68, 268, 273–74, 299, 350, 361; secession debate, 231–33; Senate reform, 141; separatism in, 134; sovereignty referendum, 166–67; sponsorship scandal, 387; and Triple-E Senate, 93
Quebec Resolution, 147-48, 158
Quiet Revolution, 53, 54, 74, 143, 174, 284

Rajotte, James, 293, 294
Reagan, Ronald, 21, 49–50, 113
Rebick, Judy, 184
Reed, John, 45
Reform Association of Canada, 63–65; formation of, 62
The Reformer, 140
Reform Party of Canada: aboriginal policy, 172–73, 218, 219; abortion, 102; accusation of racism, 218; biennial assembly (1989), 139, 141, 142–53, 158, 170; biennial assembly (1991), 168–72, 172–73, 180; biennial assembly (1994), 220–21, 235–36; bilingualism policy, 91; budget (1993), 192; capital punishment, 102; caucus chair (1994), 204; Charlottetown Accord, 174–75, 178–79, 182, 190; communications problems, 213–14; on conservatism, 263; constitution of, 73–76, 92; creation of United Alternative, 279; criticisms of, 181, 182; daycare policy, 103; and deficit, 190–91; deficit policy, 261; economic policy, 101; and economy, 210; election (1993), 189, 190, 192, 195–200, 201; election (1997), 265, 266, 267, 268–69; election campaign (1988), 105–8; electoral platform (1988), 97–103; expansion east, 160, 172; expansion into Quebec, 200; first electoral win, 131; fiscal policies, 190–91; founding, 71–87; and free trade, 87, 94–95, 108; grassroots consultation, 214–15; and Grey, 126–38; growth, 91; Harper as candidate (1988), 94; Harper in, 90, 401; Harper memo to Manning (1989), 114–25; House leader (1994), 204; House of Commons reform, 171; and immigration, 194; and joint candidates with PC Party, 269; language policy, 97, 122; leadership, 76, 86; leadership in, 125,178; Manning's "House Divided" speech, 149–53; and Meech Lake Accord, 87, 91, 92, 100, 190; MPs frustration, 215–16; MPs pay, 206, 207; MPs pensions, 102, 194, 205, 206, 207; naming of, 73; and national unity, 167–68; New Confederation proposals, 248–49; and official languages, 100–101, 158–60; as Official Opposition, 267; party platform, 111, 112; party whip (1994), 204–5; perks, 203-4, 216–17; policies, 75–76, 221;

policies re MPs, 202; policy differences, Manning and Harper, 111–25; populism in, 69, 73, 75, 76, 287; precursor to, 58–63; principles of, 169–72; and Quebec, 170, 176, 210, 269; Quebec Motion, 147–53; and Quebec Referendum (1995), 227–57; Quebec Resolution, 158; and Quebec secession, 268–69; racism accusation against, 174; reaction to deficit, 205–6; referendum policy, 69, 102; replaced by Canadian Alternative, 279; right-wing alignment, 87; same-sex marriage, 221–22; secession policy, 233–34; senatorial election in Alberta, 139; separatism policy, 96; shadow cabinet (1994), 205; social policy, 98, 102–3; and social programs, 195; and social values, 122; and Triple-E Senate, 87, 91–92, 99, 100, 190, 331; unemployment insurance policy, 103; and United Alternative, 269; vision of Canada, 100, 168–69
Regan, Geoff, 316
Reid, Scott, 248, 293, 295, 300, 304, 329, 334, 361, 392, 393
Rémillard, Gil, 155
Reynolds, John, 310
Ricardo, David, 40
Richler, Mordecai, 259–60
Riel, Louis, 74
Riley, Susan, 295
Ringma, Bob, 219
Rivard, Michel, 308
Robarts, John, 260
Roberts, Stanley, 61–62, 73, 76–77, 79–80, 86
Robertson, Lloyd, 217
Robillard, Lucienne, 244, 361
Robinson, Svend, 369
Rock, Allan, 241, 245, 275, 348
Romanow, Roy, 356
Royal commissions: on Economic Union and Development Prospects for Canada, 31, 32, 60; on Employment and Unemployment, 33–34, 60
Ryerson, Egerton, 74

Sault Ste. Marie, 156–57
Scott, Bob, 7–8, 9, 10
Sears, Val, 87, 156
Senate reform, 67, 91–92, 134, 139–40, 140–41, 175, 177, 178, 179. See also Triple-E Senate

Shaping Canada's Future Together: Proposals, 174
Sharpe, John, 367
Shaw, Gordon, 128–29
Sheppard, Jim, 217
Silye, Jim, 207, 219
Simons, Paula, 295–96
Smith, Adam, 39
Smith, Mel, 92
Social Credit Party, 78 112–13, 117
Solomon, Evan, 378
Somerville, David, 76, 258
Speaker, Ray, 63, 203, 204, 206, 208, 218, 219, 245, 286, 329
Special Joint Committee on a Renewed Canada, 174
Spencer, Larry, 362–63
St. Germain, Gerry, 297, 329
Stalin, Josef, 45
Stanfield, Robert, 15, 18, 78, 100, 260
Steffens, Lincoln, 45
Stephenson, Siân, 72, 107
Stevens, Geoffrey, 184
Stewart-Olsen, Carolyn, 343
Stoffer, Peter, 316
Strahl, Chuck, 289, 296, 309, 339
Stronach, Belinda, 329, 334, 337–38, 339, 341, 342, 343–44, 394; and Mulroney, 337, 343, 345; same-sex marriage vote, 386
Stronach, Frank, 337
Sunday Report, 259

"Taxpayers Reform Agenda," 65–68
Teskey, Laureen, 162-63, 164, 200; election campaign, 1988, 106; marriage to Harper, 207. See also Laureen Harper
Thatcher, Margaret, 49, 97, 113
Thatcher, Ross, 55
Tobin, Brian, 343
Todd, Ian, 289
Toews, Vic, 297
Toronto Star, 142, 156, 203, 302, 319, 382
Triple-E Senate, 69, 74, 75, 85, 87, 91, 94, 99, 100, 113, 114, 136, 139, 144, 170, 175, 176, 226, 284, 331
Trudeau, Pierre, 25, 27, 125, 143, 405; and Charlottetown Accord, 185; compared to Mulroney, 21; death of Lévesque, 89; election (1972), 18; federal-provincial relations, 29; Harper admiration for, 19; Harper disillusionment with, 20; and Mulroney, 30, 155;

Quebec secession, 228, 229–30; referendum (1980), 252; resignation
(1984), 17; wage and price controls,
47–48
Tu, Angela, 165
Turner, John, 27, 56, 100, 108–9, 110,
137, 157, 228; leadership of Liberals,
17; and "Western Assembly," 62
Tyler, Brent, 261–62

United Alternative, 269, 279, 304, 306,
327, 343
United States: Harper relations with, 315

Vancouver assembly, 65, 71, 72, 85, 86,
99, 112, 134
Vancouver Sun, 302–3, 400
VanderZalm, Bill, 184
Venne, Michel, 277
Verner, Josée, 381, 390
VIA Rail, 352
Vigneault, Gilles, 250
von Finkenstein, Phil, 289

Wallin, Pamela, 240
Warenko, Ken, 107
War Measures Act, 42
Waters, Stanley, 139, 140, 141, 170, 197,
260
Watson, Laurie, 179, 180, 185, 295
Watson, Paul, 8, 9
Watson, William, 358
Wayne, Elsie, 188, 318, 396
Webb, Beatrice, 45
Webb, Sydney, 45
Weissenberger, John, 293, 294, 295; dis-
enchantment with PC Party, 56; elec-
tion (1984), 22; election (1988),
107–8; expansion of Reform Party,
172; founding of Reform Party, 71-87,
88; and Harper, 41–43, 43, 90, 91;
Harper campaign manager, 196; inter-
est in Mansell, 61; letters to Mulroney,
71–72; marriage of, 165; personality,

44; political education, 58–59; political vision, 62, 266; and Quebec,
51–52, 55; resignation from PC Party,
71; "Taxpayers Reform Agenda,"
65–68; Vancouver assembly statement,
65-68, 134
Wells, Clyde, 154, 161, 185
Wells, Paul, 319
West, the: and bilingualism, 81; compared
to Quebec, 51–55; and Constitution,
55; contribution to Canada, 80–81;
effect of Quebec issue on, 268; and free
trade, 94–95, 108, 109; Harper on,
280; Manning's "House Divided"
speech, 150–53; and National Policy of
1879, 81–82; Reform Party in, 160;
Sears's comments on, 87–88; tariffs, 81;
unfairness to, 80–85; "Western
Assembly," 58–63
Western Accord, 28
"Western Assembly," 58, 59–63
Western Report, 62, 69
White, Bob, 95
White, Peter, 297
White, Randy, 369, 370, 371
Whiteside, Margaret, 107
Whyte, Kenneth, 87, 181, 216, 217
Wik, Brian, 16–17
Williams, Cynthia, 163; early relationship
with Harper, 13–14; election cam-
paign, 1984, 20–21, 23; election cam-
paign, 1988, 106; and Harper, 24, 26,
40, 57, 162; on Harper, 38–39; and
Hawkes, 15, 16
Williams, Danny, 340, 379
Wilson, Michael, 30–31
Wilson, Paul, 289
Winds of Change Conference (1996),
263, 264, 326–27
Winsor, Hugh, 302
Winspear, Francis, 62, 77, 80, 86
Wood, Ron, 179

Yaffe, Barbara, 303, 400

TRIPLE E SENATE
elected, effective + equal